In Darfur

Volume One

Letter from the General Editor

The Library of Arabic Literature series offers Arabic editions and English translations of significant works of Arabic literature, with an emphasis on the seventh to nineteenth centuries. The Library of Arabic Literature thus includes texts from the pre-Islamic era to the cusp of the modern period, and encompasses a wide range of genres, including poetry, poetics, fiction, religion, philosophy, law, science, history, and historiography.

Books in the series are edited and translated by internationally recognized scholars and are published in parallel-text format with Arabic and English on facing pages, and are also made available as English-only paperbacks.

The Library encourages scholars to produce authoritative, though not necessarily critical, Arabic editions, accompanied by modern, lucid English translations. Its ultimate goal is to introduce the rich, largely untapped Arabic literary heritage to both a general audience of readers as well as to scholars and students.

The Library of Arabic Literature is supported by a grant from the New York University Abu Dhabi Institute and is published by NYU Press.

Philip F. Kennedy
General Editor, Library of Arabic Literature

تشحيذ الأذهان بسيرة بلاد العرب والسودان

محمّد بن عمر التونسيّ

المجلّد الأوّل

LIBRARY OF
المكتبة
ARABIC
العربية
LITERATURE

In Darfur

An Account of the Sultanate and Its People

Muḥammad ibn ʿUmar al-Tūnisī

Volume One

Edited and translated by
Humphrey Davies

Foreword by
R. S. O'Fahey

Volume editor
Devin Stewart

NEW YORK UNIVERSITY PRESS
New York

NEW YORK UNIVERSITY PRESS
New York

Library of Congress Cataloging-in-Publication Data

Names: Tūnisī, Muḥammad ibn ʻUmar, author. | Davies, Humphrey T. (Humphrey Taman), translator, editor. | Tūnisī, Muḥammad ibn ʻUmar. Tashḥīdh al-adhhān bi-sīrat bilād al-ʻArab wa-al-Sūdān. | Tūnisī, Muḥammad ibn ʻUmar. Tashḥīdh al-adhhān bi-sīrat bilād al-ʻArab wa-al-Sūdān. English.
Title: In Darfur : an account of the sultanate and its people / by Muḥammad al-Tunisi ; edited and translated by Humphrey Davies.
Description: New York : New York University Press, [2018]- | Includes bibliographical references. | In English and Arabic.
Identifiers: LCCN 2017045322 (print) | LCCN 2017045917 (ebook) | ISBN 9781479811038 (v.1 ebook) | ISBN 9781479846634 (v. 1 ebook) | ISBN 9781479876389 (hardback)
Subjects: LCSH: Darfur (Sudan)--History--18th century. | Darfur (Sudan)--History--19th century. | Darfur (Sudan)--Description and travel.
Classification: LCC DT159.6.D27 (ebook) | LCC DT159.6.D27 T8613 2018 (print) | DDC 962.7/023--dc23

LC record available at https://lccn.loc.gov/2017045322

New York University Press books are printed on acid-free paper, and their binding materials are chosen for strength and durability.

Series design by Titus Nemeth.

Typeset in Tasmeem, using DecoType Naskh and Emiri.

Typesetting and digitization by Stuart Brown.

Manufactured in the United States of America
c10 9 8 7 6 5 4 3 2 1

Table of Contents

Foreword

By R. S. O'Fahey

The Darfur Sultanate emerged in about 1650 and flourished until it was first invaded and conquered in 1874 by the Sudanese warlord and slave trader al-Zubayr Pasha Raḥmah (d. 1913).[1] It was restored in 1898 by ʿAlī Dīnār (titular sultan, 1891–98; r. 1898–1916). In 1916, the British invaded the sultanate, killing its last ruler, and annexed it to the then Anglo-Egyptian Sudan (Condominium).[2] Muḥammad al-Tūnisī's 1851 travelogue, *Tashḥīdh al-adhhān*, provides an invaluable glimpse into the Darfur Sultanate at a key period in its history. For readers unfamiliar with the political and social history of the Fur people, this introduction aims to provide a broader context of the society that al-Tūnisī encountered when he lived there from 1803 to 1811.

Geography and Demography

Darfur was one of a series of African Muslim states that emerged in the eastern and central Sahel and savanna belt south of the Sahara in the sixteenth and seventeenth centuries, the major ones being, from east to west, Sinnar (or the Funj kingdom) based on the Blue Nile, Darfur, Wadai, Baqirmi, and Kanem-Borno (by far the oldest state), the latter straddling the modern Chad–Nigeria border. These states had similar structures and cut across from north to south several ecological zones, including desert, Sahel, and savanna—in Darfur's case in the far south, intruding into the Congo–Nile basin. Ethnically, they tended to be the creation of a specific ethnic group, which expanded by conquest and incorporation, mainly in the sixteenth and seventeenth centuries. All were "divine kingship" states, although the ruler's status was increasingly defined by some version of Islam. They were generally administered by elaborate title-holding elites, free and slave, with complex quasi-feudal institutions. They prospered through trans-Saharan trade, selling northward slaves and other commodities, and importing elite consumer goods such as glassware and textiles. During the partition of Africa, significantly for their future fates, they were relatively late victims. Sinnar and Darfur were conquered from the north southward; Wadai and Baqirmi from the south northward by the French. Today the region constitutes one of the poorest and least developed parts of Africa, which explains the constant emigration. While the Khartoum government has sought to dilute Darfur's past and present identity by subdividing the sultanate/province, a sense of identity transcending tribal loyalties remains.

Darfur covers 490,000 square kilometers, approximately the size of Spain. The geographic heart of Darfur is the Marrah Mountains (highest point Jabal Marrah, 3,042 meters), well-watered and fertile on the western slopes, less so on the eastern. North and east of the mountains the land is open savanna that shades northward into Sahel and desert. Rainfall is usually sufficient to sustain the growing of millet, the main staple, and other crops, especially in areas of *qoz*, stabilized sand dunes. Southwest of the mountains, along the seasonal rivers (wadis) of Azum and Barei, is the most fertile region of Darfur, and thus by far the most densely populated. South of the Marrah Massif, rainfall sustains cattle and sheep nomadism. Fundamental to the human geography of Darfur are the great distances between concentrations of fertile land, water, and people; the difficulties of movement; the harshness and precariousness of the environment; and the fluctuation in rainfall.

Earlier ethnographies of Darfur have tended to overemphasize the Arab–African divide, as has much modern reporting on conflict in the region. Ethnically, the central lands are inhabited by African peoples, of whom the Fur are now by far the most numerous. Going from west to east, the major tribes are the Masalit, Tama, and Qimr, while east of the mountains are the Berti, Birged, Daju, and numerous smaller communities.[3] Generally, the peoples west of the mountains still speak their own languages; in the east Arabic is now dominant. In the Sahel zone of the north, both the Zaghāwah and small Arab tribes (ʿIrayqāt, ʿItayfāt, Banī Hilāl, and others) live by camel and sheep nomadism, while in the well-watered southern zone substantial Arab tribes (Rizayqāt, Misīriyyah, Ḥabbāniyyah, Banī Ḥilbah, Taʿāyshah, and others) practice cattle nomadism, hence their collective name, *Baqqārah* "cattle people."

Origins

Darfur has seemingly a long but largely unknown history of state formation before the emergence of the sultanate, associated with the Daju, Tunjur, and Fur, in that chronological order. This prehistory credits the Daju as the first people to create a state in southeastern Darfur, where they still live. We have a number of references in Arab geographical writings, from al-Idrīsī writing in 1154 to Ibn Saʿīd writing just under a hundred years later (about 1240), to a people called Tajuwa living in what is approximately Darfur. After the mid-thirteenth century, the geographers simply repeat Ibn Saʿīd's report; nothing new has come in.

By the late sixteenth/early seventeenth century we have fragments of contemporary information from disparate sources—a note in an Italian geographical encyclopedia, marginalia from an Arabic manuscript, some comments from a Meccan chronicle. These can be interpreted to indicate that Wadai was newly Islamized, that there was a Tunjur kingdom in Darfur that was clearly the ancestor of the Keira Sultanate, and that the Tunjur may or may not have been Muslim, but had endowments in Mecca established in their name. The Tunjur are a mystery, an ill-defined ethnicity that today survive as sections among a number of different tribes in Darfur. The role of the Tunjur as the progenitors of the neighboring sultanate to the west, Wadai, is much more clearly remembered than their role in Darfur, where Muslim "Wise Stranger"[4] traditions appear to elide or transform the Tunjur into Keira and Fur.[5]

How little we know of this Darfur prehistory is underscored by the numerous stone buildings and related sites, especially in and around the Marrah Mountains, that have yet to be investigated, let alone excavated.[6] The Tunjur were seemingly superseded by the Keira dynasty of the Fur people in about 1650, but the traditions surrounding the transition are contradictory and ambiguous, and the survival of titles in the later sultanate of indeterminate linguistic origin compound the ambiguity.

From a Fur perspective, the foundation story of the Keira–Fur dynasty is associated with its first historical ruler, Sulaymān Solongdungo—Sulaymān "the Arab"—who is credited with introducing Islam as the state religion and conquering the lands previously ruled by the Tunjur. On seals stamped on documents from later sultans, their pedigree is traced back to Sulaymān and no further. Local traditions, especially from what are now the Fur heartlands in southwestern Darfur, by far the most fertile area of Darfur, strongly suggest that the

Fur language and identity spread with the expansion of the state, a change paradigmatically expressed in the ambiguous juxtaposition of "Fur" with "Fartīt," non-Fur pagans who could thus be enslaved, but who were somehow felt to be related to the Fur.

The Eighteenth Century: Conflict and Expansion

Sulaymān (r. ca. 1650–80) was succeeded by his son Mūsā, followed by a powerful ruler, Aḥmad Bukr (r. 1700–20), who seems to have laid the foundations of the administrative system and begun the incorporation of the Zaghāwah nomads of north-central Darfur into the state.

The early eighteenth century saw continuous tension among the Keira dynasts in succession disputes that arose among the sons of Aḥmad Bukr, who are said to have sworn an oath to their father that no son of a son would succeed until the Awlād Bukr were no more. The last son of Aḥmad Bukr to become sultan was ʿAbd al-Raḥmān, who acceded as late as 1787 or 1788. These disputes were intertwined with a series of wars with the neighboring state to the west, Wadai. Wadai emerged, based on the Maba people but also in origin a Tunjur state, somewhat later than Darfur. The two states fought a series of inconclusive wars, but with the advantage tending to go to Wadai. Two Darfur sultans were casualties of these wars: ʿUmar Lel and Abū l-Qāsim. ʿUmar Lel (r. ca. 1730–39), who was a grandson of Bukr and who became sultan in succession to his father, Muḥammad Dawra (r. ca. 1720–30), was captured in battle and died a prisoner in Wadai. His uncle and successor, Abū l-Qāsim (r. ca. 1739–52), was a son of Bukr, but sought to strengthen his position at the expense of the Fur titleholders by using slaves and by appointing a Zaghāwī as wazir. He was wounded in battle fighting a Wadaian invasion, but was put to death at the instigation of his chiefs. The wars with Wadai ended in stalemate, although occasionally tension arose between the two states, usually caused by the machinations of the tributary states along the border, Qimr, Tama, or Sila.

An important turning point came with the reign of Muḥammad Tayrāb (1752–53 to 1755–56), who moved his capital east of the Marrah Mountains and consolidated Keira rule. In the early 1780s he led his army into Kordofan, a vast area west of the White Nile under no central rule.

Tayrāb died in Kordofan, in Bara, where his army was encamped, the soldiers having refused to go any farther. As the sultan lay dying, complex negotiations between the various actors led to the emergence of ʿAbd al-Raḥmān al-Rashīd as sultan (vividly described in al-Tunisī), an otherwise unimportant son of Sultan Aḥmad Bukr. ʿAbd al- Raḥmān led the army back to Darfur to confront Isḥāq, who had been nominated (with the title caliph) as the next sultan by his father, Tayrāb. Isḥāq was backed by his mother's people, the Zaghāwah, while ʿAbd al-Raḥmān rallied the Fur. The war lasted nearly three years, with ʿAbd al-Raḥmān finally emerging victorious (1787–88 to 1803). Thereafter, succession to the sultanate was to go from father to son.

Titleholders and the Administrative System

The system through which the sultans ruled their state was complex, made the more so by the multiplicity of titles that were used. Clustered at court around the sultan were a plethora of Fur titleholders, holding titles that were seemingly largely ritual in nature and origin. More powerful in real terms were two royal women: the *iiya kuuri*, or premier wife, responsible for the preparation of food in the *fāshir*, or palace complex, a seriously labor-intensive chore; and the *iiya baasi*, or royal sister, who could play a political role. Zamzam Sendi Suttera, royal sister to Sultan Abū l-Qāsim, was executed alongside her brother. A later Zamzam, *iiya baasi* to her brother Sultan Muḥammad al-Ḥusayn (1838–73), effectively ruled the state after her brother went blind in 1856, riding around with an armed entourage and issuing court rulings under her name.[7] But when her brother died, she starved herself to death.

Some Fur titleholders were in origin very powerful clan (Fur *orre*) chiefs; the *abbo konyunga*, head of the Konyunga clan, which claimed to be Tunjur in origin, accumulated several major administrative titles and kept their preeminence throughout the sultanate's history.

The basic administrative unit was the *shartāya*, ruled by a *shartāy* (probably from the Daju, *chorti*, meaning "drum/chief"; in Fur, *kiiso*.) *Shartāya*s, which could be large and, outside the Fur areas, were usually ethnically diverse, were divided into sub-chieftainships or *dimlijiyya*s (Fur, *dilmong*). The *shartāya*s were grouped together into larger units, of which the most stable was Dār Diima, southwestern Darfur, which was and is predominantly Fur, divided into twelve *shartāya*s, ruled by a line of chiefs, the *aba diimang*.[8] Southeastern Darfur, Dār Uumo, under the *abbo uumang*, was much smaller and never had much administrative identity. The north was Dār al-Takanāwī, ruled by a line of hereditary governors, the *takanāwī* (written thus, but pronounced *takanyāwī*,[9] which is not Fur and possibly goes back to Tunjur times). The eastern province was

Dār Daali and was geographically the largest, but had very little cohesion, being vaguely under the authority of the *abbo shaykh daali,* the senior slave eunuch of the sultanate.

Around 1800, there emerged a new title/rank, the *maqdūm*, usually a senior titleholder, free or slave, who was commissioned to carry out a specific task or campaign. In northern Darfur Ḥasan Segerre, an Arab who held the Fur title *iringa,* was appointed as *maqdūm*, which position remained in his family until well into the Condominium period. The *takanāwīs* continued to function, but as subordinates to the *maqdūms*. *Maqdūms* were appointed in the south, but continual wars with the Baqqārah Arabs, where the advantage lay largely with the nomads, ensured that the *maqdūms* of the south were short-lived and never became hereditary until the Condominium period, when the *maqdūms* came from the Konyunga Fur clan. The *maqdūms* never took hold in Dār Diima.

Privilege and Estate[10]

The administrative system described above was overlaid by the late eighteenth century—and, increasingly, in the nineteenth century—by a quasi-feudal system that may have had its origins in the military-administrative organization that created the Keira state, but that increasingly served to provide the courtiers, holy families, and merchants with tax immunities, land, and income.

We do not know how the system evolved. The oldest documents so far photographed in Darfur are two from about 1700–10, written in a kind of phonetic Arabic, that seemingly grant tax immunity and protection (*jāh*) to members of the Awlād Jābir, a prominent holy family from the riverain Sudan.[11] Whether the granting of landed estates (*iqṭāʿ* or, more colloquially, *ḥakūrah*) grew out of tax immunities is not known. There is a similar ambiguity in Kanem/Borno about the evolution of the *maḥram* system there.[12] By the mid-eighteenth century, we have grants, confirmation of grants, and transcripts of court cases about disputed grants of landed estates, where the boundaries are described in increasing, not to say minute, detail by reference to trees, rocks, and bushes. Within the estates there was often a patchwork of sub-tenancies, where the tenants owed labor and where their status in some instances was similar to serfdom.[13]

Large estates were granted to the major titleholders, who often held several throughout the state. The *Ab shaykh daali,* the premier slave titleholder, held a series of estates along the eastern foothills of Jabal Marrah. Within these estates the *Ab shaykh*s granted smaller estates to holy families.[14] Other estates had their origin when new land was opened up to cultivation (*iḥyā' al-mawāt*) and was subsequently confirmed as estates. The larger estates were held by absentee holders, who usually installed a manager or factor. An important aspect of the system is that the sultans did not usually grant judicial or administrative authority to estate-holders; the *shartāy*s continued to be lynchpins of the administrative system, as they were elsewhere in the sultanate. A final comment here is that the language of the charters was culled from the Maliki lawbooks, but had specific meaning in Darfur.

How valuable these estates were to their owners is unclear. It seems that the two main areas geographically so divided were around al-Fāshir and Dār Diima, where almost all of it was divided into estates. Presumably the estates around al-Fāshir were attractive by virtue of their proximity to the sultan, while those in Dār Diima were in well-watered fertile land. One question that cannot yet be answered is whether any system of land management lay behind the granting of estates; the very meticulous demarcation of boundaries and surviving court transcripts of cases over several generations about such boundaries reenforce the suspicion that there is much about the system that we simply do not know.

When in late 1898 ʿAlī Dīnār restored the sultanate after some twenty-five years of misery and chaos, those who had claims to estates beseeched the sultan to restore their lands, which he seems to have invariably done to those who could prove their claims. With the disappearance of the sultanate after 1916, it was the smaller estates held by holy families that kept their documents, while those of the great titleholders simply evaporated. Under the British (1916–56) and during the early years of independence, such documents were treated as legally valid title deeds. In Dār Diima the British simply converted the estate managers or factors into a category of subchief (*dimlij*) under the *shartāy*s.

The estate system or, more accurately, the *ḥakūrah* came back into contention in around 2003, when conflict between Khartoum and a rebel movement broke out in Darfur. The main government proxies were the Arab nomads of northern and central Darfur (*jammāla*; the so-called *Janjawīd*), one of whose justifications for action was that they did not have secure demarcated lands or *ḥakūrah*s of their own. The term had taken on a new and highly politicized meaning.

The Nineteenth Century

When Sultan ʿAbd al-Raḥmān left Kordofan, probably in 1785, to fight the caliph Isḥāq for control of Darfur, he left behind a slave governor, Musallim, to rule the new province. Darfur and Kordofan together covered some 866,000 square kilometers, a huge area that produced animal and other products—above all, in the case of Kordofan and eastern Darfur, gum arabic. These products were the basis of a significant long-distance caravan trade from northern Darfur to Asyut on the Nile in Upper Egypt along a route across the East Libyan Desert known conventionally as the "Forty Days Road," *darb al-arbaʿīn*. The trade was ultimately organized and controlled by the sultans in cooperation with a relatively small group of rich merchants known as *khabīr*s (literally "expert, leader").[15] They were based at Kobbei, living on a string of estates along a wadi or riverbed of the same name a day's journey northeast of al-Fāshir, now established by Sultan ʿAbd al-Raḥmān as the sultanate's permanent capital. The main exports were slaves (nearly 40 percent of the total), gum arabic, alluvial gold, rhinoceros horn, ivory, and other animal products; the main imports included high-value fabrics, glassware, and specialized items like Solingen sword blades.[16] Foreign trade was primarily of concern to the elites; less well documented, but probably more significant, was interregional trade within the sultanate, animal products for grain, and the like. The Fur of Jabal Marrah traded widely in rock salt.

Darfur rule over Kordofan was to last just under forty years (1785–1821). Muḥammad ʿAlī of Egypt (1811–49) sent an expedition south to conquer the Sudan in 1820, including Darfur. While the main force occupied Sinnar, a subsidiary force under Muḥammad Bey Khusraw set off for Kordofan and Darfur. On August 19, 1821, Musallim was killed and his army crushed by Khusraw at Bāra to the north of al-Ubayyiḍ, Kordofan's capital. Darfur had not simply lost a province; it had acquired an all-too-powerful neighbor that intermittently coveted the sultanate itself—the lucrative trade links between Egypt and Darfur were enough to explain this interest.

Sultan ʿAbd al-Raḥmān died in 1800 and his son, Muḥammad al-Faḍl, was put on the throne by the slave bureaucrat, Muḥammad Kurrā, who for the next few years effectively ran the state. About three years later the young sultan challenged Muḥammad Kurrā, rallying the leading Fur titleholders around him. Muḥammad al-Faḍl and his supporters withdrew northeast of al-Fāshir to Jadīd al-Sayl, returning to the capital with an army. Muḥammad Kurrā was killed in battle.

Two long reigns followed: Muḥammad al-Faḍl (1803–38) and his son, Muḥammad al-Ḥusayn (1838–73), whose accession was smoothly arranged by Ādam Bōsh or Ṭarbūsh, a slave confidant of Muḥammad al-Faḍl, whose grandson, Ibrāhīm Qaraḍ (1873–74), was to be peacefully installed as sultan by Ādam's son, Bakhīt.

For the core sultanate, the first seventy years or more of the nineteenth century were largely peaceful and prosperous. There were occasional clashes with Wadai, and from about the mid-1830s the sultans sent armies southward against the Baqqārah in a series of campaigns that lasted into the mid-1850s. Why the southern frontier leading into the Baḥr al-Ghazāl region should become a contested region is unclear, but there is some evidence of an influx of northern Sudanese and Darfur traders into the region, which was rich in slaves and elephants. This influx was paralleled by the waterborne penetration of the sudd vegetation barrier on the White Nile by Salīm Qāpūdān in 1839. The opening up of the south by the Egyptian and European traders was followed and increasingly taken over by northern Sudanese traders and slavers turned warlords in the south.[17]

The destruction of the sultanate in 1874 was an early and relatively unknown illustration of the power of the gun. The campaigns against the cattle nomads, particularly the Rizayqāt, were fought by mailed cavalry and infantry levies. Some of the Darfur military leaders sought to create bodies of slave troops using imported guns, but it was too little too late. By contrast, the northern warlords in the south, above all al-Zubayr Pasha Raḥmah (1830–1913), recruited slaves using guns and developed a style of warfare against which knights in chain mail were doomed. By the 1860s al-Zubayr controlled the Baḥr al-Ghazāl and was sending trade goods northward through the sultanate despite attacks by the Baqqārah upon his caravans. Al-Zubayr complained to the sultan, nominal ruler of the nomads, but was powerless to curb them. It is clear from his surviving letters that al-Zubayr had an intimate knowledge of the internal politics of the sultanate.[18] In 1873, al-Zubayr began to move north against the sultanate, now ruled by Sultan Ibrāhīm Qaraḍ. The crucial battle was at Dara, capital of southern Darfur, on October 16, 1874, when the Darfur army was shattered by gunfire. Ibrāhīm escaped from the battlefield with his household troops, and made instinctively for Jabal Marrah. Al-Zubayr caught up with the sultan nine days later at Manawāshī, southeast of the mountains; on October 25 Ibrāhīm was defeated and killed, and was buried in the mosque of Shaykh Ṭāhir Abū Jāmūs, a famous holy man from Borno.

Resistance and Restoration, 1874–1916[19]

The battle of Manawāshī did not mark the end of the Keira dynasty or of a sense of Darfur identity. The Keira put up a resistance in the mountains that lasted until 1891 and seven years later, in 1898, the Keira in the person of Sultan ʿAlī Dīnār (d. 1916) successfully restored the sultanate. Whether this resistance can be characterized as a form of proto-nationalism or nationalism is a matter for discussion, but a line of Keira sultans relentlessly fought in and around the mountains seeking to restore their patrimony. As one contender was hunted down and killed, another took his place.[20] Al-Zubayr, after devastating much of western Darfur, went to Cairo to complain of his treatment by the Egyptian authorities in the Sudan; they had simply hijacked Darfur from him. The Egyptians attempted to set up an administration in the former sultanate, but were frustrated by the unremitting resistance of the Keira and the incompetence of the European officials they employed. Charles Gordon, briefly in Darfur when governor-general of the Sudan (1877–80), thought the only viable policy was to restore the sultanate as a tributary state, in some ways anticipating later British policy (1916–56).

By 1882 Darfur was beginning to be engulfed by the Mahdist revolt and revolution (1881–98) that was to decisively eject the Egyptians from the Sudan, definitively defining the Sudan as not Egypt, despite the latter's attempts in the 1930s to promote the "Unity of the Nile" (*ittiḥād wādī l-Nīl*). The history of the Mahdiyyah (meaning here both the period and the ideology) in Darfur is complex and the Keira and their supporters were only one of the protagonists involved in the endless wars of the period. A climax was reached in 1889 with a messianic movement led by Abū Jummayzah that posed the most serious challenge to Mahdist rule thus far; the threat was averted only by Abū Jummayzah's unexpected death. Finally, in 1891, the then titular Darfur sultan, ʿAlī Dīnār ibn Zakariyyah, a grandson of Sultan Muḥammad al-Faḍl, rode into al-Fāshir and surrendered to the Mahdist governor there. He was sent to Omdurman and spent the next seven years half prisoner, half courtier at the court of the Mahdi's successor, the caliph ʿAbdullāhi (r. 1885–99), himself a Taʿāyshī cattle nomad from the far southwest of Darfur.

ʿAlī Dīnār, although he fought in various Mahdist campaigns, never accepted its ideology, referring to the Mahdiyyah as "the Taʿāyshah revolt" (*al-thawrah al-Taʿāyshiyyah*) in his autobiography. When the British approached Omdurman in August/September 1898, ʿAlī Dīnār seems to have had a clear idea of the likely outcome of the battle to follow; on the eve of the encounter, he and a group of Darfur tribal leaders left and hotfooted it by camel back to Darfur (about 1,200 kilometers). Reaching al-Fāshir in late September, he took the surrender of the Mahdist garrison there and set about reestablishing the sultanate.[21]

Estates were restored to their rightful owners, mosques were rebuilt, a judicial administration was set up, and a palace was built on a ridge overlooking al-Fāshir (perhaps the most beautiful indigenous building in the Sudan,[22] now a well-maintained museum). His problem was the British, who simply regarded him as some kind of colonial subject, a status he never accepted. Although he was successful in reestablishing an administration in the core lands of the sultanate, he was faced with the recurring problem of the Baqqārah, who (especially the Rizayqāt) were very much protégés of the British, who supplied them with firearms. In 1913 Darfur faced a serious famine, while there was always the threat of would-be Mahdists. By 1916, judging from informants, ʿAlī Dīnār's letters and the subsequent actions of the British, the sultan had succeeded in reestablishing order and peace in his kingdom.

Ironically, the British now decided that the French in what is now Chad, despite being allies in the world war then raging, were threatening to move eastward into what the British saw as a potential power vacuum in Darfur, a vacuum here meaning territory not ruled by a European colonial power. After a brief propaganda campaign of vilification alleging that ʿAlī Dīnār was a bad ruler and had allied himself with the Turks, who were Germany's allies, the British invaded Darfur in 1916. The Darfur army of several thousand men was slaughtered in a battle fought just north of al-Fāshir, and ʿAlī Dīnār was hunted down and killed in November.

The British in Darfur, 1916–56[23]

The British had conquered the Sudan in 1896–98 in order to keep the French out; they had added Darfur to the Sudan for the same reason. And they had done so in the middle of a war whose scale and cost was a fearsome novelty. The result was that Darfur was to be ruled on the cheap by a few British army officers seconded first to the Egyptian army and second to serve in the Sudan.[24] This only changed in the late 1920s, when the first civilian officials arrived in the province. But the underlying principle of British administrative practice was clear: to run Darfur in the same way as the sultans. This meant a monopoly on taxation, on the use of the death penalty, and on the appointment and dismissal of chiefs; theories of "indirect rule" introduced in other parts of the Sudan were thus irrelevant in Darfur. A maqdumate held by the family of ʿAlī Dīnār's general Ādam Rijāl, head of the Konyunga Fur, was established in Nyala, and still exists; an emirate was set up under ʿAbd al-Ḥamīd, a son of Ibrāhīm Qaraḍ, to cover Dār Diima, though this did not last; while the attempt to set up a maqdumate in the north was effectively sabotaged by the Zaghāwah. The law administered in the native courts was sultanic law, in which punishments were largely fines. How embedded sultanic precedent was in the British administration can be seen in the *Western Darfur District Handbook*.[25]

Since there was no money, there was no development. Many young Darfur men went to work in the Gezira cotton scheme between the two Niles, or joined the army. It was only in the 1940s that a trickle of bright young Darfurians got to the elite schools in and around Khartoum; even fewer entered Gordon Memorial College (later to become the University of Khartoum). Northern Sudanese traders moved into centers like Nyala, which emerged as the center of the livestock industry in southern Darfur, while Darfur merchants, often from Fulani families, traded into Chad and what became the Central African Republic.[26] Darfur remained part of a central Sudanic world; this was to change in the 1950s and '60s, but in complicated and contradictory ways.

Independence

The Sudan became independent formally on January 1, 1956, under the rule of a small northern Sudanese, Arabic-speaking elite who looked northward to Cairo and vicariously took part in the excitements of Arab nationalism, Nasserism, Baathism, and the issue of Israel. But the first challenge to the northern elite came from the south in 1955–56, with a mutiny in the army there that led to an inchoate Southern political and resistance movement, the Anyanya. Nothing changed in the way Darfur was administered.

Change began to come in the 1960s; many of the rank and file of the northern army fighting in the south were from Darfur, while several Darfurian leaders from the title-holding families were coopted into Khartoum politics. The veterans from the army began to agitate in Darfur, while in 1966 an informal alliance between the chiefs and the Darfur students in Khartoum led to the establishment of the Darfur Development Front as a voice in Khartoum for Darfur concerns. Greater change came after the coup of May 1969 brought Jaʿfar al-Numayrī (1930–2009) to power as president. Al-Numayrī had served in the

Darfur garrison, and as president initiated in 1971–72 the abolition of "Native Administration" and the introduction of modern local government. This did not work in Darfur; the chiefs were too powerful and entrenched, and there were insufficient "modern" university-trained governmental workers to replace them. After the fall of al-Numayrī in 1985, the chiefs were reinstated, but now their appointment was in the hands of whoever was in power in Khartoum.

From the mid-1980s, famine became recurrent in Darfur, compounded by other factors such as the breakdown of local government, the influx of firearms from the endless wars in Chad, rapid urbanization especially in and around Nyala, and a general breakdown in law and order. Into this mix was added an ideological ingredient by President 'Umar al-Bashīr, who seized power in a military coup in 1989. There was now introduced a racial, "Arab" versus "African," dimension into the complex tribal politics of Darfur.[27] The injection of race by Khartoum was disastrous, leading to the emergence of the *Janjawīd* recruited from the northern camel nomads in response to the attack on El Fasher Airport by the Sudan Liberation Army (SLA) in April 2003, which marked the beginning of open warfare.

The United Nations and the African Union became involved in late 2004; peacekeepers from the AU were sent to Darfur, but their effectiveness was limited by the lack of helicopters. The general insecurity has speeded up urbanization, either directly into the towns or into internally displaced people (IDP) camps adjacent to the towns. At one time, Nyala was the second-largest city in the Sudan. The opposition movements in Darfur have inevitably splintered along increasingly tribal lines, with neither Khartoum nor the leaders in Darfur (or outside it) able or willing to negotiate a settlement acceptable to all sides. There are no signs that this situation will change any time soon.

Introduction

In Darfur is the result of a collaboration, undertaken in the rapidly modernizing Egypt of the 1830s and 1840s, between the work's author, the Tunisian-Egyptian Muḥammad ibn ʿUmar al-Tūnisī (1790–1857), and its instigator, copyist, and in some sense editor, the Frenchman Nicolas Perron (1797–1876). The backgrounds of these two men could hardly have been more different in terms of upbringing, language, and culture. They lived, however, in an era of convergence. Under Muḥammad ʿAlī (r. 1805–48), the Egyptian state was recruiting Arab and European professionals and deploying these to its newly created institutions. As Aḥmad Fāris al-Shidyāq, a contemporary who found employment there between 1827 and 1835, put it, Egypt had reached in those days "a peak of splendor, strength, magnificence, munificence, and glory. Those inducted into its service enjoyed a huge salary in the form of money, clothing, and provisions, more than was customary in any other state. Its viceroy awarded high rank and tokens of imperial favor to Muslim and Christian alike . . ."[28]

This was the dynamic that brought al-Tūnisī and Perron together, at the Madrasat al-Ṭibb al-Miṣriyyah (the Egyptian Medical School), the first modern institution of its kind in Egypt, founded in 1827 at Abū Zaʿbal, a military facility north of Cairo that already housed a military hospital. There, Perron worked initially as a teacher of chemistry, probably from 1829, and became director in 1839, while al-Tūnisī participated in the translation into Arabic of European medical texts, some by Perron. As colleagues, the two were part of a wide-ranging translation project based at the school that has been compared, for the importance of its role in the transfer of modern European scientific knowledge to the Arab world and for its impact on the Arabic language, to that housed at the ninth-century Dār al-Ḥikmah, or House of Wisdom, in Baghdad, celebrated as the instrument by which Greek science was translated into Arabic.[29] In addition, their relationship had a side that went beyond the normal limits of professional collaboration, since al-Tūnisī acted as Perron's *shaykh*, or teacher, for a period of half a dozen or so years, during which he gave him lessons in Arabic—lessons that acted as the incubator for the work presented here.

At the time, the Land(s) of the Blacks—as the belt of partially Islamized countries that stretched from the Atlantic south of the Sahara almost to the Red Sea was called by the Arabs—was little known to Arab scholarship and less so to European. Leo Africanus (ca. 1494–1554) had devoted a chapter of his *Description of Africa* (1550)[30] to them, but this was based more on accounts by other travelers than on firsthand experience. During the first half of the nineteenth century, French scholars and travelers began to fill the gap,[31] but the subject of al-Tūnisī's book, Darfur, which today constitutes the westernmost part of the Republic of the Sudan and lies at the center of that belt, remained largely unknown. It had taken shape as a state only in the seventeenth century and, with Wadai (now part of Chad), the other Eastern Sudanic state that al-Tūnisī visited, was less accessible than either the more Islamized states to the west or those closer to the Nile Valley to the east. Before al-Tūnisī's visit, only the Englishman W. G. Browne, who spent from June 1793 to March 1796 there, had left a description of the country; one whose value is diminished by the fact that Browne was not allowed to move freely.[32] Change, however, was afoot. In 1821, the armies of Muḥammad ʿAlī would conquer Kordofan and the Funj sultanate to its east, initiating the process that would lead ultimately to the creation, for the first time, of a country called the Sudan; in 1843, an Egyptian-sponsored army under the command of Muḥammad Abū l-Madyan, half brother of Sultan Muḥammad Faḍl, attempted to take the country but failed. The sultanate continued to maintain its independence until 1874, when it was finally incorporated into Egyptian Sudan.

Muḥammad ibn ʿUmar al-Tūnisī (1204–74/1790–1857)[33] was born into a family from the city of Tunis that claimed descent from the Prophet Muḥammad and whose male members therefore bore the title *sayyid* ("master") or *sharīf* ("of noble pedigree"); al-Tūnisī never fails to use one or other of these titles when referring to his relatives. Descent alone, however, was not the sole criterion by which they judged their lives: scholarship, and recognition for it, were also central. Al-Tūnisī's great-grandfather on his father's mother's side (named Sulaymān, as was his paternal grandfather) bore the sobriquet "al-Azharī," meaning that he had traveled to Cairo to study at the mosque-university of al-Azhar, and wrote several books (topics unspecified), while his son, al-Tūnisī's maternal great-uncle Aḥmad, was "a learned scholar, a trustworthy source, of unimpeachable authority, for the transmission of both hadiths and the law" who taught law in Tunis (§2.1.27). Al-Tūnisī's father, ʿUmar, studied with his uncle Aḥmad (§2.1.27) and later, in Darfur, gave lessons to the local men of religion and wrote scholarly commentaries for the sultan, as his son is at pains to point out (§2.3.23).

A common pattern is discernible in the lives of al-Tūnisī's grandfather and father, lives recounted in some detail in the first two chapters of the work—travel between Tunis, Cairo, the Hejaz, and Sudan; extended and ultimately permanent absences of fathers who left North Africa to settle in "the Land of the Blacks," leaving young families behind them in Tunis or Cairo; sons seeking those same absent fathers; meetings of remarkable coincidence between sons and fathers in the middle of vast, empty spaces—and al-Tūnisī himself would in some ways repeat the pattern. The travel was fueled by trade in commodities such as "mantles and tarbushes" (§2.1.1) and also, when "the Land of the Blacks" was involved, in slaves (§§2.1.28, 2.1.29, etc.). Settlement in the Land of the Blacks was facilitated by their status as learned *sayyid*s, for the rulers of the Sudanic nations, from the Funj sultanate in the east to Borno in the west, had a long tradition of encouraging the immigration of such persons, who were seen as lending religious legitimacy to their rule in a region that had been undergoing a slow process of Islamicization for hundreds of years. The coincidental meetings were occasioned by the interconnectedness, however attenuated, of the caravan system that served the trade. Absent from their lives is any but a muted sense of Europe and the non-Muslim world to the north ("French dollars"—a trading currency, and not necessarily French[34]—are one of its rare representatives). For such merchants and *sayyid*s, the non-Muslim world consisted primarily of the pagan groups living to the south, who were the source of the slaves.

Against this background, in 1803, fourteen-year-old Muḥammad al-Tūnisī set out from Cairo, to which city the family had moved, in search of his father, ʻUmar, who had left some seven years earlier for Sennar, and subsequently moved, as the boy had by this time discovered, to Darfur. Muḥammad's account of his journey, undertaken under the wing of a fortuitously met friend of his father's, and of his subsequent stay in Darfur (introduced by an overview of political events preceding his arrival), form the bulk of the work. Al-Tūnisī lived in Darfur for almost eight years, most of them without the father he had come so far to find, for the latter, a scant two months after the two were reunited,[35] sought and received the government's permission to return to Tunis, leaving Muḥammad to manage his estates. Eventually, the father would return from Tunis to the Lands of the Blacks, not to Darfur but to the neighboring Sultanate of Wadai, where he would again be welcomed by the sultan and awarded estates as tax farms. After staying on alone in Darfur, Muḥammad also moved to Wadai[36] to join his father, only to find that he had by that time returned yet again to Tunis.

On his departure from Wadai in 1813, the author, still in his twenties, went first to Tunis, then moved to Egypt (exactly when is unclear). There, after a period of unspecified length that he describes as being devoted to study and ending in insolvency (§§1.2–4),[37] he entered government service in Muḥammad ʿAlī's vigorously developing state (§1.5), by which he continued to be employed for the rest of his working life. His first job was as a chaplain (*wāʿiẓ*) in the Egyptian army that fought in Greece's Morea on behalf of the Ottomans from 1823 to 1828 (§1.6).

On his return from Greece, al-Tūnisī joined the staff of the Egyptian Medical School[38] "as a language editor[39] of medical books, specializing in pharmaceutical works" (§1.6). He also edited several canonical texts of Arabic literature[40] for the recently established government press at Būlāq, near Cairo. Toward the end of his life, he gave lessons on Fridays at the important mosque of al-Sayyidah Zaynab.[41]

Nicolas Perron (1797–1876)—at first al-Tūnisī's colleague, later his superior, and for much of the period also his student—trained in Paris initially in languages, but turned later to medicine, becoming a doctor in 1825. His interest in languages continued, however, and he took courses during the same period at the École des langues orientales, where he studied with prominent French orientalists Sylvestre de Sacy and Jean Jacques (the father) and Armand-Pierre (the son) Caussin de Perceval. He became involved with liberal intellectual circles, and in particular those of the Saint-Simonians, followers of utopian socialist Henri de Saint-Simon (1760–1825) who preached the development of a "new harmony" between religion and the scientific spirit, one in which he believed the Islamic world would play a major role. Possibly under the influence of these ideas, though also perhaps in flight from France following the banning of the radical Association Libre to which he had links,[42] Perron went, probably in 1829,[43] to Egypt, a country of special significance for the Saint-Simonians because of the promotion by the movement's founder of a project to join the Mediterranean and Red seas by a canal.[44] There he took up a position at Abū Zaʿbal as a teacher of chemistry and physics. It was while Perron was working in this capacity that he met al-Tūnisī, who would describe him as "the most brilliant man of his day in keenness of mind and understanding, the brightest of his age in industry and knowledge" (§1.6). In 1839, Perron became director of the Medical School,[45] a position he held until his return to France in 1846, having received the honorific title of Qā'immaqām from Muḥammad ʿAlī in 1845.[46]

During their time together at the Medical School, al-Tūnisī and Perron were involved, both jointly and separately, in the production of a succession of pioneering translations in the field of contemporary medicine and related sciences.[47] These works were the foundation on which the training of Egypt's new cadre of doctors, pharmacologists, chemists, and other scientists was to be erected. Their importance was not confined to the development of the sciences. Underscoring the importance of these works to the development of a modern formal Arabic language capable of transmitting the influx of new ideas that came with the opening of Egypt to European influence, Khaled Fahmy characterizes the output of the Medical School's translation program as "an impressively lucid Arabic medical prose which was as elegant as it was precise, and which was a far cry from the clumsy and awkward Arabic that was used by the nascent government bureaucracy."[48] Fahmy notes further that this style is "clear, grammatically correct, and precise,"[49] and that the translations avoid transliteration and coin clearly comprehensible new terms.[50] Notable among the works translated with al-Tūnisī's participation were Antoine Fabre's eight-volume dictionary of medicine, *Dictionnaire des dictionnaires de médicine français et étrangers* (*al-Shudhūr al-dhahabiyyah fī l-muṣṭalaḥāt al-ṭibbiyyah*), described by Fahmy as al-Tūnisī's magnum opus,[51] and *Kunūz al-ṣiḥḥah wa-yawāqīt al-minḥah* (*The Treasures of Health and Rubies of Benefaction*), based on the lecture notes of Antoine Barthélemy Clot, better known as Clot Bey, founder and director of the Medical School;[52] the latter, first published in 1844 and intended for both students and the general public, went into seven printings. Al-Shayyāl lists six more scientific works in which al-Tūnisī is credited as a language editor, and O'Fahey adds a further title.[53] A work that must have brought the two together in particularly close collaboration was Perron's *al-Jawāhir al-saniyyah fī l-aʿmāl al-kīmāwiyyah* (*The Sublime Gems Concerning Chemical Operations*), based on his chemistry lecture notes.[54]

At some point during this period of close professional contact, Perron began reading Arabic literary texts with al-Tūnisī, starting with Ibn al-Muqaffaʿ's book of animal fables, *Kalīlah wa-Dimnah* (*Kalīlah and Dimnah*).[55] In this more intimate setting, it would seem that al-Tūnisī was moved to tell Perron of some of the "splendid and amazing things" he had experienced in "the Land of the Blacks," and in response Perron urged him to "adorn the face of [his] copybook with an exposition of the marvels" he had seen and to tell him of the "strange things" that had befallen him (§1.6). These texts then became the subject matter of their lessons, and in 1845 Perron published his French translation of the part of these writings relating to Darfur under the title *Voyage au Darfour* (*Journey to Darfur*).[56] This was followed in 1850 by the publication of a lithographic edition of the Arabic text under the title *Kitāb Tashḥīdh al-adhhān bi-sīrat bilād al-ʿArab wa-l-Sūdān* (*The Book of the Honing of Minds through Consideration of the Condition of the Land of the Arabs and the Blacks*), in Perron's own hand.[57]

Following his return to France in 1846, Perron became involved in the scholarly exploration of Algeria (under French rule since 1830) through his translation of Khalīl ibn Isḥāq al-Jundī's *Epitome* (*al-Mukhtaṣar*), an advanced text on Mālikī law widely used in North and Sudanic Africa to which al-Tūnisī refers in this book (§§2.3.22–23). Perron's translation was part of a wider, unrealized, project to create a new Franco-Muslim legal code; in pursuit of this idea, he also translated the Egyptian ʿAbd al-Wahhāb al-Shaʿrānī's sixteenth-century *The Scales of the Law* (*Mīzān al-sharīʿah*), a Shāfiʿī treatise.

In 1851, Perron published a second work by al-Tūnisī, likewise the outcome of their Arabic lessons, namely, *Voyage au Ouaday* (*Journey to Wadai*),[58] in which the author describes his experiences during the two years he spent in Wadai after he left Darfur. The Arabic text of this work was never published and has never been found.[59]

Returning to Egypt in 1853, Perron took a position in the public health system in Alexandria.[60] Later, after a period in Algiers, where he directed an experimental Arabic-French school in which both languages were taught by "the direct method,"[61] he returned to France, where he retired in 1872 and died in 1876.[62]

The Darfur that Muḥammad ibn ʿUmar al-Tūnisī knew was an independent sultanate that had been ruled by one dynasty, from the Keira clan of the Fur (the largest ethnic group there), since at least the middle of the seventeenth century. It is not to be equated in any sense with the "Sudan" of the present day, of which no equivalent existed at the time. Rather, it was one of a swathe of "Sudanic" polities that stretched from the Funj sultanate, whose eastern borders reached almost to the Red Sea, followed to the west by Kordofan, then Darfur, then Wadai (now part of present-day Chad), then Borno (now parts of present-day Chad, Niger, Cameroon, and Nigeria), then smaller states stretching almost to the Atlantic (see Map 1). Darfur's links to the world north of this belt were the trading caravans; these, like the one with which the author traveled, took a route from northern Darfur across the desert to Asyut on the Nile in Egypt, following what is sometimes referred to as "the Forty Days Road"; from Asyut boats were taken to Cairo, the entire distance exceeding two thousand miles. Other caravans went east to the Hejaz (2,700 miles) and served pilgrims as well as trade. Contact with the lands to the south of Darfur was through trade and, above all, slave raiding.

Darfur was, as the title of the work signals, a land perceived as being inhabited by two groups, "Arabs" (*al-ʿArab*) and "Blacks" (*al-Sūdān*). However, what these terms meant exactly is difficult to say. O'Fahey points out that "Ethnicity is a very moveable and slippery concept, and nowhere more so than in Darfur,"[63] and goes on to say that "speaking Arabic does not necessarily mean that one is Arab."[64] The primary distinction made among their subjects by the sultans of Darfur was between those who *spoke* Arabic (*al-ʿArab*) and those who did not (*al-ʿAjam*).

The process by which *In Darfur* was created has been the subject of speculation, fueled by the facts that its French translation appeared before the Arabic original, that no original has been found,[65] and that the first, lithographed, edition of the Arabic text is in Perron's hand. Adding to these oddities is the fact that the other product of al-Tūnisī's collaboration with Perron, the *Voyage au Ouaday*, exists only in French translation. As R. S. O'Fahey notes (speaking of the work on Darfur), "The relationship between the Arabic 'original' and the French 'translation' is complicated."[66] Lurking somewhere among these anomalies may be a suspicion on the part of some that the Arabic text originated with Perron rather than al-Tūnisī, a suspicion that we, like earlier editors, reject: it is inconceivable that Perron could have written a work that stands firmly in the Arabic belles lettres tradition, with its particular strategies and conventions, just as it is impossible that he could have composed Arabic riddle poems or praise poems such as those in which the author shows off his erudition, or had the detailed knowledge of Darfur (which he never visited) displayed in the text, to mention only a few of the objections to this notion.

How the relationship between al-Tūnisī and Perron may have found expression in the language, style, and narrative content of the work is discussed in the note on the text below. However, the question of Perron's intellectual influence, if any, on the work also poses itself. That the enterprise itself, namely, the systematic "description of Darfur and its people [and] of their customs" (Book Proper, chapter one), was Perron's idea is a given, stated by al-Tūnisī (§1.6); al-Tūnisī, however, appropriates and validates that idea when he confides to the reader that he believed that "this would be in my own best interest, given the words of the author of *The Poem on Words Ending in –ā and ā'* . . . that . . . 'Man is but the words that live on after him'" (§1.6). Similarly, Perron states that "I left the form and ordering of his tales . . . as I did his judgments, entirely to"[67] al-Tūnisī. The illustrations, however, which are not intended (whatever their ultimate effect) to be decorative but simply to augment and clarify the text, and which do not occur in the French translation, are surely unique at this period of Arabic literature.[68] Thus, even if we make the large assumption that the somewhat self-consciously encyclopedic presentation of the material owes something to the author's long "embedding" in a European institution and his intense engagement with European scientific literature, we should take note too of the fact that the work as a whole is imbued with the ethos of classical Arabic literature. This is evident in the frequent pious references to the deity, the recounting of tales drawn from life and history to make a moral point, the pleasure taken in conventional verse forms such as praise poetry and puzzle poetry, and the recourse to formal strategies such as the use of poetry to encapsulate a message advanced immediately before in prose and the deployment of technical devices such as rhymed prose.

Al-Tūnisī's description of Darfur, which covers the contemporary and immediately preceding political life of the sultanate as well as its customs, garments, commerce, flora, fauna, diseases, and magical practices, is one of only three to have been made before the country's definitive incorporation into Sudan on the death of its last sultan, 'Ali Dīnār, in 1916.[69] The English traveler W. G. Browne was there from 1793 to 1796 and devotes about 130 pages of his *Travels in Africa, Egypt and Syria from the Year 1792 to 1798* to Darfur.[70] Though he covers some of the same ground as al-Tūnisī, Browne's limited knowledge of Arabic, the suspicion with which he was viewed by the authorities there, and his own dislike of the country and its people limit the reliability and comprehensiveness of his account; compare, for instance, his disdainful comment that "There are several species of trees, but none that produces fruit worth gathering"[71] with al-Tūnisī's lengthy and detailed list of Darfurian trees and fruits and their uses. Some sixty years later, between March and July 1874, on the eve of the invasion of the sultanate by Egyptian forces, a German physician, Gustave Nachtigal, stayed in the capital El-Fasher, and in volume IV of his *Sahara and Sudan* recorded his impressions with greater insight and depth of coverage than had Browne.[72]

The limited nature of these accounts, both by Christian European travelers who stayed for quite short periods, throws into relief the importance of the account of the Muslim and Arab "insider"[73] al-Tūnisī. He was not, of course, a complete insider: he was not a Darfurian, and his understanding of some aspects of the country, as well as the accuracy of his memory after more than thirty years, may be questioned. Nevertheless, as a historian, O'Fahey evaluates al-Tūnisī's works on Darfur and Wadai as "a major source on the history and peoples of the two sultanates,"[74] while another historian, Richard Hill, commends his work as "reliable but unmethodical."[75]

It is not chiefly for these reasons, however, that the work is presented here. It is rather in the belief that its larger-than-life personalities; its accounts of political events and dynastic struggles (as starkly revelatory of the forces behind the rise and fall of states and their rulers as those around which Shakespeare, for example, built his plays); its glimpses of the bewildering practices and hierarchies of an isolated, autonomous, now-vanished world; its narrative of a young person embarking on an adventure with an insatiable appetite just "to see" (§3.1.17); and its bringing back into focus of a lost world through the encyclopedic lens of the early Arab enlightenment, constitute an absorbing and rewarding work of literature.

It remains to acknowledge those who contributed time and expertise to answering my queries or providing references or other valuable support. These include Clifford Cheney, Philippe Chevrant and the staff of the library of the Institut Français d'Archéologie Orientale, Madiha Doss, Khaled Fahmy, Noah Gardiner, Daniel Jacobs, Musa Jargis, Adam Karama, Bariwarig Tooduo Kondo, Raphael Cormack, Mark Muehlhaeusler, Muhammad Shahpur, Adam Talib, Geert Jan Van Gelder, Christine Waag, Terence Walz, and Nicholas Warner. Above all, my thanks go to Rex Sean O'Fahey, who guided me in the direction of much important material and was unstinting in providing answers to my questions from his unrivaled store of knowledge of Darfur and its history. My heartfelt thanks go also to the administrative and technical team at the Library of Arabic Literature, Chip Rossetti, Gemma Juan-Simó, Amanda Yee, and Stuart Brown, who worked tirelessly, as always, to make the process go smoothly and to whose high standards I have, as always, attempted to rise. Finally, I express my deep appreciation for the efforts of Devin Stewart, my project editor, whose interventions were always for the good.

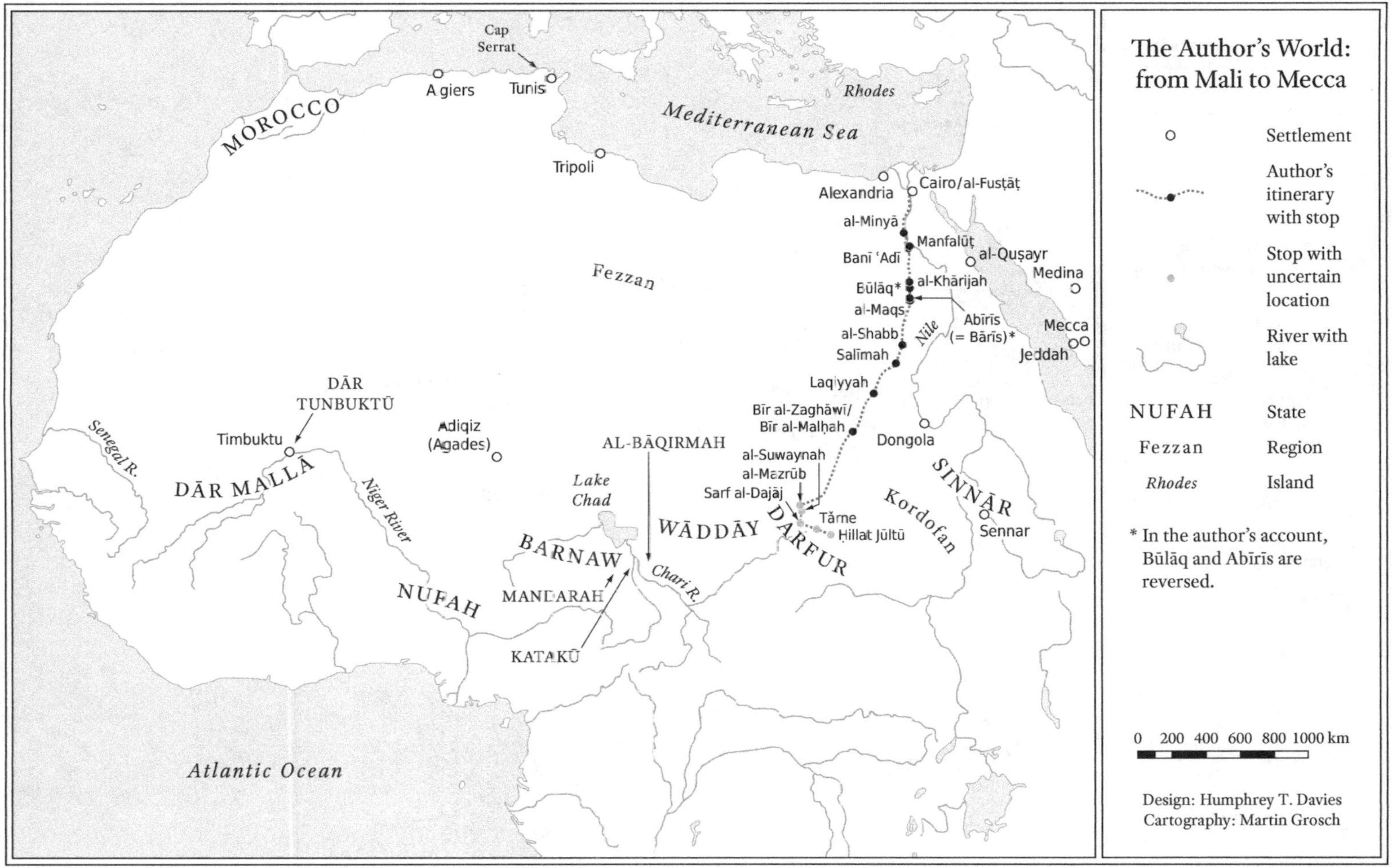
The Author's World: from Mali to Mecca
Settlement
Author's itinerary with stop
Stop with uncertain location
River with lake
NUFAH
State
Fezzan
Region
Rhodes
Island
* In the author's account, Būlāq and Abīrīs are reversed.
0 200 400 600 800 1000 km
Design: Humphrey T. Davies
Cartography: Martin Grosch
Cap Serrat
A giers
Tunis
Rhodes
Mediterranean Sea
MOROCCO
Tripoli
Alexandria
Cairo/al-Fusṭāṭ
al-Minyā
Manfalūṭ
Banī ʿAdī
al-Quṣayr
Medina
Būlāq*
al-Khārijah
al-Maqs
Abīrīs (= Bārīs)*
Nile
Mecca
Jeddah
al-Shabb
Salīmah
Laqiyyah
Fezzan
DĀR TUNBUKTŪ
Timbuktu
Adiqiz (Agades)
Senegal R.
DĀR MALLĀ
Niger River
Bīr al-Zaghāwī/ Bīr al-Malḥah
Dongola
AL-BĀQIRMAH
al-Suwaynah
al-Mazrūb
Sarf al-Dajāj
Lake Chad
SINNĀR
Kordofan
Tārne
Ḥillat Jūltū
Sennar
WĀDDĀY
DARFUR
BARNAW
Chari R.
NUFAH
MANDARAH
KATAKŪ
Atlantic Ocean

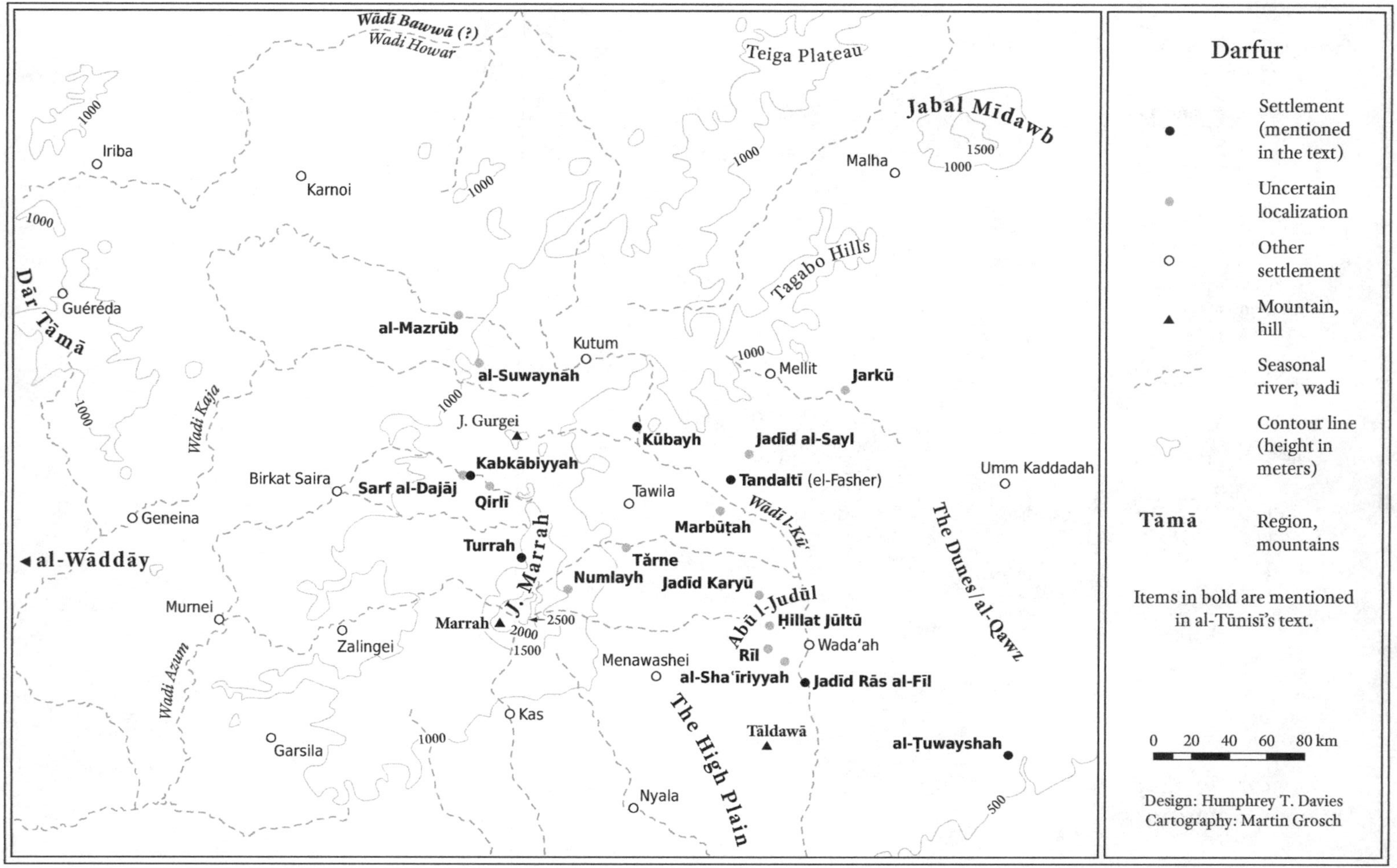
Darfur
Settlement (mentioned in the text)
Uncertain localization
Other settlement
Mountain, hill
Seasonal river, wadi
Contour line (height in meters)
Tāmā
Region, mountains
Items in bold are mentioned in al-Tūnisī's text.
0 20 40 60 80 km
Design: Humphrey T. Davies
Cartography: Martin Grosch
Wādī Bawwā (?)
Wadi Howar
Teiga Plateau
Jabal Mīdawb
1500
1000
Malha
Iriba
Karnoi
Tagabo Hills
Dār Tāmā
Guéréda
al-Mazrūb
Kutum
Mellit
Jarkū
al-Suwaynah
Wadi Kaja
J. Gurgei
Kūbayh
Jadīd al-Sayl
Kabkābiyyah
Tandaltī (el-Fasher)
Umm Kaddadah
Birkat Saira
Sarf al-Dajāj
Qirlī
Tawila
Wādī l-Kū'
Geneina
Marbūṭah
The Dunes/al-Qawz
al-Waddāy
Turrah
J. Marrah
Tārne
Numlayh
Jadīd Karyū
Abū l-Judūl
Murnei
Ḥillat Jūltū
Marrah
2500
2000
1500
Zalingei
Wada'ah
Rīl
Menawashei
al-Sha'īriyyah
Jadīd Rās al-Fīl
Wadi Azum
Kas
The High Plain
Tāldawā
al-Ṭuwayshah
Garsila
Nyala
500

Note on the Text

The Arabic Text

The text poses a number of questions and indeed quandaries for an editor. No manuscript copy of the work exists. Its earliest recension is a lithographic edition, in the hand of Nicolas Perron, the author's institutional superior and student, published in Paris in 1850.[76] An annotated edition, based, of necessity, on Perron's lithograph, was published in 1965.[77] The present edition is likewise based on Perron's "original" but differs in some respects from its excellent predecessor.

Al-Tūnisī's account of how the book came into being is that "I met the most brilliant man of his day in keenness of mind and understanding, the brightest of his age in industry and knowledge—the French teacher of chemistry, Dr. Perron. He studied *Kalīlah and Dimnah* with me in Arabic, and I told him some of the splendid and amazing things I'd endured on my travels. He then urged me to 'adorn the face of my copybook' with an exposition of the marvels I'd seen and to tell him of the strange things that had befallen me on these journeys" (§1.6).

Perron's account is essentially the same, but notes that al-Tūnisī used his "exposition of marvels" as material for their lessons and includes information about the method by which the final text was produced: "I believe . . . that I may congratulate myself on having instigated, pursued, and brought about the production in written form (*rédaction*) of this *Voyage*,[78] and that not without cost to my patience and at great sacrifice. I was taking Arabic lessons at Abū Zaʿbal from Shaykh Muḥammad. He spoke to me of his journeys to Sudan. These accounts intrigued me. I begged him to write them down. He acceded to my earnest request, and the reading of his book served thereafter for my Arabic lessons. This task was often interrupted. I gathered everything together with my own hands and made a correct copy, which I then reread with the shaykh. I left the form and ordering of his tales, as I did his judgments, entirely to him."[79]

Not long after its publication, the text caught the eye of that fighter for high linguistic standards, the Lebanese Aḥmad Fāris al-Shidyāq, whose *Leg over Leg* (*al-Sāq ʿalā l-sāq*) ends with a diatribe directed at French Arabists in which he writes that Perron has "freighted the whole book with misspellings and mistakes," of which he provides a list of twenty-seven items.[80] Crucially, he opines that these are "of a sort for which it would be unreasonable to hold even the least of the aforesaid shaykh's students responsible," implying that Perron, as a copyist and a non-Arab, should take all the blame for these canards (al-Shidyāq was presumably unaware that Perron was in fact a student of the author). Similarly, but without animus or apportionment of blame, Khalīl Maḥmūd ʿAsākir and Muṣṭafā Muḥammad Musʿad, the work's previous editors, have described al-Tūnisī's style as "unusual," with "many departures from the rules of grammar" as well as "offenses against sound Arabic style and . . . indifference to the rules of spelling."[81] They go on to say that "for the most part, the author sticks to literary Arabic norms in his book but he sometimes intersperses literary forms with colloquial, or even on occasion takes a turn toward the wholly colloquial."[82] The anomalies of language and style referred to here, when taken in combination with Perron's role in its creation, the lack of an Arabic manuscript, the appearance of the French translation before the appearance of the original on which it is supposedly based, and the fact that the other work springing from Perron's lessons with al-Tūnisī, the *Voyage au Ouaday* (1851), never appeared in an Arabic version, have combined to create a sense of unease over the integrity of the text, centering on the degree to which Perron may have influenced its form and content, and whether he should not in fact be regarded as the true author of the work.

I see this last possibility as far-fetched, for I am convinced (as were my predecessors)[83] that an Arabic original, authored by Muḥammad ibn ʿUmar al-Tūnisī, did exist at some point in some form, if only because of the innate unlikeliness that Perron, a French student of Arabic with at most twelve years of residence in Egypt, would write a lengthy, detailed work in that language about a country he had never visited.[84] In addition, the complex praise poetry, puzzle verses, and chronograms that the author attributes to himself and that figure in the early chapters; the use of rhymed prose; and the deployment of conventional literary lore indicate that the text is essentially the work of an Arab scholar. Finally, if we are to claim the work as Perron's, what are we to make of the author's occasional first-person asides,[85] some of which are addressed to Perron?[86] Spelling mistakes and divergences from standard grammar are not enough to cast doubt on the Arabic identity of the author. The issue is not whether the text was the work of one of the collaborators to the exclusion of the other, but of where al-Tūnisī stops and Perron begins.

Nonstandard aspects of the text may be categorized as follows:

- A small number of spelling mistakes so blatant that they should probably be attributed to Perron, e.g., العبن for العين;[87] فخرخ . . . وخرخ for فخرج . . . وخرج;[88] الوجود for الجود.[89]
- Divergences from standard orthography, including:
  (1) inconsistent omission or choice of "seat" for the *hamzah*, e.g., الشتا for الشتاء ["winter"][90] and نسئلك for نسألك ["we ask you"];[91]
  (2) spelling with a final *yā'* of words derived from *wāw*-final roots, e.g., دعى for دعا ["to pray"];[92]
  (3) spellings with *tā'* instead of *tā' marbūṭah* for words with "weak" roots, e.g., ملاقات for ملاقاة ["encounter"][93] and لهات for لهاة ["uvula"];[94] and
  (4) use of expanded rather than compound forms, e.g., أن لا for ألّا ["that not"][95] and كي لا for كيلا ["in order that not"].[96]

  Many of these are found in other texts of the period.
- Deviations from standard grammar such as:
  (1) *wa-baynamā hum āminīna muṭma'innīn* ("and while they were safe and at ease") instead of *wa-baynamā hum āminūna muṭma'innūn*, indicating a single sound-plural form, as in the colloquial;[97]
  (2) *hadiyyah ʿaẓīmah minhā . . . sāʿah wa-ʿulbat nushūq muraṣṣaʿatayn* ("a costly gift including . . . a watch and a snuffbox, both inlaid") instead of . . . *muraṣṣaʿatān*, indicating a single dual form, as in the colloquial;[98]
  (3) *yataṭayyabna bihā nisā' al-Sūdān* ("the women of the Blacks perfume themselves with it") with a plural verb preceding the plural subject, instead of *tataṭayyabu bihā nisā' al-Sūdān* with a singular verb;[99]
  (4) *fallāḥīn Miṣr* ("the peasants of Egypt") with final *nūn* instead of *fallāḥī Miṣr* with final *nūn* suppressed;[100]
  (5) *bi-'annahum yusāʿidūhu* ("that they help him") with absence of *nūn* as a marker of the imperfect third-person plural, as in the colloquial, instead of *bi-'annahum yusāʿidūnahu*;[101]
  (6) *wa-'in kunta fī shakk mimmā aqūlu iqlib* ("and if you have any doubt as to what I say, overturn . . .") instead of *fa-qlib*, with *fa-* marking the apodosis;[102]

(7) *ḥattā yashuqqūn* ("until they cut open") with an imperfect indicative verb instead of *ḥattā yashuqqū* with a subjunctive verb following *ḥattā*;[103] and

(8) *fa-yusammūna shawwālan bi-faṭur wa-dhī l-qaʿdah bi-*. . . ("They call Shawwāl 'Faṭur' and Dhū l-Qaʿdah . . .") instead of *dhā l-qaʿdah*, with the name of the month as a fixed lexical item rather than reflecting the syntax of the sentence.[104]

Some of these divergences are typical of the mixed, sui generis, forms associated with Middle Arabic:[105]

(1) *aʿlamtīnī* instead of *aʿlamtinī* ("you [fem. sing.] informed me"), the lengthened second-person marker of the colloquial being used with the non-colloquial Form IV verb;[106]

(2) *wa-yuwarrūna* ("and they show"), using underlying colloquial *yiwarrū* "they show" (cf. *raʾā* "to see") with the literary third-person masculine marker *-ūna*;[107]

(3) *al-bāqiyūn* ("those that remain")[108] and *al-munḥaniyūn* ("those that bend")[109] for *al-bāqūn* and *al-munḥanūn*, with sound plurals attached to fixed colloquial forms *bāqī-* and *munḥanī-*; and

(4) *fa-hal iḥdā minkunna* for *fa-hal iḥdākunna* ("so will any of you"), a partitive preposition being used as in, e.g., colloquial *waḥdah fīkum* ("one among you"), in combination with the literary form *iḥdā*.[110]

- Use of colloquialisms:[111] e.g., *fashā sirrahu* for *afshā sirrahu* ("he revealed his secret");[112] *yaʿṣā fiyya* for *yaʿṣīnī* ("he disobeys me");[113] *al-mathūm* for *al-muttaham* ("the accused");[114] *rīḥatuhā* for *rāʾiḥatuhā* ("its smell");[115] *dabbartī* for *dabbarti* ("you plotted");[116] Ḥawwā for Ḥawwāʾ ("Eve");[117] *bi-thamān sibaḥ* for *bi-thamānī sibaḥ* ("for eight strings of beads");[118] *wa-ṭāsha l-khabar* ("and the news escaped"), using the colloquial verb *ṭāsh*;[119] *fir* (written with *sukūn*, i.e., *firr*; "flee!"), where the colloquial imperative is intended;[120] and many more.
- Distortions of word endings to create rhymes in rhymed prose passages: e.g., *fa-ʿtadhara bi-ʿudhrin sāqiṭ* [for *sāqiṭin*] *lā yajidu lahu lāqiṭ* [for *lāqiṭan*] ("the man let fall an excuse too feeble for any to stoop to address");[121] *lā aʿrafu min ḥadīthihim illā l-qalīl* [for *l-qalīla*] *wa-lā arā fīhim wajhan ṣabīḥan jamīl* [for *jamīlan*] ("of whose speech I understood but little and among whom I found no cheerful, comely face").[122]

- Unusual turns of phrase, spellings, and lexical items: e.g., *naḥwa min*[123] and *bi-naḥw*,[124] both meaning "approximately"; *ayḍah* meaning "also" alongside standard *ayḍan*;[125] the repeated use of *aqṭāʿ* (اقطاع, without *hamzah* or vowels in the lithograph) as the plural of *iqṭāʿ* ("fief, estate"), as in *wa-lahum aqṭāʿ yataʿayyashūna minhā* ("and they have estates off which they live")[126] and *wa-li-hādhā l-manṣib aqṭāʿ ʿaẓīmah* ("and this office has great estates attached to it");[127] the use of *marār* in the sense of "bitterness," alongside standard *marārah*;[128] and the use of *iḥtafala fī* in the sense of "to assemble (a gift)."[129]
- Incorrect vocalization: e.g., ونُضْرَتَهُ for ونَضْرَتَهُ ("and its bloom")[130] and طَمْرَهُ for طِمِرَّهُ ("his steed").[131]
- To these should be added an occasional abruptness or jerkiness of style resulting from a paucity of copulas between sentences. For example, *wa-tuwuffiya laylata ʿīd al-fiṭr 1229 kāna mina l-ḥazm . . .* ("he himself died on the eve of the Feast of the Fast-Breaking in 1229. He was possessed of a high degree of resolve"), where one might expect *wa-* after the date (§2.1.20); *fa-nḥanā ʿalayhim . . . al-Sayyid Aḥmad kāna l-Sayyid Aḥmad* ("Sayyid Aḥmad . . . then took care of them. Sayyid Aḥmad was a learned scholar") where one might likewise expect *wa-kāna . . .* (§2.1.27); *wa-ltaḥafa l-jaww bi-l-ḍiyā . . . nahaḍnā li-l-maktūbah* ("the air was suffused with light. We rose for the prescribed prayer") where one might expect *fa-nahaḍnā* (§2.1.35); and *kharaz abyaḍ mustaṭīl fīhi baʿḍ khuṭūṭ sumr maʿrūf bi-hādhā l-ism fī Miṣr ayḍan* ("elongated white beads with brown stripes; they are known by the same name in Egypt.") where one might expect *fa-huwa maʿrūf* (§2.2.26).

The presence of supposed errors is rendered more problematic by the fact that al-Tūnisī cannot be dismissed as poorly trained in formal Arabic. As we have described elsewhere (see Introduction, p. xxvi), al-Tūnisī, as a language editor at the Egyptian Medical School, played a role in the creation of a grammatically correct yet readable and supple form of Arabic appropriate to the production of medical and other scientific texts. He was also employed by the standard-setting government press at Būlāq to edit or oversee the production of several canonical works of older Arabic literature.[132]

It is my belief that many of the "errors" and other features listed above may be attributed to the method by which the text was produced, which, I believe, allowed an element of orality to creep in, as well as by the nature of the relationship between the author and his editor, who was also his institutional superior, consciousness of which may have limited the thoroughness with which the author checked it.

Perron's description of how the work came into being raises questions. If the work was written by the shaykh, why did Perron feel compelled to write out a "correct copy" and to use this, rather than the shaykh's original, as the basis for the lithographic edition? We may assume that the literary verse with which the author embellishes the opening pages, for example, was set down by the author in finished form. Narrative passages, however, may have been less thoroughly worked. What role, then, was played by the teaching process in introducing the divergences from standard Arabic that have been noted?

I speculate that that process consisted of al-Tūnisī dictating to Perron material he had earlier prepared, perhaps in the form of notes. The dictation would likely have been accompanied by oral explanation and elaboration. Indeed, Perron provides, in addition to the numerous footnotes to the translation, seventy-six further pages of "Notes and Clarifications" regarding the text (*Voyage au Darfour*, 397–473), many of them described explicitly as being dictated by the author; the more-than-one-thousand-word addition to the original hundred-word description of how the geomancer creates the designs by means of which he foretells the future (§4.66) is a typical, if unusually long, example of these elaborations. In such a context, al-Tūnisī may have unconsciously used Middle Arabic forms and colloquialisms that, had he seen them on the page, he would have corrected. Or it may be that Perron, on writing out his "correct copy," made these errors as he attempted to recapture the full content of the discussion while lacking the command of the language that would have enabled him to recognize them as nonliterary or incorrect forms. This copy would have been the basis for the lithographic edition.

Earlier editors have concluded that "the lithographed Arabic copy . . . was checked after being printed and compared with the author's copy."[133] However, Perron states merely that he "reread" it with the author, which may imply a more passive role for the latter than that of "checking" and "comparing." More notable is that fact that this process must have taken place, according to the same editors, only *after* Perron's copy had been printed;[134] al-Tūnisī may therefore have been presented with a fait accompli. Under such circumstances, and especially given that the copyist was both his institutional superior and the person to whom he was indebted for the book's seeing the light of day, his review of

Perron's text may have been more or less pro forma. As it stands, Perron's text diverges in significant ways from standard literary norms: at one end of the range are those that are most plausibly attributable to al-Tūnisī (such as the Sudanese colloquialism *aṣbir*, "wait!")[135] and at the other those most plausibly attributable to Perron (such as the misspelling, referred to above, of خرج, "he went out," as خرخ). In between, the judgment of who was responsible for what must in the end be subjective. Does the awkward *fa-ʾin kāna dīwānan ʿāmman kāna sabʿatan al-mutarjimīn* (§3.1.41), for example, faithfully reproduce, as I have chosen to believe, an oral gloss of the author's ("If it's a public audience, they're seven—these interpreters—") or is it simply a mistake on Perron's part?

Moving on from the question of language per se, another level of complication is created when we compare the Arabic text with Perron's French translation. This differs from the Arabic in that parts of the former, called "digressions" by Perron, are relegated to notes at the back of the work.[136] On the other hand, some words, phrases, and passages found in the French translation are not to be found in the Arabic. The most glaring instance of the latter is a passage of 203 words in the translation that supplies an obvious lacuna in the Arabic;[137] here an entire page must have disappeared from Perron's notes, after Perron made his translation but before he copied the text, the disruption to the sense going unnoticed by him. Other additional material in the French, however, is limited to single words or short phrases. Earlier editors have assumed that whatever is in the French that is not in the Arabic should be regarded as material that, for unknown reasons, dropped out of the latter; they have therefore in a number of cases inserted into their edition words taken from the French and translated into Arabic. It is our feeling, in contrast, that what is additional in the French (the missing page excepted) was added by the translator to gloss and clarify the Arabic, and that by adding these words and passages Perron sought to fill in the lacunae that likely developed in the give-and-take of the orally based lessons, or that simply assumed more knowledge on the French reader's part than was reasonable to expect. This happens frequently when Perron clarifies which person is being referred to by adding a name (e.g., *Il allait trouver Mohammed-Doukkoumy, fils de l'émyn Aly* (El-Tounsy, *Voyage au Darfour*, 82) vs. *dhahaba ilā Muḥammad ibn al-amīn* (al-Tūnisī, *Tashḥīdh*, 1850, 90)) or simply expands the text when it seems overly laconic (e.g., *"J'irai, je le veux," dit-il* (El-Tounsy, *Voyage au Darfour*, 100) vs. *fa-qāla wa-lā budd* (al-Tūnisī, *Tashḥīdh*, 1850, 104), or *une habitude singulière chez les montagnards du Marrah est* (Perron, *Voyage au*

Darfour, 146) vs. *wa-min gharāʾib ʿawāʾidihim* (al-Tūnisī, *Tashḥīdh*, 1850, 143). In some cases, Perron's translation becomes a paraphrase, as with *"Volontiers, répondent-elles, nous sommes prêtes." Et la mayrem, qui connaît chaque fille et l'amant de chacune d'elles* (El-Tounsy, *Voyage au Darfour*, 235) vs. *fa-yaqulna lahā ḥubban wa-karāmatan wa-hiya taʿlamu kulla ṣabiyyatin wa-maḥbūbahā* (al-Tūnisī, *Tashḥīdh*, 1850, 215). The urgency of Perron's desire to elaborate on the Arabic text and make its unfamiliar aspects comprehensible to his French readers is evidenced by the numerous footnotes in which he quotes additional explanations provided orally by al-Tūnisī, presumably at Perron's request; particularly striking examples are the glosses to wedding songs[138] and the already mentioned thousand-word expansion on al-Tūnisī's description of how geomancers arrive at their predictions.[139]

Other factors may be in play. On occasion, Perron goes so far as to alter al-Tūnisī's text in the interests of political, perhaps specifically Saint-Simonian, correctness. Thus, al-Tūnisī's statement "Rarely, though, is a chaste woman to be found among the Blacks . . ." (§3.2.46) has no equivalent in Perron's translation except in a backhanded form: in its place, we find a passage extolling the purity of Arab women (El-Tounsy, *Voyage au Darfour*, 262–63).

This edition and that made by ʿAsākir and Musʿad in 1965 implicitly share the aim of sorting out what in the text, whether on the level of language or of content, should be attributed to the author and what to Perron. In making their many judicious and fully explained emendations to Perron's version, the earlier editors do not, however, take into consideration the element of orality that I believe helped to shape the Arabic text, nor the tendency to gloss that helped to shape the French. Where language is concerned, ʿAsākir and Musʿad tend, without being dogmatic, to show less tolerance for divergences from the written norm. Where content is concerned, they rely more on Perron's translation. This edition, in contrast, has accepted the text as it stands in the lithograph in more cases. In terms of language, this has meant reviewing ʿAsākir and Musʿad's emendations with native speakers, who were asked, in each case, whether the original could pass muster if it were understood to be the result of oral rather than written communication; if the answer was positive, the original form was allowed to stand. In terms of content, this editor has assumed that what is additional in the French translation is Perron's, and as a result the translation has been used mostly for its notes.

Unannotated changes made to Perron's text consist of:

- Corrections taken from the list of errata at the back of the lithographic edition.
- Modernization of the orthography.
- Restoration to their full forms of abbreviations such as ح for حينئذٍ and ا.هـ. for انتهى.
- Standardization of terms that are inconsistently rendered in the original (e.g., *Wādāy* (Wadai), which occurs also as *Wadāy* and even *Wadadāy*, and *Kurdufāl* (Kordofan), which occurs also as *Kūrdufāl*). This includes the title *al-ab al-shaykh* (shaykh-father), which occurs frequently in the original with one or other of the two elements seemingly randomly omitted; the full title has been used in all cases in this edition.
- Under this rubric too falls Perron's transliteration of terms in the Fur language, which is particularly inconsistent (cf. التيموركه, التاموركه, and التموركه ("the Tomorókkóngá")).
- Similarly, words that Perron persistently spells according to the pattern *faʿay-* and *faʿī-* (e.g., Ṣalayḥ, Razayqāt, Masīriyyah) have been changed to *fuʿay-* or *fiʿay-* (hence, Ṣulayḥ, Rizayqāt, Misīriyyah) in keeping with general norms, on the assumption that Perron's spellings are due to mishearing or misunderstanding.
- Addition of punctuation where needed to compensate for the lack of copulas that reflects the semi-oral nature of the text.

Annotated changes made to Perron's text include:

- Correction of misspellings affecting the ductus.
- Insertion of elements required to make the text comprehensible.
- Omission, in keeping with LAL practice, of the original voweling, except where a variation from the norm has significance for the understanding of the text.

The Translation

There are two earlier translations of this work into English. The first, by Bayle St. John, entitled *Travels of an Arab Merchant in Sudan: The Black Kingdoms of Central Africa (Darfur, Wadai)*, appeared in 1854 and is a combined and abridged translation of Nicolas Perron's French translations of both of al-Tūnisī's works, that on Darfur and that on Wadai.[140] The second is an unpublished MA thesis undertaken at Abdullahi Bayero University in 1976 by the late H. S. Umar, entitled "Al-Tūnisī, Travels in Darfur: Translation, Collation and Annotation of *Tashḥīdh al-adhhān bi-sīrat bilād al-ʿArab wa-l-Sūdān*." I have not used St. John's version since it is an abridgment and at two removes from the original. I have reviewed Umar's notes with care and quoted from them on occasion, and have also appealed to his translation for help with occasional problematic passages.[141] I also kept Perron's French translation beside me, making use of his notes and, sparingly, his text; the latter, because of its divergences from the Arabic (see above), has to be treated with care.[142]

Al-Tūnisī's prose style is mostly rather plain, with occasional rhetorical flourishes, and does not, in itself, pose major problems for a translator. Though the text contains a number of colloquialisms and other nonstandard forms, these were not intended, in most cases, to create a special effect, and no attempt has been made, generally speaking, to distinguish them in register from the rest of the text. Verse and the touches of endearingly flat rhymed prose (*sajʿ*) with which the author embellishes certain passages pose a greater challenge. I have rhymed where it came naturally, and where it did not, used assonance, rhythm, and other forms of "musicality" to distinguish these types of language. Some kinds of verse, such as chronograms (see §§2.1.23–25) and puzzle poems (see §§2.2.2–9), usually require, if their secrets are to be decoded, too close a reading to allow for any but a prose-like translation.

Arabic, or Arabized, forms are transcribed in the text according to the Library of Arabic Literature series norms, and no attempt has been made either to render colloquial Sudanese phonetic values (such as *g* for *q*) or, in the case of place and tribal names, to Anglicize (thus Masālīṭ rather than Mesalit and Wāddāy rather than Wadai); however, Anglicized or other recognized forms of names are listed in the glossary in parentheses following the form in which they occur in the text. Likewise, names occurring in both the Arab and non-Arab traditions have been kept in their Arabic forms—Ḥawwāʾ rather than Eve, Ibrāhīm rather than Abraham—in recognition of the different resonances these may carry in the Arab cultural and religious imagination; their conventional English equivalents are given in the endnotes.

Fur language items have, on the contrary, been transliterated according to a system developed by Fur linguists that avoids nonstandard characters and does not show tone, but does give the language its due as a separate presence within the text.[143] It was decided not to use al-Tūnisī's own transliterations of Fur, though he went to considerable trouble in this regard, even introducing a special character (ݣ for *ng*), because his transliteration lacks many basic features and is inconsistent. How far the modern versions provided diverge from the language underlying al-Tūnisī's transliterations is for scholars of Fur to decide.

The translation of certain words whose usage is specific to Darfur or even this particular text calls for comment, as follows:

- *Dārfūr* versus *Dār al-Fūr*: both forms occur in the text. *Dārfūr* is a compound term that denotes the state known by that name, with all its lands and ethnic groups; *Dār al-Fūr* should, by analogy with other names of the same structure, such as *Dār Rungā* and *Dār Birgid*, denote "the Land of the Fur," i.e., the territories inhabited by the Fur ethnic group. The text is not consistent, however, in maintaining this distinction, and sometimes seems to use *Dār al-Fūr* to denote the country per se (e.g., *sulṭān Dār al-Fūr* ["The sultan of *Dār al-Fūr*"], §3.2.37) or *manṣib al-bāb ghayr mukhṭaṣṣ bi-Dār al-Fūr bal fī Tūnis* ("the Door [i.e., the post of High Chamberlain] is not peculiar to *Dār al-Fūr*; it exists also in Tunis," §3.2.38) or an entity including ethnic groups other than the Fur (e.g., *wa-ajmal al-nisāʾ fī Dār al-Fūr . . . nisāʾ al-ʿArab* ["but the most beautiful women in *Dār al-Fūr* . . . are those of the Arabs"], §3.1.13). *Dārfūr* has therefore been translated consistently as Darfur, while *Dār al-Fūr* has been translated according to my reading of the context either as Darfur or as "the Lands of the Fur" (but, to reduce confusion, not as Dār al-Fūr).
- *al-fāshir*: translated as "the sultan's seat" or "the sultan's capital" rather than El-Fasher (name, from the later part of the nineteenth century, of the capital of Darfur and, more recently, of North Darfur); see note 227.
- *māl* (plural *amwāl*): translated variously as "wealth, property, assets, cattle," rather than "money," as coinage had only restricted circulation in Darfur (see §§3.3.41–55) and is never what is intended here by this word.
- *malik*: treated variously, reflecting Darfurian usage:
  (1) translated as "king" when used in its conventional sense as a designation of a monarch (e.g., "the King of Kordofan" [*Malik Kurdufāl*], §2.2.49), including the sultan of Darfur (e.g., "Sultan ʿAbd al-Raḥmān al-Rashīd, king of Darfur" [*al-Sulṭān ʿAbd al-Raḥmān al-Rashīd, malik Dārfūr*], §2.2.15).

(2) retained in its original form when used as a title of tribal chiefs (e.g., Malik Muḥammad Sanjaq, a Zaghāwah leader, §2.2.19) or leaders with links to the sultanic family (e.g., Malik Ibrāhīm wad Ramād, §2.3.38); however, such persons are called "kings" or "petty kings" when referred to collectively in order not to lose the connotations of royalty, some of whose Sudanic accoutrements, such as the right to use copper kettledrums among their insignia, still pertained to them.

(3) translated as "master of" when used as a title for an official placed in charge of a significant place or specialized group (e.g., "master of the men's door" [*malik bāb al-rijāl*], §3.1.59), "master of the royal slaves" [*malik al-ʿabīdiyyah*], §3.1.60).

- *al-Sūdān*: never translated as "Sudan," since it refers to people, not a country (and no country of that name existed at that time). Thus *bilād/arāḍī al-Sūdān* are "the Land(s)/Territories of the Blacks" and in the author's usage may refer to either Darfur specifically or the countries of the "Sudanic belt" from western Funj to the Atlantic. When preceded by *ahl* ("the people of"), *al-Sūdān* is translated as "the people of the Land of the Blacks" or simply "the Blacks." As Browne noted, "Soudan in Arabic corresponds to our Nigritia, merely general words for the *country of the blacks*."[144]

Notes to the Frontmatter

Foreword

1 See further my *The Darfur Sultanate* (with an extensive bibliography), *Darfur and the British,* and the earlier *Land in Dar Fur.*

2 After 1916, under the British, Darfur kept approximately the boundaries of the sultanate, but since the 1990s Khartoum has subdivided it into five provinces, namely Central, East, North, South, and West.

3 Ethnographically, Darfur is not well served, but the various studies of the Berti by Ladislav Holy, starting with his *Neighbors and Kinsmen: A Study of the Berti of Darfur,* are a very good introduction.

4 See Holt, *Studies in the History of the Near East*, 76–78.

5 These fragments of information are tentatively analyzed in my *Darfur Sultanate*, 24–39.

6 See further, McGregor, *Darfur (Sudan) in the Age of Stone Architecture c. AD 1000–1750.*

7 Three court transcripts (*sijill*) that I photographed were issued "under the authority of the *iiya baasi* Zamzam Umm al-Nāṣir . . ." *bi-niyaba iiya baasi Umm al-Nasir . . .*

8 Dar Diima was the only region of Darfur for which the British produced a detailed district handbook; this is given in my *Darfur and the British.* A Nyala district handbook was produced, but seemingly never circulated.

9 Similar-sounding titles are used among several peoples in Darfur and Wadai, usually with ritual or religious functions.

10 This section is largely based on the three hundred or so documents I photographed in Darfur between 1970 and 1976. All the material is available in my papers deposited in the University of Bergen Library. My *Land in Dar Fur* gives translations of some fifty documents illustrating the estate system.

11 The texts and putative translations are given in my "Two Early Dar Fur Charters."

12 See my "Endowment, Privilege and Estate on the Central and Eastern Sudan."

13 See my "A Prince and His Neighbours."

14 See my "The Archives of Shoba."

15 In contradistinction to local or petty merchants called *jallaba.*

16 See Walz, *Trade between Egypt and Bilad as-Sudan.*

17 See the early study by Richard Gray, *A History of the Southern Sudan, 1839–1889.*

18 See my "The Conquest of Darfur, 1873–82." This gives translations of the relevant al-Zubayr letters.

19 Many informants used the expression *Umm Kwakiyyah*, meaning "the time of gunfire," to characterize this period.

20 A more detailed account is given in my *Darfur Sultanate*, 275–80.

21 About two hundred letters of ʿAlī Dīnār survive; these include some hundred to be found in the Khartoum Archives and the Sudan Archive at the University of Durham. The other hundred I photographed in Darfur. Copies of all of them are among my papers at the University of Bergen.

22 See the contemporary description quoted in Theobald, *ʿAli Dinar: Last Sultan of Darfur, 1898–1916*, 194.

23 What follows is based on my *Darfur and the British*, a book that has a sad history behind it. In 1970 I spent the summer in al-Fashir going through the five hundred or more British administrative files in the Mudīriyyah or provincial headquarters (then housed in ʿAlī Dīnār's palace). I was given complete access to the files and copied about four hundred pages of notes—there was of course no copy machine nearby. I copied what I thought was relevant to my research. A few years later, the files were removed and stored in huts, where they were destroyed by the rains. Given the ethnographic interests of the handful of British officials, the destruction of the tribal files (the Zaghāwah file, for example, was in three thick volumes with many Arabic notes) was a catastrophic loss. My original notes are among my papers in Bergen.

24 Few records survive from the early years of the British occupation of Darfur either in the National Records Office in Khartoum, the Public Records Office in London, or the Sudan Archive in Durham.

25 Given in my *Darfur and the British.*

26 During my visits to Darfur in the late 1960s and '70s I found it easier to use French when interacting with the Fulani holy families, but they belonged to networks that stretched as far as west as Senegal.

27 See "The Masalit War" in Flint and de Waal, *Darfur: A Short History of a Long War*, 57–61 for a case study. See also de Waal, ed., *War in Darfur and the Search for Peace.*

Introduction

28 Al-Shidyāq, *Leg over Leg*, 2:119. In material terms, al-Shidyāq may have fared better than Perron, at least before the latter's promotion: in a letter dated August 10, 1838, Perron

complains "I am poor, with no fortune but my ink" (Artin, *Lettres du Dr Perron du Caire et d'Alexandrie à M. Jules Mohl, à Paris, 1838–1854*, 46).

29 The scope and importance of this undertaking, and the range and depth of al-Tūnisī's collaboration with Perron both within and without its component translation projects, are only now starting to be recognized. I owe my awareness of these wider dimensions of the relationship to Khaled Fahmy, who has kindly allowed me to draw on his "Translating Bichat and Lavoisier into Arabic," an unpublished paper presented at the Middle East, South Asian, and African Studies Colloquium, Columbia University, February 9, 2015.

30 See Hunwick, "Leo Africanus's Description of the Middle Niger, Hausaland and Bornu," 272–91.

31 For example, Edmé-François Jomard contributed to, edited, and helped to publish the *Journal d'un voyage à Temboctou et à Jenné dans l'Afrique Centrale* by the explorer René Caillié (Paris, 1830) and P. H. S. Escayrac de Lauture contributed a "Notice sur le Kordofan" (*Bulletin de la Société de géographie de Paris*, Series 4,1 (1851) p. 371) and a "Mémoire sur le Soudan" (Paris, 1855), which includes important interviews, made in Cairo, with pilgrims from Darfur.

32 Browne, W. G. *Travels in Africa, Egypt, and Syria, from the Year 1792 to 1798*. London: T. Caddel Junior and W. Davies, 1799. A second, enlarged, edition was published in 1806; I have not been able to examine a copy.

33 See §2.1.32.

34 See Glossary.

35 See §2.2.35.

36 Al-Tūnisī's two years in Wadai are not covered by *In Darfur*.

37 Al-Tūnisī provides little specific information about his education. He states that he studied at the mosque-university of al-Azhar in Cairo before he left for Darfur at age fourteen (§2.1.34); as he told his father when they were reunited, he had acquired there "a certain amount of scholarship" (§2.2.28). In Darfur, he took lessons with Faqīh Madanī al-Fūtāwī, his father's sponsor's brother (see, e.g., §3.3.18), but gives no information as to what these covered. On his return to Egypt, he studied once more, though he does not specify where, what, or for how long; it is likely, however, that he conducted his studies at al-Azhar and that it was during this period that he acquired the greater part of his education.

38 Heyworth-Dunne, *An Introduction to the History of Education in Modern Egypt*, 125. The earlier editors of this work, Khalīl Maḥmūd Musʿad and Muṣṭafā Muḥammad ʿAsākir, state that al-Tūnisī and Perron worked at the veterinary school associated with

the Medical School (*Tashḥīdh*, 1965, 13). This seems to be based on an ambiguous statement by al-Shayyāl ("Duktūr Birrūn (Dr. Perron) wa-l-shaykhān Muḥammad ʿAyyād al-Ṭanṭāwī wa-Muḥammad ʿUmar al-Tūnisī," 193), but neither al-Tūnisī nor Perron mention the veterinary school.

39 Al-Tūnisī describes his role as *taṣḥīḥ*, literally "correction." In this context, this means that he was one of the *muṣaḥḥiḥūn*, or scholars educated at al-Azhar who corrected the work of the original translators who, being Christians chosen primarily for their knowledge of European languages, often lacked a firm command of Arabic grammar and style (Fahmy, "Translating Bichat," 11). There is no evidence that al-Tūnisī knew French, and, despite the crucial role of the *muṣaḥḥiḥ* in the translation process, the common characterization of him as a translator is potentially misleading. On the title page of the *Voyage au Ouadây*, Perron describes al-Tūnisī as "Réviseur en Chef à l'École de Médicine du Kaire."

40 These included al-Ḥarīrī's *Maqāmāt*, al-Ibshīhī's *al-Mustaṭraf fī kull fann mustaẓraf*, and al-Fīrūzābādī's *al-Qāmūs al-muḥīṭ* (al-Tūnisī, *Tashḥīdh*, 1965, 15). On January 19, 1854, Perron noted in a letter to Jules Mohl that "Cheikh El-Tounsy's *Hariry*, printed at Bulaq, has sold out; there are only four or five copies left. . . . I have just bought the *Moustatraf* of my old teacher El-Tounsy, also printed at Bulaq. It has had a lot of success and sells very well" (Artin, *Lettres*, 107).

41 Artin, *Lettres*, 107.

42 Messaoudi, "Perron," 750.

43 Fahmy, "Translating Bichat," 13.

44 Other Saint-Simonians would follow, most notably the group led by Prosper Enfantin, known to his followers as "Le Père," who arrived in 1833 in search of "La Mère" and left again in 1836 following the failure of the group's engineering project (construction of a barrage on the Nile) and the plague; Perron involved himself in their activities (Messaoudi, "Perron," 750) and helped Enfantin find work when he was penniless (O'Fahey, "Egypt, Saint-Simon and Muḥammad ʿAlī," 21).

45 Perron wrote to Jules Mohl on September 26, 1839: "I have just been appointed director of the School of Medicine. . . . Given the knowledge of the Arabic language that I have acquired, and which corresponds to the needs of the current school set-up, the Pasha [i.e., Muḥammad ʿAlī] approved my promotion immediately" (Artin, *Lettres*, 58). In almost the same breath, however, Perron asks Mohl to find him a position in France, since "I do not want to stay here for more than a few years, if possible" (Artin, *Lettres*, 59). Perron indicates that his desire to leave Egypt was due to the country's precarious

financial situation, which had led to delays in payment of staff salaries and the downsizing of the school.

46 Al-Shayyāl, "Duktūr Birrūn," 184, 184, n. 3, 185. According to al-Shayyāl, Perron resigned in 1846; however, he is described as director of the Medical School on the title page of *Voyage au Ouaday*, published in 1851. He may have regarded himself as merely taking leave in 1846 and been relieved of the post while in France. As early as May 14, 1844, Perron confides in a letter to Jules Mohl that he is thinking of taking six months' leave (Artin, *Lettres*, 83–84), and he repeats his intention to do so in a letter dated January 14, 1845 (Artin, *Lettres*, 89).

47 Fahmy describes in detail the sophisticated methodology used to produce translations, which required the participation of foreign doctors employed by the school, such as Perron, who in some cases had authored the works in question; of Egyptian graduates of the school who had subsequently trained in France as physicians, of whom by 1832 there were twelve and who drafted the translations; and of language editors, such as al-Tūnisī ("Translating Bichat," 12–13). Another member of the team of language editors and correctors with whom Perron worked closely and whom he regarded with as much respect as he did al-Tūnisī was the latter's younger colleague Muḥammad ʿAyyād al-Ṭanṭāwī (1810–61), who would eventually (ca. 1846) leave Egypt for Russia, where he taught at the university in St. Petersburg and wrote, among a number of other works, one of the first teaching grammars of spoken Arabic for foreigners (*Aḥsan al-nukhab fī maʿrifat lisān al-ʿArab*). Perron excepted al-Tūnisī and al-Ṭanṭāwī from his criticism of the Egyptian scholars of his day, which was otherwise excoriating: "These poor *ʿulamāʾ* have nothing of scholarship but the name, are immeasurably lazy and immeasurably ignorant. . . . They do not know the names of the most ordinary Arabic books. . . . None of them writes anything" (Artin, *Lettres*, 90). Apropos of his (unrealized) project to prepare, with the help of al-Tūnisī, an edition of the renowned fourteenth-century dictionary *al-Qāmūs al-muḥīṭ* (*The Encompassing Ocean*) by Muḥammad al-Fīrūzābādī, he wrote, "there are not more than ten of these scholars who know how to use an Arabic dictionary. They do not even know the word-order system. . . . Let us then give a dictionary to the *ʿulamāʾ*" (Artin, *Lettres*, 92). Perron's negative assessment of contemporary Egyptian scholarship was not necessarily shared by other foreign scholars: Edward Lane had nothing but praise for Ibrahīm al-Disūqī, another member of the Medical School translation team, who assisted him in the preparation of his massive compendium and translation of medieval dictionaries, *An Arabic-English Lexicon* (see Lane, *Lexicon*, 1:5), while Aḥmad Fāris al-Shidyāq, who studied under Egyptian scholars from 1829 to 1832, believed that they were, at least, better than those of his homeland of Lebanon, though

their command of grammar was more theoretical than practical and they taught better than they wrote (al-Shidyāq, *Leg over Leg*, 2:383–84).

48 Fahmy, "Translating Bichat," 13.

49 Fahmy, "Translating Bichat," 32.

50 Fahmy, "Translating Bichat," 20.

51 Fabre, ed. *Dictionnaire des dictionnaires de médecine français et étrangers ou traité complet de médecine et de chirurgie pratiques, par une société de médecins.*

52 Clot Bey, *Kunūz al-ṣiḥḥah wa-yawāqīt al-minḥah.*

53 Al-Shayyāl, "Duktūr Birrūn," 221; O'Fahey, *The Writings of Eastern Sudanic Africa to c. 1900*, 67–70. O'Fahey's description of *al-Shudhūr al-dhahabiyyah* as being "based on Clot Bey's lectures" (O'Fahey, *Writings*, 70) should be applied not to this but to *Kunūz al-ṣiḥḥah* (see preceding note).

54 Perron, *al-Jawāhir al-saniyyah fī l-aʿmāl al-kīmāwiyyah.*

55 Though Perron may have known relatively little Arabic on his arrival in France, as the choice for their lessons of these relatively simple animal fables suggests, it is worth noting that he was, according to one historian at least, the only foreign teacher employed by Muḥammad ʿAlī to know any Arabic at all (al-Shayyāl, "Duktūr Birrūn," 181).

56 El-Tounsy, *Voyage au Darfour.* The volume includes material not included in the Arabic text, namely, a twenty-six-page supplement (*appendice*) concerning Muḥammad Abū Madyan, a Keira pretender whom the Egyptian government attempted but failed to place on the throne of Darfur in 1843, plus more than ninety pages of notes, comments, and clarifications, many of them dictated to Perron by al-Tūnisī. Neither al-Tūnisī nor Perron give dates for their work on what would become *The Land of the Blacks* and its sister, French-only, volume, treating al-Tūnisī's briefer stay in Wadai, the *Voyage au Ouadai.* However, Perron's French translation of the first was completed by 1842, as evidenced by Perron's statement in a letter to Jules Mohl dated March 28 of that year that he is sending the manuscript of the translation to the geographer Edmé-François Jomard, "who has allowed me to hope that it will be published" (Artin, *Lettres*, 71). Also, in a note to the translation, Perron (*Voyage au Darfour*, 316, n. 1) states that al-Tūnisī had read the text of the next-to-last chapter of the book four years previously. We may deduce, then, that the two began work no later than 1838. By July 12, 1845, the work on both volumes of translation (that for Wadai as well as that for Darfur) was well underway, Perron telling Mohl that "I have very little left to do. I am drawing the illustrations and a map. The first part of the journey [i.e., the *Voyage au Darfour*] is being printed . . ." (Artin, *Lettres*, 95). By October 5, 1845, the *Voyage au Darfour* was printed (Artin, *Lettres*, 99).

57 Al-Tūnisī ibn Sulaymān [*sic*], Muḥammad ibn al-Sayyid ʿUmar. *Kitāb Tashḥīdh al-adhhān fī sīrat bilād al-ʿArab wa-l-Sūdān* [French title page: *Voyage au Darfour ou l'aiguisement de l'esprit par le voyage au Soudan et parmi les arabes du centre de l'Afrique par le cheykh Mohamed ibn-Omar el-tounsy [*sic*], Autographié et publié par Mr. Perron*]. Paris: Benjamin Duprat, 1850.

58 El-Tounsy, Mohammed ibn-Omar. *Voyage au Ouadây*, traduit de l'arabe par le Dr. Perron, publié par le Dr. Perron et M. Jomard. Paris: Bejamin Duprat, 1851. The end matter includes vocabulary lists for several languages of the region ("Ouayen, Fôrien, Fertyt," etc.) compiled by Edmé-François Jomard.

59 In addition to his scientific translations and the works produced in collaboration with al-Tūnisī, Perron published the following: an article entitled "Tableau historique des sciences philosophiques" for Bailly de Merlieux's popular encyclopedia (1829); *Abrégé de grammaire . . . de l'arabe vulgaire* (1832); *Précis de jurisprudence* (6 vols., 1848–54), which is the above-mentioned translation of Khalīl ibn Isḥāq's *al-Mukhtaṣar* (3 vols., 1846–51); "Légendes orientales," articles published in *L'Illustration* (1850); "Récits arabes," articles published in (*La Revue orientale et algérienne* (1852); *La Perfection des deux arts, ou, Traité complet d'hippologie et d'hippiatrie* (3 vols., 1852–60), a translation of Abū Bakr ibn Badr's *Kitāb Kāmil al-ṣināʿatayn al-maʿrūf bi-l-Nāṣirī fī l-bayṭarah wa-l-zarṭaqah*; *Les Femmes arabes avant et après l'Islamisme* (1858), which draws on anecdotes from the *Kitāb al-aghānī* (*Book of Songs*); *Glaive-des-couronnes* (1862), a translation of the popular romance *Sayf al-Tījān*; *L'Islamisme, son institution, son influence et son avenir* (written in 1865 for an encyclopedia published in 1877); *Balance de la loi musulmane*, a translation of ʿAbd al-Wahhāb al-Shaʿrānī's *Mīzān al-sharīʿah*, published posthumously in 1898. He also wrote a number of articles for scholarly journals on celebrated figures of Arab lore, of which "Lettre sur les poètes Tarafah et Al-Moutalammis" in *Journal asiatique*, 3rd series, vol. XI, January 1841, pp. 215–47, may be taken as representative (compiled from Messaoudi, "Perron," and al-Shayyāl, "Duktūr Birrūn," 211–15).

60 Artin, *Lettres*, 38: "il était alors attaché comme médicin sanitaire à Alexandrie." Al-Shayyāl, however, says that he worked there as a private physician ("Duktūr Birrūn," 38). Probably he worked in both capacities.

61 Messaoudi, "Perron," 7.

62 The dispiriting coda to this life of intense engagement with the Arab world is that, during the later years of his life, Perron lost his Saint-Simonian enthusiasm for Islam's intellectual heritage. Already in 1850, he could write of Arab scholars that "the Muslims are almost all apers and parroters of the Greeks and the Indians," and by 1865 he had

dismissed Islam as a sterile and antipoetic monotheism; his hopes for the future of the Orient were now placed on Bahaism (see Messaoudi, "Perron," 751).

63 O'Fahey, *Darfur Sultanate*, 9.

64 O'Fahey, *Darfur Sultanate*, 12.

65 An Arabic manuscript with the same title housed at the Royal Library in Rabat is a copy of the first, Paris, edition (Umar, "Travels," xviii).

66 O'Fahey, *Writings*, 68.

67 El-Tounsy, *Voyage au Darfour*, lxxi–ii.

68 Though no illustrator is credited, Perron's comment in a letter that he has "only the illustrations to draw, and a map" (Artin, *Lettres*, 95) confirms that he was the artist.

69 Darfur was briefly occupied by Egyptian forces in 1843. It fell again to Egyptian forces in 1874, more than fifty years after Sennar and Kordofan, its neighbors to the east; the seven years that followed are known as the Turkiyyah, referring to the Ottoman affiliations of Egypt's rulers. In 1884, the Egyptians were driven out by the followers of the Mahdi ("the divinely guided leader sent to restore God's kingdom on earth") Muḥammad Hamad ibn ʿAbd Allāh. During the Mahdiyyah that followed, the Keira sultans maintained the resistance they had started during the Turkiyyah and, following the defeat of the Mahdist state by the British in 1898, were able to restore the sultanate, albeit under nominal British suzerainty. Darfur's independence ended with the death in battle of Sultan ʿAli Dīnār in 1916 following his 1915 rebellion against the British and in support of the Ottoman Empire.

70 Browne, *Travels in Africa*, 180–313.

71 Browne, *Travels in Africa*, 255.

72 Nachtigal, *Sahara and Sudan IV: Wadai and Darfur.*

73 O'Fahey, *Darfur Sultanate*, 69.

74 O'Fahey, *Writings*, 68.

75 Hill, *A Biographical Dictionary of the Sudan*, 278.

Note on the Text

76 Apparently only one hundred copies of the lithographic edition were printed (al-Tūnisī, *Tashḥīdh*, 1965, 16 (Foreword)), despite which it exists in two versions, one made apparently for the Arab market, the other for the French. Thus the copy in the library of the Institut Français d'Archéologie Orientale (IFAO) in Cairo ends with a four-folio list of corrections in Arabic; this list is absent from the copy made available online by the Bibliothèque Nationale Française (BNF). The latter, however, contains, on the left-hand side of the book, French short and long title pages followed by a four-folio section in

French entitled "Observations" (dealing with additions to another work, the French translation); the IFAO copy contains no material in French. The Arabic title pages of the IFAO and BNF copies also differ in orthographic detail. These differences do not, however, affect the body of the text, as each page of the latter ends and begins with the same word in both versions and the errors, as reflected in the list of corrections in the IFAO copy, are the same. Neither copy shows any sign of being incomplete or tampered with.

77 Al-Tūnisī, *Tashḥīdh al-adhhān fī sīrat bilād al-ʿArab wa-l-Sūdān,* 1965.

78 Perron gave the title *Voyage au Darfour* to both his edition of the Arabic text and his translation of it.

79 El-Tounsy, *Voyage au Darfour,* lxxi–ii ("Avant-propos").

80 Al-Shidyāq, *Leg over Leg,* 4/443. Al-Shidyāq's work appeared in 1855, only five years after *In Darfur,* and was issued by the same Paris publishing house, Benjamin Duprat, which was perhaps where al-Shidyāq saw it.

81 Al-Tūnisī, *Tashḥīdh,* 1965, 19–20.

82 Al-Tūnisī, *Tashḥīdh,* 1965, 20.

83 See al-Tūnisī, *Tashḥīdh,* 1965, 18–19.

84 It is impossible to evaluate Perron's exact degree of proficiency in Arabic when *In Darfur* was produced. With only a few years of study in Paris under his belt when he arrived in 1829, his Arabic may still have been basic, and the choice of the relatively straightforward *Kalīlah wa-Dimnah* as the material for his lessons with Muḥammad al-Tūnisī lends credence to this supposition. After seven years of residence in Egypt, in 1838, he published his notes for his physics lectures in Arabic under the title *Kitāb al-Azhār al-badīʿah fī ʿilm al-ṭabīʿah* (*The Book of Exquisite Flowers Concerning the Science of Physics*), for which he takes at least partial credit, according to al-Shayyāl, as translator. He did the same between 1842 and 1844 with his chemistry lecture notes, under the title of *al-Jawāhir al-saniyyah fī l-aʿmāl al-kīmāwiyyah* (*The Sublime Gems Concerning Chemical Operations*). In each case, however, he was assisted by a team of the Medical School's Egyptian translators and language editors (see al-Shayyāl, "Duktūr Birrūn," 214–15).

85 E.g., "as you will see on the following page, we have drawn a picture" (§3.1.91); "we have given a brief account of this earlier to which you may refer" (§3.2.4); "I witnessed this" (§3.1.45).

86 "If you want to get from me a clear exposition of Darfur and of how the home territories of these tribes and of the Bedouin who surround it are arranged, take a look at what I've drawn. . . " (§3.1.12).

87 Al-Tūnisī, *Tashḥīdh,* 1850, 3 (line 5).

88 Al-Tūnisī, *Tashḥīdh,* 1850, 229 (lines 9 and 10).

89 E.g., al-Tūnisī, *Tashḥīdh*, 1850, 5 (line 3).

90 Translations of words and phrases given here are not necessarily those given in the text but aim to allow easy recognition by the reader.

91 Both al-Tūnisī, *Tashḥīdh*, 1850, 2 (lines 4 and 6).

92 Al-Tūnisī, *Tashḥīdh*, 1850, 2 (line -3).

93 Al-Tūnisī, *Tashḥīdh*, 1850, 177 (line 4).

94 Al-Tūnisī, *Tashḥīdh*, 1850, 245 (line -4).

95 Al-Tūnisī, *Tashḥīdh*, 1850, 140 (line 7).

96 Al-Tūnisī, *Tashḥīdh*, 1850, 25 (line 3).

97 Al-Tūnisī, *Tashḥīdh*, 1850, 8 (line 13).

98 Al-Tūnisī, *Tashḥīdh*, 1850, 22 (lines -4, -3).

99 Al-Tūnisī, *Tashḥīdh*, 1850, 57 (line 7).

100 Al-Tūnisī, *Tashḥīdh*, 1850, 103 (line -3).

101 Al-Tūnisī, *Tashḥīdh*, 1850, 118 (line 1).

102 Al-Tūnisī, *Tashḥīdh*, 1850, 118 (line 2).

103 Al-Tūnisī, *Tashḥīdh*, 1850, 202 (line 5).

104 Al-Tūnisī, *Tashḥīdh*, 1850, 295 (line -2).

105 Middle Arabic indicates a variety of written Arabic that "combines standard and colloquial features with others of a third type" (Lentin, "Middle Arabic," 216). This variety was fairly common from at least the postclassical period until at least the *Nahḍah*, or renaissance in Arabic literature and sciences, in the latter half of the nineteenth century.

106 Al-Tūnisī, *Tashḥīdh*, 1850, 118 (line 4).

107 Al-Tūnisī, *Tashḥīdh*, 1850, 200 (line 11).

108 Al-Tūnisī, *Tashḥīdh*, 1850, 210 (line -7).

109 Al-Tūnisī, *Tashḥīdh*, 1850, 177 (line -5).

110 Al-Tūnisī, *Tashḥīdh*, 1850, 147 (lines 3–4).

111 In determining what constitutes a colloquialism (not always obvious given the distance in time and the lack of materials on Darfur and other possible relevant Arabics, such as Tunisian), I have been guided by the earlier editors of al-Tūnisī (*Tashḥīdh*, 1965), who give careful attention to this aspect of the text.

112 Al-Tūnisī, *Tashḥīdh*, 1850, 112 (line 10); see *Tashḥīdh*, 1965 112, n. 1.

113 Al-Tūnisī, *Tashḥīdh*, 1850, 122 (line -5); see *Tashḥīdh*, 1965, 128, n. 3 (though *Tashḥīdh*, 1965, amends in the text to *yaʿṣānī* without comment).

114 Al-Tūnisī, *Tashḥīdh*, 1850, 291 (line 6); see *Tashḥīdh*, 1965, 316, n. 1.

115 Al-Tūnisī, *Tashḥīdh*, 1850, 291 (line -6); see *Tashḥīdh*, 1965, 316, n. 3.

116 Al-Tūnisī, *Tashḥīdh*, 1850, 119 (line 6).

117 Al-Tūnisī, *Tashḥīdh*, 1850, 123 (line -4).

118 Al-Tūnisī, *Tashḥīdh*, 1850, 273 (line 9).

119 Al-Tūnisī, *Tashḥīdh*, 1850, 86 (line 8).

120 Al-Tūnisī, *Tashḥīdh*, 1850, 120 (line 17).

121 Al-Tūnisī, *Tashḥīdh*, 1850, 33 (lines 4–5).

122 Al-Tūnisī, *Tashḥīdh*, 1850, 40 (lines 2–3).

123 Al-Tūnisī, *Tashḥīdh*, 1850, 129 (line 10) and four other occurrences.

124 Al-Tūnisī, *Tashḥīdh*, 1850, 36 (line 9) and eight other occurrences.

125 Al-Tūnisī, *Tashḥīdh*, 1850, 255 (line 8) and four other occurrences.

126 Al-Tūnisī, *Tashḥīdh*, 1850, 136 (line -2).

127 Al-Tūnisī, *Tashḥīdh*, 1850, 162 (line 1).

128 Al-Tūnisī, *Tashḥīdh*, 1850, 2 (line 5), 255 (line 9), 283 (line -4), 285 (line -4).

129 Al-Tūnisī, *Tashḥīdh*, 1850, 22 (lines 8, 12).

130 E.g., al-Tūnisī, *Tashḥīdh*, 1850, 13 (line -4).

131 Al-Tūnisī, *Tashḥīdh*, 1850, 98 (line 9).

132 See p. xlviii, n. 40.

133 Al-Tūnisī, *Tashḥīdh*, 1965, 18 (foreword).

134 The writers base their assertion on the fact that "the corrections were written at the end of the book, but had it been checked after it had been copied and while still in the form of a handwritten manuscript, the corrections would have been written in the margin of the manuscript and the words and phrases corrected during the review would have been placed in the margin, in the form of insertions to be made in the text, which is the practice followed when manuscripts are corrected and checked and compared against one another" (al-Tūnisī, *Tashḥīdh*, 1965, 18 (foreword)).

135 Al-Tūnisī, *Tashḥīdh*, 1965, 221, n. 2.

136 For a list of these, see Perron's "Observations" at the front end of the BNF version of the Arabic text.

137 The lacuna occurs on page 184, line 13 of the lithographic edition, between the words رَكْ and وقد رسمنا; the passage in the French translation goes from page 200, line 16 to page 201, line 9: "du saryf . . . *meunières*." See further §3.1.91 and n. 92 in volume two.

138 See, e.g., §§3.2.11–14.

139 See §4.66.

140 See Introduction, p. xxvii.

141 I am indebted to R. S. O'Fahey for sharing with me his copy of Umar's translation.

142 I was not able to consult the notes on the work made by Sudanese historian and former official in Darfur Muḥammad ʻAbd al-Raḥīm that are housed in the National Records Office in Khartoum (see O'Fahey, *Writings*, 68).

143 I am indebted to Dr. Christine Waag, Musa Jargis, Adam Karama, and Bariwarig Tooduo Kondo of the Summer Institute for Linguistics for their efforts in this regard, which are all the more appreciated in view of the difficult conditions in which they worked.

144 Browne, *Travels in Africa*, 183.

In Darfur

Volume One

هذا كتاب

تشحيذ الأذهان

بسيرة بلاد العرب والسودان

لمؤلّفه

محمّد بن عمر التونسيّ

عفا الله عنه

This Is the Book

of

The Honing of Minds

through

Consideration of the Condition

of

the Land of the Arabs and the Blacks

by Its Author

Muḥammad ibn ʿUmar al-Tūnisī

May God Excuse His Sins

بسم الله الرحمن الرحيم

١،١ وصلّى الله على سيّدنا محمّد وعلى آله وصحبه وسلّم تسليماً كثيراً. يا من سيّر أقدام الأنام بإرادته السنيّة وجعل ﴿رِحْلَةَ ٱلشِّتَآءِ وَٱلصَّيْفِ﴾ بحكمته البهيّة نحمدك حمد من تلذّذ بحلاوة الراحة بعد مرار مشقّة السفر ونشكرك شكر من تنعّم بالإقامة بعد كدّ الرحلة والكدر ونسألك يا مالك الأملاك بما قدّرت من سير الكواكب في الأفلاك أن تُهطِل شآبيب رحمتك ورضوانك وتُنزِل غيث صلاتك وسلامك على أفضل من ارتحل وأقام وسافر من مكّة إلى الشام سيّدنا ومولانا محمّد الشفيع يوم العرض في المُذنبين الذي أُنزلت عليه ﴿قُلْ سِيرُوا فِي ٱلْأَرْضِ ثُمَّ ٱنظُرُوا كَيْفَ كَانَ عَاقِبَةُ ٱلْمُكَذِّبِينَ﴾ وعلى آله الذين رحلوا من أوطانهم في حبّه وأصحابه الذين هاجروا للمدينة رغبة في قربه وسلّم تسليماً كثيراً

٢،١ وبعد فيقول الفقير إلى رحمة ربّه المنّان محمّد بن السيّد عمر التونسيّ بن سليمان لمّا وفّقني الله تعالى لقراءة علوم العربيّة وأترع كأسي من بينها بالفنون الأدبيّة حتّى حُسِبْتُ من بني الأدب وذويه وعشيرته التي تؤويه أناخ الدهر بكلكله على ما بيدي من العين فغادره أثراً بعد عين[1] وكانت همّتي إذ ذاك مصروفة بتحصيل العلوم وجمع المنثور منها والمنظوم وحين شاهدت معاندة الزمان لمقتي تمثّلت بقول العلّامة الصفتيّ [كامل]

١ الأصل: العبن.

In the Name of God

the Merciful, the Compassionate

—and may God bless Our Lord Muḥammad and his kin and Companions, and grant them much peace. O You who move the feet of humankind by Your sublime will and have determined the times for «the winter and the summer caravan»[1] by Your radiant wisdom, we praise You as must one who has savored the sweetness of relaxation after suffering the bitterness of travel and privation, and we thank you as must one blessed with settled abode after the toil and turmoil of the road. We beseech You, O Possessor of all that may be possessed, by the course that You have decreed for the stars in their orbits, to cause the showers of Your mercy and Your acceptance to fall, to let the rain of Your blessing and Your peace descend on the best of those who journeyed and settled at journey's end, who traveled from Mecca to Syria[2]—our lord and master Muḥammad, our intercessor on the day when the wrongdoers shall be exposed, who was inspired to recite «Say, "Travel about the land and see what was the end of the deniers"»[3] and on his kin, who left their native lands for love of him, and on his Companions who migrated to Medina out of desire for his proximity, and to grant them all copious tranquility. 1.1

To proceed, the humble petitioner for the mercy of his most gracious Lord, Muḥammad son of al-Sayyid ʿUmar al-Tūnisī son of Sulaymān,[4] declares: after the Almighty had granted me success in the study of the sciences of the Arabic language and filled my cup with, in particular, the literary arts, and I'd come to be counted among the children and kinsmen of polite letters, one of that clan that opens to them their hearts, along came Fate and knelt like a camel upon my fortunes, bearing down with all its weight, leaving only ruin where once had been a solid estate.[5] All my concern at that time was devoted to the acquisition of the sciences, and the gathering of their manifestations in prose and in verse. When, therefore, I observed how Time persisted in its opposition, I quoted, to encapsulate my condition, the words of Eminent Scholar al-Ṣaftī: 1.2

هَـبَطَتْ ثُرَيَّا الشَّـارِدَاتِ لِهِمَّتِي   وَصَعِدْتُ فِي ٱلْعِرْفَانِ كُلَّ سَمَـاءِ
وَفَقَـهْتُ غَـيْرِي فِي ٱلْعُلُومِ وَإِنَّمَا   بَيْـنِي وَبَيْنَ ٱلْمَـالِ كُلُّ تَنَـائِي
فَعَجِبْتُ إِذْ عُقِدَ ٱللِّوَاءُ لِجَـاهِـلٍ   وَٱلْفَـقْرُ عَمَّ عَمَـائِـمَ ٱلْفُقَهَـاءِ

٣،١ ولمّا صفِرت الراحة وقرعت الساحة ومال المال وحال الحال وغار المَنْبَع ونبا[١] المرْبَع أنشدت من مقالي على شرح حالي شعرًا [كامل]

مَا حِيلَتِي وَلِذَا ٱلزَّمَانِ مَتَـاعِبٌ   يُؤْذِي ٱلشَّرِيفَ وَلِلْوَضِيعِ يَصُونُ
زَمَنٌ لَهُ حَـرْبٌ عَلَى أَهْلِ ٱلتُّـقَى   بِإِزَائِهِ حَـرْبُ ٱلْبَسُوسِ يَهُونُ
فَتَرَاهُ يَـرْفَعُ كُلَّ غَمْرٍ جَاهِـلٍ   وَيُسِيءُ كُـلَّ مُهَذَّبٍ وَيُهِـينُ

وتمثّلت بقول القائل [وافر]

تَبِيتُ ٱلْأُسْدُ فِي ٱلْغَابَاتِ جَوْعَى   وَلَحْمُ ٱلضَّانِ يُلْقَى لِلْكِلَابِ
وَخِـنْزِيرٍ يَنَامُ عَلَى حَـرِيـرٍ   وَذِي عِلْمٍ يَنَامُ عَلَى ٱلتُّرَابِ

٤،١ ثمّ ناجتني القرونة أن أسأل من بعض الناس المعونة فتذكّرت أن ليس كلّ أحمر لحمة ولا كلّ أبيض شحمة وربّما يريق الإنسان ماء وجهه ولا يحظى بقصده وأنّ إراقة ماء الحياة دون إراقة ماء المحيّا سيمّا إذا وقع التعس والنّكس وكان الطلب من نحْس قال الشاعر [منصرح]

١ الأصل: نبأ.

Poesy's constellations of gems well known have fallen, one by one, to
my attack—
every heaven of knowledge I've scaled.
In the sciences, I've trounced all others and yet,
'twixt me and money, lies a yawning gap.
I marvel then how the banner may go to an ignorant man[6]
while poverty flies o'er the turban of every wise one.

Given then that I was now emptyhanded and the courtyard bare, my wealth had absconded, my prospects were no longer fair, that the spring had run dry, the meadow turned sere, I recited verses of my own as a commentary on my condition, to wit: 1.3

What can I do, when these days are filled with troubles
that harm the noble and protect the lowest sort—
Days that on the pious wage a war
beside which that of al-Basūs must seem as naught?
Any ignorant greenhorn you'll find they raise,
and any man of polish you'll see they hurt and slight.

Likewise, I quoted, to encapsulate my state, the words of the poet that go:[7]

The lions in the forests go to bed hungry
while the flesh of the sheep is thrown to the hound.
Many a pig sleeps on silken sheets
while the learned sleep on dusty ground.

At this point, an inner voice urged me to seek the assistance of certain people, but I recalled that "not everything red is flesh nor everything white a truffle";[8] likewise that a man may sacrifice his self-respect and not gain his end, and that it's better to sacrifice one's life than one's self-respect, especially if doing so brings with it misery and reversal, the request being made of someone ignoble. The poet says:[9] 1.4

لَقَلْعُ ضِرْسٍ وَضَنْكُ حَبْسٍ   وَنَزْعُ نَفْسٍ وَوِرْدُ رَمْسِ
وَلَفْحُ[1] نَارٍ وَحَمْلُ عَارٍ   وَبَيْعُ دَارٍ بِرُبْعِ فِلْسِ
وَقَوْدُ قِرْدٍ وَفَرْطُ بَرْدٍ   وَدَبْغُ جِلْدٍ بِغَيْرِ شَمْسِ
وَفَقْدُ إِلْفٍ وَضِيقُ خَسْفٍ   وَضَرْبُ أَلْفٍ بِأَلْفِ قَلْسِ
أَهْوَنُ مِنْ وَقْفَةٍ لِحُرٍّ   يَرْجُو نَوَالاً بِبَابِ نَحْسِ

لا سيمّا وقد وُجد على بعض الأحجار بقلم قدرة العزيز الجبّار كلٌ مِنْ كدّ يمينك وعرق جبينك وإن ضعف يقينك اسأل الله يعينك

فدخلت في خدمة من تزيّنت بلطائفه صفحات الأيّام ونارت بعوارفه حوالك الظلام ٥،١
ظِلّ الله الظليل على البلاد والأمصار حامي ذِمار الإسلام وقامع الفجّار، من أنام الأنام في وارف حلمه وإحسانه وأذاقهم حلاوة الأمن بنجدته وأمانه [خفيف]

مَلِكٌ مَاجِدٌ حَلِيمٌ كَرِيمٌ   جُودُهُ نَاسِخٌ لِكُلِّ ٱلْجُودِ[2]
نَاشِرُ ٱلْعَدْلِ وَهْوَ لِلْجَوْرِ طَاوٍ   وَاقِفٌ فِي ٱلْأَحْكَامِ عِنْدَ ٱلْحُدُودِ
صَالِحُ ٱلْفِعْلِ صَادِقُ ٱلْقَوْلِ وَافٍ   بِوَفَا ٱلْعَهْدِ مُنْجِزٌ لِلْوُعُودِ
هَمُّهُ ٱلْقَطْعُ لِلْفَسَادِ وَإِصْلَا   حُ جَمِيعِ ٱلْبِلَادِ وَٱلتَّمْهِيدِ
نَحْنُ مِنْ رَوْضِ أَمْنِ دَوْلَتِهِ فِي   خَفْضِ عَيْشٍ بِهِ وَظِلٍّ مَدِيدِ
أَيُّهَا ٱلْمَالِكُ ٱلَّذِي يَحْتَمِي عَنْ   حَدِّ أَوْصَافِهِ ٱلْعُلَى بِحُدُودِ
أَنْتَ مِنْ حِصْنِ رَبِّنَا فِي أَمَانٍ   مِنْ عُيُونِ ٱلْعِدَى وَكَيْدِ ٱلْحَسُودِ

١ الأصل: ولفع. ٢ الأصل: الوجود.

Pulling of molars and confinement to prison,
soul's last gasp and grave vault's frenzy,
Fire's scorch and shame's reproach,
the selling off of one's house for a quarter penny,
Playing ape leader and enduring biting cold,
tanning of skin without benefit of sunlight,[10]
Loss of a loved one and narrowness of well-mouth,
a thousand blows with a thousand rope bights—
All these are easier for a noble man to stand
than waiting at a rascal's door and taking charity from an ignoble hand.

—words confirmed by the discovery, engraved on a stone somewhere by the pen of the power of the Mighty, the Omnipotent, "Eat from the toil of your right hand and the sweat of your brow, and should your confidence falter, call on God and He will come to your aid."

I therefore entered the service of one whose amicable ways each new day's 1.5
page adorn, whose deeds of kindness turn the darkest nights to dawn—God's all-embracing shade that encompasses every land and metropolis, protector of Islam's honor and suppressor of the profligate, who brings men repose under the spreading umbra of his clemency and his charity, and who through his succor and shelter has let them taste the sweetness of security:[11]

Monarch magnificent, clement, beneficent,
whose beneficence trumps all other munificence,
Sender of justice, injustice's ender,
standing by God's penalties when pronouncing sentences!
Righteous in deed, veracious in word,
true in his dealings, he fulfills his promises!
To end wrongdoing is what concerns him,
to set all lands to rights and order their territories.
We in the pastures of his state's protection
live a life free of care under a shade that encompasses.
O ruler whom sublimity protects
from the delimitation of his traits with boundaries,
You, through Our Lord's protection, are forever safe
from the eyes of your enemies and the wiles of the envious.

ألا وهو فاتح الحرمين الشريفين بجيشه المنصور ومالك الأقطار الشاميّة بإبراهيمه البطل الغضنفر المشهور، أمير المؤمنين الحاجّ محمّد عليّ باشا وليّ النعم أعلى الله سُرادِق عزّ دولته وأبّد ملكه بمجده وصولته

وكان أوّل خدمتي بوظيفة واعظ في الآلاي الثامن من المشاة وسافرت معه إلى المورة وكابدت المشقّات وكنت قبل ذلك سافرت إلى بلاد السودان ورأيت فيها من العجائب ما إذا سطر يكون كزهر بستان ثمّ استخدمت في مدرسة أبي زعبل لتصحيح الكتب الطبّيّة وخصّصت منها بتصحيح كتب الأجزاجيّة ومكثت على ذلك حتّى اجتمعت بأبرع أهل زمانه حذاقة وفهماً وأذكى أهل عصره صناعة وعلماً معلّم الكيميا الحكيم پيرون الفرنساويّ وقرأ عليّ كتاب كليلة ودمنة باللغة العربيّة فذكرت له بعض ما عاينته في أسفاري من العجائب البهيّة فحملني على أن أزيّن وجه الدفتر بأيضاح ما شاهدته من العجائب وأخبره بما حصل لي في تلك الأسفار من الغرائب فامتثلت أمره لما له عليّ من اليد البيضا ورأيت أنّ ذلك أجمل بي أيضاً لقول صاحب المقصورة ٦،١

[رجز مع كسر]

إِنَّمَا ٱلْمَرْءُ حَدِيثٌ بَعْدَهُ فَكُنْ حَدِيثاً حَسَناً لِمَنْ وَعَى

فشرعت في إبراز فرائدها من صدف الأذهان وكشف حجاب خرائدها الحسان إلى العيان وضممت لذلك من النوادر ما سمعته من الثقات أو نقلته من الكتب على سبيل الاستطراد للمناسبات لتكون هذه الرحلة روضة يانعة الأزهار لمن تأمّل فيها وحديقة دانية الثمار لمن تصغّ معانيها ولم آلُ جهداً في أيضاح معانيها للمتأمّلين ولم أتعمّق في غريب اللغة ليسهل فهمها على السامعين

Yea, he it is who conquered the two noble sanctuaries[12] with his victorious army, he who took possession of the Levantine lands through the agency of that champion, that celebrated lion, his son Ibrāhīm[13]—the Commander of the Faithful, al-Ḥājj Muḥammad ʿAlī Pasha, bestower of benefits, may God raise high the pavilion of his state's honor and cause his rule to last in all its glory and power forever!

When I began my service, I held the position of preacher in the Eighth Infantry Regiment, traveling with it to the Morea and suffering many hardships.[14] Before that, though, I'd traveled to the Land of the Blacks, where the wonders I saw, if set down in writing, would resemble a flowery bower. Then I was employed at the school at Abū Zaʿbal[15] as a language editor of medical books, specializing in pharmaceutical works. I did this until I met the most brilliant man of his day in keenness of mind and understanding, the brightest of his age in industry and knowledge—the French teacher of chemistry, Dr. Perron.[16] He studied *Kalīlah and Dimnah* with me in Arabic, and I told him some of the splendid and amazing things I'd endured on my travels. He then urged me to "adorn the face of my copybook" with an exposition of the marvels I'd seen and to tell him of the strange things that had befallen me on these journeys. I complied with his command both because of the kindnesses he had shown me and in the belief too that this would be in my own best interest, given the words of the author of *The Poem on Words Ending in -ā and a'* (*al-Maqṣūrah*)[17] that go: 1.6

> Man is but the words that live on after him,
> so let those be worthy in the eyes of those who take note.

I then set about extracting those precious pearls from the oyster of the mind and lifting the veil from those beauteous beads to expose them to view, adding anecdotes I'd heard from trusted sources or copied from books, by way of expatiations appropriate to occasions, to make this account of my travels a meadow of blooming flowers to all who upon it turn their gaze, a garden of low-hanging fruit for any who among its topics graze. Likewise, I've spared no effort to make it clear, and not gone diving after arcane words, to make it be plain to every ear.

ورتّبتها على مقدّمة ومقصد وخاتمة وفي كلّ منها أبواب كما يُعلم من الفهرسة ٧،١
وسمّيتها تشحيذ الأذهان بسيرة بلاد العرب والسودان والله أسأل أن ينشر عليها حلّة القبول ويقيها شرّ حاسد يطعن فيما فيها من المقول [وافر]

وَكَمْ مِنْ عَائِبٍ قَوْلاً صَحِيحًا وَآفَتُهُ مِنَ ٱلذِّهْنِ ٱلسَّقِيمِ

على أنّي وإن أتقنتها وهذّبتها وفي أحسن قالب سبكتها لا أقول إنّها عارية عن الخلل بريئة من الزلل لأنّي إنّما أنا بشر من الإنسان محلّ للخطأ والزلل والنسيان لكن إنّما أتعوّذ من غمر يرمقها بعين الحسد ويندد بأنّها من الخرافات عند كلّ أحد [وافر]

وَهَبْنِي قُلْتُ هذا ٱلصُّبْحُ لَيْلٌ أَيَعْمَى ٱلْعَالَمُونَ[١] عَنِ ٱلضِّيَاءِ

فرحم الله امرأً رأى الزلل فستره وشاهد الخلل فجبره [رمل] ٨،١

إِنْ تَجِدْ عَيْبًا فَسُدَّ ٱلْخَلَلَا جَلَّ مَنْ لَا عَيْبَ فِيهِ وَعَلَا

وبالله أستمدّ التوفيق إلى أقوم طريق وهو حسبي ونعم الوكيل نعم المولى ونعم النصير

---

١ الأصل: اتعْمى المعالمون.

I have organized it in the form of a prolegomenon, the book proper, and a conclusion,[18] each made up of chapters, as may be seen from the way in which I have provided it with different headings and named it *The Honing of Minds through Consideration of the Condition of the Land of the Arabs and the Blacks*, and I call on God to envelop it in the mantle of His endorsement, and protect it from attacks by the envious on what it holds by way of content, for 1.7

How many have found fault with words that are sound,
their evil thoughts the product of minds that are sick!

I do not, however, claim, even though I have worked it and refined it and poured it into the best of molds, that it is free of flaws or lacking in lapses: I am a mere mortal, liable to error, oversight, and forgetfulness. All the same, I seek refuge with God from the ignoramus who regards it with envious eyes and criticizes it by claiming to all and sundry that it is full of frivolous lies:[19]

Were I to claim this morn was night,
would no one ever again see light?

May God show His mercy to any who sees but discreetly passes over a mistake, or finds an error and sets it straight: 1.8

Should you find a blemish, pass it by—
glory be to Him without blemish, Most High.

From God I beg success in finding the straightest way—my best Proxy, the best Trustee, the best Master, the best Ally!

المقـدّمـة
وفيها ثلاثة أبواب

Prolegomenon, in three chapters

الباب الأول

في السبب الباعث لرحلتي لبلاد السودان

١،١،٢ حكى لي والدي عليه سحائب الرحمة والرضوان أنّ جدّه كان من عظماء أهل تونس وكيلاً من طرف سلطان المغرب المولى الأكمل الملك المظفّر العادل المرحوم الشريف محمد الحسنيّ فاجتمع له بذلك مال جزيل حتّى صار من أغنى أهل زمانه ولمّا مات كان قد خلف من الولد ثلاثة بنين فتنازعوا تراث أبيهم وباعوا دارهم التي كانت تؤويهم وسكن كلّ منهم على حدته بأولاده وزوجته فاتّفق أنّ أباه كان من أهل العلم جيّد الخطّ ينسخ الكتاب فيبيعه بضعف ما يبيع به غيره وكان يعرف صباغة الثياب بالألوان فكان أرفه إخوته معاشاً وأحسنهم ارتياشاً فاتّفق له أنه اشتاق لرؤية البيت الحرام وزيارة قبر نبيّه عليه السلام فباع بعض عقار كان له وتأهّب للسفر واشترى معه أحرمة وطرابيش وأعطاه الناس أموالاً كثيرة يتّجر لهم فيها لما يعلمون من صدقه وأمانته حتّى أنه وسق من السفينة جانباً عظيماً

٢،١،٢ وحين توجّه ودّعه إخوانه حتّى وصل إلى السفينة فركبها وأقلعت بهم بريح طيّبة ثمّ اختلفت الرياح على السفينة حتّى أنّهم أخذوا طريقاً غير طريقهم وذلك أنّهم جاءوا على طريق رودس وبينما هم آمنين مطمئنّين إذ هبّ عليهم قاصف ريح وكانوا إذ ذاك بجانب رودس فتلاطمت عليهم أمواج البحر وبدّل الصفو بالكدر على حدّ قول الشاعر شعر [بسيط]

Chapter 1

The Reasons That Led to My Journey to the Land of the Blacks

My father—may the clouds of God's mercy and approval hover over him!—told me that his grandfather was one of the great men of Tunis, an agent of the Sultan of Morocco, the late Perfect Lord, Just and Victorious, Sharif Muḥammad al-Ḥasanī.[20] As a result, he amassed a great fortune and became one of the richest men of his day. He died leaving three sons. They fought one another over their father's inheritance, sold the common home that had sheltered them in life, and each went to live on his own, with his children and his wife. Now my father's father was, as it happened, a man of learning, with a beautiful hand, who could copy a book and sell it for many times more than anyone else and who also knew how to dye clothes in different colors. Thus he, among all his brothers, with regard to income was the most blessed, as well as the best dressed. Now he conceived a desire to see the Sacred House and visit the tomb of His prophet, upon whom be peace, so he sold some properties he owned and prepared to travel. He bought woolen mantles and tarbushes to take with him, and others gave him large amounts of money to trade with on their behalf, knowing as they did of his honesty and trustworthiness,[21] so that a large part of the ship ended up filled with his goods. 2.1.1

When he set off, his brothers accompanied him to the ship to see him off. He embarked and it sailed off with its passengers under a good wind. Later, though, the winds turned against the ship and they were blown off course and set on a path for Rhodes. As they sat off that island, safe and at their ease, a great wind suddenly caught them, and the waves battered them and serenity turned to sorrow, as described by the poet when he says: 2.1.2

حَسَّنْتَ ظَنَّكَ بِٱلْأَيَّامِ مُذْ حَسُنَتْ   وَلَمْ تَخَفْ سُوءَ مَا يَأْتِي بِهِ ٱلْقَدَرُ
وَسَالَمَتْكَ ٱللَّيَالِي وَٱغْتَرَرْتَ بِهَا   وَعِنْدَ صَفْوِ ٱللَّيَالِي يَحْدُثُ ٱلْكَدَرُ

وكان بسفينتهم خلل فلمّا تلاطمت عليها الأمواج وسطت عليها سطوة الحجّاج تحلّل تركيبها وفسد ترتيبها وتفرّقت أجزاؤها وانفصلت أفلاذها وغرق من فيها ولم ينج إلّا القليل من راكبيها وكان ممّن نجا معهم جدّي المذكور فخلص بعد غصّ الريق إلى البلد المذكور [طويل]

إِذَا سَلِمَتْ هَامُ ٱلرِّجَالِ مِنَ ٱلرَّدَى   فَمَا ٱلْمَالُ إِلَّا مِثْلُ قَصِّ ٱلْأَظَافِرِ

فمكث في رودس مدّة ونفعه فيها هِمْيان كان في وسطه فيه بعض ذهب فكان ينفق منه مدّة إقامته ثمّ اشترى زاداً وركب في سفينة إلى ثغر إسكندريّة وكان ذلك إبّان الحجّ والذهاب إلى العجّ والثجّ فتوجّه في الحال من غير إهمال إلى ان وصل إلى تلك البقاع وبلغ مأموله جهد ما استطاع وكان لسان حاله يقول قبل بلوغ المأمول [رمل] ٢،١،٣

أَبْرَكُ ٱلْأَيَّامِ يَوْمٌ قِيلَ لِي   هٰذِهِ طَيْبَةُ هٰذِي ٱلْكُتُبُ
هٰذِهِ رَوْضَةُ طٰه ٱلْمُصْطَفَى   هٰذِهِ ٱلزَّرْقَاءُ لَدَيْكُمْ فَٱشْرَبُوا

والياء في هذي بدل عن الهاء

ولمّا قضى ما وجب عليه وتملّى بزيارة الحبيب وصاحبيه أفاق من دهشته وفاء إلى سكينته وافتكر في ضياع ماله وتشتّت حاله وافتضح من دخوله إلى تونس ذا عسر وفاقة بعد أن كان ذا يسر وإفاقة وكيف يصبر بعد الرفاهية على الكدّ أو يراه على هذه الحالة أهل البلد ولمّا تذكّر ما قد حدث أنشد على وجه الجدّ لا العبث [طويل] ٢،١،٤

You thought well of the days when they were minding their manners
and feared not the evils Fate might send.
The nights made up to you and played you for a fool—
it's when nights are clearest that clouds descend.

Their ship was unsound, and when the waves battered it, forcing it into submission as brutally as did al-Ḥajjāj the people of Iraq, its construction fell apart, its structure was undone, its parts came to bits, its heartstrings were unstrung. Those on board drowned and only a few were saved, among them my aforementioned grandfather, who was delivered, at his last gasp, to the aforementioned land:

When a man's neck's been saved from perdition,
wealth means less to him than a fingernail clipping.

My grandfather stayed on Rhodes for a while, making use of a purse in his 2.1.3
waistband that contained some gold, which he used for the duration of his stay. Then he bought provisions and sailed to the port city of Alexandria. It was the pilgrimage season, that of departure for the land of "clamor and sacrifice,"[22] so he set off without dereliction or delay and to those celebrated sites made his way, and achieved his goal, having strived as hard as he could strive, his actions expressive of the words (even before he could arrive):

The most blest of days was when I was told,
"This is Ṭaybah! This is al-Kuthub!
This is the garden of Ṭāhā the Chosen!
This, before you, is al-Zarqā', so drink!"

(In the word *hādhī,* the *yā'* is in place of the *hā'*).[23]

Once he had completed his duties and diligently made his visit to the 2.1.4
Beloved and his two companions,[24] he recovered from his dazed state, regained his equanimity, and thought of his wealth that had been lost, deciding that to reenter Tunis in hardship and poverty, after having left it in affluence and vitality, would be to expose himself to disgrace, wondering too how he could endure hard labor after a life of ease and what the people of the city would think when they saw him so debased. Then, remembering all that had passed, he recited, in earnest, not in jest:[25]

سَأَضْرِبُ فِي ٱلْآفَاقِ شَرْقًا بِغَرْبِهَا وَأَكْسِبُ مَالًا أَوْ أَمُوتُ غَرِيبَا
فَإِنْ تَلِفَتْ نَفْسِي فَلِلَّهِ رَدُّهَا وَإِنْ سَلِمَتْ كَانَ ٱلرُّجُوعُ قَرِيبَا

ومن المعلوم أنه لا[1] يسهل على المرء أن يعيش في تعب ونصب وكدّ في بلد لا يعرفه فيه أحد خصوصاً في هذا الزمن الذي يكرم به اليهوديّ لماله ويهان الشريف لفقره وسوء حاله ورحم الله القائل [كامل] ٢،١،٥

يَغْدُو ٱلْفَقِيرُ وَكُلُّ شَيْءٍ ضِدَّهُ وَٱلْأَرْضُ تُغْلِقُ دُونَهُ أَبْوَابَهَا
وَتَرَاهُ مَمْقُوتًا وَلَيْسَ بِمُذْنِبٍ وَيَرَى ٱلْعَدَاوَةَ لَا يَرَى أَسْبَابَهَا
حَتَّى ٱلْكِلَابُ إِذَا رَأَتْ ذَا ثَرْوَةٍ مَالَتْ إِلَيْهِ وَحَرَّكَتْ أَذْنَابَهَا
وَإِذَا رَأَتْ يَوْمًا فَقِيرًا عَارِيًا نَبَحَتْ عَلَيْهِ وَكَشَّرَتْ أَنْيَابَهَا

ولذا قال الإمام عليّ كرّم الله وجهه الفقر داء لا دواء له إن أذعته فضحني وإن كتمته قتلني وقد قيل إذا افتقر الإنسان خوّنه من كان يأمنه وأساء فيه الظنّ من كان يحسنه وأبعده من كان يقربه وملّه من كان يحبّه شعر [بسيط] ٢،١،٦

إِنْ قَلَّ مَالِي فَلَا خِلٌّ يُسَاعِدُنِي وَإِنْ غَنِيتُ فَكُلُّ ٱلنَّاسِ خِلَّانِي

وليت الإنسان إذا افتقر يُترك هو وشأنه ولا يُحتقر لا والله بل يُكذّب في المقال وإن كان صوابا ويُهان وإن لم يكن عابا شعر [كامل]

١ أضيف للسياق: لا.

I shall roam the horizons from east to west
and grow rich, or die in a foreign land.
Should I lose my life, Gods will give me back my soul
and should I survive, return is ever close at hand.

Everyone knows that it is not easy for a man to live through trouble, sickness, and toil in a land where he knows no one, especially these days, when the Jew is honored for his money, and the sharif despised for his indigence and poverty. God have mercy on the soul of the poet who said:[26] 2.1.5

The poor man begins his day with everything against him
and the earth shuts its doors in his face.
Observe how he's hated though he's done nothing wrong
and meets with an enmity whose cause he cannot trace.
Even the dogs, seeing a rich man,
fawn on him and wag their tails
But when they see a pauper, half-naked,
bark at him and bare their teeth.

It is this that caused Imam ʿAlī, may God honor him, to say, "Poverty is a disease that knows no cure: if I make it known, it brings me shame, and if I keep it hidden, it kills me." It is said too that "If a man becomes poor, those whom he used to trust will betray him, those who used to think well of him will think badly of him, those who used to keep him by their side will keep him at a distance, and those who used to love him will no longer find him to their taste": 2.1.6

If my wealth diminishes, no friend will help me,
but if I grow rich, everyone's my friend.

Would that a man, when he loses his money, be left alone and not despised—and not just that, I swear, but be called a liar when he opens his mouth, even if he speaks the truth, and be despised even if what he says is blameless:

مَنْ كَانَ يَمْلِكُ دِرْهَمَيْنِ تَعَلَّمَتْ شَفَتَاهُ أَنْوَاعَ ٱلْكَلَامِ فَقَالَا
وَتَقَدَّمَ ٱلْإِخْوَانَ فَٱسْتَمَعُوا لَهُ وَرَأَيْتَهُ بَيْنَ ٱلْوَرَى مُخْتَالَا
لَوْلَا دَرَاهِمُهُ ٱلَّتِي فِي كِيسِهِ لَرَأَيْتَهُ أَسْوَأَ ٱلْبَرِيَّةِ حَالَا
إِنَّ ٱلْغَنِيَّ إِذَا تَكَلَّمَ بِٱلْخَطَا قَالُوا صَدَقْتَ وَمَا نَطَقْتَ مُحَالَا
وَإِذَا ٱلْفَقِيرُ أَصَابَ قَالُوا كُلُّهُمْ أَخْطَأْتَ يَا هٰذَا وَقُلْتَ ضَلَالَا
إِنَّ ٱلدَّرَاهِمَ فِي ٱلْمَوَاطِنِ كُلِّهَا تَكْسُو ٱلرِّجَالَ مَهَابَةً وَجَمَالَا
وَهِيَ ٱللِّسَانُ[1] لِمَنْ أَرَادَ فَصَاحَةً وَهِيَ ٱلسِّلَاحُ لِمَنْ أَرَادَ قِتَالَا

وإذا كان كذلك فالموت خير لذوي الأحساب من أن تلتصق أيديهم بالتراب شعر

[مجزوء الكامل]

اَلْمَوْتُ خَيْرٌ لِلْفَتَى مِنْ أَنْ يَعِيشَ بِغَيْرِ مَالِ
وَٱلْمَوْتُ خَيْرٌ لِلْكَرِيـ ـمِ مِنَ ٱلتَّضَرُّعِ وَٱلسُّؤَالِ

ولما علم النبيّ صلّى الله عليه وسلّم أنّ الفقير يهان بعد الإكرام ويذلّ بعد العزّ والاحترام قال أكرموا عزيز قوم ذلّ وغنيّ قوم افتقر لكن كلّ ذلك بحسب ما سطر في أمّ الكتاب وقدره في علمه العزيز الوهّاب وإلّا فكم من فقير أسعفته الأقدار وكم من غنيّ أصبح لا يملك ربع دينار ومن ذلك ما حكي أنّ الوزير المهلّبيّ كان في أوّل أمره فقيراً لا يملك نقيراً واتّفق أنّه سافر راجلاً من بغداد إلى مكّة في قافلة وقد أضرّ به الجوع وأحرمه الهجوع فأنشد يقول [وافر] ٢،١،٧

١ الأصل: اسلاح.

The lips of one with two pennies to rub together
will learn all kinds of things to say and speak out loud
And stand before his brethren while they give him ear
and seem to you as one of those who steps out proud—
Yet were it not for the coins in his purse
you'd see him as the worst of the crowd.
When the rich man speaks wrong,
they say, "You speak true and have uttered no fantasy,"
But when the poor man gets it right, as one they exclaim,
"You've got it wrong, you there. You've uttered a travesty."
In every country, silver pieces
cloak a man in gravitas and make of him a pleasing sight.
They are the tongue of all who seek to persuade,
the weapon of all who wish to fight.

Things being so, those of noble line are better off dead than dirtying their hands:

Better death for the generous man
than a life of privation!
Better death for the nobly born
than pleading and supplication!

Likewise the Prophet, God bless him and grant him peace, when he learned 2.1.7
that the poor were despised when once they had been honored, and brought low when once they had enjoyed high standing and respect, said, "Honor the great man among you who has been brought low and the rich man among you who has become poor!"—all of which, however, simply reflects what the Mighty, the Bountiful, has written in the Original Book and has decreed in His foreknowledge; otherwise, how could it be that so many poor men have been rescued by the fates and so many rich ones ended up without a quarter dinar to their name? By way of example, the vizier al-Muhallabī was, in his early days, a poor man who owned less than nothing. It happened that he traveled on foot from Baghdad to Mecca with a caravan. Wracked by hunger and unable to sleep, he recited the following lines:

أَلَا مَوْتٌ[1] يُبَاعُ فَأَشْتَرِيهِ   فَهٰذَا[2] ٱلْعَيْشُ مَا لَا خَيْرَ فِيهِ
أَلَا رَحِمَ ٱلْمُهَيْمِنُ رُوحَ عَبْدٍ   تَصَدَّقَ بِٱلْوَفَاةِ عَلَى أَخِيهِ

فسمعه أحد التجّار فأعطاه رغيفاً ودرهماً ثمّ تغيّرت الأحوال فترقّى المهلّبيّ للوزارة وافتقر التاجر حتّى صار لا يملك قوت يومه وبلغه أن المهلّبيّ ترقّى للوزارة فذهب إليه وكتب له في رقعة ما صورته [وافر]

أَلَا قُلْ لِلْوَزِيرِ فَدَتْهُ[3] نَفْسِي   مَقَالًا مُذْكِرًا مَا قَدْ نَسِيهِ
أَتَذْكُرُ إِذْ تَقُولُ لِضَنْكِ عَيْشٍ   أَلَا مَوْتٌ[4] يُبَاعُ فَأَشْتَرِيهِ

وأرسلها له مع بعض خدمه فلمّا قرأها بكى واستعبر وتذكّر ما قد سلف وأمر له بعمل وسبعمائة درهم وكتب له على رقعة ﴿مَثَلُ ٱلَّذِينَ يُنْفِقُونَ أَمْوَالَهُمْ فِي سَبِيلِ ٱللَّهِ كَمَثَلِ حَبَّةٍ أَنْبَتَتْ سَبْعَ سَنَابِلَ فِي كُلِّ[5] سُنْبُلَةٍ مِائَةُ حَبَّةٍ﴾ الآية فعُلِمَ من ذلك أنّه ينبغي إكرام من افتقر بعد غناه وذلّ بعد أن بلغ في العزّ منتهاه وإذا عنت للإنسان حاجة وأراد يسأل فيها الناس فإن كان عاقلاً لا يسأل إلّا من كان ذا فضل ومروّة ولا يسأل من تموّل بعد فقره وعزّ بعد ذلّه قال الشاعر [طويل]

سَلِ ٱلْفَضْلَ أَهْلَ ٱلْفَضْلِ قِدْماً وَلَا تَسَلْ   غَنِيًّا رُبِي فِي ٱلْفَقْرِ ثُمَّ تَمَوَّلَا

٨،١،٢ ثمّ إنّ المال تميل إلى صاحبه القلوب وتنضمّ عليه أزرار الجيوب. به تتمّ الإرادات وتقضى جميع الحاجات ولقد أجاد الحريريّ في مدح الدينار حيث قال [مشطور الرجز]

---

١ الأصل: موتا. ٢ الأصل: فهذ. ٣ الأصل: فداته. ٤ الأصل: موتا. ٥ في كل – الأصل: وكل.

Is there no death for sale that I might buy it?
This is a life that holds no charms!
May the Lord of All have mercy on the soul of a mortal
who grants death to his brother as alms!

One of the merchants heard him and gave him a loaf and a silver piece. Then things changed and al-Muhallabī rose to the vizierate, whereas the merchant became so poor that he could no longer lay his hands on his daily bread. When he heard that al-Muhallabī had risen to the vizierate, he went to his residence and wrote him the following on a scrap of paper:

Do give the vizier—may my soul be his ransom—
a word to remind him of what he may have forgotten:
"Remember how you said when you wanted to die,
'Is there no death for sale that I might buy?'"

This he dispatched via a servant. When al-Muhallabī read it he wept copiously and, recalling what had gone before, ordered that the man be given work and seven hundred silver pieces, and wrote to him on a scrap of paper: «Those who spend their wealth for God's cause may be compared to a grain of corn which sprouts into seven ears, with a hundred grains in each ear.»[27] From this, one should draw the lesson that one must honor any who have become poor after being rich and been brought low after reaching the highest standing, and if need should weigh on a person's mind and he wishes to ask others for help, he will, if he has any sense, ask only those persons who are generous and chivalrous and not those who have become wealthy after being poor or reached high standing after being lowly. Says the poet:

Ask a boon of those who of old enjoyed excess,
but not of a rich man, raised in poverty, who has acquired wealth!

It is also true that money endears its owner to others' hearts and makes its owners' pockets its counterparts. Through it, wishes are realized and every need fulfilled. Al-Ḥarīrī puts it well when, praising a gold piece, he says:[28] 2.1.8

أَكْرِمْ بِهِ أَصْفَرَ رَاقَتْ صُفْرَتُهْ   جَوَّابَ آفَاقٍ تَرَامَتْ سَفْرَتُهْ
مَأْثُورَةٌ سُمْعَتُهُ وَشُهْرَتُهْ   قَدْ أُودِعَتْ سِرَّ ٱلْغِنَى أَسِرَّتُهْ
وَقَارَنَتْ نُجْحَ ٱلْمَسَاعِي خَطْرَتُهْ   وَحُبِّبَتْ إِلَى ٱلْأَنَامِ غُرَّتُهْ
كَأَنَّمَا مِنَ ٱلْقُلُوبِ نُقْرَتُهْ   بِهِ يَصُولُ مَنْ حَوَتْهُ صُرَّتُهْ
وَإِنْ تَفَانَتْ أَوْ تَوَانَتْ عِتْرَتُهْ   يَا حَبَّذَا نُضَارُهُ وَنَضْرَتُهْ[1]
وَحَبَّذَا مَغْنَاتُهُ وَنُصْرَتُهْ   كَمْ آمِرٍ بِهِ ٱسْتَتَبَّتْ إِمْرَتُهْ
وَمُتْرَفٍ لَوْلَاهُ دَامَتْ حَسْرَتُهْ   وَجَيْشِ هَمٍّ هَزَمَتْهُ كَرَّتُهْ
وَبَدْرِ تِمٍّ أَنْزَلَتْهُ بَدْرَتُهْ   وَمُسْتَشِيطٍ تَتَلَظَّى جَمْرَتُهْ
أَسَرَّ نَجْوَاهُ فَلَانَتْ شِرَّتُهْ   وَكَمْ أَسِيرٍ أَسْلَمَتْهُ أُسْرَتُهْ
أَنْقَذَهُ حَتَّى صَفَتْ مَسَرَّتُهْ   وَحَقِّ مَوْلًى أَبْدَعَتْهُ فِطْرَتُهْ
لَوْلَا ٱلتُّقَى لَقُلْتُ جَلَّتْ قُدْرَتُهْ

٩،١،٢ ولقد شوهد أنّ الألكن إذا استغنى يصير فصيحاً والأعمش إذا تموّل يعود بصره صحيحاً ومصداق ذلك أني رأيت في سفرتي هذه رجلاً يسمّى محمد المكّنيّ وكان خادماً على باب يوسف باشا صاحب طرابلس الغرب وكان أعمش العينين مُسْلَق الجفنين ترشح دموعه ويقلّ هجوعه ودام كذلك إلى أن تولّى حاكماً على إقليم فزّان فبرئ عمشه ونبت رمشه وذهب وجعه وبطل دمعه وصار أجمل أهل عصره وأوجه أهل قطره قلت ولعلّ الأمراض إنّما تعتري الفقراء لما يرونه من الذلّ والمسكنة والعري والمسغبة فيهتمّون لضيق معاشهم وعدم ارتياشهم فتتشوّش أذهانهم وتسقم أبدانهم والغنيّ ليس كذلك نعم وإن كانت له هموم لكنّها من جهة أخرى شعر [طويل]

١ الأصل: وَنُضْرَتُهْ.

How noble something yellow—a yellow pellucid—
A rover of horizons on journeys far-flung!
Its repute and its fame to us have come down,
In the lines on its brow wealth's secret is hung.
Success in endeavor keeps pace with its gait,
While men fall in love with its forehead's blaze
As though from their very hearts it was minted—
Those with a purse of it will have their ways,
Be their tribes extinct or enfeebled.
How excellent its purity and its beauty!
How excellent its sufficiency and its support!
How many commanders' commands with its help run featly!
How many coddled rich men without it would live in constant sorrow!
How many mighty armies by its attack have been tamed!
How many full moons[29] ten thousand of it have brought to heel!
How many raging furiosos, their embers aflame,
Have held secret parley with it and found their ire curtailed!
How many captives of whose release families despaired
Has it rescued and their happiness restored!
By a Lord due to whose creative genius it appeared,
I'd declare, but for the impiety, "May its power be revered!"

It has been observed that when a stutterer becomes rich he acquires fluency 2.1.9
and when a man with an eye disease acquires wealth his sight is restored. Proof of this is that while on this journey of mine I saw a man called Muḥammad al-Muknī, a client of Yūsuf Pasha, overlord of Libyan Tripoli. His eyes were diseased, his lids ulcerated, his tears never stopped, and he barely slept. He remained like this until he became governor of the province of Fezzan. At that moment, the disease disappeared, his eyelashes grew back, the pain left him, and his tears stopped. He became the handsomest man of his day and the most distinguished in the region where he lived. I would add that it may be that the diseases that afflict the poor are a result of the humiliation, poverty, nakedness, and hunger they experience, for they worry over the constraints within which they live and their lack of affluence, and as a result their minds become disordered and their bodies sick. The rich man is not so. True, he may have worries, but they arise from other causes:

وَمَنْ يَحْمَدُ ٱلدُّنْيَا لِشَيْءٍ يَسُرُّهُ   فَسَوْفَ لَعَمْرِي عَنْ قَلِيلٍ يَلُومُهَا
إِذَا أَدْبَرَتْ كَانَتْ عَلَى ٱلْمَرْءِ حَسْرَةً   وَإِنْ أَقْبَلَتْ كَانَتْ كَثِيرًا[١] هُمُومُهَا

لكنّ الغنيّ إذا بذل الدينار يبلغ الأوطار

ومن ذلك ما حكي أنّ عليّ باشا الأوّل صاحب تونس كان قبل ولايته فارًّا بالجزائر مستجيرًا بحاكمها أن يمدّه بعساكر ليأخذها من ابن عمّه حسين باشا وكان صاحب الجزائر يعدّه بذلك والأخبار تردّ على حسين باشا بذلك فكان يغتمّ إذا سمع شيئًا من ذلك لما يعلم ممّا يطرأ عليه من انحطاط شأنه وذهاب ملكه وسلطانه فاتّفق أن ورد عليه خبر أقلقه وأهمّه وأحزنه وأغمّه فركب وهو ضيّق الصدر كثير الفكر وشقّ في وسط تونس بموكبه وكان أحد وزرائه محاذيًا له يتحدّث معه فرآه على تلك الحالة فسأله عن سبب تغيّره فأخبره بما سمع من الخبر فقال الوزير أيّد الله مولانا ونصره أتهتمّ بأمر لا أصل له على أنّي أقول إنّك ما دمت موجودًا لا تقوم له قائمة والتفت عن يمينه وكان بمحلّ يسمّى سوق البلاط فرأى ساق شجرة يابسًا ملقى على الأرض فقال له إن كان هذا الساق يعود شجرة خضراء يملك عليّ باشا تونس ويصير حاكمًا عليها وأراد بذلك اطمئنان صاحبه ٢،١،١٠

فما مرّت إلّا أيّام قلائل حتّى جاء عليّ باشا بجيش كثيف من الجزائر وقتل حسين باشا واستوزر الوزير المذكور مدّة حتّى تمهّدت له الأمور فاتّفق أنّه ركب يومًا في موكبه ودخل تونس والوزير المذكور محاذيًا له كما كان محاذيًا لحسين باشا فتماديا في سيرهما حتّى وصلا إلى سوق البلاط فالتفت عليّ باشا فرأى ساق الشجرة ملقى بمكانه فقال للوزير إن عاد هذا الساق شجرة خضراء يعود عليّ باشا حاكمًا على تونس وكان بعض أعداء الوزير ألقى إليه ذلك فأسرّه في نفسه إلى ذلك الوقت ثمّ أعرض عنه ولم يحادثه بعد ذلك فعلم الوزير أنّه مقتول لا محالة لما يعلم من أخلاق عليّ باشا ٢،١،١١

---
١ الأصل: كثير.

Who praises the world for something that pleases
  will reproach it, I swear, for a trifle.
Back turned, it brings a man grief.
  Smiling, it brings no relief.

The rich man, however, can always realize his desires by spending money.

This is shown by the tale of how ʿAlī Pasha I, Lord of Tunis, before his rule 2.1.10
began, fled to Algiers to ask its ruler to lend him soldiers for support in taking Tunis from his cousin, Ḥusayn Pasha,[30] which the Lord of Algiers did. News of this reached Ḥusayn Pasha, and every time he heard anything about the matter he'd become distressed, knowing the decline in status and loss of command and authority this would mean for him. On one occasion, he received news that worried and disquieted him. Preoccupied, he rode out with his entourage through the middle of Tunis. One of his viziers, who was by his side, was speaking to him and, noticing his condition, asked him what had upset him. Ḥusayn Pasha told him of the news he had received. "God make our lord triumphant and grant him victory!" the vizier said. "Why worry over nothing? On the contrary, so long as you are still here he cannot, I assure you, do a thing." Then he turned to his right—they were in the area known as the Tile Market—and saw a dry branch lying on the ground, and said to him, "The day this branch turns green again, ʿAlī Pasha will take Tunis and become its ruler," intending by this to reassure his master.

Only a few days were to pass before ʿAlī Pasha arrived with a massive army 2.1.11
from Algiers, killed Ḥusayn Pasha,[31] and temporarily confirmed this same vizier in his position until things sorted themselves out. One day, ʿAlī Pasha happened to ride out in the midst of his entourage and entered Tunis, the said vizier at his side, as he had been at Ḥusayn Pasha's, and they proceeded till they came to the Tile Market. ʿAlī Pasha turned and saw the branch lying where it had been and said to the vizier, "If this branch turns back into a green tree, will ʿAlī Pasha come back as ruler of Tunis?"—for enemies of the vizier had told him the story, though he'd said nothing of it till that moment. After that, ʿAlī Pasha turned away from the vizier and stopped speaking to him. From this, the vizier knew he was a dead man, no doubt about it, given what he knew of ʿAlī Pasha's evil nature—for he was a bloodthirsty murderer who would kill for a trifle, let alone something of this sort. They continued on their way until ʿAlī Pasha came to his place of power and portico of pomp, and there the vizier

لأنّه كان سفّاكًا للدماء حتّى أنّه كان يقتل على الهفوة الصغيرة فضلاً عن مثل هذه وتماديا على ذلك حتّى وصل الباشا الى محلّ سلطنته وإيوان أبّهته فتقدّم إليه الوزير قبل أن يأمر فيه بأمر وقال أيّد الله مولانا إنّ ابن عمّك حسين باشا حين سمع بقدومك أودع عندي أموالاً جمّة خبأتها فى محلّ لا يعرفه غيري وأنا محقق أنّك قاتلي وأخاف إن أنا متّ وهى بمكانها لا ينتفع بها مولاي فأنّ رأى سيّدنا أن يسرّحنى لآتيه بها فليفعل

١٢،١،٢ ففرح عليّ باشا وظنّ صدقه وأمره بالتوجّه وأن تصحبه عشرة حوانب والحوانب فى لغة تونس هم القوّاصة[١] بلغة أهل مصر وقبل توجّههم قال للحوانب إن فرّ منكم قتلتكم أجمعين فتوجّهوا معه حتّى وصل لداره فأوقفهم أسفل الدار وصعد ليبعد الحريم عن الطريق فوقفوا وحال صعوده لم يكن له همّ إلّا أنّه قصد خزانة أمواله فملأ منها جيوبه ذهبًا وأخذ معه صندوقًا صغيرًا يسمّى فى عرف أهل تونس بالفنيق مملوءا ذهبًا أيضًا وصعد على السطح وتسوّر من دار أخرى وخرج الى الشارع وتوجّه الى دار قونصل الإنجليز فدخل عليه وأخبره أنّه مستجير به وأعلمه بالقصّة وأعطاه الصندوق بما فيه وقال له أريد أن تأمر بإحدى سفائنك تتوجّه[٢] بي في هذه الساعة الى إنجلاتيره فكتب له القونصل فى الحال كتابًا إلى أحد قبوداناته أن سافر الى الإنجلاتيره حال حلول جوابنا هذا إليك ولا تتأخّر دقيقة واحدة وأعطاه الكتاب ورافقه بترجمانه ونزلا البحر حتّى وصلا الى السفينة فحين قرأ مدير السفينة كتاب القونصل أقلع عن المرسى وأطلق مدفعًا علامة للقونصل بتوجّهه واستبطأه الحوانب فنادوا يا فلان انزل فقال الحريم انّه نزل من وقت صعوده فكذّبوهنّ وهجموا الدار فلم يروا فيها أحدًا وعلم عليّ باشا بإفلاته فاغتاظ وعرف أنّها حيلة وتمّت عليه فانظرْ رحمك الله الى هذه القضيّة أترى أنّ هذا الوزير لو لم يبذل هذه الدنانير أكان يبلغ مأمنه لا والله بل كان يقتل ويؤخذ

١ الأصل: القواص. ٢ الأصل: يتوجه.

presented himself to ʿAlī Pasha before he had time to issue any orders concerning him, saying, "God aid our master! When he heard of your approach, your cousin Ḥusayn Pasha deposited large amounts of money with me, which I hid in a place known only to me. I know well that you intend to kill me and I am afraid that, should I die while it is still in its hiding place, my master will not have the benefit of it. If it pleases my lord to release me so that I may bring it to him, let him do so."

ʿAlī Pasha was overjoyed and believed him, and ordered him to set off with ten *ḥawnab*s to accompany him, a *ḥawnab* being in the language of Tunis what is called a *qawwāṣ* in the language of Egypt.[32] Before they set off he told the *ḥawnab*s, "If he escapes, I shall kill you all." They went with him till they reached his house, where he made them wait below while he went upstairs to get the women out of the way. The *ḥawnab*s waited, and as soon as the vizier was upstairs he made a beeline for the safe where he kept his money and filled his pockets with gold; he also took with him a small casket of the sort that in Tunis they call a *fnīq*, which likewise was filled with gold. Then he went out onto the roof, crossed over to another house, climbed down the wall to the street, and made for the house of the British consul, informing him as soon as he was in his presence that he was seeking refuge with him, and he told him his story. Then he gave him the casket and all its contents and said, "I want you to order one of your ships to take me to England immediately." The consul promptly wrote an order to one of his commanders, which said, "Set sail for England the moment this letter reaches you. Do not delay for even one minute," and he gave the vizier the letter and sent his dragoman with him. They traveled on the water until they reached the ship. When the ship's captain read the consul's letter, he left the harborage and fired a gun as a signal to the consul that he had set off. Now, it occurred to the *ḥawnab*s that he was taking a long time so they called out, "You! Come down!" but the women told them he had left immediately after going upstairs. They thought the women were lying and stormed the house but found no one. When ʿAlī Pasha learned of his escape he was furious and realized that it had been a ruse and he'd fallen for it. 2.1.12

Ponder this case, God bless you. Do you imagine that if this vizier had not used those gold pieces, he would have made it to safety? I swear not! ʿAlī Pasha would certainly have killed him and taken his money and it would

ماله ولا ينفعه بشيء لأنّ الدرهم والدينار إذا لم يبذلا لم ينفعا ولا تقضى لصاحبهما حاجة بل إن كان واليًا عُزل وإن كان تاجرًا احتقر

١٣،١،٢ وفي هذا المعنى أنشد شيخ مشايخنا العلامة الشيخ محمّد الأمير الكبير حين عُزل خورشيد باشا والي مصر سابقًا وتولّاها صاحب السعادة لعدم إعطاء مرتّبات العساكر شعرًا [مجزوء الكامل]

عَـزَلُوكَ لَمَّا قُـلْتَ مَـا   أُعْـطِي وَوَلَّوْا مَنْ بَذَلْ
أَوَمَـا عَـلِمْتَ بِأَنَّ مَـا   حَرْفٌ يَكُفُّ عَنِ ٱلْعَمَلْ

ولقد أجاد أبو القاسم الحريريّ في ذمّ الدينار من حيث انه لا ينفع صاحبه إلّا إذا فرّ من يده حيث قال [مشطور الرجز]

وَشَـرُّ مَـا فِـيهِ مِنَ ٱلْخَـلَائِقِ   أَنْ لَيْسَ يُغْنِي عَنْكَ فِي ٱلْمَضَايِقِ[١]
إِلَّا إِذَا فَـرَّ فِـرَارَ ٱلْآبِقِ   وَاهًـا لِمَنْ يَقْـذِفُهُ مِنْ حَـالِقِ
وَمَنْ إِذَا نَاجَـاهُ نَجْوَى ٱلْوَامِقِ   قَـالَ لَهُ قَوْلَ ٱلْمُحِقِّ ٱلصَّـادِقِ
لَا رَأْيَ[٢] فِي وَصْـلِكَ لِي فَفَـارِقِ

وفي الأمثال التونسيّة إذا وضعت الدينار على فم البلا أسكته وفي الأمثال المصريّة حبيب ماله حبيب ماله أي من أحبّ ماله وخزنه لا حبيب له

١٤،١،٢ ومن هذا القبيل حكاية وقعت بتونس وهي[٣] أنّ المرحوم الأمجد أبو محمّد حمّودة باشا برّد الله ثراه كان له وزير يسمّى يوسف صاحب الطابع ومعناه المُهُرْدار أي الذي في يده الخاتم الذي تختم به الأوامر وكان يوسف المذكور قبل ذلك مملوكًا لقائد صفاقس

١ الأصل: المضائق. ٢ الأصل: ارى. ٣ الأصل: هو.

have availed him nothing, for if a gold or silver piece isn't spent, it's of no use and will provide its owner with nothing of his needs. On the contrary, if he were a governor, he'd be dismissed, and if a merchant, despised.

In the same vein, when Khūrshīd Pasha, the former viceroy of Egypt, was dismissed for failing to give the troops their pay and His Excellency[33] became the country's ruler, our shaykh of shaykhs, Erudite Scholar Muḥammad al-Amīr al-Kabīr,[34] said to the same effect: 2.1.13

They fired you when you said, "I shall not
 give," and appointed another, who knew how to spend.
Did no one ever tell you: *mā*'s
 a particle that brings regency to an end? [35]

Al-Ḥarīrī puts it well when he denounces the gold piece for being of no use to its owner until it has escaped his grasp. He says:

The worst thing about it?
It can't help in a fix,
Unless it first flees you like a slave on the run.
Woe both to the one who throws it off a high cliff
And the one to whom, as it whispers sweet nothings,
It tells it straight and says,
"Our love has no future, so up sticks!"

And there is a Tunisian proverb that goes, "A gold piece placed over the mouth of tribulation silences it," and an Egyptian proverb that goes, "Love your money, lose your friends," meaning that one who loves his money and hoards it has no friends.

There is a similar story that took place in Tunis, to wit that Abū Muḥammad Ḥammūdah Pasha of glorious memory—may God cool the earth in which he lies—had a vizier called Yūsuf the Seal Bearer (i.e., "the *Muhurdār*," meaning the official who carries the seal with which the pasha seals his orders). This Yūsuf had previously been the slave of a head of the garrison at Sfax, a man named Muḥammad al-Jallūlī,[36] and was possessed of great beauty, mannerliness, and modesty. Word of him reached the pasha, who sent to al-Jallūlī, telling him, "I hear you have a slave of such and such a description called Yūsuf. When this letter reaches you, send him to me with its bearer. Farewell." When al-Jallūlī 2.1.14

المسمّى محمّد الجلّولي وكان على جانب[١] من الجمال والأدب والحياء فنمى خبره إلى الباشا فأرسل إلى الجلّولي يقول له إنّه قد بلغني أنّ عندك مملوكاً صفته كذا واسمه يوسف فإذا وصلك كتابي هذا أرسله صحبة حامله والسلام فلمّا قرأ الجلّولي الكتاب لم يجد بدّاً من إرساله فلمّا صار في حيازة الباشا أعجبه حسنه وذكاؤه وفطنته وصدقه وأمانته

٢،١،١٥ واتّفق أنّ بعض المماليك اتّفقوا على قتل الباشا ودخلوا عليه وهو نائم ووضعوا الشفرة على مذبحه فاستغاث منهم ولبخت يوسف المذكور كان خلاص الباشا منهم على يده فنزل عنده منزلة عظيمة وأحلّه محلّ ولده وقلّده الولايات العظيمة وصارت الألوية تخفق على رأسه حتّى صار يشار إليه بأطراف البنان وكان يوسف المذكور سعيد الطالع جيّد التدبير مظفّراً في الحروب ميمون الحركة سخيّ الكفّ يجذب القلوب بلطفه حتّى أنّ الباشا جعله رئيساً على العساكر البرّيّة في محاربة صرّاط وهي محاربة وقعت بين حاكم تونس وصاحب الجزائر فَبِيُمْن صاحب الطابع كانت الدائرة على أهل الجزائر واغتنم عسكر تونس أخبية الجزائريّ وخيله وإبله وسلاحه وأسر من عسكر الجزائر في هذه الواقعة جمّ غفير ثمّ صار مدبّر الجيوش البرّيّة والبحريّة بحلق الواد وذلك حين قدم أسطول الجزائر لمحاربة تونس أيضاً فكان مقيماً ببرج حلق الواد يدبّر أمر الجيش والسفن والشواني والعسس على الشاطئ وكانت أكابر تونس تأتي إليه لقضاء أشغالهم بحلق الواد لأنّ زمام الأمور كلّها بيده

٢،١،١٦ وكان من جملة من يحضر ديوانه محمّد الجلّولي ابن سيّده سابقاً لكن كان يأتي بتيه وخفر مع عدم سلوك طريقة الأدب اللائقة بأمثاله وكان صاحب الطابع يرى منه ذلك ويتغافل عنه حتّى أنّ أكابر ديوانه تكلّموا معه في شأن ذلك وذكروا له أموراً كثيرة حتّى قالوا إنّه يراك إلى الآن مملوك أبيه وقد صرّح بهذا مراراً فنقم ذلك عليه وتحيّل في طريق الانتقام منه فأخبر أنّه يدخل داره راكباً ولا ينزل خارج الدار كبقيّة الأمراء وأنّ سائسه يأخذ بغلته ويربطها في مربط دوابّه فدعا برئيس السيّاس وقال له

---

١ أضيف للسياق: جانب.

read the letter, he could see no alternative but to send the man, and when the pasha had him in his possession, he delighted in his good looks, intelligence, quick-wittedness, honesty, and trustworthiness.

Now it happened that some slaves, having agreed among themselves to kill the pasha, entered his room while he was sleeping and put the blade to his throat.[37] He called out for help and it was this Yūsuf's good fortune to be the one who saved the pasha. The latter raised him to high estate and treated him as he did his own children, bestowing upon him posts of great importance, so that banners now fluttered above his head[38] and men took to pointing at him with the tips of their fingers.[39] This Yūsuf was so charming, so deft in his dealings, so victorious in war, so blessed in all he did, so openhanded, that his polished ways appealed to all men's hearts. The pasha made him commander of land forces at the Battle of Serrat, between the ruler of Tunis and the master of Algiers.[40] To Yūsuf's good fortune, the Algerians suffered a calamitous defeat. The Tunisian forces captured their tents, horses, camels, and weapons, and a huge number of Algerian soldiers were taken prisoner. After this, he became the commander of land and sea forces at Ḥalq al-Wād, at a time when the Algerian fleet was advancing, once again, to do battle with Tunis. He lived in the fortress of Ḥalq al-Wād, and organized the army, ships, stores, and nightly patrols along the coast. The notables of Tunis used to seek him out there and have their affairs attended to, as he controlled everything. 2.1.15

One man who used to come to his court was Muḥammad al-Jallūlī, the son of his former master, but he would arrive with an arrogant air, with guards, and without following the code of etiquette appropriate to an official of Yūsuf's importance. The seal bearer noticed this in him but paid no attention until the leading members of his court spoke to him about it, citing many instances. They even said, "He still looks upon you as his father's slave and has said so openly many times." This annoyed Yūsuf, and he schemed to have his revenge. He was told al-Jallūlī would enter his house mounted, not dismounting outside like the other emirs, and that al-Jallūlī's groom would take his mule and tether it alongside Yūsuf's own mounts. Yūsuf therefore summoned the chief groom and said, "They tell me that al-Jallūlī's groom tethers his mule with my mounts. If after today I hear that he has tethered it with my horses, you will have only yourself to blame for the consequences." "I hear and obey," said the man. One day, al-Jallūlī came and dismounted as was his wont, and his groom took his mule and tethered it as was his wont (Yūsuf's groom being absent), 2.1.16

قد بلغني أن سائس الجلّولي يربط بغلته في مربط دوابّي. إن بلغني أنّه ربطها في مربط خيلي بعد اليوم لا تلومنّ إلّا نفسك فقال سمعاً وطاعة ثمّ إنّ الجلّولي جاء ونزل على عادته وأخذ سائسه البغلة والسائس كان غائباً وصعد هو إلى مجلس صاحب الطابع وجلس وبينما هو جالس إذ سمع هيصة[1] وصياحاً فنظر من أحد الشبابيك فرأى بغلته تركض عائرة وسائسه مضروباً والدم ينبع من رأسه فانزعج ونزل فأخبره سائسه أنّ كبير السيّاس[2] جاء ووجد البغلة مربوطة فأطلقها وضربها فخرجت عائرة فسمعت بذلك فقلت له لِمَ تطلق بغلة سيّدي فشتمني وشتمك فرددت عليه فضربني وترك حالي كما ترى

١٧،١،٢ فرجع الجلّولي إلى صاحب الطابع وهو مغضب وقال له أتطلق بغلتي ويضرب خادمي وأنت موجود فلم يلتفت إليه ولم يردّ عليه جواباً فزاد حنقه وعلم أنّ الخادم لا يفعل مثل هذا الفعل إلّا بإذن سيّده فنزل وركب من ساعته وتوجّه إلى الحضرة ودخل على المرحوم حمّودة باشا وشكا له جميع ما قد جرى عليه من صاحب الطابع فما أشكاه ولا التفت إليه فكاد يتميّز من الغيظ ونزل من الحضرة وتوجّه لداره كئيباً حزيناً لا يدري ماذا يصنع فاجتمع عليه بعض أصحابه ورآه على تلك الحالة فسأله عن سبب حزنه فأخبره الخبر فلام عليه فيما صنع لا سيّما في شكواه للباشا وقال له أما تعلم أنّ صاحب الطابع هو المقبول وكلمته هي المسموعة أتريد أن تعاديه وتشكوه للباشا ويسمع لك عليه دعوى بئسما فعلت وساء ما توهّمت أدرك نفسك وتلافَ أمرك وإلّا حلّ بك ما يحلّ من التلف وأنت المذموم أما سمعت قول الشاعر [كامل]

وَإِذَا ٱلْعِنَايَةُ صَادَفَتْ عَبْدَ ٱلشَّرَا   تَمْشِي عَلَى سَادَاتِهِ أَحْكَامُهُ

١٨،١،٢ فقال الجلّولي والخروج من هذا الأمر والحيلة في الخلاص منه؟ قال له صاحبه اعلم أنّ المال إذا لم يبذله صاحبه في مثل هذا المهمّ كان هو وحجارة[3] الدار سواء

١ الأصل: هيظة. ٢ الأصل: السايس. ٣ الأصل: كان حجارة.

and al-Jallūlī went upstairs to the seal bearer's meeting chamber and sat down. While he was thus seated he heard a ruckus and cries, so he looked out of a window and saw that his mule was running loose and that his groom had been beaten, blood welling from his head. He went downstairs in a fury, and his groom told him that the chief groom had come and found his mule tethered, and that he had set it loose and struck it, causing it to run off. "When I heard this," the man said, "I asked him, 'Why did you set my master's mule loose?' and he swore at me, so I swore back at him. Then he beat me and left me in the condition you find me in."

Al-Jallūlī went back in a rage to the seal bearer and said to him, "How could my mule be set loose and my servant be beaten before your eyes?" Yūsuf, however, did not look at him and gave no reply. Al-Jallūlī became even angrier, realizing that the servant would never have done what he did without his master's permission. He went down, mounted forthwith, and set off for an audience with the pasha. He went in to see the late Ḥammūdah Pasha and complained of all he had suffered at the seal bearer's hands. The pasha, however, paid no attention to his complaints and would not even look at him. At this point, al-Jallūlī was bursting with rage. He left the pasha's presence and went home depressed and distressed, at a loss as to what to do. One of his friends came to see him, and finding him thus asked him why he was upset. He told him what had happened, and the man chided him for what he had done, and especially for complaining to the pasha. "Are you not aware," he said, "that the seal bearer is his favorite and it's his word that is heard? Do you want to make him your enemy? Do you think you can complain about him to the pasha and have your petition against him heeded? How wretchedly you have acted, and what foolish delusions you have harbored! Bethink yourself and put things right, or you will suffer the harm that is coming to you and will have only yourself to blame. Have you not heard the words of the poet that go: 2.1.17

> Should God's favor fall on the purchased slave,
> his commands will govern his masters?"

"So how do I get out of this situation?" asked al-Jallūlī. "What strategy should I use to escape my predicament?" "Know this," his friend told him. "If a man doesn't spend his money when it comes to a critical business such as this, it's of no more use to him than the stones of his house. Your strategy should be to put together a dazzling gift, present it to the seal bearer, and beg 2.1.18

والحيلة أن تحتفل في هديّة سنيّة وتقدّمها بين يدي صاحب الطابع وتتوسّل إليه بأعزّ أحبابه عليه كحضرة ابن أبي الضِيَاف وقاسم البوّاب وصالح أبي غُدَيْر وأضرابهم وتبذل لهم من المال ما يرضيهم وينشّطهم للشفاعة لأنّ المال لا يطلب إلّا لمثل هذا المهمّ فأخذ الجلّولي نصيحته بقبول واحتفل في هديّة عظيمة منها سيف لا يُقوَّم بمال لحسن جوهره وخاتم من الماس عظيم لا يقوّم أيضاً وخنجر مرصّع بماس وياقوت وعلبة نشوق وساعة مرصّعتين وعشرة آلاف محبوباً وأخذ مالاً جزيلاً غير هذا وتلطّف حتّى اجتمع بأصحاب صاحب الطابع وأخبرهم أنّه متوسّل بهم إليه أن يتوسّلوا له في العفو وبذل لهم ما أرضاهم وسلّمهم الهديّة فأخذوها وذهبوا إلى صاحبهم وأخبروه أنّ الجلّولي جاء معتذراً يطلب عفو سعادته وأطلعوه على الهديّة وزيّنوا له أمر الصلح والعفو عنه وترك الانتقام منه إلّا إن عاد لمثلها

١٩،١،٢ فشرهت نفسه الهديّة وقبلها وعفا عنه وأمرهم بإحضاره وأن يبالغوا في وصيّته على سلوك طريق الأدب وأن يترك ما كان عليه من التكبّر ولا يرى لنفسه على غيره فضلاً بل يقف على قدم العبوديّة لأنّه هو وأحد القوّاد عندنا على حدّ سواء وإن عاد إلى مثلها لا يلومنّ إلّا نفسه فامتثلوا أمره وأحضروه وبالغوا في وصيّته ثمّ أدخلوه على صاحب الطابع فلمّا رآه بشّ في وجهه وأمره بالجلوس وأجلّ مجلسه واعتنى به ولم يفاوضه في شيء ممّا كان ثمّ إنّ صاحب الطابع كتب إلى مخدومه الباشا وأعلمه بما وقع من الجلّولي ومنه وأنّ الجلّولي استرضاه بهديّة وأنّه رضي عنه وأرسل الهديّة صحبة الكتاب فلمّا وصله الكتاب قرأه وأحضر الهديّة ونظرها ثمّ ردّها إليه وكتب له ما صورته قد بلغنا كتابك وفهمنا ما انطوى عليه ووقعت منّا الهديّة أحسن موقع لكنّنا رأينا كلّ ما فيها يصلح لك لا لنا فقد رددناها عليك وسامحناك فيها لأنّك شابّ وتحبّ الزينة ونحن بمَعزَل عن ذلك وأمّا العشرة آلاف فاصرفها في مصالح العسكر وقد رضينا عن الجلّولي لرضاك عنه والسلام ولمّا كان من الغد دخل الجلّولي على

his forgiveness through his dearest friends, such as His Excellency Ibn Abī al-Ḍiyāf,[41] Qāsim the Doorman, Ṣāliḥ Abū Ghudayr, and their like, spending enough money on them to make them contented and active intercessors on your behalf: what is money for, if not critical situations like this?" Al-Jallūlī accepted his advice and prepared a costly gift, including a sword that was beyond price by virtue of the beauty of its gems, a huge seal ring made with diamonds that was likewise beyond price, a dagger inlaid with diamonds and rubies, a snuffbox and a watch, both inlaid, and ten thousand gold sequins. Taking a large sum of money, he wheedled away until he obtained a meeting with the seal bearer's friends and informed them he wanted to use them to gain access to the seal bearer so that they could entreat him to forgive him. He gave them presents to win their good will and handed over to them the gift, which they took to their friend, informing him that al-Jallūlī had come to apologize and seek His Excellency's forgiveness. They showed him the gift and outlined the advantages of calling a truce with the man and of excusing him and not seeking vengeance, so long as he didn't do it again.

The gift excited Yūsuf's greed, so he accepted it and forgave the man. He **2.1.19**
ordered them to have him brought before them and to counsel him forcefully that he must follow the rules of etiquette, abandon his former arrogance, and cease to regard himself as better than everyone else; rather, he should adopt a servile manner, since "to us, he's no different from any other commander in the army, and if he reverts to his old ways he will have only himself to blame for the consequences." They obeyed his command, fetched him, and counseled him. Then they brought him into the presence of the seal bearer who, when he saw him, gave him a friendly smile, ordered him to be seated, made much of his having come, paid him every attention, and made no reference to what had happened. Then the seal bearer wrote to his master the pasha and told him what had taken place with al-Jallūlī—that al-Jallūlī had sought his favor with a gift and that he had granted him his favor—and he sent the gift with the bearer of the letter. When the letter reached the pasha, he read it and he had the gift brought and inspected it; then he returned it to Yūsuf, writing to him as follows: "Your letter has reached us, and we have understood what it contains and found the gift to be excellent. However, we think its contents better suited to you than to us, so we have returned it to you and give you permission to enjoy it, for you are a young man and love adornment, while we have nothing to do with such things. As for the ten thousand, spend them on the needs of the army. We grant

الباشا فأعظم ملقاه ورحّب به وأضاف له عملاً على ما بيده من الأعمال وصار في أحسن حال فتأمل رحمك الله في هذه القضيّة بعين الاعتبار. أترى أنّ الجلّولي لو لم يبذل هذا المال أكان يرجع لحاله الأوّل لا والله بل تؤخذ من يده الأعمال وربّما قُتِلَ في الحال

٢،١،٢٠ وإذ قد انجرّ الكلام إلى سيرة المرحوم حمّودة باشا ووزيره المرحوم يوسف صاحب الطابع فلنذكر نبذة من سيرتهما لأنّ المقصد ألّا تخلو رحلتنا عن الفوائد الجميلة ولا أجمل من ذكر الملوك العادلين الذين حسنت سيرتهم فتنعّمت بهم رعيّتهم ونبدأ بذكر الباشا فنقول هو المولى الأجلّ الفاضل العادل الفطن الحازم أبو محمّد حمّودة باشا بن عليّ باشا بن حسين باشا بن عليّ ولد ليلة السبت الثامنة عشر من ربيع الثاني سنة ١١٧٣ وبويع له يوم وفاة أبيه سنة ١١٩١ وتوفّي ليلة عيد الفطر ١٢٢٩. كان من الحزم وحسن الرأي والعدل بمكان شجاعاً مهاباً عفيف النفس عالي الهمّة. أنشأ بستان منوبة المشهور الآن الذي أخفى ذكر بستان أبي فِهْر الذي قال فيه أبو عبد الله محمّد الوِرْغي [بسيط]

وَقِفْ هُنَا بِأَبِي فِهْرِ ٱلْجَمِيلِ فَقَدْ ... مَضَتْ بِهِ دَوْلَةُ ٱلشُّمِّ ٱلْعَرَانِينِ
تَرَى ٱلْحَنَايَا كَسَطْرِ ٱلنَّخْلِ مَدَّ بِهِ ... بَعْضٌ لِبَعْضٍ بِحَنْيِ ٱلْعَرَاجِينِ
أَوْ خُرَّدٍ نَهَضَتْ لِلرَّقْصِ فَٱعْتَنَقَتْ ... كَيْلَا تَجِيءَ بِرَقْصٍ غَيْرِ مَوْزُونِ

٢،١،٢١ وسوّر على تونس السور العظيم وحصّنها بالأبراج والمدافع وشحن الأبراج بالعسكر ورفع التلال التي كانت بين تونس والبحيرة وقد كانت مثل الجبال العظيمة مانعة لجودة الهواء يخشى على البلد منها وهي من مدّة دولة بني حفص فاجتهد في نقلها في مدّة سبع سنين حتّى ترك محلّها مزرعة عظيمة وكشف بذلك غمّة أهل تونس وأنشأ

al-Jallūlī our favor because you have granted him yours. Farewell." The following morning, al-Jallūlī went in to see the pasha, who made much of seeing him and welcomed him and gave him a further district to administer in addition to those he already had, and the man found himself very well off.

Observe this case and give it due consideration. Do you think that if al-Jallūlī hadn't spent his money he'd have been restored to his former station? I swear he wouldn't! On the contrary, he would have been stripped of his estates and might well have been killed on the spot.

Since our discussion has led us to the life of the late Ḥammūdah Pasha and 2.1.20
his vizier Yūsuf the Seal Bearer, let us record a small portion of their history, for we are determined that this travel narrative of ours not be without attractive and informative parables, and there is nothing more enjoyable than talk of just kings whose conduct was good and whose subjects led comfortable lives because of them. We begin with mention of the pasha, as follows:

The Resolute, Sagacious, Just, Virtuous, Sublime Master Abū Muḥammad Ḥammūdah Pasha, son of ʿAlī Pasha, son of Ḥusayn Pasha, son of ʿAlī, was born on the eve of Saturday, Rabiʿ al-Thani 18, 1173 [December 8, 1759]. Allegiance was paid to him the day his father died in 1191 [1777–78].[42] He himself died on the eve of the Feast of the Fast-Breaking in 1229 [September 15, 1814]. He was possessed of a high degree of resolve, discrimination, and justice, and was courageous, inspiring of respect, chaste, and bold. He constructed the Manūbah Garden that is now so famous and that has eclipsed the Garden of Abū Fihr, of which Abū ʿAbd Allāh Muḥammad al-Wirghī said:

> Stand here, at lovely Abū Fihr—
> no stranger to the days of prideful beaux!
> Observe the curves and those they grace—like a line of palms, each touching
> another as, weighed down by clusters, they're brought low,
> Or like well-bred virgins who, rising to dance, have placed their arms around each other's necks
> lest they fall to dancing out of step.

It was he too who built the great wall around Tunis, fortified it with towers 2.1.21
and cannons, and manned the towers with soldiery. He removed the mounds of refuse that lay between Tunis and the lake, which had been like mighty mountains, blocking the good air and putting the city at risk, since the days of

محلاًّ لإنشاء المدافع العظيمة وحصّن حلق الواد بالأبراج والأبنية العجيبة بحيث صار لا تدخله فلوكة إلّا ويفتح لها بابان وبنى قلعة الكاف وأخرج تونس وأعمالها من ربقة الرقّ من أهل الجزائر إلى الحرّيّة المطلقة وكان مظفرًا ميمونًا لا يعاديه أحد إلّا خذل فلم تقدر له أهل الجزائر على شيء ومن سعادته أنّه استوزر يوسف صاحب الطابع المذكور وأطلق يده في جميع الأمور كما قدّمناه فكان يوسف المذكور جيّد الرأي حسن التدبير عالي الهمّة محبًّا للعلماء وأهل الفضل مجبولاً على فعل الخير جوادًا مهابًا

بنى الجامع المشهور به الآن بسوق الحلفاوين[١] بتونس وبنى بإزائه مدرسة عظيمة لطلب العلم ورتّب فيها وفي الجامع رواتب جليلة منها أنّه جعل نظر المدرسة لأوحد أهل زمانه علماً وديانة المولى الأجلّ الأديب البارع سيّدي الشيخ إبراهيم الرِياحيّ شيخنا وشيخ المشايخ الآن بتونس وشرط عليها قراءة درسين في كلّ يوم درس في الفقه ودرس في التفسير وزاد الشيخ من نفسه درساً في الحديث ودرساً في النحو وصرف صاحب الطابع على بناية الجامع والمدرسة المذكورين مالاً جزيلاً حتّى أنّ جامعه الآن في الحسن والإتقان أعظم جامع يوجد بتونس بل يمكن ألّا يوجد أتقن منه ولا أعجب منه وإن كان صغيراً إلّا فيما لم نشاهده ولقد رأيت عدّة جوامع بالقاهرة وبطرابلس الغرب وبالمورة والحجاز فلم أر أتقن منه اللّهمّ إلّا أن يقال إنّ الجامع الأمويّ بدمشق أو جامع القرويّين بفاس أو جامع أياصوفيا بقسطنطينيّة أعظم منه وبنى أمام الجامع سوقاً عظيماً للتجّار وبنى فوقه سراية عظيمة لجلوسه وأنشأ عدّة مكاتب وموارد في جملة مواضع ٢٢،١،٢

١ الأصل: الحَلْفَاوِيِّين.

the Hafsids. For seven years, he went to great lengths to have them removed and replaced with a huge plantation, thus relieving the people of Tunis of a great nuisance. He also built a place for the construction of large guns and fortified Ḥalq al-Wād and its wondrous towers and buildings, with the result that now not even a small sailing ship can enter without two gates first being opened to let it through. He also built the citadel at al-Kāf and released Tunis and its possessions from the slaver's noose imposed by the Algerians[43] so that they could enjoy absolute freedom. He was victorious, favored by fortune, and dashed the hopes of any who attacked him—so the Algerians could do nothing against him. Among his felicitous acts was the appointment of the previously mentioned Yūsuf the Seal Bearer as a vizier, whom he granted freedom to act in all things, as we have already mentioned. Yūsuf was very judicious, an excellent planner, zealous, a lover of scholars and learned men, predisposed by nature to acts of charity, generous, and inspiring of respect.

Yūsuf built the mosque in Tunis's al-Ḥalfāwīn market that now bears his 2.1.22
name[44] and a large school for the acquisition of knowledge next to it, providing lavish salaries for its administrators and those of the mosque. For example, he awarded the directorship of the school to the man of his day most outstanding in both learning and piety, the Most Sublime Master and Skilled Man of Letters, My Master Shaykh Ibrāhīm al-Riyāḥī, our teacher and currently the shaykh of shaykhs of Tunis. The latter made it a condition at the school that two classes be given each day, one in law, the other in Qur'anic commentary. The shaykh himself contributed two further classes, one in Hadith, the other in grammar. The seal bearer spent vast sums to build the aforementioned mosque and school, with the result that the mosque is now the greatest in all of Tunis in terms of beauty and perfection of construction. Indeed, there may be nothing more perfectly constructed or wonderful, despite its small size, unless it is one I haven't yet seen, and I have seen many mosques, in Cairo, Libyan Tripoli, the Morea, and the Hejaz. Despite this, I have never seen any more perfectly constructed, though it is said that the Umayyad mosque in Damascus, the Qarawiyyīn mosque in Fez, and the mosque of Hagia Sophia in Constantinople are more impressive. In front of the mosque he built a great market for merchants, and above it a mighty palace for himself to sit in. He also built several schools for young children and placed drinking fountains everywhere.

ولقد رأيت أحد الموارد التي أنشأها مكتوب عليها تأريخ لشيخنا العلامة الشيخ ٢٣،١،٢
إبراهيم الرياحيّ وصورته [مجزوء الرجز]

ذَا مَوْرِدٌ جَادَ بِهِ رَاجِي ثَوَابِ رَبِّهِ

يُوسُفُ خُوجَةُ ٱلرِّضِي صَاحِبُ طَابَعِ ٱلْبَهِي

فَخْرِ ٱلْعُلَى حَمُّودَةٍ بَاشَا وَذَا مِنْ سَيْبِهِ

يَا وَارِدًا أُدْعُ وَقُلْ تَارِيخُهُ بِشُرْبِهِ

١٢٠٩

وهو على طريقة أيقش أي طريقة حساب المغاربة قلت وهذا التأريخ أعني قوله بشربه غير بليغ أي ليس فيه من المعنى شيء حسن وأين هذا من تأريخ الأديب البارع المولى الشيخ محمد شهاب الدين المصريّ في السبيل الذي أنشأه محمود أفندي بالمحروسة الكائن بين الأزهر والمقام الحسينيّ وصورته [بسيط]

يَا وَارِدًا سَلْسَبِيلاً رَاقَ مَنْهَلُهُ اِشْرَبْ هَنِيئًا فَهٰذَا ٱلْعَذْبُ مَوْرُودُ

وَٱنْظُرْ إِلَى حُسْنِهِ وَٱلسَّعْدُ أَرَّخَهُ سَبِيلُهُ عَاطِفٌ لِلْخَيْرِ مَحْمُودُ

١٠٧ ١٦٠ ٨٧٠ ٩٨

١٢٣٥

ومن بعض تواريخ أديب زمانه الشيخ عليّ الدرويش في كسوة البيت الحرام ونصّه ٢٤،١،٢
[مجزوء الرجز]

I saw one of the fountains he constructed. It bore a chronogram[45] written by our teacher, Erudite Scholar Ibrāhīm al-Riyāḥī, which went as follows: 2.1.23

This is a fountain generously donated
by one who hopes for his Lord's reward:
Yūsuf, Counselor of Him Who Is Most Content with God's Favors[46]
and seal bearer of the magnificent,
Nobility's boast, Ḥammūdah
Pasha, and is of his largesse.
O you who drink, pray and speak
its date *on drinking of it.*

The individual words yield the date 1209 [1794–95] and are composed using the *ayqash* system, i.e., that used by westerners for calculation.[47] I declare: this chronogram (i.e., the words *bi-shurbihī*) is ineloquent, i.e., contains no pleasing sense. It is nothing compared to that written by the outstanding man of letters, Master Shaykh Muḥammad Shihāb al-Dīn al-Miṣrī, on the public drinking fountain constructed by Maḥmūd Effendi in Cairo the Protected between al-Azhar and the Shrine of al-Ḥusayn,[48] which goes as follows:

O you who drink from a spring whose source is pure,
quaff and good health to you, for this sweet water has been brought especially,
And see how excellent it is and how dated
His well inclines to good, is worthy of praise with felicity.[49]

The individual words yield the values 107, 160, 870, and 98, i.e., 1235 [1819–20].[50]

A chronogram by the Great Writer of His Day, Shaykh ʿAlī al-Darwīsh, on the covering of the Sacred House goes: 2.1.24

يا نُورَ نَاظِرِ كِسْوَةٍ   يَزْهُو بِهَا خَزٌّ وَبَزْ
بُشْرَى خَلِيلٍ نَاظِرًا   فَلَهُ بِهَا سَعْدٌ نَجَزْ
وَٱلسَّعْدُ قَالَ مُؤَرِّخًا   سِتْرٌ لِبَيْتِ ٱللهِ عَزْ

٦٦٠ ٤٤٢ ٦٦ ٧٧

١٢٤٥

وأين هذا التاريخ من تاريخيَ اللذين[1] نظمتهما للمرحوم السيّد محمّد المحروقيّ حين أنشأ الزاوية التي تجاه زاوية الشيخ العفيفيّ بالقرافة الصغرى والمورد الذي أنشأه ببركة الرَّطْليّ بالمحروسة ونصّ الأوّل [كامل]

أُنْظُرْ لِزَاوِيَةٍ تَكَامَلَ حُسْنُهَا   وَصَبَا إِلَيْهَا لُبُّ كُلِّ مَشُوقِ
وَبَدَتْ بِإِتْقَانٍ فَأَعْجَزَ وَصْفُهَا   ذَا ٱلنُّطْقِ بِٱلْمَفْهُومِ وَٱلْمَنْطُوقِ
وَقَدِ ٱسْتَضَاءَتْ بِٱلسِّيَادَةِ أَرِّخُوا   مَلِئَتْ بِنُورِ ٱلسَّيِّدِ ٱلْمَحْرُوقِي

٤٨٠ ٢٥٨ ١٠٥ ٣٩٥

١٢٣٨

ونصّ الثاني [طويل]

تَأَمَّلْ لِمَا شَادَتْ يَدُ ٱلْعِزِّ وَٱلْبَهَا   تَرَى مَوْرِدًا بِٱللُّطْفِ وَٱلْحُسْنِ قَدْ زَهَا
وَقَدْ شَادَهُ مِنْ نَسْلِ أَكْرَمِ مُرْسَلٍ   هُمَامٌ لَهُ مَجْدٌ عَلَا[2] ذُرْوَةَ ٱلسُّهَا
مُحَمَّدُ ٱلْمَحْرُوقِيُّ أَنْشَاهُ رَاجِيًا   ثَوَابَ إِلٰهٍ حَدُّهُ مَا لَهُ ٱنْتِهَا
وَمُذْ تَمَّ قَالَ ٱلسَّعْدُ لِلشُّرْبِ أَرِّخُوا   زُلَالُ شِفَاءٍ جَيِّدٌ وَهْوَ مُشْتَهَى

٦٨ ٣٨١ ١٧ ١٧ ٧٥٥

١٢٣٨

١ الأصل: الذين. ٢ الأصل: على.

Ah, how brightens the eye that beholds a covering
that fine stuffs are proud to adorn!
Glad tidings from al-Khalīl[51] to any who looks upon it,
for by so doing he acquires good fortune—
And Fortune declared, to date it,
A seemly covering for the House of God, may He be glorified.

The individual words yield the values 660, 442, 66, and 77, i.e., 1245 [1829–30].

And even that is nothing compared to the two chronograms I composed for the late Sayyid Muḥammad al-Maḥrūqī when he constructed the Sufi hospice opposite that of Shaykh al-ʿAfīfī in the Lesser Cemetery[52] and the water source at al-Raṭlī Pond in Cairo the Protected. The first goes:

Behold a Sufi hospice whose beauty's complete
and to which all yearning hearts aspire!
It emerged so perfect as to beggar description
by any who speaks by sign or word
And it is illumined by the grace of a *sayyid*. Date it:
It has become filled with the light of Sayyid al-Maḥrūqī!

The individual words yield the values 480, 258, 105, and 395, i.e., 1238 [1822–23].

The second goes:

Observe what the hand of might and pride has built
and you will see a water source made magnificent by grace and beauty,
Its builder, of the line of the noblest messenger,
a gallant man whose glory tops al-Suhā's zenith.[53]
Muḥammad al-Maḥrūqī erected it, in hope of
reward from a god whose limits know no end.
When it was finished, Fortune said to those who drank, "Date it:
Sweet water, curative, excellent, to be desired."

The individual words yield the values 68, 381, 17, 17, and 755, i.e., 1238 [1822–23].

توفّي المرحوم يوسف خوجة صاحب الطابع في شهر صفر سنة ١٢٣٠ ومات قتيلاً وطيف بِشِلْوِهِ يُجَرّ في الأسواق بعد أن كان البصر يخشى أن يمتدّ إليه فسبحان المعزّ المذلّ ورثاه شيخنا العلاّمة الشيخ إبراهيم الرياحيّ بأبيات كتبت على قبره وهي هذه [مجزوء الكامل] ٢،١،٢٥

لله قَدْ وَجَبَ ٱلدَّوَامْ　　وَسِوَاهُ نَهْبٌ لِلْحِمَامْ

سِيَّانِ فِي تَنْغِيصِهِ　　عَالٍ وَمُنْخَفِضُ ٱلْمَقَامْ

أَيْنَ ٱلْمُلُوكُ وَأَيْنَ مَنْ　　كَانَتْ لَهُمْ تُرْعَى ٱلذِّمَامْ

لَمْ يَظْفَرُوا بِسِوَى ٱلَّذِي　　عَمِلُوهُ مِنْ خَيْرٍ فَدَامْ

هَذَا ٱلَّذِي بِصَنِيعِهِ　　قَدْ رَامَهُ هذَا ٱلْهُمَامْ

مِنْ فِعْلِ خَيْرٍ عَزَّ أَنْ　　يَغْنَى ٱلْأَنَامُ عَنِ ٱلْغَمَامْ

وَجَوَامِعٍ وَمَكَاتِبٍ　　وَمَوَارِدٍ تَسْقِي ٱلْأُوَامْ

اَللهُ يَرْحَمْ يُوسُفاً　　خَتْمَ ٱلْكِرَامِ بِلَا كَلَامْ

لَا غَرْوَ أَنْ أَرَّخْتُهُ　　بِمَمَاتِهِ يَتِمُّ ٱلْكِرَامْ

٤٨٨ ٤٥٠ ٢٩٢

١٢٣٠

ولنرجع إلى ما نحن بصدده ثمّ إنّ جدّي خرج من مكّة المشرّفة إلى بندر أي مرسى جدّة ومكث ينسخ الكتب بالأجرة وكان جميل الخطّ كما قدّمنا فاتّفق أنّه اجتمع في تلك المدّة بأناس من أهل جزيرة سِنّار وتودّد إليه بعضهم وارتبطت بينهم صحبة فسأله من أيّ البلاد أنت فقال من تونس فسأله عن سبب إقامته بجدّة ٢،١،٢٦

The late Yūsuf Khōjah the Seal Bearer died in the month Safar 1230 [January 1813].[54] A man to whom men once feared to raise their eyes, he was murdered and his body dragged through the markets, so glory to Him who raises and brings low! Our teacher, Erudite Scholar Ibrāhīm al-Riyāḥī, elegized him in lines that were written on his tomb, as follows: 2.1.25

God alone may last forever;
  others are death's booty.
Equal are they in their discomfiture,
  whether their station be high or low.
Where are the kings; where those
  whose rights were honored?
They took naught with them save what
  they did of good, which therefore lasted.
This is what this great soul hoped to obtain
  by his good deeds
    —and rarely can man dispense with generosity!—
And by mosques and schools for the young
  and water sources to quench the thirst.
May God have mercy on Yūsuf,
  Seal of the Noble,[55] which no one can deny.
Small wonder that I have expressed the date as:
  With his death, the noble have ceased to exist.

The individual words yield the values 488, 450, and 292, i.e., 1230 [1814–15].

Let us now return to the matter at hand. My grandfather then traveled from Mecca the Ennobled to the *bandar*—meaning port[56]—of Jeddah, and stayed there copying books for money; as we have mentioned, he had a beautiful hand. During this period, chance threw him together with people from the Island of Sinnār,[57] one of whom became fond of him, and a bond of friendship was formed. This man asked him, "What country are you from?" and he answered, "Tunis." The man asked him why he'd settled in Jeddah, so my grandfather told him all that had befallen him, and the man from Sinnār asked him, "Why don't you go with us to the city of Sinnār? There you will find respect and esteem, for our *makk*—meaning 'our king'—is an openhanded man who cares nothing for the glitter of gold or silver's gleam. He loves, on the contrary, learning and its fraternity, assigning to each his rightful place and 2.1.26

فأخبره بقصّته وما جرى عليه فقال له السنّاريّ ألا تتوجّه معنا إلى مدينة سنّار ويحصل لك العزّ والافتخار لأنّ مَكًّا أي مَلِكَنا رجل مبسوط اليد لا يبالي بلجين ولا عسجد. يحبّ الفضل وأهله ويحلّ كلاًّ منهم محلّه وينيل الأشراف بما يقدر عليه من الإسعاف وأنا ضامن لك إن ذهبت معنا أن يجبر كسرك ويسدّ خللك وتصبح ذا مال ونوال ورقيق وجمال فطمع جدّي في نوال الملك المذكور وتوجّه معهم يأمل الفرح والسرور وحين وصل معهم إلى جزيرة سنّار قابلوا به الملكّ وأعلموه أنه رجل من أهل العلم غريب الديار قد انكسرت سفينته وضاع ما كان حيلته فرحّب به وأعظم ملقاه وبشّره باليسر وهنّاه وأنزله دار إكرامه وأمر له بجزيل إنعامه فكان فيما أنعم عليه به جارية مَكاديّة بهيّة سنيّة غالية القيمة تسمّى حليمة فتسرّاها جدّي لجمالها فجاءت بغلام وجارية مثالها وأجرى عليه رزقًا فاستقرّ جدّي بسنّار ونسي أهله بتونس وأولاده الصغار

٢٧،١،٢ وكان حين خروجه من تونس ترك ثلاثة أولاد مع أمّهم أكبرهم عمّي المرحوم السيّد محمّد كان عمره تسع سنين وأوسطهم المغفور له والدي وكان عمره ستّ سنين وأصغرهم عمّي المرحوم السيّد محمّد طاهر وعمره ثلاث[1] سنين هكذا سمعت من والدي وجدّتي عليهما سحائب الرحمة والعهدة عليهما فانحنى عليهم خالهم المولى الأجلّ الأكمل الأمثل الفقيه المحدّث العالم الفاضل السيّد أحمد ابن العلامة الرُحَل السند السيّد سليمان الأزهريّ صاحب التصانيف العديدة والتآليف المفيدة. كان السيّد أحمد عالمًا فاضلاً ثقة حجّة في المنقول عرض عليه منصب القضاء بتونس فامتنع منه وكان مشتغلاً بالتدريس وولي وظيفة التدريس بمدرسة عليّ باشا الأوّل فلازمها وأصيب في آخر أمره بداء أزمنه فكان يقرأ الدروس في داره وتحضره أكابر طلبة العلم والفضلاء ولم يزل كذلك حتّى شبّ والدي وبلغ مبلغ الرجال وكان حفظ القرآن وحضر بعض دروس في العلم على خاله وغيره وبينما هو كذلك إذ تحرّك شوقه إلى الحجّ

١ الأصل: ثلاثة.

giving what aid he can to the Prophet's posterity. I guarantee that if you go with us he will console you and compensate you for your lost chattels, and you will find yourself possessed of wealth and gifts, slaves, and camels." Coveting the largesse of the aforementioned *makk*, my grandfather set off with them, hoping for joy and pleasure, and when they reached the Island of Sinnār, they took him to meet the *makk* and informed him that he was a man of learning and a stranger in their country, one whose ship had foundered on the main, leaving not a penny to his name. The *makk* welcomed him, made much of meeting him, assured him of a life of ease to come, congratulated him, put him up in his guesthouse, and ordered that the best of his favors be bestowed upon him. Among the things so bestowed was a gorgeous, superb, extremely valuable Abyssinian slave girl called Ḥalīmah. She was so beautiful my grandfather took her as his concubine and she bore him a boy and a girl as beautiful as she. The *makk* also allocated him an income. So my grandfather settled down in Sinnār, oblivious of his family and young sons in Tunis, now so far.

On his departure from Tunis, he had left behind three sons, as well as their **2.1.27**
mother. The oldest of them was my uncle, the late Sayyid Muḥammad, who was nine at the time; in the middle was my late lamented father, who was six; and the youngest was the late Sayyid Muḥammad Ṭāhir, who was three. This is what I heard from my father and my grandmother—may the clouds of God's mercy rain upon them—and I report this on their authority. Their maternal uncle, the exemplary, perfect, outstanding master, the expert in law, Hadith scholar, and adept of both the religious sciences and the literary arts, Sayyid Aḥmad, son of the scholar, traveler, and reliable source of hadiths, Sayyid Sulaymān al-Azharī, author of numerous works and informative compositions, then took care of them. Sayyid Aḥmad was a learned scholar, a trustworthy source, of unimpeachable authority, for the transmission of both hadiths and the law, who was offered a post as a judge in Tunis. This, though, he refused, being more concerned with teaching. Instead, he assumed a position at the college of law established by ʿAlī Pasha I, and this he stuck to. At the end of his life, he was afflicted by a chronic sickness, so he gave his lessons at home, and these were attended by the most advanced students and learned men. This uncle continued to look after my grandfather's sons until my father became an adolescent and attained manhood. My father had memorized the Qur'an and attended some classes in the religious sciences with his maternal uncle and others. While thus occupied, he was seized by a desire to make the

فاستشار خاله في السفر فتحرّك شوقه هو أيضاً فتجهّزا للسفر معاً وركبا البحر من تونس إلى إسكندريّة ومنها إلى مصر ومن مصر توجّها إلى القُصَيْر وكان ذلك قبل أشهر الحجّ

٢،١،٢٨ وبينما هما سائران في القافلة إذ عرضت لهما قافلة قادمة من سنّار فناداهما مناد يا أيّها المغاربة هل فيكم أحد من تونس فقال أبي نعم نحن منها فقال هل تعرفون السيّد أحمد بن سليمان فقال أبي نعم نعرفه ومن أنت قال أنا نسيب أحمد قد خرجت من تونس منذ كذا وكذا وتركت أولادي وأهلي ولا أدري أهم أحياء أم أموات وكان خال أبي في شِبْرِيَّة مرخى عليها ستر فسمع ذلك كلّه فقال لأبي يا عمر سلّم على أبيك فأكبّ والدي يسلّم على أبيه ويقبّل يده وأعلمه أنّه خاله في الشبرية فجاء جدّي وسلّم على نسيبه[1] وبعد انقضاء السلام قال أبي لوالده أيسوغ لك أن تتركنا هذه المدّة بدون نفقة ونحن صغار ولولا أنّ الله سخّر لنا خالنا كنّا ضائعين فقال والده[2] ما حيلتي والقضاء والقدر يجريان على وفق الإرادة العليّة مفرد [كامل]

إِنَّ ٱلْمُقَـدَّرَ كَائِنٌ لَا يَنْـمَحِي   وَلَكَ ٱلْأَمَانُ مِنَ ٱلَّذِي مَا قُدِّرَا

فقال أبي لوالده ألم يَأْنِ لك أن ترجع إلى بلدك وتقرّ أعيننا برؤيتك فقال يكون ذلك إن شاء الله قال له والدي متى قال أنا الآن متوجّه إلى القاهرة أبيع ما معي من الرقيق وأرجع إلى سنّار وآخذ متاعي وأولادي وآتي إلى القاهرة وأنتما توجّهان للحجّ وترجعان إلى القاهرة فنجتمع هناك وكلّ من سبق صاحبه انتظره هناك ثمّ ودّعهما وتوجّه كلّ منهم إلى سبيله على حدّ قول الشاعر [كامل]

لَمْ أَسْتَتِـمَّ سَـلَامَهُ لِقُـدُومِهِ   حتّى ٱبْتَدَأْتُ سَـلَامَهُ لِوَدَاعِـهِ

٢،١،٢٩ فتوجّه والدي وخاله إلى الحجّ وتوجّه جدّي إلى المحروسة أمّا جدّي فباع رقيقه وتسوّق ورجع إلى سنّار وأمّا والدي وخاله فتوجّها إلى الحجاز ومكثا بالطائف حتّى

١ الأصل: ان. ٢ الأصل: والدي.

pilgrimage, so he consulted his uncle about the journey, and his uncle was seized by the same desire. They therefore prepared themselves for the journey and sailed on the boat from Tunis to Alexandria, then to Cairo, and from Cairo they set off for al-Quṣayr.[58] This was before the pilgrimage months had begun.

While on the road with their caravan, another, coming from Sinnār, crossed their path, and someone called out to them, "You westerners, is there anyone with you from Tunis?" so my father said, "Yes. We're from there." The man said, "Do you know Sayyid Aḥmad ibn Sulaymān?" "Yes," said my father, "we know him. And who are you?" The man replied, "I am Aḥmad's kinsman by marriage. I left Tunis thus-and-so-many years ago, leaving behind my sons and my parents, and I have no idea whether they are alive or dead." My father's uncle was in a camel litter, lying down and out of sight, and he overheard all this and told my father, "ʿUmar, say hello to your father!" and my father threw himself at his father's feet and greeted him, kissing his hand and informing him that his uncle was in the litter. Then my grandfather went and greeted his in-law. When the greetings were over, my father said to his father, "Is it nothing to you that you left us all this time without support, when we were still young, and that, if God in his generosity hadn't sent us our uncle, we would have been destitute?" "What was I to do," said his father, "when fate and destiny follow the courses set for them by the Divine Will? 2.1.28

What is decreed is a created fact that cannot be erased.
One is safe, though, from what has not been decreed."

Then my father asked his father, "Isn't it about time you returned to your country and gave us the joy of laying our eyes on you?" "So be it," said his father, "God willing." "When?" asked my father. "Right now," said the other, "I'm on my way to Cairo to sell the slaves I have with me. After that, I'll return to Sinnār, gather my belongings and my children, and come to Cairo. You are on your way to make the pilgrimage and will be returning to Cairo, so we'll meet there, and let the first to arrive wait for the other." Then he bade them farewell and each party went its way, as the words of the poet describe:[59]

Barely had I finished greeting him on his arrival
than I began bidding him farewell on his departure.

My father and his uncle then set off for the pilgrimage, while my grandfather set off for Cairo the Protected. There he sold his slaves, bought what he 2.1.29

جاء وقت الحجّ فقدما مكّة وحجّا وبعد انقضاء الحجّ توفّي خاله في مكّة المشرّفة ودفن بباب المَعَلّى ثمّ رجع والدي إلى القاهرة فما وجد أباه فأقام ينتظره مدّة فلم يأت وكان أبي في هذه المدّة يحضر دروساً في[1] العلوم بالجامع الأزهر ولمّا أعياه الانتظار توجّه إلى سنّار مع قافلة أتت فلمّا وصل إليه وجدّه قارّاً في داره مغتبطاً بأولاده وعياله لا يسأل عن غيرهم ولا يخطر له السفر على باله فسأله عن سبب خُلَف الوعد ولِمَ جعل الهزل مكان الجِدّ فاعتذر بعذر ساقِطٍ لا يجد له لاقِطٌ فقال له يا بنيّ إنّ لي ديوناً على بعض الناس ماطلوني في دفعها ولا يمكنني الارتحال إلّا بعد خلاصها على كلّ حال ليستقيم بها أودي ويقوى في السفر عضدي فمكث معه نحو ستّة أشهر وبعد ذلك تجهّزت قافلة إلى الأقطار المصريّة فسأل أبي والده في أحد أمرين بأن قال له هذه القافلة متوجّهة فإمّا أن تتوجّه بنا صحبتها أو تأذن لي بالتوجّه معها فأبى عليه فيهما[2] وقال أمّا الذهاب فلا سبيل إليه لما عليّ في تونس من الأموال لا سيّما وقد أُخبِرتُ بأنّ أمّك تزوّجت وأمّا الإذن لك فيكون لكن في قافلة أخرى إن شاء الله تعالى حتّى أجمع لك ما تسافر به من الرقيق والجمال والذهب والأحمال بحيث أنّك لا تعود إلّا مجبور الخاطر فأبى والدي المكث واستطالة[3] اللبث وقال إنّي مشتاق أطلب العلم وفي إقامتي هنا ضياع زمن بغير فائدة فاختلف رأيهما وحصلت بينهما وحشة

٣٠،١،٢ فخرج والدي مغضباً وتوجّه مع القافلة لا يملك شيئاً فألحقه والده بعد ثلاثة أيّام بثلاثة جمال وأربع جواري وعبدين وعلى الجمال أهبة السفر من مؤونة وماء وعلى أحد الجمال حمل صمغ فأخذها والدي وسار صحبة القافلة وبينما هم سائرون إذ ضلّوا عن الطريق وأدركهم العطش وطال عليهم الأمد فمات الرقيق والجمال ورجع إلى مصر فقيراً كما كان مفرد [طويل]

١ أضيف للسياق: دروس في. ٢ الأصل: فيها. ٣ الأصل: استطال.

needed, and went back to Sinnār, while my father and his uncle made their way to the Hejaz and stayed in al-Ṭā'if until the time of the pilgrimage, when they proceeded to Mecca and performed the rites. After they'd done so, my uncle died in Ennobled Mecca and was buried at Bāb al-Muʿallā. My father returned to Cairo, only to find that his father wasn't there. He waited for him for a time, but the man never came. During this period, my father was attending lessons at the mosque of al-Azhar. When he grew tired of waiting, however, he set off for Sinnār with a caravan that had come from there. On his arrival, he found his father settled in his house, reveling in his children and dependents, giving no thought to anyone else and with no intention of leaving. My father asked him why he'd broken his promise—why for earnestness he'd substituted jest, and the man let fall an excuse too feeble for any to stoop to address, saying, "My son, some people owe me money and have been dilatory in paying it back. I cannot travel, whatever might befall, until I have received what I am owed, in total and in full, that my needs be provided for, even at the lowest level, and my backbone stiffened, at least enough to travel." My father stayed with him for about six months. Then a caravan prepared to depart for the land of Egypt, so he gave his father two options, saying, "A caravan is preparing to leave. Either you and I both go with it or you grant me permission to go alone." His father refused him on both counts, however, saying, "It is impossible for me to go myself because of the monies that I owe in Tunis, and all the more because word has reached me that your mother has married again. As to your going, so be it, but with another caravan, the Almighty willing, to give me time to assemble slaves, camels, gold, and merchandise, so that you don't return empty-handed." My father, though, refused to prolong his stay, saying, "I long to study, and by staying here I am wasting time with nothing to show for it." Their views differed, and a coolness arose between them.

My father left in a temper and set off with the caravan with nothing to his 2.1.30
name, but three days later his father sent after him three camels along with four female slaves and two male, the camels bearing all the provisions and water he would need for the journey. One of the camels was loaded with gum arabic. My father took these things and continued with the caravan. On their way, they got lost[60] and were overtaken by thirst. They were late in reaching their destination, the slaves and the camels had died, and my father reached Cairo as poor as he had left it:

إِذَا أَقْبَلَتْ كَانَتْ تُقَادُ بِشَعْرَةٍ   وَإِنْ أَدْبَرَتْ كَانَتْ تَقُدُّ ٱلسَّلَاسِلَا

فمن لطف الله عزّ وجلّ مرض خبير القافلة بصداع أحرمه الهجوع وعجز عن شفائه الجموع وبلغ والدي هذا الخبر فكتب رقعة وأخذها الخبير باعتقاد ووضعها على محلّ الألم فبرئ لوقته فاعتقد في والدي الصلاح وأمر أن يُحمل ويُحمل له عِدل صمغ على إبله

٣١،١،٢ فوصل والدي إلى القاهرة بعد غصّ الريق وباع عدل الصمغ بخمسة وسبعين فُنْدُقْلِيّ ودخل الجامع الأزهر لطلب العلم وتزوّج والدتي إذ ذاك ومكث معها نحو سنتين جاءت منه بولد سمّاه أحمد عاش سنة وثلاثة أشهر ثمّ مات فحزن عليه وتمثّل بقول الشاعر مفرد [الشطر الأول من الطويل والشطر الثاني من الرجز]

لَقَدْ خَانَتِ ٱلْأَيَّامُ فِيكَ فَقَرَّبَتْ   يَوِمَ ٱلرَّدَى مِنْ لَيْلَةِ ٱلْمِيلَادِ

وبقول الآخر [كامل]

عَجَباً لِمَوْلُودٍ قَضَى مِنْ قَبْلِ أَنْ   يَقْضِي لِأَيَّامِ ٱلصِّبَا مِيقَاتَا
فَكَأَنَّهُ مِنْ نُسْكِهِ وَصَلَاحِهِ   وَهَبَ ٱلْحَيَاةَ لِوَالِدَيْهِ وَمَاتَا

وبقول التهاميّ في ولده [كامل]

يَا كَوْكَباً مَا كَانَ أَقْصَرَ عُمْرَهُ   وَكَذَا تَكُونُ كَوَاكِبُ ٱلْأَسْحَارِ

٣٢،١،٢ ثمّ إنّ والدي توجّه إلى تونس وأخذ أمّي وأمّها معه وكنت إذ ذاك حملاً فلمّا وصل إلى تونس نزل بدار أخيه المرحوم السيّد محمّد وكان من مشاهير المعلّمين بسوق الشواشيّة أي الطرابيشيّة[١] فولدت بعد ذلك بخمسة أشهر في الساعة

١ الأصل: طرابيشة.

When the world looks with favor upon you, it can be led by a thread.
When it turns against you, it breaks chains.

Now, through the grace of God, Mighty and Sublime, the leader of the caravan happened to fall ill: he had a headache that prevented him from sleeping and no one could cure him. When news of this reached my father, he wrote something on a slip of paper[61] and the leader took it with faith in his heart, placed it on the place that hurt, and was immediately cured. He then became convinced that my father was one of the righteous, ordered that he be given a mount, and had a sack of gum arabic loaded onto his camel.

After all these tribulations, my father returned to Cairo, sold the sack of gum for seventy-five sequins, and enrolled at the mosque of al-Azhar to continue his studies. At that time too, he married my mother, with whom he lived for about two years, during which she bore him a boy whom he named Aḥmad, who lived for one year and three months and then died. Mourning for him, my father summed up the situation by quoting the words of the poet that go: 2.1.31

The days betrayed you and closed the gap
between the day of death and the night of nativity

and the words of another that go:

Marvel at a babe who died ere
he could see the days of childhood to an end—
As though, so selfless and good was he,
he gave his life back to his begetters, and died

and also the words of al-Tuhāmī on his son:

Ah star! How short its life—
but so it is with stars that rise at dawn.

My father then set off for Tunis, taking with him my mother and her mother, my mother being then pregnant. When he got there, he stayed in the house of his brother, the late Sayyid Muḥammad, who was a well-known shopkeeper in the market of the *shāshiyyah*—meaning the tarbush—makers. I was born five months later at the third hour of a Friday in mid-Dhū l-Qaʿdah of the year 1204.[62] My father stayed there three more years. Then a coolness developed between him and his two brothers, so in 1207 [1792–93] he took us by caravan 2.1.32

الثالثة من يوم الجمعة منتصف ذي[1] القعدة سنة ١٢٠٤ ومكث بعد ذلك نحو ثلاث سنين ثمّ حصلت بينه وبين أخويه وحشة فقفل بنا إلى القاهرة سنة ١٢٠٧ فصار يطلب العلم في الأزهر ويحضر[2] درس العلامة المرحوم الشيخ عرفة الدسوقيّ المالكيّ وشيخ مشايخنا العالم الأوحد المرحوم الشيخ محمّد الأمير الكبير وتولّى نقيباً برواق السادة[3] المغاربة وكان في عيش متوسّط وما زال كذلك إلى أن دخلت سنة ١٢١١ وورد عليه كتاب من أخيه لأبيه من سنّار مع القافلة مضمونه بعد السلام إنّ والدنا توفّي إلى عفو الله تعالى وترك جملة من الكتب فسرقها منّا رجل يسمّى بأحمد البَنْزَرْتيّ أمّناه على بيتنا لأنّه ادّعى القرابة لوالدنا وبقينا في حالة تسرّ العدوّ وتسيء[4] الصديق فإذا وصلك كتابي هذا عجّل بالقدوم علينا لتأخذنا معك نعيش بما تعيش به والسلام فلمّا قرأ الكتاب بكى واستعبر وأخذته الشفقة على أخويه فتعجّل وسافر إليهما وكنت إذ ذاك ابن سبع سنين قد ختمت القرآن بداية ووصلت في العيادة[5] آخر آل عمران وكان لي أخ عمره أربع سنين وترك لنا نفقة تكفينا ستّة أشهر فمكثنا سنة باعت فيها والدتي أشياء كثيرة من نحاس وحليّ

ثمّ جاء عمّي الصغير المسمّى بالطاهر فانحنى علينا يربّينا وكان قد جاء للحجّ والتجارة ومعه ولد كالشمس الضاحية في السماء الصاحية اسمه محمّد وكان أسنّ منّي بنحو سنة ونصف فكان يذهب معي إلى المكتب لقراءة القرآن حتّى سافر به والده إلى الحجّ آخر سنة ١٢١٢ ثمّ دخلت الفرانسيس القاهرة وملكوها في أوّل سنة ١٢١٣ وكان عمّي إذ ذاك مع الحجّاج فهربت الغُزّ وتمزّقوا كلّ ممزّق ودخل الحجّاج فوجدوا الفرنسيس في مصر وأعمالها ومكثوا كذلك إلى أوّل سنة ١٢١٦ ثمّ جاء الوزير بالعساكر وخرجت الفرنساويّين وكان ابن عمّي المذكور قد حفظ القرآن وابتدأ يحضر دروس العلم وكان من الحياء والأدب بمكان فوقعت في تلك السنة أمراض وبائيّة وألمّت بابن عمّي المذكور فأخرجته من القصور إلى القبور بل للملاعبة مع الحور ٣٣،١،٢

---

١ الأصل: ذا. ٢ الأصل: تحضر. ٣ الأصل: لسادة. ٤ الأصل: تسيء. ٥ الأصل: العبادة.

to Cairo and studied at al-Azhar, where he attended the lessons of the late Erudite Shaykh ʿArafah al-Dusūqī al-Mālikī, and of our shaykh of shaykhs, the late Unique Scholar Shaykh Muḥammad al-Amīr al-Kabīr.[63] Then he assumed the deanship of the hall[64] of the Maghrebi *sayyid*s and became moderately well off. He continued like this until the beginning of 1211 [1796–97], when he received a letter from his half brother brought by the caravan from Sinnār, which read as follows: "Greetings. Know that our father has died and passed into the mercy of the Almighty. He left a quantity of books, but these were stolen from us by a man named Aḥmad al-Banzartī, in whose trust we had placed our house because he claimed to be related to our father. We now find ourselves in a position to bring pleasure to our enemies and disquiet to our friends. If this letter reaches you, hasten to us so that you can take us back with you and we can live the life you live. Farewell." When my father read the letter, he wept and shed tears and was overcome with pity for his brothers, so he hastened to them. I was seven years old at the time—I had been through the Qur'an once to learn it by heart and had gotten as far as the end of Āl ʿImrān[65] on the second time round; and I had a brother aged four. My father left us enough money to last six months, but we survived on it for a year, during which my mother sold much of her copperware and jewelry.

Then my youngest paternal uncle, the one called al-Ṭāhir, came and devoted himself to our upbringing. He had come for the pilgrimage[66] and to trade, and brought with him a son like a blazing sun in a clear sky, whose name was Muḥammad. He was about a year and a half older than me and used to go to Qur'an school with me, until his father took him to perform the pilgrimage at the end of 1212.[67] Then the French entered Cairo, taking it at the beginning of 1213,[68] when my uncle was still with the pilgrims. The Turkish soldiery fled and were ripped to shreds, and the pilgrims returned to find the French in Egypt and its provinces. There they remained until the beginning of 1216 [May 1801], when the vizier came accompanied by his soldiers, and they left.[69] My aforementioned cousin had memorized the whole of the Qur'an and had begun to attend lectures in the higher sciences; he was extremely modest and polite. In the same year, epidemics broke out and they seized this cousin of mine, taking him from palace to grave; nay, to that place where he could sport forever with many a sloe-eyed maid.[70] When he died, his father grieved greatly; indeed, he almost perished of sorrow and was in such pain and anguish that he 2.1.33

ولمّا قضي عليه حزن عليه والده أشدّ الحزن حتّى كاد يهلك أسفاً ويدخل رمسه توجّعاً ولهفاً ورحم الله القائل [رجز]

اَلنَّاسُ لِلْمَوْتِ كَخَيْلِ ٱلطِّرَادْ   فَٱلسَّابِقُ ٱلسَّابِقُ مِنْهَا ٱلْجَوَادْ
وَٱلْمَوْتُ نَقَّادٌ عَلَى كَفِّهِ   جَوَاهِرٌ يَخْتَارُ مِنْهَا ٱلْجِيَادْ

وكره المقام بمصر لخلوّها من ولده وفلذة كبده وفى ذلك قلت [وافر]

إِذَا رَحَلَ ٱلْحَبِيبُ مِنَ   ٱلدِّيَارِ كَرِهْتُ لِبُعْدِهِ تِلْكَ ٱلدِّيَارَ

فأراد أن يبرّد ناره ويوارى أواره بحجّ بيت الله الحرام ورؤية قبر نبيّه عليه الصلاة والسلام ولله درّ من قال [كامل]

نَقِّلْ فُؤَادَكَ حَيْثُ شِئْتَ مِنَ ٱلْهَوَى   مَا ٱلْحُبُّ إِلَّا لِلْحَبِيبِ ٱلْأَوَّلِ

وفى هذا المعنى قال عليه الصلاة والسلام إذا أصيب أحدكم بمصيبة فليذكر مصيبته بي فانها أعظم المصائب [كامل]

اِصْبِرْ لِكُلِّ مُصِيبَةٍ وَتَجَلَّدِ   وَٱعْلَمْ بِأَنَّ ٱلْمَرْءَ غَيْرُ مُخَلَّدِ
وَإِذَا أُصِبْتَ بِفَقْدِ مَنْ أَحْبَبْتَهُ   فَٱذْكُرْ مُصَابَكَ بِٱلنَّبِي مُحَمَّدِ

فتوجّه الى الحجاز وتركني بمصر لطلب العلم بالأزهر وأبقى لى نفقة تكفينا أربعة أشهر ومكث هو أكثر من ذلك فنفدت وضاق ذرعي لذلك وأنا إذ ذاك فى شرخ الشباب فبقيت متحيّراً لا أدري ما أصنع واستنكفت أن أترك طلب العلم وأتعلّم إحدى الصنائع وبينما أنا متحيّر فى طلب المعاش وضيق الصدر لعدم الارتياش إذ بلغنى أنّ قافلة وردت من بلاد السودان من دارفور وكان قبل ذلك بلغنا أنّ والدى توجّه من سنّار ٣٤،١،٢

was on the verge of going to his own tomb—and may God extend His mercy to the poet who said:[71]

People are to death as horses to a race—
the first to arrive is in quality the first.
Death's an assayer with gems in his hand
from which he picks those of greatest worth.

He could not abide the thought of remaining in Egypt because it no longer contained his son, the apple of his eye—on which topic I myself have said:

Should the beloved depart the homeland,
For his absence, I should hate that homeland.

Consequently, he decided to seek relief from his pain and to dampen his anguish by making pilgrimage to God's Holy House and by looking on the tomb of His prophet, upon whom be blessings and peace—and how excellently he put it who said:[72]

Shift your affections as you will,
the only true love's the first.

And the Prophet, peace and blessings be upon him, said to the same effect, "If any of you is stricken by a catastrophe, let him remember the catastrophe with which he is stricken by loss of me, for that is the greatest of them all."

Bear patiently each mishap and endure
and know that no man lives forever.
If stricken by the loss of a beloved
remember what you have lost in the Prophet Muḥammad.

My uncle therefore went to the Hejaz, leaving me in Cairo to continue my studies at al-Azhar with enough money to last four months, but he stayed there longer than that. I ran out of money and could accomplish nothing—I was in the prime of my youth at the time—and found myself at a loss, not knowing what to do and scorning the idea of abandoning my studies and learning a craft. While thus at a loss and surviving in straitened circumstances due to my lack of wherewithal, I heard that a caravan had arrived from the Land of the Blacks, from Darfur—for which, we had heard earlier, my father had left Sinnār, accompanied by his brother. When the caravan had settled itself at the 2.1.34

إليها صحبة أخيه فلمّا استقرّت بوكالة الجلّابة توجّهت إليها لأسأل عن أبي أهو حيّ يُتوقّع أم أودع اللحد البلقع فلقيت على سبيل المصادفة رجلا من أهل القافلة مسنّاً ذا هيبة ووقار يسمّى السيّد أحمد بدويّ فقبّلت يده ووقفت أمامه برهة فسألني بلطف وقال لى ماذا تريد قلت أسأل عن رجل غائب لي في بلدكم لعلّ يعرفه منكم أحد يدلّني عليه فقال من هو وما أسمه فقلت اسمه السيّد عمر التونسيّ وهو رجل من أهل العلم فقال على الخبير به سقطت هو صاحبي وأنا أعرف الناس به وأرى بك شبهاً له فكن ابنه فقلت أنا هو على تغيّر حالي وتبلبل بالي فقال يا بنيّ ما يقعدك عن اللحاق بأبيك لترى عنده ما يهنّئك قلت قلّة ذات يدي واعتدادي وعُدَدي فقال إنّ أباك من أعظم الناس عند السلطان وأكرمهم عليه دون أهل الديوان وإن أردت التوجّه إليه فأنا عليّ مؤونتك ومركوبك وراحتك حتّى تصل إليه وتقف بين يديه فقلت أحقّ ما تقوله فقال إي وحياة الرسول لأنّ أباك فعل معي معروفاً لا أقدر على مكافأته فيه ولو بذلت جميع ما تملكه يدي وتحويه فقلت أنا أطوع لك من نعلك وأتبع من ظلّك فعاهدته على ذلك واستوثقت منه هنالك وجعلت أتردّد عليه حتّى تأهّب وقال لي السفر غداً فإن شئت بتّ عندنا لنصبح على السفر مُبَكِّرين فقلت على الرأس والعين

٢،١،٣٥ فبتّ عنده في ألذّ عيش وأهناه وأحسن حال وأصفاه إلى أن لاح ابن ذُكا والتحف الجوّ بالضيا. نهضنا للمكتوبة فأديناها وأبرزنا الحمول وأخرجناها وجيء حينئذ بالجمال وحُمّلت عليها الأحمال فما ذَرّ قرن الغزالة إلّا وقد تمّ التحميل وأخذت العيس في الذَّمِيل ولا زالت كذلك حتّى أُنيخت بالفسطاط على شاطئ النيل وابتدئ في شحن الفُلْك بها حتّى تمّت كلّها ثمّ صبرنا حتّى صلّينا الجمعة خلف الإمام ونزلنا الفلك وودّعنا مصر بسلام

Caravanserai of the Jallābah,[73] I went there to ask after my father, to find out if he was still alive and might yet arrive, or had been placed in the bare-walled vault on his demise. By coincidence, I came across a man—elderly, imposing, and dignified—called Sayyid Aḥmad Badawī, who was with the caravan. I kissed his hand and stood before him for a while, until he asked me gently, "What do you want?" I replied, "I'm looking for a man I know who has disappeared into your country. Perhaps one of you knows him and can guide me to him." "Who is he?" he asked, "and what is his name?" "His name is Sayyid ʿUmar al-Tūnisī, and he is a man of learning," I replied. "It so happens that you've come upon one who knows him well!" he said. "He is my friend and no one knows him better than I. I see a resemblance in you to him. I think you must be his son." "I am," I answered, "though my outward appearance is changed, my inner self deranged." "Then what prevents you, dear boy," he next asked, "from setting off to seek your father and finding, when you meet him, joy?" "Lack of means," I replied, "and of provisions and the necessary gear." "Your father," said the man, "is regarded by the sultan as a very great man and is among those to whom he is most generous, more than any other at his court. Should you wish to go to him, I'll take care of your provisions, your mount, and your comfort till you reach him and stand before him." "Do you really mean that?" I asked him. "By the life of the Messenger, I do!" he replied. "Your father once did me a favor I could never repay were I to spend all that I own, every penny I possess." "I am your obedient servant," I said, "and will follow you in everything." I therefore made a pact with him to that effect, and gave him my word then and there, and took to visiting him often until he was ready and told me, "Tomorrow we leave. Spend the night with us, if you like, so we can make an early start!" to which I replied, "That will I do, with all my heart!"

I spent the night at his lodgings in the most luxurious and comfortable of 2.1.35
circumstances and best and happiest of states till morning came and the air was suffused with light. We rose for the prescribed prayer and performed it, and uncovered the camel litters and brought them out. Then the camels were brought and the loads put on them so that before the sun's disk could peep above the horizon, the loading was done and the golden-white camels had set off at an easy stride, which they kept up until they were kneeled at al-Fusṭāṭ,[74] on the banks of the Nile, and the men set about loading them onto the boat, till all were on board. Then we waited till we'd performed our Friday prayers behind the imam, and went on board, having bade Cairo salaam.

الباب الثاني[1]

الرحلة من الفسطاط إلى دارفور[2]

لمّا امتطينا الدهماء لهذا السفر العظيم قلنا ﴿بِسْمِ اللَّهِ مَجْرَاهَا وَمُرْسَاهَا إِنَّ رَبِّي لَغَفُورٌ رَّحِيمٌ﴾ ولمّا أقلعنا عن ساحل الفسطاط ناوين البعد والشطاط تذكّرت متاعب الأسفار وما يحصل فيها من الأخطار خصوصاً لمن كان حاله كحالي في الفقر المُدْقِع والعسر المُصْقِع وتوسوس صدري وانزعج وبقيت في مشقّة وحرج لا سيّما وقد وجدت نفسي مع غير أبناء جنسي بل بين أقوام لا أعرف من حديثهم إلّا القليل ولا أرى فيهم وجهاً صبيحاً جميل فقلت ودمعي بادي [وافر] ١،٢،٢

فَجِسْمُكَ مَعْ ثِيَابِكَ وَٱلْمُحَيَّا   سَوَادٌ فِي سَوَادٍ فِي سَوَادِ

وندمت على تغريري بنفسي مع أبناء حام وتذكّرت ما بينهم من العداوة لأبناء سام فداخلني من الهلع ما لا أقدر على وصفه حتّى كدت أن أطلب الرجوع إلى الربوع

ثمّ أدركتني ألطاف الله الخفيّة وتذكّرت ما مُدحت به الأسفار على ألسنة البلغاء الأدبيّة خصوصاً ما ورد في الأثر عن خالق البشر سافِرْ أُحْدِثْ لك رزقاً جديداً وإنّ أفضل الأنام سافر من مكّة إلى الشام وقد قالت العلماء إنّ السفر يسفر عن أخلاق ٢،٢،٢

١ الأصل: الباب الثاني من المقدمة. ٢ أضيف للسياق: الرحلة من الفسطاط إلى دارفور.

Chapter 2

The Journey from al-Fusṭāṭ to Darfur

On mounting our ash-gray she-camel[75] for this great journey, we declared, «In God's Name shall be its course and its berthing; surely my Lord is Merciful and Forgiving.»[76] Yet, as we set sail from the shore of al-Fusṭāṭ, heading for faraway places and distant lands, I thought of travel's travails and of the dangers that it brings, especially to those in a state of grinding poverty and harrowing hardship such as myself, and my heart filled with misgivings and distress, and I found myself overwhelmed by oppressive feelings and stress, all the more so because I found myself without any of my own race—among, indeed, nations of whose speech I understood but little and among whom I saw no cheerful, comely face. Tears welling, I recited: 2.2.1

> Your body, your clothes, and your countenance
> are black upon black upon black

and I regretted that I'd exposed myself to danger with the sons of Ḥām, recalling the antagonism that existed between them and the sons of Sām,[77] and was overcome by such panic as I cannot describe—so much so that I came close to asking if I might return to where I normally reside.

Then God's hidden graces caught me by surprise, and I remembered how eloquent literary tongues have spoken of journeying with praise, and in particular the saying found among those attributed to the Creator of Humankind which goes, "Travel, and I will create a new source of livelihood for you." I recalled too that the Best of Humankind journeyed from Mecca to Syria,[78] and that scholars have said that "travel reveals a man's morals and divides the males from their ankleted sisters." Furthermore, it has been said that "were pearls 2.2.2

الرجال وهو المميّز للذكور عن ربّات الحجال وقد قيل إنّ الدرّ لو لم ينقل من معدنه لما رُصعت به التيجان ولو لم يسر البدر لكان في غاية النقصان قال الشاعر [كامل]

سَافِرْ تَنَلْ رُتَبَ ٱلْمَكَارِمِ وَٱلْعُلَى   فَٱلدُّرُّ سَارَ فَصَارَ فِي ٱلتِّيجَانِ
وَٱلْبَدْرُ لَوْلَا سَيْرُهُ فِي أُفْقِهِ   مَا كَانَ إِلَّا زَائِدَ ٱلنُّقْصَانِ

وقال الآخر [طويل]

تَغَرَّبْ عَنِ ٱلْأَوْطَانِ فِي طَلَبِ ٱلْعُلَى   وَسَافِرْ فَفِي ٱلْأَسْفَارِ خَمْسُ فَوَائِدِ
تَفَرُّجُ هَمٍّ وَٱكْتِسَابُ مَعِيشَةٍ   وَعِلْمٌ وَآدَابٌ وَصُحْبَةُ مَاجِدِ
وَإِنْ قِيلَ فِي ٱلْأَسْفَارِ ذُلٌّ وَغُرْبَةٌ   وَتَشْتِيتُ شَمْلٍ وَٱرْتِكَابُ شَدَائِدِ
فَمَوْتُ ٱلْفَتَى خَيْرٌ لَهُ مِنْ حَيَاتِهِ   بِأَرْضِ هَوَانٍ بَيْنَ وَاشٍ وَحَاسِدِ

ولله درّ الطُغرائيّ حيث يقول [بسيط]

إِنَّ ٱلْعُلَى حَدَّثَتْنِي وَهْيَ صَادِقَةٌ   فِيمَا تُحَدِّثُ أَنَّ ٱلْعِزَّ فِي ٱلنُّقَلِ
لَوْ كَانَ فِي شَرَفِ ٱلْمَأْوَى بُلُوغُ مِنًى   لَمْ تَبْرَحِ ٱلشَّمْسُ يومًا دَارَةَ ٱلْحَمَلِ

على أنّي لو كنت أقمت بالقاهرة في هذا الحال ما كنت أرى فيها إلّا الوبال وحينئذ تمثّلت بقول الطغرائيّ المفضال حيث قال [بسيط] ٣،٢،٢

فِيمَ ٱلْإِقَامَةُ بِٱلزَّوْرَاءِ لَا سَكَنِي   فِيهَا وَلَا نَاقَتِي فِيهَا وَلَا جَمَلِي

وبقول الآخر [بسيط]

never taken from their beds, they would ne'er adorn crowns" and "if the full moon didn't move, it would be forever on the wane." As says the poet:

Travel, for pearls have moved and found themselves in crowns,
and you too may reach the ranks of the noble and high.
Likewise, the full moon, if it ne'er moved in its course,
would be forever waning in the sky.

And another[79] says:

Leave your lands and seek high station!
Journey—for five good things come from travel:
Escape from care, a way to earn your living,
knowledge, savoir faire, and the friendship of the noble.
Though some say travel means abjection in exile,
and loss of friends and a life of trouble;
Still, better a young man die than live
in a land of ignominy, midst jealousy and tittle-tattle.

And how well al-Ṭughrāʾī[80] put it when he said:

High Standing addressed me and spoke true:
"Glory," said she, "lies in change of location.
If hopes could be attained through nobility of domicile,
the sun would never leave its ovine station."[81]

The point being that, had I stayed in Cairo in the state I was in, I would have 2.2.3
met with nothing but evil. At this, I encapsulated my feelings in the words of that most excellent poet al-Ṭughrāʾī when he says:

Wherefore should I reside in Baghdad of the Concave Gates? I have no house there,
neither is my she-camel there, nor yet my he-camel![82]

And in the words of another, who says:[83]

اِرْحَلْ بِنَفْسِكَ مِنْ أَرْضٍ تُهَانُ بِهَا   وَلَا تَكُنْ مِنْ فِرَاقِ ٱلْأَهْلِ فِي حُرَقِ
أَلَمْ تَرَ ٱلتِّبْرَ تُرْبًا فِي مَعَادِنِهِ   وَفِي ٱلتَّغَرُّبِ مَحْمُولًا عَلَى ٱلْعُنُقِ

فوطّنتُ نفسي على الأسفار ولوكنت أُكْوى بالنار

وكنّا قد أقلعنا بريح طيّب ظلّ معنا يومه وسفينتنا تميس به عجبًا وتمايل بحسنه طربًا وقد ملأ شراعها وأطال في المسير باعها وعلى ذكر السفينة ووصف سيرها تذكّرت لغزي الذي كنت سألت فيه العلّامة الشيخ مصطفى كسّاب شيخ مدرسة الطبّ البيطريّ التي أنشأها صاحب السعادة بإزاء مدرسة الطبّ البشريّ بأبي زعبل وهو هذا [طويل] ٤،٢،٢

أَمَوْلَايَ يَا كَسَّابُ لِلْعِلْمِ وَٱلتُّقَى   وَيَا بَحْرَ عِرْفَانٍ لَدَى ٱلنَّاسِ يَعْذُبُ
سَأَلْتُكَ عَنْ شَيْءٍ ثُلَاثِيِّ أَحْرُفٍ   بِهِ كَلِفٌ قَلْبُ ٱلشَّقِيِّ[1] مُعَذَّبُ
لَقَدْ جَاءَ فِي ٱلتَّنْزِيلِ وَٱلْأَمْرُ وَاضِحٌ   وَمِثْلُكُمُ يَتْلُوهُ دَوْمًا وَيَكْتُبُ
وَأَيْضًا لَهُ إِسْمٌ خُمَاسِيٌّ قَدْ أَتَى   مُؤَنَّثُ لَفْظٍ لِلْبَرِيَّةِ يُعْجِبُ
يَهِيمُ بِهِ ٱلْمُضْنَى وَتَجْرِي دُمُوعُهُ   وَمَادَّتُهُ يُشْتَقُّ مِنْهَا ٱلْمُهَذَّبُ
كَذَاكَ لَهُ إِسْمٌ شَهِيرٌ لَدَى ٱلْوَرَى   رُبَاعِيُّ حُرُوفٍ وَهْوَ مِنْهَا مُرَكَّبُ
مُسَمَّى ٱلَّذِي قَدْ قُلْتُ يَا حَبْرُ وَاحِدٌ   وَأَنْتَ لَبِيبٌ لَيْسَ ذَا عَنْكَ يُحْجَبُ
مَطِيَّةُ عَزْمِي ٱلْآنَ دَهْمَاءُ قَدْ أَتَتْ   إِلَيْكَ فَرِيدَ ٱلْعَصْرِ وَٱلْحَلَّ أَطْلُبُ
وَأَوْصَافُ مَا قَدْ قُلْتُ أَضْحَتْ شَهِيرَةً   لِجَارِيَةٍ حَسْنَاءَ لِلُّبِّ تَسْلُبُ
تَمِيسُ مَتَى تُكْسَى وَيَكْثُرُ سَعْيُهَا   وَإِنْ جُرِّدَتْ لِلسَّعْيِ تَخْشَى وَتَرْهَبُ

١ الأصل: السقى.

Take yourself off from a land where you're despised
and on parting from your people do not mourn.
See you not that gold, in the mother lode, is but dust,
yet, when it travels, on men's necks is borne?

Thus did I reconcile myself to journeying to distant lands, though I be scorched in the doing by fiery brands.

We set off with a good wind that stayed with us through the day, our ship surging majestically to it in a wondrous way, moving, so fine it was, with a joyful sway, while it filled its sail, causing the ship to lengthen its stride as it pursued its way—and apropos of ships and how to describe their progress I'm reminded of my riddling poem that I addressed to Erudite Shaykh Muṣṭafā Kassāb,[84] the shaykh at the school of veterinary medicine established by His Excellency next door to the Medical School at Abū Zaʿbal, to wit:[85] **2.2.4**

O Master, "Acquirer"[86] of knowledge and godliness,
O sea of wisdom that men find sweet to drink,
What's something three letters long
with which my rascally heart's enamored, tormented?[87]
It comes in the Revelation[88] and the matter's clear,
and such as you constantly recite it, and write it too.
It has another name, of letters five, that comes
in the feminine, men to delight.[89]
The one who pines goes into raptures at its sound, and his tears run down
and from its radicals the swiftly moving draws its name.[90]
Likewise, it has a name, well-known among humankind,
of four letters,[91] from which it's composed.
The thing of which I speak, erudite scholar, is but one[92]
and you are wise, so this can't from you be hidden.
The mount of my resolve,[93] an ash-gray she-camel, has reached you now,
you who are unique in your age, and the answer I ask.
The characteristics of that of which I speak have become renowned
as those of a pretty maid, a stealer of hearts:[94]
It struts when decked out and runs with great speed,[95]
but when stripped it fears to run and is dismayed.[96]

وَتحمِلُ مَا يَعْسُرُ عَلَى ٱلنَّاسِ حَمْلُهُ وَمحْمُولَةً يَا قَوْمُ مِنْهَا تَعَجَّبُ
وَفِي سَعْيِهَا تَمْشِي عَلَى حُرِّ ظَهْرِهَا وَأَرْجُلُهَا لِلْبَطْشِ قَدْ تَتَجَنَّبُ
تُطِيعُ ٱلْهَوَى تَخْشَى ٱشْتِدَادَ عُصُوفِهِ وَلٰكِنْ بِهِ تَزْهُو وَتَلْهُو وَتَلْعَبُ
وَحَسْبُكَ تَوْضِيحِي فَهَاتِ جَوَابَهُ فَلَا زِلْتَ يَا مِفْضَالُ لِلْحَلِّ تُطْلَبُ

٥،٢،٢ فأجاب[1] حفظه الله بما نصّه [طويل]

أَيَا عَالِمًا بِٱلْعِلْمِ مِنْهُ وَبِٱلنُّهَى وَبِٱلْفَضْلِ عِنْدَ ٱلْعَالَمِينَ مُحَبَّبُ
وَمَنْ حِذْقُهُ قَدْ شَاعَ شَرْقًا وَمَغْرِبًا وَمَنْ هُوَ بِٱلشِّعْرِ ٱلْمُهَذَّبِ يُغْرِبُ
وَلِمْ لَا وَقَدْ حَازَ ٱلْقَرِيضَ[2] بِأَسْرِهِ وَطَاوَعَهُ مَا قَدْ يَضِلُّ وَيَعْزُبُ
وَأَنَّى لِقُسٍّ وَٱمْرِئِ ٱلْقَيْسِ مِثْلُهُ كَلَامٌ يُثِيرُ ٱلْعَاشِقِينَ وَيُطْرِبُ
أَتَيْتَ بِشِعْرٍ كَٱلنَّسِيمِ لَطَافَةً فَمَنْ يَدَّعِيهِ فَهْوَ لَا شَكَّ كَاذِبُ
وَأَلْغَزْتَ فِي ٱسْمٍ عَمَّ فِي ٱلْبَحْرِ نَفْعُهُ وَيَحْمِلُ أَثْقَالًا تُكِلُّ وَتُتْعِبُ
وَنُوحٌ تَوَلَّاهُ وَأَبْدَعَ صُنْعَهُ وَنُجِّيَ مِنَ ٱلطُّوفَانِ وَٱلْمَوْجُ لَاعِبُ
وَقَالَ ٱرْكَبُوا فِيهَا فَبِٱللهِ مَجْرَاهَا كَذٰلِكَ مُرْسَاهَا فَلَا تَتَرَسَّبُ
وَقَدْ حُلَّ لُغْزُ ٱلتُّونُسِيِّ مُحَمَّدٍ إِمَامٌ لَهُ ٱلْعَلْيَاءُ تُنْمَى وَتُنْسَبُ
فَلَا زَالَ يُبْدِي مِنْ نَتَائِجِ فِكْرِهِ نَفَائِسَ دُرٍّ تَنْبُ عَنْهَا ٱلْمَطَالِبُ

٦،٢،٢ وقد ألغزت في لفظ بحر فقلت [طويل]

---

[1] الأصل: فاحاب. [2] الأصل: جاز الفريض.

It bears what others find impossible to bear
and a cargo, O people, at which you wonder.[97]
When it runs, it moves on the flat of its back[98]
while its legs, for walloping, stick out on each side.[99]
It obeys the wind[100] while fearing the rising of the storm
while in the winds of love she revels, makes merry, and plays.
Enough then of my clues. Out with the answer,
for Your Eminence is still requested to provide the solution.

He, God preserve him, replied with the following: 2.2.5

O scholar who for his knowledge, wits,
and learning is by all other scholars loved,
Whose intelligence has been bruited both east and west,
and who puzzles the mind with verse refined—
And how could it not be so when he has mastered poesy in its entirety
and when all that is errant and ungraspable obeys his command?
Where in the works of Quss and Imruʾ al-Qays is one to find their like,
words like these, fit to excite lovers and send them into ecstasy?—
You have offered verses like the breeze in delicacy
(and any who claims them as his own is without doubt a liar)
And made your riddle on the name of a thing whose benefits to the sea are everywhere,
that carries loads that exhaust and tire,
And that Noah took in hand and excelled at fashioning[101]—
Noah who was saved from the Flood while the waves played
And said, "Embark on it, for in God's name shall be its course
and likewise its berthing, so it will not sink!"[102]
Muḥammad al-Tūnisī's riddle now is solved—
a beacon of scholarship he, to whom great deeds are attributed and ascribed
And who forever produces from the fruits of his thinking
precious gems, unlike the grammarians' wrangles.

I also made up a riddle on the word *baḥr* ("sea"), saying: 2.2.6

أَلَا قُلْ لِنِحْرِيرِ[1] ٱلْعُلُومِ وَمَنْ غَدَا   لَهُ ٱللُّغْزُ طَوْعًا قَدْ يَزُولُ نِقَابُهُ
فَدَيْتُكَ مَا ٱسْمٌ مِنْ ثَلَاثَةِ أَحْرُفٍ   مُسَمَّاهُ يَسْطُو بِٱلْأَنَامِ عُبَابُهُ
وَفِي قَلْبِهِ مَعْنَى ٱتِّسَاعٍ لِمَنْ أَتَى   وَإِنْ شِئْتَ فِعْلًا مَاضِيًا لَا تَهَابُهُ
وَأَوَّلُ حَرْفٍ مِنْهُ إِنْ كُنْتَ حَاذِفًا   فَسَمٌّ بِضِدِّ ٱلْبَرْدِ وَهْوَ ٱنْقِلَابُهُ
بِتَشْوِيشِهِ تَبْدُو مَعَانٍ ثَلَاثَةٌ   تَأَمَّلْ لَهَا فَهْوَ ٱلْعَجِيبُ عُجَابُهُ
إِمَامُ عُلُومٍ وَٱلْمِدَادُ وَثَالِثُ ٱلْـ   ـمَعَانِي أَمْرٌ لَا يَسُرُّ مُصَابُهُ[2]
وَإِنْ تَحْذِفِ ٱلثَّانِي فَضِدٌّ لِإِسْمِهِ   يَصِيرُ فَلَا يَعْسُرْ عَلَيْكَ جَوَابُهُ

٧،٢،٧ وقلت مُلْغِزًا في مصباح [طويل]

أَلَا قُلْ لِمَنْ حَازَ ٱلْبَلَاغَةَ وَٱلْفَهْمَا   وَأَعْطَاهُ رَبُّ ٱلْعَرْشِ بَيْنَ ٱلْوَرَى عِلْمَا
فِدَاكَ أَبِي مَا ٱسْمٌ خُمَاسِيُّ أَحْرُفٍ   بِهِ ٱلنَّفْعُ يَا حَبْرُ ٱلْبَرِيَّةِ قَدْ عَمَّا
صَغِيرٌ كَأُنْمُلَةٍ إِذَا قِسْتَ جِسْمَهُ   وَيَمْلَأُ بَيْتًا وَهْوَ فِي حَجْمِهِ جَزْمَا
إِذَا مَا نَسِيمٌ هَبَّ مَالَ صَبَابَةً   وَمَهْمَا تَقَوَّى مَاتَ مِنْ وَجْدِهِ حَتْمَا
فَرِيدٌ بِأَوْصَافٍ حِسَانٍ سَمَا بِهَا   وَأَحْسَنُهَا إِرْشَادُ شَخْصٍ لَهُ أَمَّا
وَيَمْرَضُ مَهْمَا طَالَ يَا صَاحِ أَنْفُهُ   وَإِنْ قُطِعَتْ يَصْحُو وَلَا يَذْكُرُ ٱلْغَمَّا
وَيَزْهُو مَتَى حَلَّ ٱلْبَهِيمُ وَإِنْ رَأَى ٱلْغَـ   ـزَالَةَ ذَرَّتْ نَالَ مِنْ ضُعْفِهِ وَصْمَا
وَمِنْ إِسْمِهِ حَرْفَانِ شَيْءٌ مُحَبَّبٌ   إِذَا كَانَ مِنْ حُلْوِ ٱلْمَرَاشِفِ أَيِ أَلْمَى
وَبَاقِيهِ فِعْلٌ مَاضٍ كُنْ مُتَفَطِّنًا   وَفَاعِلُهُ فِي ٱلنَّاسِ يَسْتَوْجِبُ ٱلذَّمَّا

[1] الأصل: لتحرير. [2] الأصل: مصبابه.

To one proficient in the sciences and to whom
riddles are become obedient and have dropped their veil,
Say, God save you, what is three letters long
that names something by whose billows people are buffeted
And that, if you reverse it, means room[103] for any who come
and, if you wish, may be a past-tense verb,[104] not to be feared,
And if you omit the first of its letters,
then name it the antonym of "cold," that is, its opposite.[105]
If you scramble it, three meanings appear
—observe them, for this is a wondrous thing:
A leader in the sciences, and ink, and the third
of its meanings is something unpleasing to any afflicted by it[106]
And if you drop its second letter, then the opposite of its name
is what it becomes[107]—so the answer cannot be hard for you.

I also composed a riddle on the word *miṣbāḥ* ("lamp"), saying: 2.2.7

Do say, to one who has achieved good style and understanding
and to whom out of all humankind the Lord of the Throne has granted knowledge,
"I'd give my father for you—what has five letters
whose benefits, Eminent Scholar, have extended to all mankind,
Small as a fingertip, if you measure its body,
yet which, despite its size, can fill a house most definitely?
When a breeze arises, it bends in ardent love,
and however much it is strengthened, it must die of its passion inevitably.
It is unique in excellent qualities with which it is raised to the heavens,
and the best of these is that it guides a person to his destination.
The longer its nose[108] gets, my friend, the sicker it becomes,
yet if it is trimmed, it revives and has no memory of its distress.
It shines brightly when deepest darkness descends, and when it sees
the sun risen in splendor, it becomes weak from shame.
Two letters, taken from its name, yield something much liked
from one whose lips are pretty, that is, a cool-saliva'ed lover.[109]
The remaining part is a past-tense verb (now exercise your wits!)
whose subject, if a person, merits censure.[110]

وَأَوَّلَ حَرْفٍ مِنْهُ فَٱحْذِفْ تَرَ[1] ٱلَّذِي تَبَقَّى رَدِيفاً لِلْغَدَاةِ فَكُنْ شَهْمَا
وَحَسْبِي لَقَدْ أَوْضَحْتُ هَاتِ جَوَابَهُ وَقَدْ جَاءَ فِي ٱلتَّنْزِيلِ فَٱنْظُرْهُ قَدْ تَمَّا

وقلت ملغزا في السماء [بسيط] ٨،٢،٢

يَا مَنْ رَقِيَ لِسَمَاءِ ٱلْعِلْمِ وَٱلْحُكُمِ وَفَضْلُهُ قَدْ غَدَا يَنْهَلُّ كَٱلدِّيَمِ
بَيِّنْ لَنَا مَا ٱسْمُ شَيْءٍ رَاقَ مَنْظَرُهُ وَحُسْنُهُ قَدْ بَدَا لِلْعُرْبِ وَٱلْعَجَمِ
لٰكِنَّهُ ذُو ٱرْتِفَاعٍ لَا يُحَلُّ بِهِ إِلَّا ٱلَّذِينَ حُبُوا مِنْ بَارِئِ ٱلنَّسَمِ
مِنْهُ ٱلْمَصَابِيحُ تَبْدُو وَهْيَ زَاهِيَةٌ بِهَا ٱلْهِدَايَةُ فِي دَاجٍ لَنَا بَهِمِ
وَحُسْنُهُ ٱلْبَاهِرُ ٱلزَّاهِي نَقَرُّ بِهِ لِأَنَّهُ جَاءَ فِي ٱلتَّنْزِيلِ ذِي ٱلْحِكَمِ
مُرَكَّبٌ مِنْ حُرُوفٍ أَرْبَعٍ رُسِمَتْ فِي ٱلنَّظْمِ كُنْ فَاهِماً لِلنَّظْمِ وَٱلْكَلِمِ
قَدْ تَمَّ أَرْجُو جَوَاباً شَافِياً حَسَناً لَا زِلْتَ يَا حَبْرُ فِي عَالٍ مِنَ ٱلْهِمَمِ

وقد تذكّرت بهذه الألغاز ما ألغز[2] به خاتمة المحقّقين الإمام ابن حجر الشافعيّ رحمه الله في لفظة مُدام ونصّه [وافر] ٩،٢،٢

وَمَا شَيْءٌ حَشَاهُ فِيهِ دَاءٌ وَأَوَّلُهُ وَآخِرُهُ سَوَاءُ
إِذَا مَا زَالَ آخِرُهُ فَجَمْعٌ[3] يَكُونُ ٱلْحَدُّ فِيهِ كَذَا ٱلْمَضَاءُ[4]
وَإِنْ أَهْمَلْتَ أَوَّلَهُ فَفِعْلٌ لَهُ بِٱلرَّفْعِ وَٱلنَّصْبِ ٱعْتِنَاءُ

ولنمسك عنان القلم عن جريه في هذا الميدان إذ لو تتبّعت ما قلته من الأشعار والألغاز لطال الحال وجلب الملال ونرجع إلى ما نحن بصدده

١ الأصل: ترى. ٢ الأصل: للغز. ٣ الأصل: بجمع. ٤ الأصل: المعناء.

Throw out its first letter and you'll find that what
remains is a synonym of 'morrow,'[111] so be astute.
Enough clues have I given now, so out with the answer!
It comes also in the Revelation,[112] so look for it there! Now I'm done."

And I also made up a riddle on *al-samāʾ* ("the sky"), saying: 2.2.8

You who have risen to the heavens of knowledge and wisdom
and whose bounty has come to pour down like steady rains,
Reveal to us the name of a thing the sight of which brings pleasure
and whose beauty is clear to both Arabs and others,
Though it is of such a height that none alight there
save those who have been rewarded by the creator of life.
Out of it lamps[113] appear and brightly burn,
providing guidance for us in gloomy darkness.
We delight in its shining dazzling beauty
because it is mentioned in the Revelation,[114] with its wise words.
It is composed of four letters when written out
one after the other. Take note of the ordering and the wording!
Now I'm done—please provide an answer nice and clear,
may you ever continue, great scholar, to aspire to greatness!

Remembering these riddles made me think of one by that ne plus ultra of critics, the Shāfiʿī imam Ibn Ḥajar, God have mercy on him, on the word *mudām* ("wine"), which goes as follows: 2.2.9

What is a thing whose insides are a disease[115]
And whose first and last are the same.
If its last is taken away, it's a plural[116]
which would have an edge, and likewise sharpness![117]
And if you ignore its first, it's a verb,[118]
capable of being either imperfect or subjunctive.

But let us here rein in our pen, halt its gallop across this maidan—for were I to follow the track of everything I've composed by way of poems and riddles, it would take forever and be conducive to torpor—and return to our topic.

فنقول وعند المساء سكن الهواء وبطل هبوبه وفقد شماله وجنوبه وقد جئنا مقابل المِنْيا[١] وكان فيها جماعة من الغُزّ الذين ابتزّ الله منهم حلّة العزّ فأخذونا بالقوّة والقهر وأمالوا سفينتنا إلى جانب البرّ وكان معسكرهم مخيّماً في عرض البلد على النيل وكانوا مقيمين هناك لنهب السفّار المارّين فغرموا صاحبنا جملة من المال وبعد الخلاص أقلعنا عنهم في الحال ١٠،٢،٢

وفي اليوم الثالث حللنا منفلوط فأخذنا منها ما احتجنا[٢] إليه ثمّ أقلعنا حتّى دخلنا بني عديّ فأقمنا فيها حيثما[٣] تأهّبت القافلة وخرزوا أسقيتهم وصنعوا زادهم ثمّ جيء بالمطيّ فحملت أحمالها وضربنا مَهْمَهاً قَفْرًا حتّى وصلنا إلى الخارجة في عشيّة اليوم الخامس فوجدناها قد دار بها النخيل دورة الخلخال بالساق أو التفاف يدي العاشق على معاطف المعشوق للعناق وفيها من التمر ما تشتهيه الأنفس وتلذّ به الأعين مع رخص الأسعار وحسن تلك الأثمار[٤] فأقمنا بها مدّة خمسة أيّام وفي صبيحة اليوم السادس ارتحلنا وسرنا نحو يومين وفي الثالث حللنا بلدة يقال لها أَبِيرِيس وهي بلد قد استولى عليها الخراب من ظلم الحكّام وتمزّق شمل أهلها بعد الانتظام ففسد ما به من النخيلُ وذهب رونقه بعد أن كان جميلْ ١١،٢،٢

فأقمنا بها يومين حتّى أفاقت دوابّنا وزال عنها العنا ثمّ سافرنا يومين ونزلنا في ثالثهما بلداً يقال لها بولاق وهي[٥] من الساكن في إملاق قد درست معالم أكثرها وتصدّع بناء أقومها وأشهرها ومن العجائب أنّ نخلها في غاية القصر وهو حامل للتمر لا يتكلّف جانيه القيام بل يتناول منه ولو في هيئة النيام فتذكّرت باسمها بولاق مصر المحميّة حرسها الله من كلّ آفة وبليّة فانهملت دموعي وهاج وجدي وولوعي فأنشدت أقول شعراً [طويل] ١٢،٢،٢

تَـذَكَّرْتُ بُولَاقًـا وَمِـصْـرَ وَأَهْلَهَـا وَأَذْكَرَنِي هـذِي ٱلَّتِي تُـدْعَى بُولَاقَـا

فَبِـاللهِ يَا عَيْـنِي ٱسْـعِفِينِي بِأَدْمُعٍ[٦] عَسَى يَبْرُدُ ٱلْقَلْبُ ٱلَّذِي زَادَ إِحْرَاقَـا

---

١ الأصل: المنية. ٢ الأصل: احتاجنا. ٣ الأصل: ريثما. ٤ الأصل: الثمار. ٥ الأصل: وهو. ٦ الأصل: يا دمع.

We therefore declare: in the evening the breeze died down, it ceased to gust, and neither northerly nor southerly remained. We were opposite al-Minyā, where there was a gang of Turkish soldiers whom God had relieved of the garments of glory.[119] They seized us by naked force and compelled our ship to pull in to shore. Their camp was pitched in the open space between the town and the Nile, and there they resided so that they could plunder passing voyagers. They made our friend pay a large sum of money. When we were released, we set sail again immediately. 2.2.10

On the third day, we alighted at Manfalūṭ,[120] from which we took what we needed, then sailed until we came to Banī ʻAdī, where we stayed while the caravan equipped itself, the men sewing the waterskins and putting together their provisions. Then the camels were brought, their loads loaded, and we set off across an arid waste. On the evening of the fifth day, we reached al-Khārijah, which we found to be surrounded by palm groves—as a leg by an anklet is encased, or the beloved's cloak by the hands of a lover seeking an embrace. It is full of the most delicious and beautiful dates; their price is low, and their quality excellent. We stayed there for five days, departed on the morning of the sixth, and proceeded for about two days, alighting on the third at a town called Abīrīs[121]—a settlement overtaken by ruin due to rulers' tyranny, its people scattered when once they lived a life of harmony; its palm groves therefore are now in disrepair, the splendor gone from what was once so fair. 2.2.11

We stayed there for two days, until our mounts had recovered and cast off their fatigue, then traveled two days and on the third set up camp at a town called Būlāq, whose inhabitants have been reduced to poverty.[122] Most of its landmarks have disappeared and most of its finest and most celebrated buildings are full of cracks. An odd thing is that its palm trees are extremely short: when they bear dates the gatherer doesn't have to go to the trouble of climbing—he can simply pick them by hand, even lying on his back. Its name made me think of the Būlāq of Cairo the Protected, may God secure her from every infestation and disaster, and my tears poured out, my passion, love, and yearning were excited, and I declaimed: 2.2.12

I thought of Būlāq and of Cairo and its people,
moved by this other Būlāq to recollection.
I beg you, O my eye, come to my aid with tears
that haply my heart may cool once more, after its incineration!

ثمّ سافرنا مجدّين من غير لبس حتّى نزلنا عشيّة النهار على بلد يسمّى المَقْس مفرد ١٣،٢،٢
[رجز]

وَبَلْدَةٍ لَيْسَ بِهَا أَنِيسُ إِلَّا ٱلْيَعَافِرُ وَإِلَّا ٱلْعِيسُ

قيل إن هذا البلد كان أعمر من كلّ بلد فأخنى عليه الذي أخنى على لبد وتمزّق شمل أهله ولم يبق به أحد وليس به من الأشجار إلّا ما قلّ وهو بعض أَثْل وعَبَل فأقمنا فيها يومين وملأنا القرب وارتحلنا وللمفازة الحقيقيّة دخلنا فمكثنا خمسة أيّام في مهامه[1] قفرا وبيداء غبرا ليس فيها من الحشائش إلّا عاقول قليل كما لا يوجد بها شجر يصلح للمقيل وكان يطبخ لنا في تلك المدّة بما تلتقطه الخدم من بعر الإبل الجاف لقلّة الوَقُد الذي يحصل به الإسعاف وفي عشيّة اليوم الخامس وردنا محلّا يقال له الشبّ وهو محلّ بين غرود من الرمل عليه ريح الوحشة قد هبّ فأرحنا فيه يومين وارتحلنا وللمفازة الثانية دخلنا

١٤،٢،٢ فقطعناها عَنَقاً وذَمِيلاً في مدّة أربعة أيّام نزلنا في ضحى خامسها[2] ببئر يقال له سليمة وبهذا البئر رسوم أبنية قديمة وهو في عرض جبل يسمّى بهذا الاسم أيضاً فمكثنا فيه يومين حتّى قضينا منه غرضاً ومن خواصّ[3] هذا المحلّ أنّ الحالّ به يستأنس به ولا يستوحش منه ومن العجائب أنّ الشبّان من أهل القافلة يصعدون على الجبل الذي هناك ويضربون الحجارة بعصيّ صغار كما يضربون الطبول فيسمع لها صوت كالطبل ولا يعرف سبب ذلك أهو تجاويف في الحجر أو هي موضوعة على خلوّ فسبحان من يعلم حقيقة ذلك وأخبرني أهل القافلة أنّ في بعض الليالي وأظنّهم قالوا في ليلة كلّ جمعة يسمع من الجبل أصوات طبول وكأنّه عرس ولا يعرفون حقيقته

١٥،٢،٢ ثمّ ارتحلنا صبيحة اليوم الثالث بعد ملء أدوات الماء ودخلنا مفازة سافرنا فيها خمسة أيّام وصلنا في ضحى سادسها إلى محلّ يقال له لَقِيَّة فوجدنا هناك آبارًا محاطة بالرمل

١ الأصل: مهمه. ٢ الأصل: خاسسها. ٣ الأصل: خواض.

Then we traveled some more, pressing on hard without hesitation till we made camp on the evening of the same day in a town called al-Maqs: 2.2.13

> And many a town there is that holds no friendly presence,
> only the antelope, only the white-gold camel.

It's said that this was once a most flourishing town. Then it went the way of Lubad,[123] its people were scattered, and no one remained. It has few trees, mainly kinds of tamarisk. We stayed there two days, filled our waterskins, and set off again, entering now into the true desert, and we continued for five days in arid wastes and a dust-blown wilderness in which the only plants were a little camel-thorn, and where no trees suitable as resting places were to be found. During this period, our cooking was done using whatever dry camel dung the servants could glean, there being so little by way of vegetal matter on which to depend for help. On the evening of the fifth day, we reached a place called al-Shabb[124] (set among sandy dunes o'er which the lonesome zephyr croons). We rested there two days, then departed, and our entry into the next desert started.

This we crossed, moving now fast, now slow, over a space of four days, setting up camp on the forenoon of the fifth at a well called Salīmah. At this well are ancient buildings. It lies opposite a mountain of the same name. We stayed there two days till we had rested, for it is one of the peculiarities of the place that anyone who alights there settles down comfortably and feels no unease. A wonder to be noted is that the young men of the caravan climb to the top of the mountain there and strike the stones with small sticks, as one would a drum, and the stones make drumlike sounds. No one knows why this is so—because of cavities in the stones, or because they are set over empty spaces; glory to Him who knows the truth of the matter! The people with the caravan told me that on certain nights—I think they said on the night preceding each Friday—the sounds of drums would be heard coming from the mountain, as though a wedding were taking place, and no one knows the explanation.[125] 2.2.14

Early on the morning of the third day, after filling the waterskins, we set off again and entered a desert through which we traveled for five days, arriving in the late morning of the sixth at a place called Laqiyyah, where we found wells with sweet clear water amid the sands. Before we reached it, a caravan coming from the natron well called al-Zaghāwī crossed our path,[126] the people of the caravan being Arabs of the tribe known as al-ʿAmāyim. They received us with 2.2.15

وماؤها عذب زلال وقبل وصولنا لهذا المحلّ عرضت لنا قافلة صادرة من بئر النطرون المسمّى بالزغاويّ وأهلها من عرب يقال لهم العمايم فقابلونا بالسلام ثمّ انصرفوا عنّا بسلام فمكثنا في لقيّة يومين وفي صبيحة اليوم الثالث ارتحلنا للزغاوي قاصدين وإذا[1] بهجّان أقبل من ناحية دارفور يخبر بوفاة المرحوم الملك العادل المجيد السلطان عبد الرحمن الرشيد ملك دارفور وما والاها وسلطان أقصاها وأدناها وأنّه ذاهب إلى مصر لتجديد الخاتم الذي تختم به الأوامر السلطانيّة لعدم من يتقنه هناك لابنه السلطان محمّد فضل وذلك لليال مضت من رجب الفرد سنة ١٢١٨ فحزن أهل القافلة على موت سلطانهم وخافوا من وقوع الفتن في أوطانهم لأنّه كان سلطاناً عادلاً كريماً محبّاً للعلم وذويه مبغضاً للجهل ومن يليه وسنتكلّم على عدله وأحكامه فيما يأتي بأبسط عبارة إن شاء الله تعالى

ثمّ سافرنا من هناك خمسة[2] أيّام أنخنا في سادسها ببئر الزغاويّ وهو بئر النطرون ١٦،٢،٢ وبينه وبين دارفور مسيرة عشرة أيّام كاملة فأقمنا به أحد[3] عشر يوماً نصلح شؤوننا ونرتاح وترعى دوابّنا[4] لتقوى على قطع هذه المفازة الدهماء ونُحرت في إقامتنا تلك عدّة جُزُر وفُرّق لحمها على أهل القافلة واجتمعنا هناك بأعراب البادية من دارفور وأتونا بلبن الإبل وسمنها فاشترينا منهم ما احتجنا إليه وكانوا أتوا لهذا البئر ليأخذوا[5] منه ملحاً ونطروناً لدارفور لأنّ النطرون وأكثر الملح لا يُجلب لها إلّا من هناك وكنّا قبل حلولنا بالزغاويّ أرسلت أهل قافلتنا هجّاناً لدارفور بأوراق إلى الدولة وإلى أهاليهم تعلمهم بالمجيء وأنّهم قد قفلوا سالمين وكنت قدكتبت معهم كتاباً لوالدي ونصّه

إلى حضرة والدي وأعزّ الناس عندي السيّد عمر التونسيّ أبقاه الله آمين بعد تقبيل أياديه الشريفة إنّي قد أتيت مع قافلة الخبير فرج الله صحبة السيّد أحمد بدويّ صاحبكم وحبيبكم وفعل معنا من المعروف من أجل خاطركم ما لا نقدر على وصفه لسعادتكم والسلام كاتبه ولدكم محمّد عمر ابن سليمان

١ الأصل: واذ. ٢ الأصل: ثم سافرنا من هناك ثم سافرنا خمسة. ٣ الأصل: احدى. ٤ الأصل: دوبنا. ٥ الأصل: لياخذون.

greetings, then left us in peace. We stayed two days in Laqiyyah, and set off early on the morning of the third, making for al-Zaghāwī, crossing paths on the way with a rider on a swift camel coming from Darfur, who informed us of the death of the late just and glorious monarch, Sultan ʿAbd al-Raḥmān al-Rashīd, king of Darfur and its dependencies, sultan of its farthest and nearest reaches. The rider said he was on his way to Cairo to have a new seal ring made for the sultan's son, Sultan Muḥammad Faḍl, as there was no one in Darfur with the skills to do so. It was of the sort with which the sultan's commands are stamped.[127] The sultan had died early in the month of Rajab the Separate, 1218 [October 17–November 16, 1803]. The people of the caravan mourned the death of their sultan and feared the outbreak of conflict in their lands, as he had been a just and generous sultan who loved scholarship and those who practice it and hated ignorance and those who pursue it.[128] We shall speak later, God Almighty willing, of his justice and his rule, and in the most expansive terms.[129]

We traveled on from there for five days, kneeling our camels on the sixth at Bīr al-Zaghāwī, also called Bīr al-Malḥah,[130] which is a full ten days' travel from Darfur. We stayed there eleven days putting ourselves to rights and resting, while our animals grazed so as to be strong enough for the crossing of that forbidding waste. During our stay, many meat camels were slaughtered and their flesh distributed among the people of the caravan, and we met with desert Arabs from Darfur, who brought us camel's milk and clarified butter, and from whom we bought what we needed. They come to this well to get salt and natron for Darfur, since all the natron and most of the salt is brought from there and there alone. Before alighting at al-Zaghāwī, our caravan had sent a rider on a fast camel ahead to Darfur with papers addressed to the state and its inhabitants informing them of our coming and of the caravan's safe return. I too sent a letter, addressed to my father, of which the following is the text: 2.2.16

> To my honored father and the dearest person to me, ʿUmar al-Tūnisī, may God preserve his life, amen. I first kiss your noble hands, then inform you that I have come with the caravan led by Khabīr Faraj Allāh in the company of your dear friend Sayyid Aḥmad Badawī, who for your sake has shown me such kindnesses as are too numerous to describe to Your Excellency. Farewell. Signed, your son, Muḥammad ʿUmar ibn Sulaymān.

١٧،٢،٢ فأخذها الهجّان وارتحل من وقته ولم أر في أسفاري التي سافرتها أهون منها لأنّي كنت فيها في غاية الراحة وذلك أنّ حال خروجنا من بني عديّ أمر السيّد أحمد بدويّ عبيده أن يضعوا الخيمة على أهدأ جمل وأن يوطّئوها للركوب توطئة حسنة ففعلوا وأخذ بيدي إلى أن سلّمني خطام الجمل وأمر أن يأتوا بزمزميّة ملآنة ماء فجيئت وعلّقت على الجمل وقال هذا جملك تركبه مهما أردت وتنزل عنه مهما أردت وهذه الزمزميّة تشرب منها كلّما احتجت إلى الشرب وكلّما فرغت مُرْ أحد العبيد يملأها لك وأمر جميع العبيد والخدمة بطاعتي في ذلك

١٨،٢،٢ وكان معه من العبيد الكبار سبعة وعبد صغير وثمانية من الخدمة ومعه من الجمال ثمانية وستّون جملاً قد أعدّ منها ثمانية للماء وأربعة للزاد وفي وقت الدخول إلى المفازة كان يعلّق على كلّ جمل قربتين وكان معه من السراري خمسة وسادستها ابنة عمّه السيّدة جمال وكانت من أجمل النساء[1] وكان معه حصان دنقلاويّ أسود لا يُقوّم بمال لحسنه وعليه سرج غشاؤه قطيفة خضراء يقوده عبد خاصّ به وكان السيّد أحمد يلاطفني ملاطفة الوالد لولده فكنت إذا نزلت القافلة ربّما نمت من تعب الركوب وهزّ الجمل وحرّ الشمس فكان يدثّرني وإذا جيء بالعشاء يوقظني بلطف ويطلب ماء ويغسل وجهي ويدي ويأمرني بالمضمضة لأفيق من النوم ويأخذ يدي ويضعها في الإناء وربّما أخذ الطعام ووضعه في فيّ ولم يزل هذا دأبه معي حتّى وصلنا بالسلامة

١٩،٢،٢ ثمّ ارتحلنا من بئر الزغاويّ. سافرنا عشرة أيّام سفر الجِدّ نأخذ من أوّل الليل قِطْعَة ومن آخره دَلْجَة حتّى وصلنا ضحى حادي عشرها إلى المزروب وهو بئر في أوّل أعمال دارفور وقبله بنحو ثلاث ساعات أو أربع جاءتنا أعراب بقرب من الماء واللبن فاستبشرنا بالسلامة ثمّ نزلنا البئر المذكور فأقمنا فيه يومنا وفي صبيحته ارتحلنا نحو أربع ساعات ووردنا بئرًا يقال له السُوينة وهناك قابلنا قائد الولاية وحاكمها وكان يسمّى الملك محمّد سَنجَق وهو قائد الزغاوة وهي قبيلة عظيمة من السودان وأهل السودان

١ الأصل: نساء.

The camel rider took the papers and set off right away. And here I have to say that in all my travels, I never had an easier journey, or one on which I enjoyed greater comfort. This was because, on our departure from Banī ʿAdī, Sayyid Aḥmad Badawī ordered his slaves to put my tent on the calmest camel and make it kneel nicely for mounting. They did so, and he took my hand and placed in it the camel's reins. He also ordered them to bring a canteen full of water, which they did, and it was hung on the camel. "This is your camel," he said, "Ride it whenever you want and dismount whenever you want. Drink from this canteen whenever you need to, and whenever it becomes empty tell one of the slaves to fill it for you." And he ordered all the slaves and servants to obey me in this. 2.2.17

He had with him seven adult male slaves and one young one, plus eight servants. He also had sixty-eight camels, of which eight were equipped to carry water, four to carry provisions;[131] on moving into the desert, two skins of water would be hung on each camel. He also had five concubines with him and a sixth woman, his niece, Mistress Jamāl, a most beautiful woman. He also had a black stallion from Dongola,[132] of a beauty beyond price, which wore a saddle with a green velvet saddlecloth and was led by its own special slave. Sayyid Aḥmad treated me as kindly as a father would his son: when the caravan set up camp I would sometimes fall asleep, exhausted by the riding, the rocking of the camel, and the heat of the sun, and he would cover me with a blanket. Then, when dinner was brought, he would wake me gently and call for water and wash my face and hands and tell me to rinse out my mouth to wake myself up, and he would take my hands and place them on the dish and on occasion take food and place it in my mouth. He treated me like this all the while until we had safely arrived. 2.2.18

Then we left Bīr al-Zaghāwī. We pressed on hard for ten days, spending the first part of the night in travel and marching likewise in the last part, until, in the late morning of the eleventh day, we reached al-Mazrūb, which is a well in the first district of Darfur. Some three or four hours before we got there we were met by Bedouin with skins of water and milk who were filled with joy at our safe arrival. We alighted at the aforementioned well and stayed there the rest of the day. Early on the following morning, we proceeded for about four hours and arrived at a well called al-Suwaynah,[133] where we were met by its governor, "Malik" Muḥammad Sanjaq by name; he is the leader 2.2.19

يسمّون القائد مَلِكًا ومعه جيش كثيف أظنّه نحو خمسمائة فارس فسلّم على أهل القافلة وهنّأهم بالسلامة فأقمنا في هذا المحلّ يومين ثمّ ارتحلنا وتفرّقت الناس فكلّ أناس أخذوا طريق بلادهم لأنّ أهل القافلة كلّهم ليسوا من بلدة واحدة فأكثرهم من بلدهم المشهور المسمّى كُوبَيْه وبعضهم من كَبْكَابِيّة وبعضهم كالسيّد أحمد بدويّ صاحبي من سَرْف الدجاج وبعضهم من الشَعِيرِيَّة وبعضهم من جديد كَرْيُو وبعضهم من جديد السَّيْل

فذهب كلّ منهم في مذهبه وأخذنا طريق سرف الدجاج فسافرنا سفرًا هيّنًا نحو ثلاثة أيّام ونزلنا في رابعها قرب الظهر في ظلّ جبل بقرب بئر فقِلْنا هناك وجاءت أناس كثيرون يهنّوننا بالقدوم وجاء هناك بدويّ ابن السيّد أحمد ومعه عبيد وخدم بأطعمة كثيرة فسلّم على والده وهنّأه بالسلامة وتغدّينا وأقمنا حتّى أنهر النهار وأخذ الشمس الطَفَل والاصفرار ثمّ[1] حُمِلت الأحمال[2] ورُفعت الأثقال فلم يأت المغرب إلّا ونحن على ظهر رواحلنا[3] مُقلّون وعلى[4] الجادّة سائرون فدخلنا سرف الدجاج بعد العشاء مفرد [طويل] ٢٠،٢،٢

فَأَلْقَتْ عَصَاهَا وَٱسْتَقَرَّ بِهَا ٱلنَّوَى   كَمَا قَرَّ عَيْنًا بِٱلْإِيَابِ ٱلْمُسَافِرُ

وبتنا تلك الليلة في مشقّة من كثرة المُسلّمين وازدحام الداخلين والخارجين ومع ذلك لم يتهاون السيّد أحمد بأمري ولا شغله ما هو فيه عنّي بل أفرد لي حجرة وجعل فيها من الفرش والآنية ما أحتاج إليه وأنا لا أعلم ذلك بل حين طال عليّ السهر دخلت عليه وقلت له أين أنام فنادى بأحد العبيد وقال له أرِ[5] سيّدك حجرته فأخذني وأدخلني حجرة رأيت فيها سريرًا وفرشًا وآنية بل وجميع ما أحتاج إليه وبتّ بأنعم ليلة حتّى إذا أصبحت لبست ثيابي ودخلت عليه فوجدته جالسًا في أبّهة عظيمة بين خدمه وجواريه وأولاده قارًّا سارًّا كأنّه لم يكن مسافرًا

---

١ أضيف للسياق: ثم. ٢ الأصل: الاحملا. ٣ أضيف للسياق: رواحلنا. ٤ الأصل: علي. ٥ الأصل: أري.

of the Zaghāwah, who are a mighty tribe among the blacks, in whose lands the people refer to a tribal leader as Malik, meaning "king." He had with him a massive army, of around five hundred horsemen, I think. The governor greeted the people of the caravan and congratulated them on their safe arrival. We stayed there two days,[134] then left, and everyone dispersed, each party taking the road that led to its own country, for not all the people of the caravan were from the same place. Most of them were from a town well-known there called Kūbayh, some from Kabkābiyyah, some, like my friend Sayyid Aḥmad, from Sarf al-Dajāj, some from al-Shaʿīriyyah, some from Jadīd Karyū, and some from Jadīd al-Sayl.[135]

Everyone went his own way, and we took the road to Sarf al-Dajāj, making 2.2.20
easy going for about three days and alighting around noon on the fourth in the shadow of a mountain close to a well, where we took a siesta. Many came to congratulate us on our arrival. Badawī, Sayyid Aḥmad's son, appeared too, accompanied by slaves and servants with large quantities of food. He greeted his father and congratulated him on his safe arrival, and we lunched—staying till day had begun to wane and yellow to o'ertake the setting sun, turning all to flame. Then the loads were loaded, the burdens hoisted, and by the time sunset had arrived, we were atop the backs of our trusty steeds and moving down the track. Thus we entered Sarf al-Dajāj after the evening prayer:

> Then she threw down her stick, her destination thereby settling,
> just as the traveler's eye finds settled comfort on his return.

We spent an uncomfortable night, what with so many well-wishers and others coming in and out, despite which Sayyid Aḥmad didn't forget me or allow himself to be distracted from me. On the contrary, he gave me my own room and filled it with all the bedding and vessels I could need. I was unaware of this, and when I felt I had stayed up long enough, I went to him and asked, "Where am I to sleep?" He called one of his slaves, told him, "Show your master his room," and the man took me and led me into a room where I found a bed, bedding, and vessels—everything indeed that I might need. I spent a very comfortable night, and when morning came I got dressed and went to see him. I found him sitting in great splendor among his servants, slave women, and children, as settled and happy as though he'd never left.

فرحّب بي وأكرمني فقبّلت يده وجلست معه ثمّ قال لي إنّ ابن أخي السيّد أحمد الصغير قد صنع في هذا النهار وليمة القدوم والتمس منّي أن تتوجّه إليه وتشرّف مجلسه بحضورك فإن رأيت بك نشاطاً وأردت جبر خاطره فذاك إليك وما أريد أن أشقّ عليك فقلت سمعاً وطاعة لكنّي لا أعرف منزله فأمر أحد غلمانه أن يعرّفني منزله فذهبت وحضرت ضيافته فأعظم ملقاي ورحّب بي وكان يوماً عظيماً ثمّ إنّ جميع أهل القافلة صاروا يصنعون الولائم فتوالت وكلّ وليمة يدعونني فأحضرها حتّى جاء عمّي وتوجّهت صحبته إلى والدي ٢،٢،٢١

وذلك أنّي كنت في ضيافة بعض الأصحاب وأتيت قرب المساء فدخلت الحجرة المعدّة لي فرأيت فيها رجلين وعبدين أمّا الرجلان فأحدهما أسمر قصير ذو هيئة حسنة جميل البزّة يقرب لونه من لون الحبشة والآخر أسود رثّ الهيئة فسلّمت عليهما فردّا عليّ السلام وجلست متعجّباً كيف دخلا في حجرتي بغير إذني فرأيتهما يتغامزان ويقول أحدهما للآخر أهو هو فيقول الآخر نعم هو ولا أعرف علام يقولان ذلك ثمّ سألني الرجل الأوّل وقال لي أنت من هنا فقلت لا أنا من مصر جئت ملتمساً لأبي فقال ومن أبوك فقلت أبي السيّد عمر التونسيّ ٢،٢،٢٢

فقال لي السودانيّ سلّم على عمّك السيّد أحمد زرّوق فسلّمت عليه حينئذ وبعد السلام أخرج لي مكتوباً فيه ٢،٢،٢٣

بعد السلام إنّه قد جاءنا كتاب من ولدنا السيّد محمّد أخبرنا فيه أنّه قدم صحبتك وفعلت معه من المعروف ما أنت أهله فجزاك الله عنّا خيراً وهذه منّة لا أكاد أقوم بشكرها وصنيعة لا أقدر على مكافأتها ومن المعلوم أنّ المهاداة سنّة من أوّل الزمان وقد قبل الهديّة سيّد ولد عدنان لذا قال عليه صلاة ربّنا المنّان تهادوا تحابّوا وتذهب الشحناء من

He welcomed me warmly and I kissed his hand and sat with him. "My nephew," he said, "young Sayyid Aḥmad, is putting on a welcome banquet today and has asked me to invite you to honor his gathering hall with your presence. If you have the energy, and would like to oblige him, it's up to you. I don't want you to put yourself to any trouble." "I hear and obey," I said, "but I don't know his house," so he ordered one of his young male slaves to show me the house. I attended his party and he welcomed me and made a great fuss over me—it was a great day. Then everyone who had been in the caravan started putting on banquets one after another, and they'd invite me to every banquet and I'd go. This went on until my uncle arrived and I set off with him to see my father. 2.2.21

This came about as follows: I'd been at a party given by some friends. I came home close to evening and entered the room that had been prepared for me to find two men and two slaves. One of the men was short and dark-complexioned, his color about that of an Ethiopian, well-dressed and in handsome clothes. The other was black and shabbily dressed. I greeted them, they returned my greeting, and I sat down, wondering how they could enter my room without my permission. Then I noticed them winking at one another and one said to the other, "Is that him?" "Yes," the other replied, "that's him," though I didn't know why they said this. Then the first man asked me, "Are you from here?" "No," I answered, "I'm from Cairo and have come to look for my father." "And who is your father?" he asked. "My father is Sayyid ʿUmar al-Tūnisī," I replied. 2.2.22

The black-skinned man said, "Salute your uncle, Sayyid Aḥmad Zarrūq,"[136] so I saluted him and he showed me a letter that said: 2.2.23

> Greetings. We have received a letter from our son, Sayyid Muḥammad, informing me that he has come here in your company and that you have done him the kindnesses we would expect of you—may God reward you with good fortune for what you have done for us! This is an act of generosity for which I can scarcely find words to thank you, one I shall never be able to repay. It is well known that the exchange of gifts is a custom practiced from the beginning of time, and that the Lord of ʿAdnān's Offspring[137] accepted presents. This is why he said, may he enjoy the blessings of our Ever-Generous Lord, "Give each other presents and you will

قلوبكم وقد أرسلت لحضرتك صحبة أخي السيّد أحمد زرّوق عبدين سُداسيّين ومُهرًا أحمر أرجو من سعادتكم قبولهم وهم على قدر مقامي لا على قدر مقامك ولله درّ[1] القائل شعرًا [بسيط]

جَاءَتْ سُلَيْمَانَ يَوْمَ ٱلْعَرْضِ هُدْهُدَةٌ   أَتَتْ لَهُ بِجَرَادٍ كَانَ فِي فِيهَا
وَأَنْشَدَتْ بِلِسَانِ ٱلْحَالِ قَائِلَةً   إِنَّ ٱلْهَدَايَا عَلَى مِقْدَارِ مُهْدِيهَا
لَوْكَانَ يُهْدَى إِلَى ٱلْإِنْسَانِ قِيمَتُهُ   لَكَانَ قِيمَتُكَ ٱلدُّنْيَا وَمَا فِيهَا

ومنّا السلام عليكم وعلى أولادكم وأهل منزلكم ومن يحويه مجلسكم السعيد

٢،٢،٢٤ وقال لي خذ هذا الكتاب واقرأه على عمّك السيّد أحمد فذهبت به وقرأته عليه وأحضرت الهديّة فرآها وبارك فيها ثمّ قال إنّي قبلتها ووهبتها لابني هذا يعنيني فألححت عليه أنا وعمّي في قبولها فأبى إلّا ذلك وقال إنّي لو أفنيت أموالي كلّها في مرضاته لما كان ذلك جزاء له بما صنع معي من المعروف فتجاسرت عليه حينئذ وسألته بالله العظيم إلّا ما أخبرني عن هذا المعروف الذي صنعه معه فقال لي اعلم يا ولدي أنّ أعدائي وشوا بي إلى حضرة السلطان بأنّي أبيع الأحرار[2] وزخرفوا له القول حتّى استقرّ في ذهنه أنّ الأمر صحيح فغضب لذلك وقال تاجر مثل هذا في غنائه يفعل هذا الفعل الفقر أولى به فأحضرني من داري على غير صورة وحين دخلت عليه وبّخني وقرّعني بالكلام المؤلم وطلبت تحقيق ما قيل فيّ فلم أتمكّن من ذلك ولا سمع لي قول بل أمر بالقبض عليّ وأن توضع الأغلال في عنقي ويُضيّق عليّ في الحبس

٢،٢،٢٥ وكان من لطف الله تعالى أنّ أباك حاضر بالمجلس فلم يتجاسر أحد على أن[3] يشفع لي عنده لما قام به من الغضب وحين رأى والدك ذلك تقدّم وتنحنح وذكر أحاديث في العفو عن الجاني وتلا ﴿يَا أَيُّهَا ٱلَّذِينَ آمَنُوا إِنْ جَاءَكُمْ فَاسِقٌ بِنَبَإٍ فَتَبَيَّنُوا﴾ ثمّ شفع في

١ أضيف للسياق: در. ٢ الأصل: الاحرارا. ٣ أضيف للسياق: على أن.

love each other, and the rancor will leave your hearts." I have sent your honored person, in the company of my brother Sayyid Aḥmad Zarrūq, two *sudāsī* slaves[138] and a red foal. I hope Your Excellency will accept them, though they are more in keeping with my station than with yours—and how well the poet put it when he said:

The lark on parade day to Sulaymān came[139]
  and gave him a locust it had in its beak.
Then with nature's tongue[140] it spoke these words:
  "Gifts are proportionate to the giver, be he mighty or meek.
If each according to his worth were given,
  your gift would be the World and all you therein seek!"

Greetings from us to you, to your children, to the people of your household, and to all who fill your happy assembly.

Sayyid Aḥmad Zarrūq then said to me, "Take this letter and read it to your uncle Sayyid Aḥmad,"[141] so I did, taking along the gift, which he saw and expressed thanks for. Then he said, "I accept it and give it to this son of mine," meaning me. My uncle and I insisted that he should take the gift but he refused any such thing, saying, "Were I to spend every penny I own on making him happy, it would not repay his father for the kindnesses he has shown me." At this, I was so bold as to say to him, "For the Almighty's sake, do please tell me about this kindness that my father did for you!" "You should know, dear boy," he replied, "that my enemies spread false rumors about me to His Highness the Sultan, to the effect that I was selling free men as slaves, and they painted such a picture of me that it became fixed in his mind that it was true. He was furious and said, 'That a merchant as rich as he should do such a thing! Poverty is more fitting for him.' They brought me from my house in disarray and when I entered his presence, he upbraided me and chided me harshly. I asked for an investigation into what had been said about me but was unable to secure this, and he wouldn't listen to a word I said. On the contrary, he ordered that I be seized, that chains be placed around my neck, and that I be confined to jail. 2.2.24

"It was a blessing from the Almighty that your father was present at the gathering, as the sultan was so furious with me that no one had the courage to intercede on my behalf. When your father saw this, he came forward, cleared his throat, quoted hadiths concerning pardon for offenders, and recited: 2.2.25

فشفعه السلطان وأمر بإطلاقي وبعد ذلك ظهرت له براءتي ولكن لولم يسخّره الله لي في تلك الساعة لذهبت نفسي وأموالي كلّها فأيّ جميل أكبر من هذا أو أيّ صنيع[1] أعظم من هذا ومع ذلك كلّه فأجر أبيك فيما فعله معي على الله وإنّي طالما كنت أترقّب له حاجة تأتي على يدي فأقضيها له فلم[2] يتيسّر لي إلّا هذه الخدمة وعسى أن يكون فيها قضاء بعض ما وجب عليّ ولا أظنّ ذلك

٢،٢،٢٦ ثمّ أراد عمّي أن يسافر صبح ذلك النهار فأبى السيّد أحمد فمكثنا بعد ذلك ثلاثة[3] أيّام وفي صبيحة اليوم الرابع دخلت عليه لأودّعه فأعطاني خرزاً كثيراً يضعنه نساء السودان في أوساطهنّ من قبيل الزينة يسمّى عندهنّ رُقاد الفاقة ومعناه نوم الراحة وأعطاني خرزاً آخر غالي الثمن يجعلنه في أجيادهنّ وهو على أنواع. منه ما يسمّى بالريش وهو خرز أبيض مستطيل فيه بعض خطوط سمر معروف بهذا الاسم في مصر أيضاً ومنه ما يسمّى بالمنصوص وهو خرز أصفر من كهربان مستدير مفرطح ومنه خرز كرويّ الشكل أحمر غير ناصع يسمّى بالعقيق فأعطاني منها ما يزيد على عقدين وثمنه ينوف عن ثلاثة رؤوس من الرقيق وأعطاني عمامة خضراء من الشاش جديدة وسنبلاً ومحلباً وصندلاً كثيراً وهذه الثلاثة من العطريات يتطيّبن بها نساء السودان وقال فرّق هذه الأشياء بين نساء أبيك واذبح[4] لنا شاة وحنّذها وبلغتهم يقال لها نصيص. زوّدناها وودّعنا وركبنا

٢،٢،٢٧ وكان مع عمّي عبد آخر كبير فركبت الفرس وركب عمّي هجيناً وركب الرجل حماراً فارهاً وسعت العبيد أمامنا وسرنا قاصدين محلّ أبي وكان بمحلّ يقال له أبو الجُدُول وبينه وبين سرف الدجاج ستّة أيّام سفر فخرجنا من سرف الدجاج ومررنا بالبلد المسمّى بكَبْكَابيّة وهي بلد أشبه ببلاد ريف مصر إلّا أنّها أعمر منها وأخصب لأنّها آهلة بالساكن مغتصّة بالقاطن وأهلها تجّار أغنياء وعندهم من الرقيق ما لا يحصى كثرة ولهم نخيل وأرض واسعة[5] فيها آبار قريبة الماء يزرعون بها أنواع الخضروات

١ الأصل: صنع. ٢ الأصل: لم. ٣ الأصل: ثلاثا. ٤ الأصل: وذبح. ٥ الأصل: واسع.

«Believers, if an evildoer brings you news, ascertain the correctness of the report fully.»[142] Then he interceded for me, and the sultan accepted his intercession and ordered that I be released. Later, he realized I was innocent, but if God hadn't at that moment used your father as His instrument, I would have lost my life and all my money. What favor could be greater than that, or what action of greater import? Yet, despite all this, your father's true reward for what he did for me will come from God. For a long time now I have been waiting for some need of his to come to my attention so that I might satisfy it for him, and the only thing to have been vouchsafed me is this service. Perhaps, by fulfilling it, I have discharged some of the duty that I owe, though I do not believe so."

My uncle wanted to set out the morning of the next day, but Sayyid Aḥmad refused to allow this, so we stayed three more days. Early on the morning of the fourth I went to see him and say goodbye. He gave me a large supply of the beads that the women of the Blacks put around their waists as a kind of adornment and which they call *ruqād al-fāqah,* meaning "restful sleep." He also gave me another costly kind of bead that they place around their necks, which is of various types. One type is called *rīsh*; these are elongated white beads with brown stripes; they are known by the same name in Egypt. Another kind is called *manṣūṣ*; these are round, flattened, yellow beads made of amber. A further kind is a matte-red bead of rounded shape called *ʿaqīq*; he gave me enough of these for more than two necklaces, with a value of around three hundred slaves. He also gave me a new turban of green muslin, as well as some spikenard and mahaleb and a great quantity of sandalwood, which are three aromatic substances the women of the Blacks use to perfume themselves. "Divide these things up among your father's womenfolk," he told me, "and slaughter a ewe on our behalf and roast it on hot stones" (in their language[143] this is called *naṣīṣ*). He added even more things of the same sort to our supplies and bade us farewell and we mounted. 2.2.26

My uncle had another slave with him, so I rode the horse, my uncle rode a camel, the other man rode a tall donkey, and the slave ran in front of us. We proceeded thus, heading for where my father was, a place called Abū l-Judūl, six days' journey from Sarf al-Dajāj. We exited Sarf al-Dajāj and passed by the town called Kabkābiyyah, which resembles a town of the Egyptian Delta, though more prosperous and fertile, its streets thronged with inhabitants, its people rich merchants with slaves too many to count.[144] They have palm groves and extensive lands, with wells whose water is close 2.2.27

والبقول من بامية وملوخيّة وقرع وباذنجان وفقوس وقثّاء وبصل وحلبة وكمّون وفلفل وحبّ رَشاد وكلّه كما نعهد إلّا الفلفل فإنّه حبّ رفيع أغلظ من الشعير بقليل وعندهم بعض شجر الليمون الحامض وبقربهم جبل يقال له مَرّة وهو جبل يشقّ إقليم الفور من أوّله إلى آخره مع الاستقامة وله عدّة طرق تصعد الناس منها إليه ولكلّ قطعة منه اسم خاصّ به غير الاسم[1] العامّ والفور يسكنون في أعلاه ولا يألفون الوهاد بل يرون أنّ ذلك أصون لهم ولأموالهم وسيأتي لهذا مزيد توضيح

٢،٢،٢٨ وحين مرورنا بكبكابيّة وجدنا سوقها عامرًا فأخذنا منه ما احتجنا إليه ثمّ توجّهنا فسافرنا ثلاثة أيّام في عرض جبل مرّة وصرنا نبيت ببلاد أقوام مستوحشين يكرهون الضيوف خصوصاً إن كانوا من أولاد العرب فأصابتنا منهم مشقّة عظيمة حتّى صرنا لا نبيت عندهم إلّا كرهاً عليهم مع أنّ معنا أزوادنا ولا نحتاج لهم في شيء فكانوا ينفرون منّا بالطبع وبعد ذلك خرجنا إلى السهل فبتنا ليلة واحدة بمحلّ يقال له تارْنِيَه فأكرمونا هناك وصنعوا لنا ضيافة عظيمة وفي ضحى اليوم السادس دخلنا البلدة التي فيها والدي المسمّاة بِحِلّة جولتو وهي من جملة حلل أبي الجُدول فرأينا على باب دار والدي خيلاً وحميرًا وخدماً لأضياف كانوا عنده فدخلنا الدار وعرضنا جواري وعبيدا يسلّمون علينا ويهنّوني بالسلامة ثمّ جاء والدي بعد أن ركب أضيافه وسلّم عليّ فقمت وقبّلت يده ووقفت أمامه خدمة له فأمرني بالجلوس فجلست فسألني ما الحرفة التي تعلّمتها فقلت له القرآن وشيئاً من العلم فسرّ لذلك وصنع ثاني يوم مجيئي وليمة ذبح فيها عدّة شياه وبقر ودعا الناس فجاء خلق كثير فأكلوا وكان يوم سرور

٢،٢،٢٩ ثمّ إنّه بعد ثلاثة أيّام جهّزني وعمّي السيّد أحمد إلى الأعتاب السلطانيّة بهدايا من عنده إلى حضرة السلطان ووزيره الأعظم إذ ذاك الأب الشيخ محمّد كرّا والفقيه مالك الفوتاويّ وهو وكيل أبي وحوائجه التي تعرض للدولة كلّها على يده وهو من قبيلة تسمّى الفُلّان وأهل دارفور يسمّونها الفلّاته وفَلّاتا بالألف في الآخر أصحّ والفقيه

---

١ الأصل: اسم.

to the surface. On these lands, they grow vegetables and pulses such as okra, Jew's mallow, squash, eggplant, long cucumber, pumpkin, onions, fenugreek, cumin, pepper, and cress, all of them in the varieties with which we are familiar, except for the pepper, which has a small berry slightly fatter than barley. They also have some lemon trees. Next to them is a mountain range called Jabal Marrah, which runs a straight course through the middle of the Fur region from beginning to end and through which run several roads people use to climb it. Each part of the range has its own name, different from the overall name. The Fur live at the top and know nothing of the lowlands; indeed, they believe that doing so is safer for them and their properties. We shall explain this point in greater detail below.[145]

When passing through Kabkābiyyah, we found its market in full swing, so we bought everything we needed there. Then we set off again and traveled for three days across Jabal Marrah, spending the night in the towns of wild peoples who hate guests, especially if they're Arabs. We had to put up with a great deal of aggravation from them; so much so that in the end we were staying overnight in their towns against their will, even though we had our own provisions and needed nothing from them—it was just in their natures to hate us. After this, we descended to the plain, where we spent one night in a place called Tărne, where they treated us well, putting on a huge party for us. Late in the morning of the sixth day, we entered the town my father was in, called Ḥillat Jūltū, one of the villages of Abū l-Judūl. At the gate of my father's house, we found the horses, donkeys, and servants of some guests who were visiting him. We entered the house, passing by male and female slaves, who greeted us and congratulated us on our safe arrival. After his guests had mounted, my father came out to greet me. I rose, kissed his hand, and stood before him at his service. He ordered me to sit and I did. He asked me what professional skills I had acquired and I said, "The Qur'an and a certain amount of scholarship." This pleased him, and the second day after my arrival he put on a banquet for which he slaughtered several ewes and cows. He invited everyone, so large numbers came and ate, and it was a happy day. 2.2.28

Three days later, my father provisioned my uncle and me for the journey to the Sultanic Portals,[146] bearing gifts for the Sultan's noble person, for the Grand Vizier (who at that time was Shaykh-Father Muḥammad Kurrā[147]), and for Faqīh Mālik al-Fūtāwī,[148] who was my father's agent and in charge of all my father's business with the state.[149] He belonged to a tribe called the Fullān, 2.2.29

مالك المذكور أعظم الوزراء من أولاد العرب وكان يومئذ السلطان محمّد فضل ابن المرحوم السلطان عبد الرحمن صغيرًا وكان زمام الأمور كلّها بيد الأب الشيخ محمّد كرّا معناه بالفوراويّة الطويل لأنّه هو الذي عضد السلطان محمّد فضل بعد موت أبيه وأجلسه على سرير ملكه وناب عنه في الأحكام وتدبير المملكة لصغر سنّه وقد شاع على ألسنة الناس أهل دارفور أنّه من عبيد السلطان وليس كذلك بل هو حرّ خدم السلطان وأُغْنِيَ في خدمته وقام بأعباء[1] الأمور حتّى ترقّى للوزارة العظمى بحسن تدبيره وتصرّف في مملكة دارفور حتّى كان لا تعلو على كلمته كلمة غير كلمة[2] السلطان وكان رحمه الله فيه دهاء ومكر وشجاعة وإقدام وحيل على الأمور حتّى ينفذ أغراضه وستأتي سيرته وسيرة السلطان عبد الرحمن وابنه السلطان محمّد فضل وأخيه السلطان محمّد تَيْراب مفصّلة إن شاء الله تعالى

فركبنا من أبي الجدول إلى تَنْدَلْتي وهو المقرّ[3] السلطانيّ في أوّل شعبان سنة ٣٠،٢،٢
١٢١٨ ويسمّى بلغتهم الفاشر وكلّ محلّ سكنه السلطان يسمّى فاشرًا فسافرنا يومين سفرًا غير شطيط ودخلناه ضحوة الثالث فوجدنا بلدًا يموج بالساكن ويرتجّ بالقاطن ما بين راكب وماشي وجالس وغاشي وطبول ترعد وخيول تركض فدخلنا دار الفقيه مالك فوجدناه جالسًا بين خدم وحشم وأرباب الحوائج محتفّون به فدخلنا عليه فسلّم عليه عمّي فأعظم ملقاه ورحّب به فعرّفه عمّي بي فسلّم عليّ وبشّ في وجهي ورحّب بي ثمّ إن عمّي أعطاه الكتاب الذي له والكتب التي للدولة فقرأ كتابه ورحّب بنا[4] وأفرد لنا محلًا وضعنا فيه متاعنا ثمّ أخذنا في الحال إلى دار الأب الشيخ محمّد كرّا فرأينا دارًا على بابها من الخيل والدوابّ ما لا يحصى كثرة ودخلنا فرأيناه جالسًا في مجلس حفل وأرباب الدولة محتفّون به فسلّم علينا ولم يعلم من أنا ثمّ سأل وقال من هذا فقال له الفقيه مالك هذا ابن الشريف عمر التونسيّ العالم المقيم بأبي الجدول

١ الأصل: بعبآء. ٢ أضيف للسياق: كلمة. ٣ الأصل: مقر. ٤ أضيف للسياق: بنا.

whom the Darfurians call the Fallātah (though Fallātā, ending in a long *ā*, is more correct). This Faqīh Mālik was the greatest of the viziers of Arab descent.[150] In those days, Sultan Muḥammad Faḍl, son of the late Sultan ʿAbd al-Raḥmān, was young and the management of affairs was entirely in the hands of Shaykh-Father Muḥammad Kurrā, whose last name means "the Tall" in the language of the Fur; it was he who supported the claim of Sultan Muḥammad Faḍl after his father's death, placed him on his throne, and, in view of his young age, acted as his regent in making rulings and managing the realm. A rumor has spread on the tongues of the Darfurians that he had once been a slave of the sultan, but that is not the case. The truth is he was a freeborn man who served the sultan, grew rich in his service, dealt with the burden of affairs, and eventually rose to the grand vizierate through his good management, one who controlled the Darfurian realm to the point that no word, after that of the sultan, carried greater weight than his.[151] He possessed, God have mercy on his soul, a shrewdness, cunning, courage, boldness, and vigor in the execution of affairs that ensured that his intentions were seen through. His history, along with those of Sultan ʿAbd al-Raḥmān, his son Sultan Muḥammad Faḍl, and the former's brother Sultan Muḥammad Tayrāb, will be told in detail, God Almighty willing.[152]

On the first of Shaʿbān, 1218 [November 16, 1803], we rode from Abū l-Judūl to Tandaltī, the seat of the sultanate. Such a seat is known in their language as a *fāshir*: any place where the sultan resides is called a *fāshir*.[153] We traveled at an easy pace for two days and entered the place on the morning of the third to find a town teeming with people—some mounted, some on foot, some seated, some coming, some going, with drums thundering and horses galloping. We entered the house of Faqīh Mālik and found him sitting among his servants and entourage, surrounded by those who had business to conduct with him. We approached, my uncle saluted him, and he welcomed us with much ceremony. My uncle told him who I was, and he greeted me, smiled at me, and welcomed me. Then my uncle gave him the letter addressed to him and the letters addressed to the government. He read his letter, welcomed us, and had a private room assigned to us in which to put our things. Then he took us right away to the house of the Shaykh-Father Muḥammad Kurrā, which had at its gate horses and other riding animals too many to count. We went in and found him sitting in a crowded gathering hall surrounded by the chief officers of the state. He greeted us but didn't know who I was, so he asked, 2.2.30

وقد أرسله صحبة عمّه ليسلّم على سعادتك وهذا كتاب أبيه فأخذ الكتاب وفتحه ولمّا علم ما فيه صار يلاطفني ويحيّيني[1] إكراماً لوالدي وقدّمت له الهديّة فقبلها وأمر بإدخالها إلى خزائنه وأقبل يلاطفني بالتحيّة إكراماً لوالدي ثمّ أمر الفقيه مالك أن يبقينا عنده حتّى يأذن لنا في التوجّه فبقينا عند الفقيه مالك ثلاثة أيّام ونحن في أكرم ضيافة وألذّ ائتناس

٣١،٢،٢ وفي اليوم الرابع دعانا الأب الشيخ محمّد كرّا على يد الفقيه مالك وكساني كشميراً أخضر وجبة خضراء وقفطاناً من القطن الهنديّ وأمر لي بجاريتين وعبد وكتب لأبي كتاباً قرأته بعد ذلك عند أبي وصورته

من حضرة من أكرمه الكريم ولا يفارقه الخير والنعيم الوزير الأعظم المتوكّل على من يسمع ويرى الأب الشيخ محمّد كرّا إلى حضرة الأستاذ الأعظم والملاذ الأفخم علامة الزمان ونخبة سلالة سيّد ولد عدنان السيّد الشريف عمر التونسيّ دام مجده آمين أمّا بعد إنّه قد حضر لدينا نجلكم المكرّم صحبة أخيكم المحترم المعظّم بما أهديتموه لنا حسبما هو مشروح في جوابكم ففرحنا غاية الفرح بأمرين الأوّل اجتماع شملك بقرّة عينك والثاني بأنّنا نأمل إقامتك في بلدنا وهذا هو المقصود الأعظم لتحصل لنا البركة بكم أهل البيت وقد أتحفناه بما صحبه ونرجو أن يكون مقبولاً لديكم ولولا ما نحن فيه من الأشغال لكان الأمر أبلغ من ذلك فالمعذرة إليك وآمل ألّا تنساني من صالح دعواتك والسلام عليك ورحمة الله وبركاته

[1] الأصل: ويحيني.

"Who is that?" and Faqīh Mālik answered. "This is the son of Sharif ʿUmar al-Tūnisī, the scholar who lives at Abū l-Judūl. He's sent him with his uncle to salute Your Excellency; this is a letter from his father." The shaykh-father took the letter and opened it, and once he'd read it, talked to us indulgently and spoke kind words to us, out of respect for my father. I presented him with the gift, and he accepted it, ordered that it be put away in his treasure house, and went on conversing indulgently and kindly to us out of respect for my father. Then he ordered Faqīh Mālik to keep us at his house until he gave us leave to go, so we remained at Faqīh Mālik's three days, during which we enjoyed the most generous hospitality and delightful company.

On the fourth day, Shaykh-Father Muḥammad Kurrā summoned us through 2.2.31
Faqīh Mālik and presented me with a green cashmere shawl,[154] a green open-fronted gown, and a caftan of Indian cotton, and commanded that I be given two girl slaves and a male. He also wrote a letter to my father that I read to him later, and which went as follows:

> From one to whom the Generous Lord has been generous and who is never without His blessings and favors, Grand Vizier Shaykh-Father Muḥammad Kurrā, who places his trust in Him who hears and sees all, to the Grand Teacher and Most Eminent Refuge, the Erudite Scholar of the Age, the Flower of the Progeny of the Lord of ʿAdnān's Offspring,[155] Sharif ʿUmar al-Tūnisī, may his glory last forever, amen. Your most noble son has come to us, accompanied by your respected and venerated brother, bringing the gifts you have sent us as set out in your letter. We have thus experienced the utmost joy, for two reasons: first, that you have been reunited with the apple of your eye, and second (and this is the burden of what we intend to convey) because we place high hopes on your presence in our land, that we may experience grace through you, O People of the House.[156] He bears with him what we have presented to him and we hope you find it acceptable. Were we not so busy, more would have been done to show our esteem. Our excuses, then, to you, and we hope that you will not deprive us of the benefit of your prayers. And may peace be upon you and the mercy of God and His blessings.

ثمّ إنّ الفقيه مالك قدّم لي جارية ناهداً وجواباً قرأته بعد ذلك أيضاً مضمونه ٣٢،٢،٢

بعد السلام إنّه قد ورد علينا كتابكم صحبة نجلكم وأخيكم وقدّمناهما إلى حضرة الأب الشيخ محمّد كرّا وقد دخل عليه من السرور ما لا يعلمه إلّا الله بقدوم نجلك كما يفصح لك كتابه عن ذلك ونحن أشدّ فرحاً منه لما بيننا من المودّة وما أهداه الأب الشيخ محمّد كرّا لنجلك يُتْلَى عليك ويصل بين يديك وها نحن قد أتحفنا نجلك الكريم بجارية كوعبة مترِبة

أراد هنا كاعبة وأمّا قوله مـتربـة لا معنى له هنا وذلك من جهل الفقيه وهذا أي كاعبـة ومـتربـة مذكور في القرآن في وصف الحور وأراد الفقيه أن يُدْعى[1] عالماً فإنّه غلط وقال هنا قولاً بدون معنى

واسمها حميدة عسى أن تُلْحَظ بالقبول كما هو المأمول والسـلام

٣٣،٢،٢ فأخذنا جميع ذلك وتوجّهنا لوالدي فرحين مسرورين ففرح بقدومنا ثمّ أقمنا جميعاً مدّة شهر رمضان وحين انقضائه توجّه أبي إلى الفاشر للسلام وقابل الأب الشيخ محمّد كرّا وطلب منه الإذن في التوجّه إلى تونس ليرى أمّه وأخويه ويجتمع بهم قبل وفاة أمّه وأعلمه أنّه سيتركني في بيته وبلاده لأنّ البلد التي كان فيها أقطاع له أقطعها له المرحوم السلطان عبد الرحمن قبل وفاته وكان قبل ذلك أقطعه بلاداً في المحلّ المسمّى بِقرلي فأبى والدي الإقامة فيه لعجمة لسان أهله وعدم معرفتهم العربيّ فنقله إلى هذه البلد وهذا الإقطاع يشتمل على ثلاثة بلاد حلّة جولتو الذي فيه بيتنا والدبّة وأمّ بعوضة فاتّفق مع الأب الشيخ محمّد كرّا أن يتركني في هذه البلاد أجمع خراجها وأنتفع بـزرعها فأخذ عليه المواثيق بالعود وأذن له وكتب له عدّة أوامر إلى العمّال الذين

[1] الأصل: أنه يدّعى.

Then Faqīh Mālik presented me with a perky-breasted slave girl and a letter, which I also read later and which went as follows: 2.2.32

> Greetings. Your letter has reached us, accompanied by your son and your brother, and we have presented them to the honored Shaykh-Father Muḥammad Kurrā. He experienced such joy at the coming of your son as only God can understand, as his letter will make clear to you, we being even more overjoyed than he in view of the affection that exists between us. What Shaykh-Father Muḥammad Kurrā presented to him will be handed over to you and will be yours to dispose of. I myself have presented him with a slave called Ḥumaydah,[157] a distressed damsel, *kawʿabah matrabah*, for a slave—

He should have said *kāʿibah* for the first word, while *matrabah*, as used here, has no meaning. This was due to the Faqīh's ignorance. These words, i.e., *kāʿibah* and *matrabah*, occur in the Qurʾan in descriptions of the houris of Paradise.[158] The Faqīh wanted to be reckoned a scholar, but committed an error and produced nonsense.

> Perhaps she will be regarded with approval, which is our hope. Farewell.

We then took all these things and set off in high spirits to return to my father, who rejoiced at our arrival. Thereafter, we stayed together for the whole of Ramadan. When the month was over, my father set off for the seat of the sultan, to make his salutations. He met the Shaykh-Father Muḥammad Kurrā and requested permission to leave for Tunis to see his mother and brothers and be together with them before his mother died. He informed him that he would leave me in his house and on his lands, because the town he was in was one of the fiefs[159] granted to him by the late Sultan ʿAbd al-Raḥmān before his death. Before that he'd granted him villages in the area called Qirlī, but my father had refused to live there because its inhabitants spoke a different language and had no knowledge of Arabic,[160] so the sultan transferred him to this place. The fief embraced three villages—Ḥillat Jūltū, where our house was, al-Dibbah, and Umm Baʿūḍah. He agreed with Shaykh-Father Muḥammad Kurrā that he would leave me on these lands, to collect their tax and reap the benefits of farming them. Then my father gave the shaykh-father pledges that 2.2.33

بطريقه أن يعطوه جميع ما يحتاج إليه وأن يرسلوا معه جنداً يوصّله إلى محلّ الأمن وودّعه ورجع إلينا مهتمّاً بأمر السفر

فجهّز نفسه في أقرب وقت وذلك أنّه باع ما عنده من القطن وكان عنده قطن ٣٤،٢،٢
كثير ينوف عن مائة قنطار لأنّه كان زارعاً قطعة أرض تزيد عن عشرين فدّاناً من أفدنة برّ مصر قطناً وكانت هذه القطعة يجمع منها وقت هجوم القطن في كلّ يوم أربع عشرة ريكة والريكة في عرف أهل دارفور كالقُفّة في عرف أهل مصر وهي ربّما لو صُبّت فيها غلال تَسَعُ[1] نحو خمسة أرباع بالربع المصريّ فباع كلّ ذلك وباع مُراح غنم كان عنده وكذا باع البقر والحمير وأخذ جواريه وعبيده وما حُصل لي من السيّد أحمد بدويّ ومن الأب الشيخ محمّد كرّا ولم يترك لي إلّا جارية بعينيها بياض تسمّى فرحانة وعبدين وامرأتيهما وحماراً وهجيناً ضعيفاً وترك لي إحدى نسائه تسمّى زهرة وامرأة أخيه وكلّ منهما[2] معها بنت وباع مطامير الغلال ولم يبق لي إلّا مطموراً واحداً وأعطاني وثيقة الإقطاع التي كتبها له المرحوم السلطان عبد الرحمن حين أقطعه الأرض المذكورة ونصّها

من حضرة السلطان الأعظم والملاذ الأفخم سلطان العرب والعجم ومالك رقاب الأمم سلطان البرّين والبحرين وخادم الحرمين الشريفين الواثق بعناية الملك المبدي المعيد السلطان عبد الرحمن الرشيد إلى حضرة الملوك والحكّام والشَّرَاتِي والدمالج[3] وأولاد السلاطين والجبّايين وأهل دولة السلطان من العرب والسودان أمّا بعد فإنّ السلطان المذكور المبرور المؤيّد المظفر المنصور تفضّل وأمدّ بمعونته وأعطى العلّامة السيّد الشريف عمر التونسيّ قطعة من الأرض كائنة بأبي الجدول حاوية لثلاث حلل من حلّة جولتو والدبّة وأمّ بعوضة بحدودها المعروفة وأتخامها الموصوفة

١ الأصل: يسع. ٢ الأصل: منها. ٣ الأصل: الرماج.

he would return, and the shaykh-father gave him permission to leave, writing for him a number of orders addressed to the tax collectors along his route that instructed them to give him everything he needed and send mounted soldiers with him to escort him to the next safe place. My father bade him farewell and returned to us, his mind preoccupied with travel.

My father equipped himself in the shortest possible time, achieving this by selling his cotton; he had a lot of it, around a hundredweight, because he'd sown a piece of land, of more than twenty feddans by the Egyptian measure, from which he would gather fourteen *réékas* every day at the height of the cotton season, the *rééka* being in Darfurian parlance what they call a *quffah* in Egypt; if one were to fill it with grain, it would perhaps take around five *rubʿ*s as these are measured in Egypt.[161] All of this he sold, and he also sold a sheep pasture and likewise the cattle and the donkeys. He took all his female and male slaves and everything I'd been given by Sayyid Aḥmad Badawī and Shaykh-Father Muḥammad Kurrā and left me only a female slave with cataracts in both eyes called Farḥānah, plus two male slaves and their wives, a donkey, and a weak riding camel. He also left with me one of his wives, called Zuhrah, and his brother's wife, each of whom had a daughter. And he sold the granaries, leaving me only one, and gave me the deed to the fief that had been written for him by the late Sultan ʿAbd al-Raḥmān when he'd granted him the land.[162] It went as follows: 2.2.34

> From the Grand Sultan and Most Eminent Refuge, sultan of the Arabs and the non-Arabs, in whose grasp are the necks of the nations, sultan of the two lands and the two seas, servitor of the two noble sanctuaries, who places his trust in the solicitude of the King who creates and recreates, Sultan ʿAbd al-Raḥmān al-Rashīd, to the petty kings, governors, *shartays*, *dimlijs*, sons of sultans, tax collectors, and people of the sultan's realm, be they Arabs or Blacks. Now, the above-named sultan—by God blessed, aided, made victorious, and supported—has deigned to extend his assistance to Erudite Scholar Sharif ʿUmar al-Tūnisī and grant him a parcel of land located at Abū l-Judūl and embracing the three villages of Ḥillat Jūltū, al-Dibbah, and Umm Baʿūḍah, according to their recognized boundaries and frontiers as demarcated by Malik Jawhar for Malik Khamīs ʿArmān,[163] no subject of the realm

حسبما حدّده الملك جوهر للملك خميس عَرْمان[1] لا يعارضه فيها معارض
ولا ينازعه منازع من أهل المملكة خصوصاً جبّايي العيش يتصرّف
فيها بأيّ نوع من وجوه التصرّفات شاء هبة لوجه الله تعالى وطلباً للثواب
في دار المآب والحذر ثمّ الحذر من الخلاف والتعرّض من الخاصّ أو العامّ

ثمّ إنّ والدي حمل أثقاله وأخذ رقيقه وسريّته وأخاه وتوجّه وأبقاني في الحلّة

وفي شهر رجب سنة ١٢١٩ قُتِلَ الأب الشيخ محمّد كرّا في حرب عظيم وقع بينه وبين السلطان محمّد فضل وسببه أنّ أعداء الأب الشيخ محمّد كرّا دخلوا بالفتنة والسعاية بينه وبين السلطان وقالوا للسلطان إنّ الأب الشيخ يريد نزع المملكة من يدك ويولّي عليها أخاه باسي عوض الله فأظلم الجوّ بينهما واحتال السلطان وجماعته في القبض عليه فلم يتيسّر له ذلك وانعزل الأب الشيخ بجماعته في بيت آخر كان له بتندلتي بعيداً عن بيت السلطان وأرسل له السلطان أن يأتي إليه فأبى فلمّا لم يجد السلطان وجماعته حيلة للقبض عليه وامتنع عنهم منعوه الماء فمكث ثلاثة أيّام يستقي من جديد السيل ثمّ لمّا اشتدّ العطش بجماعته قالوا له إنّا قد عطشنا وليس عندنا من الدوابّ والقِرَب ما يأتي لنا بالماء الذي يكفينا فارحل بنا إلى محلّ آخر نشرب منه الماء أو دبّر لنا حيلة ٣٥،٢،٢

فركب حينئذ هو وعسكره وتوجّه للرهد وهو غدير الماء بتندلتي فوجد عليه حارساً من دولة السلطان مع عسكر كثيف يمنع جماعته وهو الملك محمّد دلدن ابن عمّة السلطان محمّد فضل فقتله وقتل جماعته قتلاً ذريعاً وسمع بذلك جماعة السلطان فخرجوا عليه ونشب الحرب بينهما فانكشفت جماعة السلطان وكان ظهر يوم الخميس وخاف السلطان على نفسه ففرّ إلى جديد السيل وكان يوماً على السلطان وجماعته لا لهم وما زال الحرب بينهم حتّى أمسى المساء فنزل الأب الشيخ محمّد كرّا بجماعته في ٣٦،٢،٢

[1] الأصل: عزفان.

> being permitted to stand against him or challenge his right to these places, and specifically not those who collect the tax on the staple grains.[164] This is his to administer in any way he wills, as a gift for the sake of Almighty God and in the hope of reward in the Hereafter. Beware and beware again of any disagreement or objection, from noble or commoner!

Then my father loaded up his belongings, took his slaves, his troop of soldiers, and his brother, and set off, leaving me on my own in the village.[165]

In the month of Rajab 1219 [October–November 1804], Shaykh-Father Muḥammad Kurrā was killed in a great battle that broke out between him and Sultan Muḥammad Faḍl. Shaykh-Father Muḥammad Kurrā's enemies had driven a wedge between him and the sultan, using intrigue and slander and telling the latter that the shaykh-father wanted to wrest the kingdom from his hands and place over it his own brother, Báási ʿAwaḍ Allāh.[166] The atmosphere between them was fraught and the sultan and his men schemed to arrest him.[167] This was not easily done, however, as the shaykh-father had secluded himself and his men in another compound that belonged to him in Tandaltī, far from that of the sultan. The sultan sent someone to bring him in but he refused to go. When the sultan and his men could find no way to arrest him and he refused to obey their demands, they cut off his water supply and for three days he drank from Jadīd al-Sayl. When his men could stand the thirst no longer, they told him, "We're thirsty and don't have the animals or waterskins to bring us enough water—either take us to some other place, where there's water for us to drink, or come up with some other plan." 2.2.35

So he and his soldiery mounted and set off for al-Rahad, which is the pool at Tandaltī.[168] There he found a guard sent by the sultan's government with a mass of soldiery, barring their way. This was Malik Muḥammad Daldan, son of Sultan Muḥammad Faḍl's aunt. The shaykh-father killed him and his men in a dreadful slaughter. When the sultan's men heard about this, they set out against him and a battle broke out. The sultan's men were exposed—this was at noon on the Thursday—and the sultan, fearing for his safety, fled to Jadīd al-Sayl: it was a day that went against, not for, the sultan and his men. The fighting continued until evening, at which point Shaykh-Father Muḥammad Kurrā pitched camp with his men along the stream and the sultan's men pitched camp on the other side, opposite them, waiting for morning. During the night, the shaykh-father 2.2.36

عرض الغدير ونزل جماعة السلطان قبالتهم من الجانب الآخر حتّى أصبح الصباح وكان الأب الشيخ افتقد بالليل جماعته فوجد أخاه باسي عوض الله قد قتل في الحرب فحزن لذلك وقال لمن أقاتل وقد مات أخي وأعزّ الناس عندي وكان قد أخرج معه باسي طاهر بن السلطان أحمد بُكُرعمّ السلطان محمّد فضل وبايعه على السلطنة وتلك حيلة عملها لئلّا تنفر منه أهل دارفور لأنّ من عاداتهم ألّا يتولّى عليهم إلّا من كان من أولاد الملوك من بيت سلطنتهم[1]

٣٧،٢،٢ ولمّا علم بقتل أخيه قال لمن حوله إنّي قد كرهت الحياة في غد إيّاكم أن تقاتلوا بل أدخلوني في الحرب وانجوا أنتم بأنفسكم فحين شاع عنه ذلك فرّت جميع عساكره الأباعد ولم يبق معه إلّا ذوو قرابته في نفر يسير تبلغ عدّتهم ألفاً أو أكثر بقليل فلمّا أصبح ضربت طبول الحرب وركبت جماعة السلطان وركب هو أيضاً في جماعته وأدخلوه في الحرب والتحم القتال وغاص الأب الشيخ في جماعة السلطان واخترق الصفوف حتّى لم يبق بينه وبين السلطان أحد ولو أراد قتله لفعل ولكن تذكّر معروف أبيه فمنع يده عنه ووقف أمامه برهة وقال له يا ابن الفاعلة أتسمع فيّ كلام الناس ويكون هذا جزائي معك وخاف السلطان حينئذ على نفسه منه وأراد أن يفرّ ونادى قد جاء ليقتلني فانطبقت عليه الناس من كلّ جانب وداروا به كالخاتم بالإصبع ولم يجد معيناً ولا مساعداً فقاتل حسب طاقته وقتل عدّة أبطال وجرح جراحات غير بالغة فلم يكترث بها وخافوا أن يدركه أحد من جماعته فيخلص من أيديهم مع أنّ جماعته كلّها انكشفت عنه وبقي فيهم وحده فصار يقاتلهم نحو ساعة ثمّ لمّا عجزوا عنه عقروا جواده فوقع على الأرض فما استطاع النهوض لثقله لأنّه كان لابساً درعين من الحديد فتكاثروا وتكالبوا عليه بالرماح والسيوف حتّى قُتل رحمة الله عليه ولقد جُرّد بعد موته فوجد فيه ما ينوف عن مائة جرح من ضربة سيف وطعنة رمح ورجع ابن زوجته محمّد شيلفوت ظنّاً منه أن يجده حيّاً فينقذه من أيديهم فوجده قد قُتل

[1] الأصل: سلطانتهم.

inspected his men and discovered that his brother, Báási ʿAwaḍ Allāh, had been killed in the battle. He was grief-stricken and said, "For whom shall I fight when my brother, the person dearest to me, is dead?" Among those who had taken up arms with him was Báási Ṭāhir, son of Sultan Aḥmad Bukur, uncle of Sultan Muḥammad Faḍl, to whom he had pledged allegiance as sultan. This was a ruse by the shaykh-father to ensure that the Darfurians wouldn't regard him with aversion, for it was their custom that only someone who was the offspring of a royal personage from their sultanate's ruling family should rule over them.

When the shaykh-father learned of the death of his brother, he said to those around him, "I have come to hate this life. Tomorrow I forbid you to fight! Let me enter the battle and you save yourselves." When word of this got out, all his despicable soldiers fled and the only ones left were his relatives, who made up a small band not exceeding a thousand in number, or a little more. When morning came, the war drums sounded and the sultan's men mounted. The shaykh-father mounted too, in the midst of his men. They went into battle with him and the fighting began. The shaykh-father plunged into the midst of the sultan's men, breaking through the ranks till no one stood between him and the sultan—had he wanted to kill him he could have. However, he remembered the sultan's kindnesses toward him and stayed his hand, standing before him for a little while and addressing him as follows, "You son of a whore, would you listen to the lies people tell about me? Is this how you reward me?" At that moment, the sultan, fearing for his life at his hands and seeking to flee, called out, "He has come to kill me!" and people closed in on him from all sides and formed a circle around him, tight as a ring on a finger. Finding none to come to his aid, the shaykh-father fought them with all his might, killing several champions and sustaining only light wounds, to which he paid no heed. For their part, they were afraid that one of his own men would reach him and that he would escape them, even though all his men had been cut off from him and he was alone among the enemy. He therefore set to and fought them for about an hour. When they failed to reach him, they hamstrung his horse, which fell to the ground. He could not get up because of the weight—he was wearing two suits of chain mail—and they fell upon him in great numbers with spears and with swords until they had killed him, may God have mercy on his soul.[169] After his death, they stripped him and found on his body around a hundred wounds, sword blows, and lance thrusts. His wife's son, Muḥammad Shīlfūt,[170] returned, thinking he would find him alive and be able to save him, 2.2.37

فجرّد سيفه وغاص فيهم فقتل منهم عدّة أبطال وهو ينادي يا لثارات الأب الشيخ محمّد كرّا وأخيرًا تكالبوا عليه وقُتل هو الآخر بعد أن قتل أكثر من عشرين من المعدودين

٣٨،٢،٢ وإذ قد ذكرنا مقتل الأب الشيخ محمّد كرّا فلنذكر مبدأ أمره وكيف ترقّى به الحال ونتعرّض لسلاطين دارفور حسبما علمنا من ثقاتهم وأخبرني به الجمّ الغفير من مسنّيهم فأقول إنّ السلطان محمّد فضل هو ابن السلطان عبد الرحمن بن السلطان أحمد بكر. قيل إنّ السلطان أحمد بكر كان له من الولد سبعة بنين وهم عمر وأبو القاسم ورِيِّز ورِيفا وتَيْراب وطاهر وعبد الرحمن وهو المدعوّ باليتيم لأنّ أباه مات وتركه حملا فلما حضرته الوفاة جمع أرباب دولته وجعل ولاية العهد لجميع أولاده يتولّاها كلّهم الأكابر فالأكابر وشرط ألّا يتولّى هذا الأمر أحد من أولادهم إلّا بعد انقراضهم فلمّا توفّي تولّى أكبرهم المسمّى بعمر فمكث في الملك سبع سنين ثمّ قُتل في حرب كان بينه وبين السلطان جودة سلطان دار صُلَيح المسمّاة بدار واداي وبدار بَرْقو ثمّ تولّى بعده أخوه أبو القاسم فمكث ثمان سنين وقُتل في الحرب مع سلطان برقو أيضاً

٣٩،٢،٢ ثمّ تولّى بعده السلطان محمّد تيراب فكَرِهَ الحرب وأقام في بلده آمرًا ناهيًا سلطانًا ثلاثًا وثلاثين سنة إنّما سمّي تيراب أرض الشام لأنّ الفور يسمعون أنّ أرض الشام مخصبة وأنّها من أرض الجنّة سيّما وفيها المحشر وهي عشّ الأنبياء فلقّبوه بهذا اللقب لصدور الأفعال الجميلة منه كما أنّ أرض الشام نباتها كلّها جميل ومعنى التيراب بلغتهم الحبوب التي تزرع في التراب التي يعبّر عنها أهل مصر بالتقاوي وأهل المغرب بالزّريعة ولقّبوه بذلك لأنّه كان رجلاً كريماً حليماً واسع الصدر جيّد التدبير شفوقًا على المساكين وكان ذا أناة[1] وكان فيه مجون يحبّ الزينة وأنواع الملاهي وكانت أيّامه كلّها خصباً ودعة ورخاء أسعار إلّا أنّ آخر أمره كرهته الناس لظلم أولاده لأنّ له ما ينوف عن ثلاثين ولدًا ذكرًا[2] غير الإناث فصاروا يركبون ويجوسون خلال البلاد وكلّما سمعوا بشيء جميل أخذوه من صاحبه ويكلّفون الرعيّة ما لا تطيق حتّى كان فيهم ابن له

١ الأصل: كان اناءة. ٢ الأصل: ولد ذكر.

but he found he'd been killed, so he unsheathed his sword and plunged into their midst, killing a number of champions and calling out, "Revenge for Shaykh-Father Muḥammad Kurrā!" In the end, they fell upon him, and he too perished, but only after he'd killed more than twenty of those present.

Now that we've spoken of how Shaykh-Father Muḥammad Kurrā was killed, let us speak of his beginnings and of his rise to power. Let me also pass in review the sultans of Darfur according to the information we received from trustworthy informants among the people there and what I was told by most of their old people. Sultan Muḥammad Faḍl was the son of Sultan ʿAbd al-Raḥmān, son of Aḥmad Bukur. It is said that Sultan Aḥmad Bukur had seven sons—ʿUmar,[171] Abū l-Qāsim, Rīz, Rīfā, Tayrāb, Ṭāhir, and ʿAbd al-Raḥmān, known as the Orphan because his father died and left him while he was still in the womb. When death was close, Sultan Aḥmad Bukur gathered the high officers of the state and bestowed the succession on all his sons, who were each to rule the country, one after the other in order of age, and made it a condition that none of their children should take over until all the fathers were dead. Thus, when Aḥmad Bukur died, the oldest of them, ʿUmar, became the ruler. He reigned for seven years. He was killed in a battle between him and Sultan Jawdah,[172] sultan of Dār Ṣulayḥ, also known as Dār Wādday and Dār Barqū.[173] Then his brother al-Qāsim succeeded him and he too was killed in a war with the sultan of Barqū. 2.2.38

Al-Qāsim was succeeded by Sultan Muḥammad Tayrāb, who hated war and exercised absolute power in his country for thirty-three years. He was known as "Seed of Syria's Soil" because the Fur had heard that the earth in Syria was fertile, and was taken from the soil of Paradise, especially because it is there that the dead will be marshaled for judgment on the Last Day. It is also "the nest of the prophets." They gave the sultan this title because beautiful deeds issued from him, just as all the plants produced by the soil of Syria are beautiful.[174] The meaning of *tayrāb* in their language is "the seed that grows in the dirt (*turāb*)," or what Egyptians call *taqāwī* and western Arabs *zarrīʿah*.[175] They also gave him this title because he was a clement, generous man, forbearing, an excellent manager of affairs, and solicitous of the lowly. He was full of kindliness and enjoyed ribaldry, loving adornment and all kinds of sport. His rule was all abundance, peacefulness, and low prices—though toward the end of his days people hated him because of the injustices meted out by his offspring—he had around thirty male children, not to mention the females. These took to riding out and poking around in the country. 2.2.39

يقال له مساعد كان من عتوّه وتجبّره يأبى أن يركب الخيل بل كان يركب ظهور الآدميّين فكلّما وجد شاباً أمر بالقبض عليه وركبه حتّى أعياه وربّما سافر السفر البعيد لا يركب فيه جواداً ولا حماراً بل ينتقل على الناس حتّى ينتهي سفره وإذا لم يجد غريباً ركب من جماعته وكانت الرعيّة ترفع شكايتهم[1] لأبيهم فكان لا يُشْكيهم ولا يقبل منهم بل ربّما غضب وقال إنّ هذا لهو العجب إقليم مثل هذا لا يتحمّل أولادي وكلّما عملوا صغيرة يشكون إليّ فلمّا رأى الناس ذلك أبطلت الشكوى ورفعت أمرها إلى الله عزّ وجلّ

٤٠،٢،٢ وكان قد ولّى المناصب الجليلة لأقارب أزواجه فكانت جميع وزرائه أقارب زوجاته وكان أكبر أولاده إسحاق المسمّى بالخليفة. كان إسحاق المذكور شجاعاً مهاباً ذا رأي وحزم إلّا أنّه كان فيه نوع ظلم وجور وسبب تسميته بالخليفة أنّ أباه جعله خليفة بعده ولقّبه بهذا الاسم وجعل له دولة كدولته ووزراء كوزرائه فكلّ وزير كبير له ولد كان السلطان يأمره أن يأتي بابنه للخليفة ليكون عنده بمنزلة أبيه عند السلطان ومكث على ذلك مدّة حتّى سافر السلطان تيراب إلى كردفال وأبقاه خليفة في دارفور كما يأتي بيانه إن شاء الله تعالى وكان السلطان تيراب يحبّ الخلاعة والانبساط حتّى كانت الشبّان تلعب مع البنات أمامه أي يرقصن البنات والشبّان وهو ينظر إليهم فممّا اتّفق أن جاءت أمامه طائفة من البِرْقِد وهم قبيلة من السودان لهم رقص معلوم يسمّى تَنْدَكَّهْ ومن عاداتهم إذا تعبوا من الرقص تجلس كلّ فتاة وشابّ معاً على حدة فلعبوا حتّى تعبوا وتفرّقوا وجلسوا على عادتهم فقال الشابّ للفتاة أترضي أن أكون لك زوجاً فقالت نعم ما الذي تعطيني من المهر فقال لها أنا رجل فقير ولا أجد شيئاً أعزّ من المقابل لنا هذا وأشار إلى السلطان وكان السلطان جالساً على كرسيّ مقابلا لهما فقالت الفتاة قد رضيت ونظر السلطان لإشارتهما له فدعا بهما فلمّا مثلا بين يديه سألهما عن ذلك فقال الشابّ إنّي سألت محبوبتي هذه في أن تتزوّجني

[1] الأصل: وشكوهم.

Whenever they heard of something beautiful, they'd take it from its owner, and they imposed on their subjects more than the latter could bear. There was even one son, called Musāʿid, who in his arrogance and tyranny refused to ride horses, riding instead on the backs of men: whenever he found a young man, he would have him seized and ride him till he had worn him out. Sometimes he would cover great distances without mounting either horse or donkey but instead moving around on people, until his journey's end. If he couldn't find a stranger, he'd ride one of his own men. The subjects took their complaints to the father,[176] who refused to listen and would accept nothing they said; indeed, sometimes he'd grow impatient and say, "Now here's a wonder! A territory this big, and it can't support my sons? Whenever they commit some petty offense, the people come complaining to me?" When people saw this, they stopped complaining and referred their affairs to God, Great and Glorious.

Sultan Muḥammad Tayrāb used to appoint his wives' relations to high positions; all his viziers were relatives of his wives. His oldest son was Isḥāq, known as "the Successor." This Isḥāq was brave, inspired deference, and was a man of insight and resolve, but there was something of the tyrant and the despot in him. He was called the Successor because his father had appointed him to succeed him, given him that title, and created a government for him just like his own, with viziers like his, the sultan commanding every senior vizier who had a son to bring him to the Successor so that the boy could play the same role for him as the boy's father did for the sultan. This went on for a while, until Sultan Tayrāb traveled to Kordofan and left Isḥāq behind to rule Darfur, as we shall describe later, the Almighty willing. Sultan Tayrāb loved licentiousness and fun, to the point that boys would sport with girls in front of him, meaning that the girls and boys would dance together while he watched. Once it happened that a group of Birqid, a tribe of the Blacks who have a well-known dance called the *tindinga*, came before him. Now, it is a custom of theirs for each couple to go and sit together on their own when they tire of dancing, and so they did on this occasion. One of the boys said to his girl, "Would you like to have a husband?" and she said, "Yes. What will you give me as a dowry?" "I'm a poor man," he answered, "and see nothing more valuable to give you than the man sitting opposite us," and he pointed to the sultan, who was seated on a chair opposite them, and the girl said, "I accept." The sultan noticed that they were pointing at him and summoned them. When they stood before him, he asked them about it, and the boy said, "I asked my sweetheart here to marry me, and she agreed 2.2.40

فرضيت وطلبت منّي المهر فقلت لا أملك شيئاً أعزّ من هذا المقابل لي وأشرت إليك فانبسط لقوله وقال رضيت بي مهراً لها قال نعم فقال السلطان أترضيني بالفداء وأنا أفدي نفسي قالت نعم أرضى فدعا بأبيها وخطبها منه وعقد له عليها وأمهرها جاريتين وأعطى الرجل عبداً وأمر لهما برزق يعيشان فيه وهذا نهاية مكارم الأخلاق إذ لا شيء أعظم من جمع بين متحابّين في الحلال

ومن ذلك ما حكي عن أبي بكر الصدّيق رضي الله عنه أنّه كان في أيّام خلافته ٤١،٢،٢
يطوف في المدينة المنوّرة بالليل ليقف على أحوال الناس ويعلم مظلومهم من ظالمهم[١] وبينما هو في طوافه إذ سمع جارية تغنّي وتقول شعراً [كامل وإنّما الشطر الرابع من الطويل]

وَهَوِيْتُهُ مِنْ قَبْلِ قَطْعِ تَمِيمَتِي   مُتَمَايِسٌ مِثْلُ ٱلْقَضِيبِ ٱلنَّاعِمِ
فَكَأَنَّ نُورَ ٱلْبَدْرِ يُشْبِهُ وَجْهَهُ   يَغِيبُ وَيَبْدُو مِنْ ذُؤَابَةِ[٢] هَاشِمِ

فطرق رضي الله عنه الباب وقال لها من هويت فقالت إليك عنّي فقال لا بدّ وأن تعلميني فقالت له بحقّ صاحب القبر إلّا ما انصرفت عنّي فقال والله لست بزائل من مكاني هذا حتّى تعلميني فتنفّست الصعداء وقالت [كامل]

وأَنَا ٱلَّتِي قَرَحَ ٱلْغَرَامُ بِقَلْبِهَا   فُتِنَتْ بِحُبِّ محمّد بْنِ ٱلْقَاسِمِ

فقال لها أحرّة أنت فقالت لا بل مملوكة فقال لمن قالت لفلان سمّته له فتوجّه رضي الله عنه ولمّا أصبح سأل عن محمّد بن القاسم فوجده غازياً بالعراق فأرسل إلى مولاها واشتراها منه وأرسلها إلى محمّد بن القاسم بالعراق وكتب له القصّة ثمّ قال واعلم يا بنيّ أنّ كم مات بهنّ سقيم وعطب بهنّ سليم

---

١ الأصل: ظالم. ٢ الأصل: ذوابة.

and asked me what the dowry would be, so I said I own nothing more valuable than this man sitting opposite me and I pointed to you." The sultan was pleased with his words and said, "Do you agree that I be her dowry?" and the boy said, "Yes." Then the sultan said, "Will you agree to a swap, and that I buy myself back?" and she said, "Yes, I agree." Then he summoned her father, asked him for her hand, concluded the contract for her, paid her a dowry of two female slaves, gave the groom a male slave, and commanded the couple be given an income on which to live. This is the height of noble manners, for there is nothing greater than to bring two lovers together in sanctioned matrimony.

A similar example is to be found in the story told of Abū Bakr al-Ṣiddīq, may God be pleased with him, to the effect that when he was caliph, he would roam Medina the Illumined by night to find out how people were living and to discover which were oppressed and which oppressors. While on his rounds, he suddenly heard a young woman singing the following verses: 2.2.41

I loved him before the cutting of my amulet[177]—
whippy as a peeled wand,
A boy of Hāshim's best,[178] the moon's effulgence mimicking, it seemed
to me, his face
as it waxed and waned.

He then, may God be pleased with him, knocked on her door and asked her, "With whom did you fall in love?" to which she replied, "Leave me alone!" "You must tell me," he said. "By the dweller in the grave,"[179] she said, "leave me alone!" "I will not stir from where I stand till you tell me!" he said, so she heaved a sigh and said:

I am she whose heart by passion has been galled—
she who's in love with Muḥammad ibn al-Qāsim.[180]

"Are you a free woman?" he asked her. "No," she answered, "a bought slave." "Belonging to whom?" he asked, and she gave him the man's name. He left, may God be pleased with him, and the next morning asked after Muḥammad ibn al-Qāsim and found that he was raiding the infidels in Iraq, so he sent to her master, bought her from him, and sent her to Muḥammad ibn al-Qāsim in Iraq with a letter telling him the story. Then he recited, "Know, dear boy, that it's a matter of 'How many a one has died for them when sick and how many a one has perished at their hands though sound!'"[181]

٤٢،٢،٢ ومن ذلك ما حكي أنّ سليمان بن عبد الملك بن مروان كان غيورا على النساء جدّاً حتّى أنّه ربّما سفك دم من ظنّ أنّه نظر لبعض محاظيه نظر عشق فاتّفق له أن أحضر مغنيّاً في بعض الأيّام وكان في النهار فأجلس المغنّي تحت السرير وأمره أن يغنّي واستلقى على ظهره على السرير وكانت معه جارية تروّح عليه من شدّة الحرّ فأخذه النوم فرفع المغنّي رأسه على حين غفلة فرأى الخليفة قد نام والجارية تروّح عليه فتأمّلها فوجدها كالشمس في رابعة النهار فافتتن بها ولم يقدر على التكلّم خوفاً من الخليفة فانهملت دموعه وهاج ولوعه فأخذ قرطاساً وكتب فيه شعراً [كامل]

إِنِّي رَأَيْتُكِ فِي ٱلْمَنَامِ ضَجِيعَتِي   مُسْتَرْشِفاً مِنْ رِيقِ فِيكِ ٱلْبَارِدِ
وَكَأَنَّنَا وَكَأَنَّنَا وَكَأَنَّنَا   بِتْنَا جَمِيعاً فِي فِرَاشٍ وَاحِدِ

ثمّ ألقاه عليها فأخذته وقرأته وكتبت له فيه [كامل]

خَيْرًا رَأَيْتَ وَكُلُّ مَا أَمَّلْتَهُ   سَتَنَالُهُ مِنِّي بِرَغْمِ ٱلْحَاسِدِ
وَتَبِيتَ بَيْنَ خَلَاخِلِي وَدَمَالِجِي   وَتَحُلُّ بَيْنَ مَرَاشِفِي وَسَوَاعِدِي
وَنَكُونُ أَوَّلَ صَاحِبَيْنِ تَلَاقَيَا   رَغْمَ ٱلزَّمَانِ بِلَا مَخَافَةِ حَاسِدِ

ورمت القرطاس إليه فالتقفه الخليفة قبل أن يصل إليه فلمّا قرأه احمرّت عيناه وكاد يتميّز غيظاً وقال ما حملكما على ما صنعتما أحبّ قديم بينكما أم عشق خامركما في هذه الساعة فقالا بل والله في هذه الساعة ولم يكن لنا به عهد قبل ذلك وانهملت دموعهما فلمّا رأى منهما ذلك رقّ لهما وقال للمغنّي خذها ولا تعد تقاربنا انتهى

٤٣،٢،٢ فعاش السلطان تيراب مدّة مديدة كما ذكرنا وأكثر من الأزواج والسراري حتّى كان له من الولد أكثر من ثلاثين ذكراً راكبين الخيل غير الإناث والصغار وفي أيّامه تلك خدمه الأب الشيخ محمّد كرّا وكان غلاماً مراهقاً فأمره أن يكون في الكوركوا أي

Likewise, the story is told that Sulaymān ibn ʿAbd al-Malik ibn Marwān was extremely jealous where women were concerned—so much so that he was capable of shedding the blood of anyone he suspected of looking amorously at one of his concubines. Once he had a musician brought (this was during the day), had him seated below his couch, and ordered him to sing, while he lay back on the couch. He had a slave girl fanning him because it was so hot, and he fell asleep. The musician raised his head without warning and, seeing that the caliph was asleep while the slave girl fanned him, took a good look at her and found her to be as radiant as the sun at its prime. Enchanted, yet unable to talk to her for fear of the caliph, his tears gushed and his desire surged, so he took a sheet of paper and wrote on it: 2.2.42

In my dreams I saw you in my bed
while I drank up the cool saliva of your mouth—
As if . . . as if . . . as if . . .
we' d spent the night as one, upon a single couch.

Then he tossed the piece of paper to her. She took it, read it, and wrote on it:

How well you saw, and all that you desire
of me you'll get, in spite of any who may envy.
You'll spend the night between my anklets and my bracelets
and melt between my lips and you'll embrace me,
And we shall be the first two lovers to meet,
despite the times, without fear of any jealousy.

She tossed the paper to him but the caliph caught it before it got to him. When he read it, his eyes turned red, he almost exploded with fury, and he said, "What drove you to do this? Is this a longstanding love between you or a passion that has just taken hold?" "Not at all," they said. "It took us, we swear, at this very moment, and we knew nothing of it before," and their tears gushed. When he saw their state, he felt pity for them and told the singer, "Take her, and let us never see you again."

Sultan Tayrāb lived long, as we have mentioned, and took many wives and concubines, such that he had more than thirty male children old enough to ride horses, not to mention females and younger ones. It was during this period that Shaykh-Father Muḥammad Kurrā entered his service, though he was still only an adolescent. The sultan ordered him to join the *kóór kwa*, or warriors, 2.2.43

أهل الحرب أي يكون مع الجماعة الذين يحملون الحراب خلف السلطان حين يركب وحين يجلس للحكم ولا خصوصيّة للسلطان في ذلك بل كل ملك من ملوك الفور وقائد من قوّادهم له جماعة يحملون الحراب خلفه حين يركب أو يجلس للحكم مسمّون كوركوا ويرون أنّ ذلك من تمام نظام المُلْك حفظاً للناموس وهيبة للمخدوم في قلوب رعاياه فخدم الأب الشيخ محمّد كرّا في تلك الخدمة مدّة وظهرت منه علامات النجابة فأحبّه السلطان تيراب ونقله إلى سُومِينْدُقَلَهَ والسوم هو الدار وين هو علامة الإضافة والدقله هو العيال ومعناه دُرا العيال والدرا بلغتهم العربيّة اسم للمحلّ أو الدار وأهل سوميندقله هم الأمناء على مصالح المخدوم يرسلهم في أسراره. رئيسهم أعظم مقاماً من رئيس كوركوا

فأغنى في خدمته حتّى أنّ السلطان كان لا ينادي في أكثر حوائجه غيره فحسده بعض أهل الدار فسعى به إلى السلطان قائلاً[1] إنّ محمد كرّا خائن غدّار وأنا أراه يجتمع هو وفلانة الحظيّة في كلّ ليلة وتأتيه بالطعام الجميل فغضب السلطان لذلك وهمّ بالبطش به فبلغ الخبر إلى كرّا فأخذ مدية واختلى بنفسه في حجرة واستأصل مذاكير نفسه بيده وجاء بها إلى السلطان وكان قريباً منه وألقاها بين يديه وقال إنّما قيل فيّ ما قيل لمصاحبتي لهذه وها أنا قد استأصلتها لئلاّ يبقى في قلب مولاي منّي ريب ثمّ سقط مغشيّاً عليه فرحمه السلطان وأمر بمداواته فعولج حتّى برئ ثمّ إنّ السلطان أمره أن يكون صحبة الأمين عليّ وَدْ جامع أحد الوزراء العظماء ووصّى عليه الأمين المذكور بأن قال له خذ هذا الغلام إلى دُراك واعتنِ به وأكرمه وإيّاك أن تتهاون به فإنّي أرجو أن يخلفك في منصبك فأخذه الأمين على مضض منه ووضعه في سوميندقله كما كان عند السلطان وقد ذكرنا قريبا أنّ أهل سوميندقله هم الأمناء على المصالح المهمّة يرسلهم المخدوم في أسراره ٤٤،٢،٢

[1] الأصل: قائل.

meaning he should be one of the company who carry spears behind the sultan when he rides out and when he sits in judgment. This is not something peculiar to the sultan: every one of the petty kings of the Fur as well as every one of their commanders has men called *kóór kwa* who carry spears behind him when he rides out or sits in judgment. In their eyes, it is an essential part of the apparatus of royal rule, required to preserve the natural order and inspire dread of the overlord in his subjects' hearts. Shaykh-Father Muḥammad Kurrā served in this role for a period, and showed signs of promise. Sultan Tayrāb therefore loved him and transferred him to the *soom'íng dogólá*. *Soom* means "house," *–íng* is the marker of the genitive, and *dogólá* means "children," and it means, as they would say, "the *durā* of the children," *durā* being a word for "place" or "house" in their dialect of Arabic.[182] The people of the *soom'íng dogólá* are the agents who oversee their master's business; he sends them on his confidential missions and their chief is of higher standing than the chief of the *kóór kwa*.

Shaykh-Father Muḥammad Kurrā grew rich in the sultan's service, and eventually the sultan would call on no one else for most of his needs. As a result, a member of the household became jealous of him and told tales against him to the sultan, saying, "Muḥammad Kurrā is a traitor and an ingrate, and I see him meeting every night with so-and-so, the concubine, who brings him delicious food." This infuriated the sultan, who decided to take ruthless action against him. Word of it reached Kurrā, who took a knife, went into a room on his own, and cut off his genitals with his own hand. Then he took them to the sultan, who was nearby, and threw them down in front of him, saying, "The only reason rumors have spread about me is that I am equipped with these. See, now I have cut them off so that the heart of my master the sultan can harbor no further suspicion of me." Then he fainted. As a result, the sultan had mercy on him and ordered that he be cared for until he was better. Subsequently, the sultan commanded that he be attached to Counselor[183] 'Alī wad Jāmi', one of the grand viziers, recommending him to him with the words, "Take this youth into your household. Look after him, treat him well, and woe betide you should you treat him with disrespect, for I expect him to succeed you in your office." The counselor therefore took him, against his will, into the *soom'íng dogólá*, with the same rank he had held with the sultan. As we just explained, the people of the *soom'íng dogólá* are the agents of the sultan who oversee important business and whom the master of the household sends on confidential missions. 2.2.44

٤٥،٢،٢ فجلس محمّد[١] كرّا في ذلك المحلّ مدّة وكان لا يغيب عن باب مخدومه وكلّما نادى الأمين على أحد من أهل سوميندقله يجيبه محمّد كرّا بل ربّما لم يجد غيره فكان يرسله في قضاء مصالحه وكان من عادته ألّا يذهب لقضاء مصلحة إلّا نجح وأغنى فيها فأحبّه الأمين قهرًا عنه لما رأى من كفايته فجعله ملكًا على أهل سوميندقله وميّزه عنهم فصارت جميع الخدمة تحت يده يأتمرون بأمره وحين ولي هذا المنصب اجتهد في الخدمة زيادة عمّا كان عليه ولازم باب مخدومه

٤٦،٢،٢ وكان في الأمين نوع إهمال للأمور منه أنّه كان يأتيه من الطعام وقت الغداء والعشاء ما ينوف عن ألف إناء فكان لا يلتفت إلى ذلك بل كان يأتيه هو ومن معه ما يكفيهم والباقي تتوزّعه الخدمة بغير ترتيب وكثير من الآنية ما يرجع إلى الحريم ملآنًا فالتفت محمّد كرّا إلى ذلك ورتّبه أحسن ترتيب وهو أنّه كان يبثّ الخدمة في أتباع سيّده ينظرون من عنده ضيف منهم فيأتونه بالأخبار ويقولون فلان عنده ضيف وفلان وهلمّ جرًّا فكان إذا حضر الطعام اختار لمخدومه من أحسنه ما يكفيه هو ومن معه ثمّ يوزّع على الخدمة كفايتهم ثمّ يوزّع الباقي على محالّ الضيوف كلّ منها على حسب حاله في المرتبة والغنى والجاه والعلم ويوصّي الحاملين أن يقولوا إنّ الأمين أرسل لكم هذا ضيافة والأمين لا يعلم شيئًا من ذلك فصارت الناس تشكر الأمين وتتمدّح به وحين يأتون إليه يقولون جزاك الله خيرًا أرسلت لنا الضيافة العظيمة فلا يوجد نظيرك في أمناء السلطان ويثنون عليه غيبة وحضورًا

٤٧،٢،٢ فكان الأمين يتعجّب من ذلك ويقول هؤلاء يثنون عليّ ويقولون إنّي أرسلت لهم الطعام مع أنّي لم أفعل شيئًا من ذلك لأنّه لا يعلم سببه وبقي متحيّرًا كيف يعلم سبب ذلك حتّى اتّفق له أن كان في الحريم عند المساء وجاء خارجًا إلى الديوان فرأى محمّد كرّا يوزّع الأطعمة فلمّا أحسّ بذلك تربّس وأكمن[٢] في محلّ فسمع الأب الشيخ محمّد يقول للخدمة كم في بيت الملك فلان من الضيوف فقالوا له كذا وكذا فقال احملوا

---

[١] أضيف للسياق: محمد. [٢] أي: تربص وكمن.

Muḥammad Kurrā remained there for a while. He would never leave his master's door, and whenever the counselor called for someone from the *soom'íng dogólá*, Muḥammad Kurrā would answer; often, indeed, he would find no one else. He would therefore send him to see to his affairs. It was Muḥammad Kurrā's custom never to set out to take care of some business without ensuring that he did so successfully and made himself useful. Thus, despite himself, the counselor came to love him for the competence he saw in him and he put him in charge of the people who worked in the *soom'íng dogólá*, giving him a special status. All the servants thus ended up under his command. On assuming this position, Muḥammad Kurrā made even greater efforts to serve than he had before and never left his master's door. 2.2.45

Now, the counselor was a bit lax. For example, at lunch and at dinner, about a thousand dishes of food would be sent to him. He gave no thought to this. On the contrary, he'd be sent enough for him and anyone with him, and the rest the servants would distribute haphazardly. Often the dishes would return to the women's quarters full. Muḥammad Kurrā noticed this and organized things very well: he'd send the servants in among his master's followers and see which of them had a guest; the servants would then let him know and say, "So-and-so has a guest, and also so-and-so," and so on. Then, when the food came, he'd select enough of the best of it to satisfy his master and those with him, give that amount to the servants to give to them, then distribute the rest among the guests, each according to his condition in terms of rank, wealth, standing, and learning, instructing the bearers to tell them, "The counselor has sent you this hospitality," though the counselor was quite unaware of what was going on. Then everyone would thank the counselor and sing his praises, and when they came to see him they'd say, "God reward you with good fortune! You sent us wonderful hospitality. There's no one else like you among the sultan's agents," and they'd praise him, in his presence and out of it. 2.2.46

Since he didn't know why, the counselor was astonished and said, "These people thank me and say I sent them food when I did nothing of the sort!" For a while he was at a loss as to the reason. When he happened to be in the women's quarters one evening, he came out into the public offices and saw Muḥammad Kurrā distributing the different dishes. As he became aware of what was going on, he concealed himself in a chamber and waited. Then he heard Shaykh-Father Muḥammad ask the servants, "How many guests are there in the house of such and such a high official?" and heard them answer 2.2.47

لهم كذا وكذا إناء وقولوا لهم قد أرسل هذا العشاء الأمين حتّى وزّع الطعام كلّه فقال من هنا جاء العمل فضنّ به وأكرمه وأعلى رتبته وجعله على الكورايات وفي عرفهم هو الذي يحكم على الخيل وجميع الخدمة وهو منصب جليل عندهم وإن كان في عرف غيرهم لم يخرج عن كونه رئيس السُيّاس وأقام محمّد كرّا في صحبة الأمين عليّ على هذه الحالة حتّى سافر الأمين عليّ إلى كردفال صحبة السلطان تيراب وسافر معه الأب الشيخ محمّد كرّا

سبب سفر السلطان محمّد تيراب إلى كردفال

٤٨،٢،٢ قد حكى لي الثقة العارف بالأنساب أنّ السلطان سَلوگ المدعوّ سليمان الجدّ الأوّل لسلاطين دارفور كان له أخ يقال له المسبَّع فاقتسم هو وأخوه الإقليمين فأخذ السلطان سليمان إقليم دارفور وأخذ المسبّع إقليم كردفال وتعاهدا ألّا يخون أحد منهما صاحبه فبقيا كذلك حتّى كان في زمن السلطان محمّد تيراب. كان الوالي على كردفال من أولاد المسبّع السلطان هاشم المسبّعاويّ وكان فيه شهامة وشجاعة وإقدام على الأمور الشاقّة فأكثر الغزوات على بلاد التُروج والعرب البادية حتّى صار ذا مال عظيم وصار عنده من العبيد ما ينوف عن عشرة آلاف عبد حامل للسلاح واجتمعت عليه أوباش[1] الناس من الدناقلة والشايجية والكبابيش وعرب الرُزيقات حتّى صار في جند كثيف فطمعت نفسه في تملّك دارفور واستشار أرباب دولته في ذلك فأشاروا عليه أن يبثّ السرايا أوّلاً على أطراف البلاد ليضعفوا أهل مملكة دارفور ثمّ بعد ذلك يتوجّه إليها فسمع قولهم وبثّ السرايا على أطراف مملكة دارفور فقتلت وسبت واغتنمت أموالاً عظيمة فأرسل السلطان تيراب إلى السلطان هاشم يقول له

١ الأصل: ارباش.

with this or that figure, at which the shaykh-father would say, "Take them such and such vessels and tell them, 'The counselor sends you this dinner.'" In this way he distributed all the food. "So this is where it all comes from!" said the counselor, and after that he clung to him as to a precious object, treating him magnanimously, raising his rank, and putting him in charge of the *kūrāyāt*, who, in their parlance, are the persons who manage the horses and all the servants. It is a position held in great esteem among them, though in the practice of other nations he would simply be head groom. Muḥammad Kurrā stayed with Counselor ʿAlī in this capacity until the latter traveled to Kordofan in the entourage of Sultan Tayrāb, at which point Shaykh-Father Muḥammad Kurrā went with him.

Why Sultan Muḥammad Tayrāb Went to Kordofan

A trusted authority on pedigrees told me that Sultan Solóng, known as Sulaymān, the original ancestor of the sultans of Darfur, had a brother called al-Musabbaʿ, and that he and his brother divided up the two territories: Sultan Sulaymān took Darfur and al-Musabbaʿ took Kordofan,[184] and they made a pact that neither would betray the other, and the two territories remained thus until the reign of Sultan Muḥammad Tayrāb. The ruler of Kordofan then was Sultan Hāshim al-Musabbaʿāwī, a descendant of al-Musabbaʿ. Possessed of great manliness, courage, and enterprise in the execution of demanding affairs, he carried out numerous raids against the lands of the Turūj and the Bedouin of the desert and became very wealthy. He had some ten thousand armed slaves, and a rabble made up of people from Dongola, and the Shayijiyyah,[185] Kabābīsh, and Rizayqāt Arab tribes rallied to him. Together they formed a massive army.[186] His greed then urged him to take over Darfur. He consulted the chief officers of his government and they advised him to first dispatch squadrons of troops to harry the borders and thus weaken the Darfurians, and then go there himself. He accepted their advice and the squadrons he sent to the Darfurian borders murdered, took captives, and made off with large herds of animals. Sultan Tayrāb then sent Sultan Hāshim a letter in which he wrote: 2.2.48

بعد السلام يا ابن عمّي أرسلت سراياك على أطراف بلادي وأنت تعلم ما بيننا من المودّة ولم يقع منّا ما يخالف المودّة مع أنّك تعلم أنّ الذين أخذت أموالهم مسلمون والذين قتلوا موحّدون وهذا الفعل لا[1] يبيحه أحد ولا يفعله عاقل فإذا وصلك كتابي هذا فانته وإلّا سيلقى الباغي مصرعه والسـلام

٤٩،٢،٢ فلمّا وصله الكتاب ما زاد إلّا عتوًّا واستكبارًا وبثّ السرايا ثانيًا فعلم السلطان تيراب أنّه إن لم يتداركه ويستأصل شأفته زاد شرّه وأخرب البلاد فتجهّز وتوجّه إليه وهذا هو السبب الظاهر والسبب الباطن أنّه يعلم أنّ الناس غير راضيين عنه ولا يرضون بتولية أحد من أولاده خصوصًا مع وجود أولياء عهد السلطان أحمد بكر الذين هم أعمامهم ولا سيّما إذا تذكّروا ما وقع منه ومن أولاده من الظلم وهو يريد أن يعهد إلى أكبر أولاده المسمّى بإسحاق الخليفة كما تقدّم فاغتنم الفرصة حين وقع من هاشم ملك كردفال هذا الأمر واغتاظ في الظاهر وأعلن أنّ هذا الأمر لا يقوم به غيره مع أنّه لو بعث الأمين عليّ أو أحد وزرائه لكفاه مؤونة السفر[2] والمشقّة ولكن أراد أن يسافر ويأخذ معه جميع أولاد السلطان كبارًا وصغارًا ويقتحم بهم الحروب حتّى يهلكهم ويهلك الوزراء الذين لا يحبّون الولاية لابنه ليتمكّن إسحاق من البلاد والأموال والرجال وينفرد بالذكر

٥٠،٢،٢ ولمّا كانت هذه نيّته جمع جميع أولاد السلطان والوزراء الكبار وأبقى مع الخليفة أولاد الوزراء كلّ منهم في منصب والده وارتحل بهم على هذه النيّة وإن كان أخفاها فقد ظهرت على حدّ قول القائل [طويل]

١ الأصل: لم. ٢ الأصل: للسفر.

> Greetings, Cousin. You have dispatched your squadrons to the borders of my country though you know of the love between us and that we have done nothing to violate that love. At the same time, you know that those whose animals have been taken are Muslims and those who have been murdered acknowledged the oneness of God. These are deeds that no man regards as lawful and that no man in his right mind would undertake. Desist, therefore, when this letter of mine reaches you, or the wrongdoer shall meet his end. Farewell.

When the letter reached him, Sultan Hāshim's insolence and arrogance only increased and he dispatched his squadrons a second time. Sultan Tayrāb realized that if he didn't take steps to prevent him and remove him root and branch, his evil deeds would only increase and would lead to the ruination of the country. He therefore made his preparations and set off against him. This was Sultan Tayrāb's overt motive. His covert motive was that he knew his people were unhappy with him and wouldn't agree to be ruled by any of his sons, especially since the signatories to the pact of Aḥmad Bukur, namely, his uncles, were still alive,[187] and especially when they thought of the injustices he and his sons had committed. The sultan himself wanted the succession to pass to his eldest son, known as Isḥāq the Successor, as previously noted.[188] So, when Hāshim, King of Kordofan, did what he did, he seized the opportunity and put on a show of anger, proclaiming that only he could take care of the matter, though had he sent Counselor ʿAlī, or one of his viziers, he could have saved himself the supplies for the journey and its hardships. He was, however, determined to make the journey and take with him all the sultan's sons, young and old,[189] and to plunge them into battle and thus destroy them, and with them the viziers. The latter did not want the succession to go to his son, as it would mean that Isḥāq would take control of the country, its wealth and its men, and be the only one to go down in history.[190] 2.2.49

Having decided on this, he gathered all the sons of Sultan Aḥmad Bukur and the grand viziers, and set off with them, leaving the viziers' children with the Successor, each in the office held by his father[191]—yet even though he hid his intentions, they still become apparent in the end, in keeping with the words of the poet who said: 2.2.50

وَمَهْمَا تَكُنْ عِنْدَ ٱمْرِئٍ مِنْ خَلِيقَةٍ وَإِنْ خَالَهَا تَخْفَى عَلَى ٱلنَّاسِ تُعْلَمِ

مع أنه عومل بخلاف قصده وأعقبه الله تعالى بقتل ولده ولم ينفع تدبيره بشيء ورحم الله القائل [مجزوء الرمل]

إِنَّ أَلْطَافَ إِلٰهِي لَمْ تَدَعْ فِي ٱلْكَوْنِ ضَنْكَا
كُلَّمَا رُمْتُ ٱحْتِيَالًا لِي قَالَتْ خَلِّ عَنْكَا
سَلِّمِ ٱلْأَمْرَ إِلَيْنَا نَحْنُ أَوْلَى بِكَ مِنْكَا

وفي كون الأمور دائماً تأتي على خلاف المراد قال المتنبي [بسيط]

مَا كُلُّ مَا يَتَمَنَّى ٱلْمَرْءُ يُدْرِكُهُ تَأْتِي ٱلرِّيَاحُ بِمَا لَا تَشْتَهِي ٱلسُّفُنُ

٥١،٢،٢ فلمّا سمع ملك كردفال بقدومه فرّهو وجماعته واستجار بملك سنّار وأقام عنده فدخلها بغير حرب وصار يبثّ السرايا والجند في أطراف البلاد حتّى دوّخها وجبى الأموال واستقامت الأحوال فمكث على ذلك حتّى حال الحول وملّت الناس من المقام وسألوه العود إلى بلادهم فغضب لعدم ظفره بما أمل لكنّه أخفى ذلك وقال لهم كيف ترجعون وقد بلغني أنّ هاشم استجار بملك سنّار والملكّ قد جهّز له جيشاً ويريد القدوم علينا فإن رجعنا وجاء بعدنا ظنّ أنّا فررنا منه ونال من البلد مراده وبعد ذلك يغزونا ويحُوجنا إلى الرجوع له ثانياً وأنا الآن مضمر أنّي أتوجّه إليه قبل أن يأتي ولكن حتّى أتحقّق الخبر

٥٢،٢،٢ ومكثوا بعد ذلك مدّة فلم يظهر لما قاله أثر فتنكّرت قلوبهم وساءت أحوالهم واشتاقوا إلى أهلهم وعيالهم وتذاكروا مع بعضهم في ذلك خلوة فقال الوزير الأمين عليّ ود برقو وكان صهر السلطان أي أنّ السلطان كان متزوّجاً بابنته

Any qualities a man may have,
    though he think them hidden from others, will become well
        known.[192]

In reality, however, the treatment he received from God was the opposite of what he intended: the Almighty punished him with the death of his son, and all his planning went for nothing. God bless the poet who said:

Verily, the kindnesses of my God
    have left not a strait in the world for me to suffer.
Whenever I wish to pull off some gambit
    they tell me, "Have done!
Leave things to us—
    we've a better right to you than you yourself, or any other."

In this world, things always work out the opposite of what one wishes. As al-Mutanabbī says:[193]

Not all a man hopes for does he attain—
    the winds may blow in ways the ships do not desire.

When the King of Kordofan heard that Sultan Tayrāb was coming, he fled with his men and sought refuge with the King of Sinnār, in whose country he took up residence. The sultan thus entered the land without a fight and set about sending out squadrons and cavalry troopers to all corners of the country, until he had subjugated it and collected taxes, and things were quiet. He remained there a full year, by the end of which his forces had become fed up with inactivity and asked if they could go back to their own country. This angered him, as he hadn't achieved his goal, but he hid this and asked, "How can we go back when I'm told Hāshim has taken refuge with the Makk of Sinnār, who has raised him an army and is planning to attack us? If we go back and he comes after we've left, he'll think we fled before him and that he has gotten what he wanted from the country. Then he'll raid us and force us to go back again. I am presently mulling over whether I should set off against him before he comes—but let us wait till the news is confirmed." 2.2.51

They went on like this for a while, but nothing the sultan told them materialized, so their hearts became estranged and their morale worsened. Homesick for their wives and children, they conspired in secret. The vizier, Counselor 2.2.52

ماذا جعلتم لي إن قتلته وأرحتكم منه وتولّون بعده عليكم من شئتم فضمنوا له مالاً عظيماً وتعاهدوا معه على ذلك وجعل بينه وبينهم العلامة صوت الطبل فمهما سمعوا الطبل يكونوا على أهبة مستحضرين فصبر الأمين عليّ حتّى جنّ الليل ولبس درعين سابغين متينين ولبس ثيابه عليهما وتقلّد بسيفه ودخل دار السلطان وقصد حجرة ابنته لما يعلم من حبّ السلطان لها لأنّ السلطان كان له بها مزيد اعتناء فكثيرًا ما كان يجده عندها فلمّا دخل عليها عرفت الشرّ في وجهه وخانه جدّه. إنّ السلطان لم يكن عندها في تلك الليلة فسألها عن السلطان فقالت لا أعلم أين هو ولكن إن أردت بحثت لك عنه وأعلمته[1] بقدومك فقال لها نعم ما تصنعين لأنّي شديد الاحتياج إليه في هذه الليلة وكانت في وقت محادثتها له رأت طوق الدرع من تحت طوق الثوب فتأكّدت الشرّ وذهبت إلى محلّ السلطان وأعلمته أنّ أباها جاء طالباً له وأنها رأت منه أمورًا أنكرتها منها أنّه لابس درعاً تحت ثيابه ومتقلّد سيفه مع أنّ العادة أنّهم[2] لا يدخلون على السلطان بسيف أبدًا ومنها أنّ في وجهه علامة الغضب فأحسّ السلطان بالشرّ لأنّه هو الذي كان يلحّ عليه بالعود ويبالغ في القول له فأمرها ألّا تعود إليه وخرج السلطان ونادى كبراء العسس وأمرهم بالقبض على من جاء خارجاً عن الدار وإن أفلت منهم لا يلومون إلّا نفسهم وأخذ هو جماعة منهم حرساً له متأهّبين[3] بأسلحتهم وغاص في لُجّة داره ودخل في حجرة[4] بعض نسائه واحتاط الحرس بها

٥٣،٢،٢ فجلس الأمين عليّ في انتظار ابنته تعود فلم تعد إليه بخبر السلطان أو أنّ السلطان يأتي إليه ليبلغ أربه منه فلم يأته أحد بل كان كالباحث عن حتفه بظلفه والجادع مارنَ أنفه بكفّه على حدّ قوله [مجزوء الوافر]

إِلَى حَتْفِي سَعَى قَدَمِي أَرَى قَدَمِي أَرَاقَ دَمِي

١ الأصل: واعلمه. ٢ أضيف للسياق: أنّهم. ٣ الأصل: متأهيين. ٤ الأصل: حجر.

ʿAlī wad Barqū, the sultan's in-law (the sultan being married to his daughter), said to them, "What will you do for me if I kill him and rid you of him, leaving you free to appoint whomever you like to rule over you?" and they gave him guarantees of great wealth and made a pact with him to that effect. They agreed that the sign for them to act should be the sound of the drums, and that they would be ready and listening out for them. Counselor ʿAli waited until night fell, then dressed in two coats of strong, body-length chain mail, over which he put his clothes. He buckled on his sword, entered the sultan's house, and made his way to his daughter's chamber, knowing full well how the sultan loved her, for the sultan was extremely solicitous of her, and he had often found him there. When he entered, she saw the evil in his face, and his luck let him down too: the sultan wasn't with her that night. He asked her about the sultan and she said, "I don't know where he is, but if you like I'll look for him and tell him you've come." "That would be a good thing for you to do," he replied, "as I need to see him urgently tonight." While they were talking, she noticed the collar of the coat of mail underneath the collar of his top clothes and became convinced that evil was afoot. She went to the sultan and informed him that her father had come looking for him and that she had noticed things that made her suspicious, among them that he was wearing chain mail under his clothes, had his sword strapped on—even though it was their custom that no one ever went to see the sultan wearing a sword—and that she had seen signs of anger in his face. The sultan now realized that evil was afoot, for it was Counselor ʿAlī who had been urging him to go back, speaking to him in the strongest terms. The sultan ordered her not to go back to him and went out and summoned the chief officers of the watch, ordering them to arrest anyone who tried to leave the house, saying that if any escaped they would have only themselves to blame for the consequences. He himself took several of them, fully armed, as guards, plunged into the depths of his house, entered the bedchamber of one of his wives, and placed a guard around it.

Counselor ʿAlī sat waiting for his daughter to come back, but she did not, and neither did the sultan, that ʿAlī might have his way with him. Indeed, no one came and he was like the sheep that digs its grave with its own hoof,[194] or the man who cuts off his nose with his own hand. As the poet[195] says: 2.2.53

> To my demise my foot has led me—
> meseems my foot has shed my blood.

ولمّا أعياه الانتظار قام يريد الذهاب إلى داره خوفاً من أن يطلع النهار عليه ويفتضح فمشى قليلاً حتّى إذا قارب العسس نهضوا إليه وقالوا له ارجع حيث كنت فأبى وعرّفهم بنفسه لأجل أن يخلوا سبيله فما أمكن بل قالوا له نحن مأمورون بالقبض عليك إن لم ترجع إلى المحلّ الذي جئت منه فسبّهم وأراد أن يخرج قهراً عنهم فهجموا عليه ليُوثِقوه حتّى يصبح فقاتلهم وجرح أناسا منهم فتكالبوا عليه وقتلوه ولم يستفد من بغيه إلّا فناء أجله ولهذا قال عليه الصلاة والسلام لكلّ باغٍ مصرع أو كما قال رحمه الله السيّد عليّ الغراب حيث يقول [خفيف]

زَارِعُ ٱلْبَغْيِ حَاصِدٌ لِلنَّدَامَهْ فَٱطْلُبِ ٱلسِّلْمَ إِنْ أَرَدْتَ ٱلسَّلَامَهْ
لَا تَثِقْ بِٱلْمُنَى فَمَا كُلُّ بَاغٍ نَالَ مَا يَرْتَجِي وَوُفِّي مَرَامَهْ
رُبَّمَا كَانَتِ ٱلْأَمَانِي مَطَايَا لِلْمَنَايَا وَمَوْرِدًا لِلنَّدَامَهْ
رُبَّمَا خَيَّلَتْ لِرَاجٍ مَنَالًا مِثْلَمَا خَيَّلَتْ لِرَاءٍ مَنَامَهْ
رُبَّ سَاعٍ لِيَجْتَنِي طِيبَ عَيْشٍ وَهْوَ يَجْنِي وَلَيْسَ يَدْرِي حِمَامَهْ

٥٤،٢،٢ وأُخبر السلطان حينئذ بموت الأمين فقال اجعلوه في رداء وضعوه في محلّ حتّى يصبح وحين بزغ الفجر أمر السلطان بإحضار عبيده كلّهم لابسين السلاح فحضروا ورتّبهم على الأبواب وأمر البوّابين أن يفتحوا الأبواب حتّى إذا لم يبق أحد أغلقوها عليهم وأمرهم ألّا يدعوا[1] حواشي القوّاد يدخلون معهم بل لا يدخل إلّا الأمراء فقط ووصّى العبيد إذا أغلقت الأبواب تأتي جماعة منهم ويقفون أمامه محيطين بالعالم الذين يكونوا في المجلس ثمّ أمر أن تضرب الطبول ضرب حزن وإزعاج لأنّ لهم في حال السرور ضرباً معروفاً وفي حال الحزن كذلك فضُربت الطبول كما أمر وجاءت الوزراء والملوك على طبقاتهم ظنّاً منهم أنّ عليّ ود برقو فعل ما اتّفق معهم عليه

١ الأصل: يدعون.

When he grew tired of waiting, he rose to go home, afraid that daylight would come and he'd be discovered. He walked a little way until he found himself confronted by the watch, who told him, "Go back where you came from!" He refused and told them who he was, expecting that they'd let him through, but he couldn't persuade them. In fact, they said, "We have orders to arrest you if you don't go back to where you came from." He cursed at them and tried to force them to let him leave, so they set upon him, meaning to tie him up till morning came, but he fought them, wounding a number. At that they fell upon him and killed him. Thus, all he gained from his evil action was his preordained annihilation. Because of such things he upon whom be God's peace and blessings has said, "Every evildoer will meet with a violent death," or as Sayyid ʿAlī al-Ghurāb, God bless him, says:

> To sow evil deeds is to reap regret,
> so seek peace if you hope for salvation.
> Trust not in fate, for not all who do evil
> get what they wish for and their dreams' consummation.
> Many a wish is a mount that brings us
> to our fates, and a wellspring for contrition.
> Many a time the attainment they picture to the wisher
> is no more than a dreamer's vision.
> Many a one strives to garner life's perfume
> while, all unknowing, what he harvests is his perdition.

When the sultan was informed of the counselor's death, he said, "Wrap him in a cloak and put him in a room until morning." When dawn came, the sultan ordered that all his slaves be brought, fully armed. They came, and he set them at the doors. Then he ordered the doorkeepers to open the doors, leave them open till no one was left inside, then close them upon him and his men. He also forbade them to allow any of the army commanders' bodyguards to enter and told them to allow only the emirs in. And he ordered a group of slaves to go to him, once the doors had been closed, and stand in front of him and surround any who might be in the assembly hall. Then he ordered that the drums be beaten in a mournful and distressing rhythm—for they have a recognized beat for glad times, as they have another for sad—and the drums were beaten as he commanded, and the viziers and the kings came, all according to their various ranks, thinking that ʿAlī wad Barqū had done what he'd agreed with them. 2.2.54

فجاءوا متهيّئين[١] فحين وصلوا إلى باب دار السلطان رأوا الأمر على غير ما يعهدون فلم يجدوا بدّاً من الدخول ودخلت أتباعهم معهم فمُنعوا وبقوا منفردين عن أتباعهم وجاء العبيد الذين أوصاهم بالإحاطة بهم فأحاطوا بهم شاكّين السلاح مظهرين الغضب وخرج السلطان عليهم غارقاً في ثياب سود متطيلساً بكشمير أحمر وهذا نهاية الغضب فجلس السلطان في محلّه المعدّ له وأمر بإحضار القتيل فأُحضر ملفوفاً بالرداء فأمر بوضعه في وسط الحلقة وقال أريد منكم أن تعرفوا هذا من هو فبادروا إليه وكشفوا وجهه فعرفوه ولم يتجاسر أحد منهم على التكلّم لما قام عنده من الغضب فقال لهم السلطان هل عرفتم هذا فسكتوا كلّهم

٥٥،٢،٢ فقام رجل منهم ذو دهاء صهر السلطان أيضاً فقال قد عرفناه وهو الأمين عليّ ود برقو وقد دخل عليك باطّلاعنا أجمعين فإن أردت قتلنا فها نحن بين يديك وإن عفوت فالأمر إليك فقال السلطان وما حملكم على ذلك قال إنّك أتيت بنا إلى هنا وتعلم أنّ لنا في بلادنا أهلاً وعيالاً وأولاداً قطعتنا عن رؤيتهم والتمتّع بمعاشرتهم وليس لنا هنا شغل نعذرك في الإقامة بسببه ولسنا نراك ناوياً أوبة ولا يطيب لنا عيش إلّا بمكاننا فأجلّ ما تصنع معنا أن تردّنا إلى أوطاننا فإنّ قلوبنا أنكرت الغربة وحنّت إلى الأوطان شعر [طويل]

حَـنِيني وَأَشْوَاقِي لِأَوَّلِ تُـرْبَـةٍ   وَأَوَّلِ أَرْضٍ مَسَّ جِلْدِي تُرَابُهَا

لا سيّما وقد ورد عن سيّد ولد عدنان حبّ الوطن من الإيمان فلمّا سمع مقال ذلك الرجل عرف صدقه وخاف إن بطش بأحد منهم قامت عليه القيامة لأنّهم معذورون في ذلك فتخلّص منهم بأن قال لا تستعجلوا[٢] موتي فإنّي ميّت لا محالة لأنّي مريض مرضا لا يمكنني إطلاعكم عليه وهو الذي يمنعني عن السفر فإن عافاني الله في هذه المدّة رجعت بكم وإيّاكم أن تفعلوا مثل هذه والسلام

---

١ الأصل: متهيين. ٢ الأصل: تستعجلون.

They came armed, but when they arrived at the door of the sultan's house, they found that things weren't as they'd expected. They could see, however, that they had no choice but to enter; their followers tried to enter with them, but they were stopped and separated from their commanders. The slaves the sultan had ordered to surround them now came and did so, bristling with arms, their faces showing their fury; and the sultan came out to them swathed in black garments and with a red cashmere shawl draped over his head and shoulders—a mark of extreme anger. The sultan took his seat in the place prepared for him and ordered them to bring the murdered man. He was brought, wrapped in the cloak, and the sultan ordered them to place him in the middle of the circle. "I want you to identify this person," he said, so they went up to him and uncovered his face, and they recognized him. None of them dared speak, so furious was the sultan. When the sultan asked them, "Do you know him?" all remained silent.

Then one of them, a man of unusual shrewdness, stood up and said, "We 2.2.55
know him. He is Counselor ʿAlī wad Barqū, and he entered your house with the knowledge of us all. If you want to kill us, here we stand before you. If you decide to pardon us, the decision is yours." "What drove you to do this?" asked the sultan. "You brought us here," the other replied, "knowing full well that we have wives and children in our country, and have been deprived of the sight of them and of the enjoyment of their company. We have nothing to excuse you in our eyes for keeping us here and we can see no intention on your part to return, even though life has no sweetness for us anywhere but in our homeland. The best thing you can do is to send us back to our own country—our hearts are sick for it and will have no more truck with exile. As the poet says:

My hankering and my longing are for the first dirt
    and for the first land whose dust made contact with my body.

"This is especially true, given that the Lord of ʿAdnān's Offspring[196] is reported to have said, 'Love of homeland is intrinsic to faith.'" When the sultan heard the man's words, he perceived the truth of them and feared that, if he were to deal violently with any of them, all hell would break loose, for in their own eyes they were in the right. He only got out of the predicament they posed for him by saying, "Don't be in a hurry to kill me for I'm a dead man in any case. I have a sickness whose nature I cannot reveal to you. It is that which prevents me from traveling, but if God saves me in the coming days, I will take you back. Please do nothing more of this sort. Farewell."

ثمّ إنّه بعد ذلك بأيّام أظهر أنّه مريض وصار لا يخرج إلى الديوان ولا ينظر في أحوال الناس مع أنّه معافى الجسم ولم يعلم أنّ من تمارض انقلب الهزل جدّاً ومرض حقيقة وربّما مات وقد قال عليه أفضل الصلاة وأتمّ التسليم لا تمارضوا فتمرضوا فتموتوا فانقلب عليه الدست وحلّ به المرض والمقت وأيقن أنّه هالك لا محالة وكتب حينئذ للخليفة كتاباً يقول فيه بعد السلام اعلم يا ولدي أنّه قد اعتراني مبادئ ما لا بدّ منه ولا محيص عنه فإذا وصلك كتابي هذا فخلف ولدك خليل على دارفور وعجّل بالقدوم عسى أن تدركني وبي رمق لعلّي أدبّر لك شيئاً ينفعك والسلام وختم الكتاب وأرسله صحبة هجّان وطاش الخبر أنّ السلطان ثقل عليه المرض وأرجف بموته وصارت الناس لا يتحدّثون إلّا بذلك ٥٦،٢،٢

وكان محمّد كرّا كثيرًا ما يدخل دار السلطان ويجتمع على نسائه وكان ممّن يجتمع عليها إيا كري كنانة أعظم نساء السلطان صاحبة الرتبة الجليلة لأنّ كلّ سلطان يتولّى لا بدّ وأن يحبّ أحد نسائه ومن أحبّها وقلّدها أمور الحكم في بيته هي التي تسمّى إيا كري حقيقة وهذا اللفظ معناه السيّدة الملكيّة وإن قيل لغيرها من نساء السلطان إيا كري فذلك من قبيل التعظيم لا غير وهذه كنانة كانت صاحبة رأي وتدبير. كان السلطان تيراب لا يألف غيرها إلّا لِماماً[١] ولهذا قلّدها هذا المنصب لأنّ هذا المنصب له أقطاع ومعاليم وأموال تُجبى لها منه وتصدر منها أوامر ولها قوّاد يضبطون أموالها وأحوالها فلمّا رأت أنّ السلطان ميّت لا محالة خافت على نفسها وكان لها ولد يسمّى حبيب خافت عليه أيضاً فاجتمعت على محمّد كرّا وقالت له يا محمّد هل لك فيّ حيلة تخلّصني وولدي من هذا الأمر قال لها نعم الحيلة أنّك تصلين حبلك باليتيم لأنّه هو صاحب الدولة بعد السلطان تيراب لأنّ كلّ الناس راضون عنه فقالت هل لك أن تجعل بيني وبينه عهداً وتتوثّق منه بأنّه إذا تولّى يجعلني إيا كري ويجعل ولدي حبيب خليفة فقال لها محمّد[٢] كرّا أفعل ذلك ولك ما يسرّك إن شاء الله ٥٧،٢،٢

---

١ الأصل: لماسا. ٢ أضيف للسياق: محمد.

A few days later, he pretended to be sick, even though his body was in good health, and stopped going to the court or dealing with people's business, unaware that those who fake sickness may find that their joke has turned serious, become truly sick, and even die. He upon whom be the most perfect peace and the best of blessings has said, "Do not feign sickness, for then you will indeed become sick and die." Now the tables were turned, sickness and aversion became his lot, and he felt sure that he was doomed to perish. At that point he wrote a letter to the Successor saying, "Greetings. Know, my son, that the first signs of that from which there is neither escape nor sanctuary have descended upon me, so when this letter reaches you, leave your son Khalīl in your place as ruler of Darfur and come quickly. You may reach me before I breathe my last and I shall perhaps be able to arrange something for you that will be to your advantage. Farewell." He sealed the letter and sent it by swift camel rider. News that the sickness had taken the sultan hard and that he was on the point of death got out, and it was the only thing anyone could talk about. 2.2.56

Now, Muḥammad Kurrā often used to visit the sultan's house and meet with his womenfolk. Among them was Iyā Kurī Kinānah, the greatest of the sultan's women and the highest in rank—for every sultan who ever ruled has surely loved one of his women, and the one whom he loves and to whom he entrusts the management of his household is called "the true *Iyā kurī*." *Iyā kurī* means "royal lady,"[197] and if any other of the sultan's women is called *Iyā kurī* it is simply as a courtesy. This Kinānah was gifted with insight and good management. Sultan Tayrāb was only passingly intimate with the other women, which is why he bestowed this office on her, for this is an office that comes with fiefs, customary dues, and assets from which taxes could be levied on her behalf, and she issued orders and had officers to keep her wealth and affairs in order. When Iyā Kurī Kinānah saw that the sultan was bound to die, she feared for her life; she had a son called Ḥabīb for whom she also feared. She therefore met with Muḥammad Kurrā and said, "Muḥammad, have you thought of a plan to save me and my son from what's going on?" "I have," he replied. "You should call on your relationship with the Orphan, because he will be master of the state after Sultan Tayrāb, seeing that everyone accepts him." "Can you," she asked, "make a pact between him and me that when he becomes ruler, he will make me *Iyā kurī* and my son Ḥabīb his successor?" and Muḥammad Kurrā said, "That I shall do. God willing, you will be pleased." 2.2.57

٢،٢،٥٨ وكانت كنانة تخاف على ولدها حبيب من الخليفة إسحاق لأنّه ابن ضَرّتها وعرفت أنّ اليتيم لا ولد له فقالت يربّي ولدي فذهب إليه محمّد كرّا وأقرأه سلامها وأخبره أنّها تريد أن تعينه على التولية بشرط أن يتزوّجها ويجعل ولدها خليفة فعاهده على ذلك فقال محمّد كرّا وماذا لي أنا أيضاً إن كتمت سرّكما وأعنتك بجهدي على التولية ودبّرت بحيلتي على قدر طاقتي [طويل]

وَلا تَحْتَقِرْ كَيْدَ ٱلضَّعِيفِ فَرُبَّمَا   تَمُوتُ ٱلْأَفَاعِي مِنْ سُمُومِ ٱلْعَقَارِبِ

فقال اليتيم إن فعلت ذلك وأغنيت فيه قلّدتك منصب الأب الشيخ وعاهده على ذلك فرجع إليها محمّد كرّا وأعلمها أنّه استوثق منه بما أرادت فاطمأنت لذلك وصارت ترسل معه أخبار السلطان وقتاً فوقتاً

٢،٢،٥٩ ولمّا ثقل مرض السلطان تيراب ويئس من مجيء ولده إسحاق الخليفة أحضر الأمين عليّ ود جامع، سيّد محمّد كرّا، والأمين حسب الله جِران والأمين إبراهيم ود رَماد والأب الشيخ عبد الله جُثا وأميناً آخر نسيت اسمه وقال اعلموا أنّي صنعت معكم معروفاً وأرجو أن تكافئوني عليه بتنفيذ وصيّتي التي أريد أن أوصيكم بها فقالوا سمعاً وطاعة فقال للأمين عليّ إنّي أوصيك إذا أنا متّ بأن تجمع العساكر كلّهم تحت يدك وتُوصلهم إلى إسحاق ولدي بدارفور فقال سمعاً وطاعة وقال للأمين حسب الله قد جعلتك أميناً على خزائن أموالي. إذا أنا متّ توصلها إلى ولدي فقال سمعاً وطاعة وقال للأمين إبراهيم ود رماد قد جعلتك أميناً على دوابّي وخيلي إذا أنا متّ توصلها إلى ولدي بدارفور وقال للأب الشيخ قد قلّدتك الحريم والعيال والخدم إذا أنا متّ توصلها إلى ولدي وقال للآخر قد جعلتك أميناً على أسلحتي وملبوساتي وأولادي إذا أنا متّ توصّلها إلى ولدي فقبلوا منه ذلك بالسمع والطاعة ودعوا له بالعافية وبكوا لما هو فيه من المرض لأنّهم أصهاره ما عدا الأب الشيخ لأنّه خصيّ ثمّ ذهبوا إلى

Kinānah feared what Isḥāq the Successor might do to her son Ḥabīb because the former was the son of her co-wife. Knowing that the Orphan had no children, she thought, "He can raise my son as his own." Muḥammad Kurrā therefore went to him, passed on to him her greetings, and informed him that Kinānah wanted to help him accede to the throne, but with one condition—that he marry her and make her son his successor. He made a pact with her to that effect, and Muḥammad Kurrā then said, "And what will you do for me if I keep this secret of yours, use my good offices to help you gain the throne, and devote my energies to devising schemes to that end? 2.2.58

Do not belittle the cunning of the weak—
many a viper has died from a scorpion's venom!"

The Orphan said, "If you do this and are of help, I shall bestow on you the office of shaykh-father," and he made a pact with him to that effect. Then Muḥammad Kurrā returned and informed her that he had gotten from him what she wanted. This put her mind at ease, and as events unfolded she began sending the Orphan news of the sultan through him.

When Sultan Tayrāb's illness grew worse and he despaired of the arrival of his son Isḥāq the Successor, he had Counselor ʿAlī wad Jāmiʿ,[198] Muḥammad Kurrā, Counselor Ḥasab Allāh Jirān,[199] Counselor Ibrāhīm wad Ramād, Shaykh-Father ʿAbd Allāh Juthā,[200] and another counselor whose name I've forgotten brought to him and said, "I have done each of you favors, and I hope that you will repay me for this by carrying out my last wishes, which I am about to entrust to you." "We hear and obey," they said. To Counselor ʿAlī he said, "I ask that when I die you gather all my soldiers under your command and deliver them to my son Isḥāq in Darfur." "I hear and obey," he said. To Counselor Ḥasab Allāh he said, "I hereby place in your charge the coffers of my wealth. When I die, deliver them to my son." "I hear and obey," he said. To Counselor Ibrāhīm wad Ramād he said, "I hereby place in your charge my animals and my horses. When I die, deliver them to my son in Darfur." To the shaykh-father he said, "I hereby bestow on you guardianship of the harem, the young children, and the servants. When I die, deliver them to my son." To the remaining counselor he said, "I hereby place in your charge my weapons, my clothes, and my sons. When I die, deliver them to my son." They acceded obediently to his request, prayed that God grant him good health, and wept for his illness, for they were all his in-laws, except for the shaykh-father, who was a eunuch. Then they returned to 2.2.59

محلّهم وقضى السلطان نحبه وهم غائبون وحين توفّي أرسلت كنانة إلى اليتيم بسبحة السلطان ومنديله وخاتمه وحجابه تُعلمه بموته على يد محمد كرّا

٦٠،٢،٢ وجاء أولئك الوزراء الذين أوصاهم فوجدوه قضي عليه فندموا على خروجهم من عنده ودبّروا حيلة وأجمعوا أمرهم أن يجعلوا السلطان في تخت بعد فتحه والقاء ما في أمعائه[١] وتصبيره ثمّ[٢] يُغطّى ويُحفّ بالعساكر ولا يتركون أحداً يصل إليه وكلّ من سأل عليه قيل له مريض حتّى يصلوا إلى دارفور ويسلّموا كلّ ذلك إلى ولده إسحاق الخليفة

٦١،٢،٢ والأب الشيخ محمد كرّا أخذ الأشياء المذكورة وتوجّه إلى اليتيم وقال له عوّضك الله في أخيك خيراً وأعطاه الخاتم والسبحة والمنديل فتحقّق موت أخيه وأخذ الأشياء وذهب إلى أخيه الأكبر المسمّى ريز فحين أعلمه نهض قائماً وأخذ ريفا وطاهراً وتوجّهوا إلى دار السلطان فلم يقدر أحد على منعهم وما زالوا داخلين حتّى وصلوا إلى المحلّ الذي فيه الجماعة والسلطان تيراب مسجّىً أمامهم وهم يبكون عليه فدخلوا عليهم ولم يخاطبوهم بل جلسوا حول أخيهم وبكوا حتّى فاؤوا ثمّ التفتوا إلى الجماعة وقال لهم ريز أما كفاكم أنّ مدّة حياة أخينا كان خيره لكم والآن تريدون أن تأخذوا شِلْوه أيضاً لأجل أن يكون لكم حيّاً وميّتاً ها نحن قد اطّلعنا على موته فافعلوا ما بدا لكم فقد تركناه لكم ثمّ خرجوا وتركوهم

٦٢،٢،٢ فاختلف رأي الجماعة بعدهم وقالوا قد فسد تدبيرنا واطّلعوا على موت السلطان فلا يمكننا أن ننفذ وصيّته الآن فقال الأمين عليّ ود جامع لا بدّ لي من تنفيذ وصيّته أو أموت دونها ثمّ نادى يا محمد كرّا اذهب إلى محمد ولدي وقل له يجمع عساكري ويلبسوا دروعهم وأسلحتهم ويأتون إلى باب السلطان فقال سمعاً وطاعة وذهب إلى محمد ابن الأمين وقال له إن حضرة الأمين يأمرك أن تجهز العساكر وتركب معهم وتذهب إلى أولاد السلطان وتكون معيناً لهم حتّى يأتيك أمري فقال الأمين محمد

١ الأصل: امائه. ٢ أضيف للسياق: ثم.

their quarters, and the sultan expired in their absence. When he died, Kinānah sent the sultan's prayer beads, kerchief, seal ring, and amulet to the Orphan, by hand of Muḥammad Kurrā, to let him know.

The viziers to whom he had revealed his last wishes returned and found that he'd passed away. Regretting they'd left him, they devised a stratagem, agreeing to place his corpse in a litter after first opening it, removing the innards, and embalming it; after that, it was to be covered, and a cordon of soldiers placed around it, with no one allowed to get to it. Any who asked would be told he was sick, until they reached Darfur and had handed everything over to his son, Isḥāq the Successor. 2.2.60

Shaykh-Father Muḥammad Kurrā took the things that were mentioned above, went to see the Orphan, and told him, "God compensate you with good for the loss of your brother!" and he gave him the ring, the prayer beads, and the kerchief. The Orphan was thus apprised of his brother's death and he took the things and went to his older brother, whose name was Rīz. When he told him, Rīz arose and took Rīfā and Ṭāhir, and they went to the sultan's quarters. No one could stand in their way. They went on through the house until they got to where the sultan's men were, as well as Sultan Tayrāb himself, who was laid out in front of them while they wept over him. They entered the room without speaking. In fact, they sat down around their brother and wept till they regained their composure. Then they turned to his men, and Rīz asked them, "Isn't it enough that you profited from our brother's benevolence throughout his life? Yet now you want to take his cadaver too so that he can be yours in death as well? We have seen with our own eyes that he's dead, so do what you like. We leave him to you." Then they exited, leaving them. 2.2.61

When they'd gone, his men changed their minds, saying, "Our plan has gone awry and they've seen that the sultan is dead. We can't carry out his last wishes now." But Counselor ʿAlī wad Jāmiʿ said, "I shall carry out his wishes, or perish in the attempt," and called out, "Muḥammad Kurrā, go to my son Muḥammad and tell him to assemble my soldiers and have them put on their chain mail and their swords and come to the sultan's door." "I hear and obey," replied Muḥammad Kurrā, and he went to Muḥammad, the counselor's son, and told him, "The honorable counselor orders you to ready the soldiers and ride with them to the sons of the sultan and assist them till you receive further orders from him." "I hear and obey," said Counselor Muḥammad,[201] and he called for his soldiers and they readied themselves, mounted, and went to join 2.2.62

سمعاً وطاعة ونادى في العساكر فتأهّبوا وركبوا وتوجّهوا إلى أولاد السلطان ورجع هو بعد ذلك للأمين وقال له قد ذهبت فوجدت سيّدي قد أخذ العساكر وتوجّه إلى أولاد السلطان فاغتاظ الأمين على ذلك وعلم أنّه لا يقدر على تنفيذ وصيّة السلطان تيراب[1] وخاف من الإيمان والعهود فأخرج علبة صغيرة كانت معه وفتحها واستفّ منها شيئاً ممّا كان فيها فوقع ميتاً ولمّا مات انخذل الباقون وتفرّق رأيهم وهذه أقوى مكيدة عملها محمّد كرّا في الأمين وولده وبسببها وقعت العداوة بينه وبين الأمين محمّد بن الأمين عليّ المذكور

٦٣،٢،٢ ثمّ إنّ الجماعة تفرّقوا وذهب كلّ منهم إلى جيشه وهاجت الناس وماجت وعلموا أنّه لا بدّ للدولة من سلطان يقوم بأمرهم ويجمع كلمتهم وكانت أولاد السلطان أحمد بكر الذين هم إخوان المتوفّى جالسين هم وأتباعهم على حدة وأولاد إخوانهم وأتباعهم على حدة والرعايا على حدة فنهضت جماعة من المدبّرين ودعوا بالقاضي والعلماء وأرسلوهم إلى أولاد السلطان أحمد[2] بكر لأنّهم هم الكبراء وأولياء العهد من أبيهم وقالوا لهم قولوا[3] لهم بعد السلام اعلموا أنّه لا بدّ لهذا الأمر من سلطان يجمع كلمة الناس ويقوم بأمرهم والملك لكم وأنتم أربابه فعيّنوا لنا سلطاناً نرضى نحن وأنتم به[4] فتوجّهت العلماء والقاضي وأخبروهم بذلك فقالوا قد عيّنّا لهم أخانا ريزًا لأنّه هو أكبرنا وسيّدنا ونحن تحت أمره ونهيه

٦٤،٢،٢ فتوجّهت العلماء لأولاد السلاطين الصغار وأخبروهم أنّ باسي ريزًا يكون عليهم سلطاناً فأبوا وقالوا إن باسي ريز عمّنا ووالدنا لكن لا نريد أن يتولّى علينا لأنّه صعب المراس فيه حدّة تُخشى غائلته خصوصاً ونحن أولاد صغار نريد سلطاناً حليماً يربّينا وإن صدر من أحدنا بادرة يعاملنا فيها بالحلم وقالت الرعيّة إنّ باسي ريز ملكنا وابن ملكنا ولكن به حدّة والأولى أن يختار هو غيره لأنّه هو سلطان تولّى أم لم يتولّ فرجعت العلماء وأخبروهم بذلك فقال باسي ريز قبلنا عذرهم وولّينا عليهم باسي

١ الأصل: تيرب. ٢ أضيف للسياق: أحمد. ٣ الأصل: قلوا. ٤ أضيف للسياق: به.

the sons of the sultan. Muḥammad Kurrā, meanwhile, returned to the counselor and told him, "I went and I found that my young master had already taken the soldiers and gone to the sons of the sultan." The counselor was enraged and realized that he would be unable to carry out Sultan Tayrāb's wishes. He was also struck by dread because of the oaths and pacts he'd made. Pulling out a little box that he had on his person, he opened it and swallowed some of its contents. Then he fell down dead. With the counselor dead, the others were left in the lurch and couldn't agree. This was a great trick that Muḥammad Kurrā played on the counselor and his son, and because of it he and Counselor Muḥammad, son of the aforementioned counselor, became enemies.

After this, the sultan's men split up, and each went to his own army, while 2.2.63
the people simmered and seethed, everyone knowing that the state had to have a sultan to take care of their affairs and to speak for the people with one voice. The sons of Sultan Aḥmad Bukur, the brothers of the deceased, were assembled with their followers in one place, the sons of their brothers with their followers in another, and the commoners in a third. A group of those who manage the affairs of state then arose and called for the judge and religious scholars and sent them to the sons of Sultan Aḥmad Bukur because they were the elders and parties to the pact made by their father. These high officials told the judge and the scholars, "Say to the sons of Sultan Aḥmad Bukur, 'Greetings. Know that this matter requires a sultan, to speak for the people with one voice and to see to their affairs. You hold supreme authority, and you are those who dispose of it. Appoint us, therefore, a sultan whom both you and we can accept.'" The scholars and the judge then went and gave them this message, and the sons of Sultan Aḥmad Bukur said, "We appoint our brother Rīz because he is the oldest among us and our lord, and we are at his command."

Next, the scholars went to the young sons of the sultans[202] and informed 2.2.64
them that Báási Rīz would be sultan over them, but they refused, saying, "Báási Rīz is our uncle and like a father to us, but we don't want him to rule us because he is intractable and impetuous, and the havoc he may cause is to be feared, especially because we're young. We want a mild-natured sultan to raise us, one who will treat us with clemency should any of us step out of line." The commoners said, "Báási Rīz is one of our royal princes and the son of our king, but he is impetuous, and it would be better if he himself were to choose someone else, because he is a sultan whether he rules or not." The scholars then returned and informed the sons of Sultan Aḥmad Bukur of all this.

طاهرًا فأخبروا به أيضاً أولاد السلاطين[1] فقالوا لا نرضى بعمّنا طاهر لأنّ له أولادًا كثيرة لا ينتبه لتربيتنا بسببهم وقالت الرعيّة إنّما كرهنا السلطان تيراب لكثرة أولاده فإن يولّوا علينا طاهرًا فنحن نرضى بالخليفة أن يكون سلطانًا لأنّه أقلّ أولادًا منه فرجعوا وأخبروهم فقال ريز قد ولّينا عليكم اليتيم فأخبروهم فرضوا به كلّهم رعيّة وأولاد ملوك وانعقد أمرهم عليه وأخذوه وتوجّهوا به إلى دار السلطان وألبسوه الخاتم وأقعدوه على كرسيّ المملكة ولم يختلف عليه اثنان

١ الأصل: السلطان.

Báási Rīz said, "We accept their reservations and appoint Báási Ṭāhir to rule over them." They informed the sons of the sultans of this, but these said, "We do not accept our uncle Ṭāhir because he has many sons and he will be too busy with them to pay attention to our upbringing." The commoners said, "We hated Sultan Muḥammad Tayrāb precisely because he had so many sons. They may appoint Ṭāhir to be our sultan, but we would prefer the Successor as sultan because he has fewer sons." So the scholars went back and informed the sons of Sultan Aḥmad Bukur, and Rīz said, "We appoint the Orphan to rule over you," so they informed the others of this, and everyone, commoners and royalty, was satisfied and the matter was made official. They took him, conveyed him to the sultan's house, placed the ring on his finger, and sat him on the throne of the kingdom, and no two disputed his right.[203]

الباب الثالث

في ذكر نبذة من سيرة السلطان عبد الرحمن الملقّب بالرشيد وأوّل أمره وولايته ووفاته

١،٣،٢ قد ذكرنا فيما مضى أنّ السلطان أحمد بكر خلّف سبعة من الولد منهم السلطان عبد الرحمن المذكور وهو أصغرهم لأنّ أباه توفّي وهو حمل في بطن أمّه ولذلك سمّي باليتيم. نشأ على أحسن حال حفظ القرآن وقرأ في الفقه وعرف الحلال والحرام ولم ينتبه إلى ما انتبه له أولاد الملوك في دارفور لأنّ أولاد الملوك هناك متى كبر الواحد منهم يخوض في البلاد يتضيّف وينهب أموال الناس وكلّما رأى شيئاً أعجبه أخذه بدون ثمن ويقول إنّ جميع ما في دارفور من العالم عبيد لأبيه إلّا عبد الرحمن فإنّه من صغر سنّه كان صالحاً تقيّاً نقيّاً عفيف النفس وكان في غاية من ضيق العيش وكان إذا سافر وأمسى عليه المساء في بلد قال لمن ينزل عنده أنا ضيف الله فإنّ قبله مكث وإلّا ذهب إلى محلّ آخر ولم يُسمع عنه أنّه ظلم أحداً قطّ وكان لا ينسى الصنيعة لمن فعلها معه بل يتذكّرها ويجازيه عليها

٢،٣،٢ ومن ذلك أنّه كان مسافراً فنزل عند رجل من قبيلة يقال لها البِرّتي فعرفه الرجل وذبح له كبشاً سميناً ولاطفه ولمّا جاء العشاء وحضر الطعام رأى السلطان عبد الرحمن أنّ الرجل قد تكلّف له فقال له يا هذا أما كان يغني عن هذا ما هو أقلّ منه

Chapter 3

A Brief Excerpt from the History of Sultan ʿAbd al-Raḥmān, Called the Rightly Guided: His Early Days, His Rule, and His Death

We have mentioned above that Sultan Aḥmad Bukur left seven sons,[204] among them the aforementioned Sultan ʿAbd al-Raḥmān, who was the youngest of them because his father died while he was in his mother's belly, which is why he was called the Orphan. He grew up to be a fine young man, learned the Qur'an by heart, studied religious law, and knew what religion allowed and what it forbade. He had no interest in the things that interested royal sons in Darfur. When any of these grows up, he launches himself on the country, imposing himself as a guest and plundering people's wealth. Every time he sees something that he likes, he takes it without paying, with the words, "Everyone in Darfur is my father's slave." In contrast, ʿAbd al-Raḥmān was, from his earliest days, righteous, God-fearing, purehearted, and virtuous. He lived in greatly straitened circumstances. If he was on a journey and evening found him in a village, he would say to the person in whose house he was to stay, "I am God's guest." Then, if the man accepted him, he'd stay, and if the man did not, he'd go elsewhere. He was never heard to have treated anyone unjustly and he never forgot to return a favor. On the contrary, he'd remember it and reward the doer.[205] 2.3.1

Once, for example, he was on a journey and put up at the house of a man from a tribe called the Bartī. The man recognized him, slaughtered a fat ram for him, and treated him kindly. When dinnertime came and the food was brought, Sultan ʿAbd al-Raḥmān saw that the man had put himself to great expense for him and said, "Friend, wouldn't less have been enough? If you'd slaughtered us a chicken, it would have fed us just as well and you would still have performed your duty." "No, my lord," the man said. "I swear, if I owned a meat camel, 2.3.2

لو ذبحت لنا دجاجة لقامت مقامه وكنت أدّيت ما وجب عليك فقال لا يا مولاي والله لو ملكت جَزوراً لنحرتها لك ألست عبد الرحمن اليتيم ابن سلطاننا فقال له اليتيم ومن أين تعرفني قال عرفتك بحسن خلقك وتقواك وإنّه سيصير لك شأن فقال اليتيم لئن ملكت لأطعمنّك أسمن ممّا ذبحت لنا وكان الأمر كذلك فإنّه لمّا ولي دعا بالرجل وكان يسمّى محمّد دَرْدُوك وولّاه منصباً جليلاً وأخرجه لجباية أموال قبيلة العرب المجانين وهي قبيلة عظيمة أهلها أصحاب إبل فحصل منها من الأموال والنوق والجمال ما لا يوصف

٣،٣،٢ ومنها أنّه مرّ ببلاد الريح ونزل على رجل فقير يقال له جِدّو فأكرمه على قدر طاقته وكان هذا الرجل من بيت كبير وأبوه كان ملكاً عظيماً يقال لمن تولّى في منصبه التَكِنْيَاوِي فلمّا ولي اليتيم ولّاه منصب أبيه ورأيته واجتمعت به ومنها أنّ الفقيه مالك الفوتاويّ الذي أسلفنا ذكره كان رأى له مناماً وصورته أنّه رأى قمراً في السماء والناس ينظرون إليه ويقولون هذا اليتيم فأوّله أن يلي المُلْك وذهب وبشّره بذلك فقال إن صدقت رؤياك لأرفعنّ قدرك فكان كما قال وكان يصوم الخميس والاثنين على الدوام ويصوم رجب وشعبان ورمضان وكان يحبّ أهل العلم ويكرمهم

٤،٣،٢ وقبل ولايته بأيّام شاع عند المنجّمين وأصحاب خطّ الرمل أنّ اليتيم هو الذي يتولّى السلطنة بعد السلطان تيراب وسمع السلطان بذلك فحقد عليه وأراد قتله مراراً والله يمنعه منه وكان يدعوه للطعام ويجعل له السمّ فيه فكان اليتيم يقول إنّي صائم ولا يأكل منه شيئا ولقد أخبرني من شاهد وقت توليته حين أدخلوه لدار السلطنة أنّه كان عليه قميص قد بلي حتّى أن كتفيه ظاهران منه وبيده سبحة من خشب تساوي في برّ مصر عشرين فضّة ومكث عزبا حتّى بدا الشيب في لحيته وما ذاك إلّا لفقره

I would slaughter her for you! Are you not ʿAbd al-Raḥmān the Orphan, son of our sultan?" "By what did you recognize me?" asked the Orphan. "I recognized you by your virtuous nature and your godliness. One day you will be a man of consequence." The Orphan said, "If I ever come to power, I will feed you with something fatter than what you slaughtered for us," and that is exactly what happened. When he assumed power, he summoned the man (whose name was Muḥammad Dardūk), appointed him to high office, and sent him out to collect the taxes from the Majānīn Arabs, a great tribe whose members have many camels. The man collected from them cattle and both cow and bull camels in numbers too large to count.

Similarly, he was once passing through Dār al-Rīḥ and put up at the house of a poor man called Jiddū.[206] The man provided him with the best hospitality he could. Now, the man was from a great house, and his father had been a great lord, holding the office of Tikináwi. When the Orphan assumed power, he appointed the man to his father's office. I saw him and met with him. Likewise, Faqīh Mālik al-Fūtāwī, whom we have mentioned above, once had a dream, as follows: he saw a moon in the sky and everyone was looking at it and saying, "It's the orphan,"[207] which he interpreted to mean that ʿAbd al-Raḥmān would assume power. When he went and gave him the good news, ʿAbd al-Raḥmān averred, "If your vision turns out to be true, we shall certainly raise your standing," and it was as he promised. He also fasted every Thursday and Monday and during the months of Rajab, Shaʿbān, and Ramaḍān, and he loved and was generous to men of religion. 2.3.3

A few days before he assumed power, word went around among astrologers and geomancers that the Orphan was the one who would assume the sultanate after Sultan Muḥammad Tayrāb. The latter heard this and hated him for it and tried to kill him several times, but God prevented him from doing so. He'd invite him to take food and poison it, but the Orphan would say, "I'm fasting,"[208] and eat none of it. I was told by a witness that at the time of his assumption of the sultanate, when they took him into the palace, he was wearing a shirt so tattered that his shoulders showed and that he was carrying wooden prayer beads worth but half a piaster in Egypt. He remained a bachelor until gray hairs began to appear in his beard, by reason of poverty and lack of money to take a concubine or marry. He didn't know a woman until he went to Kordofan in the company of his brother Sultan Muḥammad Tayrāb. When he passed through 2.3.4

وعدم المال الذي يتسرّى أو يتزوّج به ولم ير النساء إلّا حين سافر إلى كردفال صحبة أخيه السلطان محمّد تيراب فمرّ على بلاد يقال لها البِيقُو فأعطاه ملكها جارية وَخْشاء تسمّى أنبوسة فغشيها فولدت منه السلطان محمّد فضل

٥،٣،٢ ولمّا انعقد الأمر عليه أجلسوه على سرير الملك كما تقدّم وبايعوه وكان أوّل من بايعه أخوه الأكبر ريز ثمّ ريفا ثمّ طاهر ثمّ أولاد السلاطين فبايعوه ثمّ القاضي والعلماء ثمّ الأمراء وضربت طبول الحزن إعلانًا بموت السلطان تيراب ثمّ بطلت قليلاً وضربت طبول الهناء إعلاما بتولية السلطان عبد الرحمن وكان من عادة ملوك الفور أنّ السلطان إذا تولّى يمكث سبعة أيّام في بيته لا يسأل عن حكم ولا أمر ولا نهي بل يجلس للتهنئة والسرور تدخل عليه العلماء والوزراء وأرباب الدولة فلمّا تولّى السلطان عبد الرحمن أبطل تلك العادة وخرج صبيحة توليته فجاءت الوزراء فرأوه جالساً في ديوانه وتناول بعض أحكام فلاموه وقالوا ليست العادة كذا فقال بئس العادة ليست في كتاب الله ولا في سنّة رسوله ثمّ جمع جميع أرباب الدولة وقال لهم إن كان لكم أَرَب في أن أكون سلطانا عليكم تُبْطِلوا الظلم ولا تحدّث به أنفسكم وتتوبوا إلى الله تعالى منه فإنّ الظلم يخرب الدول ويقصر أعمار الملوك فقالوا سمعاً وطاعة

٦،٣،٢ ثمّ لمّا كانت صبيحة اليوم الثالث أمر بإخراج خزائن السلطان تيراب فأخرجت ففرّق ما كان فيها من العين من ذهب وفضّة وثياب على العلماء والأشراف والفقراء ووجد فيها من الكشمير والجوخ الذي عثّ شيء كثير فأمر أن يرمى خارج الديار وكلّ من وجد شيئا ينفعه أخذه فأخرج فكان كالطود العظيم واجتمعت عليه الفقراء ينهبونه وبسطوا أيديهم بالدعاء للسلطان عبد الرحمن ثمّ لمّا كان سابع يوم أخرج جواري السلطان تيراب وفرّقها أيضاً ولم يترك إلّا الحرائر وأمّهات الأولاد التي تزوّجها أخوه

a land called al-Bīqū, its lord gave him an uncouth slave girl called Anbūsah.[209] He slept with her and she bore him Sultan Muḥammad Faḍl.

When he was recognized, they sat him on the royal throne, as previously 2.3.5
mentioned, and pledged their allegiance to him. The first to do so was his eldest brother, Rīz, followed by Rīfā, then Ṭāhir, then the sons of the sultans. After these had pledged allegiance, so too did the judge and the scholars, followed by the commanders of the army. The mourning drums were beaten to announce the death of Sultan Tayrāb. Then they stopped and the drums of good tiding were beaten to announce the succession to the throne of Sultan ʿAbd al-Raḥmān. It had been a custom of Fur royalty that when the sultan assumed power, he would stay seven days in his house, giving no thought to government or to the issuance of commands or prohibitions. Instead, he'd simply sit to receive congratulations and expressions of joy, and the scholars, viziers, and officers of state would come in to visit him. When Sultan ʿAbd al-Raḥmān came to the throne, he abolished this custom. He went out early on the morning of his accession, and when the viziers came, they found him sitting in his court, dealing with cases. They chided him, saying, "This is not the custom," but he replied, "That was a bad custom, not to be found in God's Book or the practice of His Prophet." Then he gathered together all the officers of state and told them, "If you want me to be your sultan, in authority over you, abandon injustice and don't let your appetites seduce you into it, but repent to God of it and give it up. Injustice is the ruin of states and brings untimely ends to kings." "We hear and obey," they said.

Early in the morning of the third day, he ordered all Sultan Tayrāb's coffers 2.3.6
brought out and this was done. Everything in them by way of gold, silver, and clothes he distributed to religious scholars, descendants of the prophet, and the poor. He found a great quantity of moth-eaten cashmere and broadcloth, which he ordered thrown down in front of the houses for anyone who found anything of use to take. They took it out and there was so much it looked like a mighty mountain. The poor gathered around and plundered it, stretching out their hands in blessing for Sultan ʿAbd al-Raḥmān. On the seventh day, he brought out Sultan Tayrāb's slave girls and distributed them too; no one was left but the free women and the mothers of children whom his brother had contractually married. Next he distributed the offices, making Muḥammad Dukkumī a counselor with the same responsibilities as his father, Counselor

بالعقد ثمّ نصب المناصب فجعل محمّد دُكُّي أميناً في منصب أبيه الأمين عليّ ود جامع وأمرهم بالأهبة للرحيل إلى دارفور فتجهّزوا

٢،٣،٧ وحين خرج من كردفال مرّ على جبل التروج فأوقع بهم وأخذ جميع ما فيه من الشباب والبنات ولم يترك فيه إلّا المسنّين واجتمع بمشايخ عرب البادية من الرزيقات والمِسيريّة فالتمس منهم المسير معه لحرب الخليفة وكلّ ما اكتسبوه من المال والسلاح والخيل فهو لهم فاجتمع عليه منهم ألوف وتوجّه إلى دارفور لكنّه لم يأتها من جهة المشرق بل أتاها من جهة الجنوب وقبل وصوله كتب إلى الخليفة كتاباً يقول فيه

من عبد الرحمن سلطان دارفور إلى ولد أخيه إسحاق أمّا بعد فإنّي أعزّيك في والدك وإن كان أخي لأنّك أقرب منّي إليه وأوصيك ببرّ الوالدين فإذا علمت هذا فاعلم أنّي عمّك وحرمتي كحرمة أبيك وعار على الولد أن يصادر أباه أو عمّه فضلاً عن أن يجرّد في وجهه حساماً فأنهاك عن القتال وإيّاك أن تستفزّك رعونة الشباب وتسمع قول المفسدين فيحولوا بيني وبينك ولك عليّ عهد الله وميثاقه أن أقرّك خليفة كما كنت في أيّام أبيك وأجعلك وليّ عهدي كما كنت وليّ عهد أبيك فاسمع قولي واحقن دماء المسلمين وإن خالفت حلّت بك الندامة ﴿وَسَيَعۡلَمُ ٱلَّذِينَ ظَلَمُوٓاْ أَيَّ مُنقَلَبٖ يَنقَلِبُونَ﴾

٢،٣،٨ فلمّا وصل الكتاب إلى الخليفة وعلم ما فيه كتب إلى السلطان عبد الرحمن

بعد السلام أمّا بعد فإني عاهدت الله تعالى ألّا أطأ غير بساط أبي وأنا وليّ عهده ولا حقّ لك عليّ وإن قاتلتني فأنا مظلوم والسـلام

ʿAlī wad Jāmiʿ. Then he ordered the office holders to prepare to leave for Darfur, and they readied the army for travel.

When they left Kordofan, they went by way of Jabal al-Turūj, falling upon it, taking every young man and girl there, and leaving only the old. Sultan ʿAbd al-Raḥmān met with the shaykhs of the Rizayqāt and the Misīriyyah Bedouin tribes and requested they march with him to do battle with the Successor, on the basis that whatever property, weapons, and horses they might take would become theirs. Thousands of them rallied to his banner and he set off for Darfur. However, instead of coming to it from the east, he came to it from the south, and before arriving, he wrote the Successor a letter saying: 2.3.7

> From ʿAbd al-Raḥmān, Sultan of Darfur, to his nephew Isḥāq. I offer you my condolences on the death of your father, even though he was my brother, because you are closer kin to him than I, and I commend to you the virtue of filial respect. If you understand this, you will understand too that I am your uncle and as inviolate to you as your own father and that it is shameful for a son to stand in the way of his father or his uncle, to say nothing of drawing his sword in his face. I forbid you therefore to fight, and beware lest the rashness of youth provoke you into listening to the words of any evildoers who may strive to come between us. You have my word before God and His covenant that I will designate you successor to the throne as you were in the time of your father and that I will make you my crown prince just as you were your father's. Listen to my words and spare the blood of the Muslims. If, however, you oppose me, you will regret it «and the wrongdoers will soon know how evil a turn their affairs will take.»[210]

When the letter reached the Successor and he was apprised of its contents, he wrote to Sultan ʿAbd al-Raḥmān, saying: 2.3.8

> Greetings. I gave my word before the Almighty that I would tread no carpet but my father's.[211] I am his appointed successor, and you have no rights over me. If you fight me, I shall be the injured party. Farewell.

ثمّ جهّز له جيشاً كثيفاً بنظر الحاجّ مفتاح داداه وأكبر عبيده فتلاقى هو وجيش السلطان عبد الرحمن في محلّ يقال له تبلديّة فكان مع كلّ إنسان من جيش السلطان عبد الرحمن سَفْرُوك والسفروك قطعة من العصا صورتها هكذا  فحين التقى الجمعان ألقى جماعة السلطان السفاريك على جماعة الخليفة وقالوا الله أكبر ففرّوا وتبعهم جماعة السلطان يأسرون ويأخذون الأسلاب والخيول وتبعهم العرب أيضاً فاغتنموا منهم غنيمة عظيمة ونجا الحاجّ مفتاح وفلّ من أصحابه برأس طِمِرّه[1] وحين دخل الحاجّ مفتاح على الخليفة قال له ما وراءك قال يا سيّدي إنّي ناصح لك صالح عمّك وإن طلب منك مالاً فأعطه إيّاه واجعلني أوّل ما يُعطى فأنا فداؤك فلمّا سمع الخليفة منه هذا الكلام زجره وقال رجعت إلى أصلك يا عبد السوء لكنّ اللوم عليّ في أن أقدّمك على العساكر ثمّ إن الخليفة حشد الحشود وفتح الخزائن وفرّق الأموال وأعطى الأقطاع فجمع جيشاً عظيماً لا أوّل له ولا آخر وبرز يؤمّل النصرة على السلطان

فوصل إلى محلّ يقال له تالْدَوَا فأدركه السلطان هناك ولمّا عاين كلّ منهما صاحبه ٩،٣،٢
رتّبا جيوشهما وصفّا صفوفهما وكان مع جماعة الخليفة رجل من الملوك يقال له بحر الجبّاي وهو الذي يجبي الغلال للسلطنة ومعه أتباعه ما ينوف عن عشرة آلاف من الخيل خلاف الرجّالة فلمّا تلاقى الجمعان أخذ جماعته وزحف على جيش السلطان عبد الرحمن كأنّه يريد قتالهم ودخل فيهم وألصق صفّه بهم وبقي يقاتل الخليفة فترك في صفوف الخليفة ثلماً عظيماً وفرجة ما قدروا على سدّها فانكسرت قلوب عسكر الخليفة بما فعل الملك بحر والتحم القتال فلم يكن إلّا كلمحة بارق حتّى تقهقر جيش الخليفة وحين رأى الخليفة ذلك خرج يقاتلهم بنفسه فكان كلّ من عرفه يعرض عنه إكراماً له ولأبيه وما زال يفعل كذلك حتّى رأى جيشه انهزم وبقي هو في نفر قليل فلحق بجيشه فرأى

[1] الأصل: طَمْرة.

Then he mustered a massive army under al-Ḥājj Muftāḥ,[212] who had been his governor as a child and was the most senior of his slaves, and this army and that of Sultan ʿAbd al-Raḥmān came face to face at a place called Tabaldiyyah.[213] Each man in Sultan ʿAbd al-Raḥmān's army had a *safrūk*, a *safrūk* being a piece of stick that looks like this,  and when «the two hosts met,»[214] the sultan's men threw their *safrūk*s at the Successor's men, crying, "God is greater!"[215] and the others fled and the sultan's men chased them, taking captives, spoils, and horses. The Bedouin chased them too, and seized large quantities of plunder. Al-Ḥājj Muftāḥ survived and fled headlong from his companions on his fleet steed. When al-Ḥājj Muftāḥ went in to see the Successor, the latter asked him, "What do you leave behind you?" and the former replied, "My lord, take my advice. Make peace with your uncle, and if he asks you for compensation, give it to him. Make me the first thing given to him. Let me be your ransom." When the Successor heard these words, he rebuked him, saying, "You have reverted to your origins, evil slave! But it is my fault for having put you in charge of the troops." Then the Successor marshaled great numbers, opened his coffers, distributed wealth, and gave out fiefs. Thus, he gathered an army so immense it had neither beginning nor end, and he marched out, expecting victory over the sultan.

He reached a place called Tāldawā, where the sultan caught up with him, and 2.3.9
when each had looked the other over, they set their armies in order and drew up their ranks. Among the Successor's men was a *malik* called Baḥr the Tax Collector;[216] he was the person responsible for collecting the grain tax for the sultanate. With him were his followers, numbering some ten thousand horsemen, not to mention foot soldiers. When the two hosts met, he took his men and marched against Sultan ʿAbd al-Raḥmān's army as if intending to engage them, but instead joined them and added his ranks to theirs and started fighting the Successor. This took a great swathe out of the Successor's army and made a breach that they couldn't fill, and the courage of the Successor's soldiery deserted them in the face of what Malik Baḥr had done. Battle was joined, but the Successor's army retreated in a flash. When the Successor saw this, he went out to fight them himself, and everyone who recognized him turned aside from him out of respect for him and his father. He continued to fight till he saw that his army had been defeated and he was left surrounded by a small company. He followed after his army but found that most had been killed. The sultan's soldiers pursued them, taking captives and plunder, till evening came. Someone

أنّه[1] قد قتل أكثره وتبعتهم عساكر السلطان يأسرون ويسبون حتّى أمسى المساء وحكى لي من كان حاضرًا أنه وقت التحام القتال بينهما رأى النجوم في السماء وكان الوقت ضحى ولقد شاهدت محلّ الواقعة فرأيته جدبًا في وقت الربيع فسألت عن سبب ذلك فقيل لي إنّه لا ينبت فيه نبت لما سال فيه من الدماء

ثمّ إنّ الخليفة توجّه بأصحابه إلى الجهة الشماليّة وترك السلطان بالجهة الجنوبيّة ولمّا انفرد الخليفة عن السلطان وأبعد عنه ظلم وتعدّى وجار وصار يخرج الناس معه قهرًا عليهم وكلمّا عثر بجواد أخذه أو بمال استأصله فاجتمع له بذلك مال عظيم وخلق كثيرون وعظم شرّه واستغاث الناس منه إلى السلطان فأراد أن يتوجّه إليه بنفسه فمنعه أرباب دولته فكتب له كتابًا يقول فيه ٢،٣،١٠

بعد ما يليق فإنّك طغيت وبغيت وظلمت وتعدّيت وقد نصحتك أوّلًا أن تحقن دماء الناس فأبيت وكان منّا ما كان والآن فقد استعنت على قتالنا بظلم العالم ونهب أموالهم وأنا أنصحك ثانيًا أن تترك ما أنت عليه من الرعونة والجبر والعتوّ فإن رجعت إلينا ثانيًا قبلناك وجعلنا لك ما جعلناه أوّلًا وإن أبيت فالإثم عليك وأنت المذموم وإن أصررت على القتال فالرعيّة لا ذنب لها فعِفَّ نفسك عن أموال الناس وها هو مالي بين يديك. خذ منه ما شئت حتّى يحكم الله والسلام

فلمّا وصل إليه الكتاب وعلم ما فيه مزقه ولم يردّ له جوابًا وزاد شرّه وكثر شاكوه فأرسل إليه ملك الجهة الشماليّة ويسمّى بالتكنياوي في جيش فذهب إليه التكنياوي فأدركه في محلّ يقال له بوًّا فحين رأى الخليفة الجيش قد أقبل رتّب صفوفه ووقف حتّى وصل إليه الجيش والتقى الجمعان وكان جيش الخليفة قد أثّر فيه الرعب من وقعة تالدوا ٢،٣،١١

[1] أضيف للسياق: أنه.

who was present told me that, at the moment when the two armies joined battle, he saw stars in the sky though it was late in the morning. I saw the battlefield and found it bare of vegetation, though it was spring; I asked why and was told no plants could grow there because there was too much blood.

The Successor then set off for the north with his companions, leaving the sultan in possession of the south. Once the Successor had disengaged from the sultan and put distance between them, he acted like a tyrant, transgressor, and oppressor. He began forcing people to join him, and whenever he came across a fine horse he would take it, and any assets he found he would carry off. Thus, he accumulated great wealth and many followers. As his evil grew ever greater, the people appealed to the sultan for help against him. The sultan wanted to go after him himself, but the high officers of the state prevented him, so instead he wrote him a letter, saying, 2.3.10

> After whatever greeting may be appropriate: you have tyrannized, oppressed, mistreated, and transgressed. I advised you the first time to spare the people's blood, but you refused and you suffered at our hands what you suffered. Now you have decided to mistreat the people and loot their possessions instead of fighting us. I hereby advise you, a second time, to abandon the rashness, the use of force, and the arrogance in which you are embroiled. If you return to us again, we shall accept you and reward you as we promised to do the first time. If you refuse, the sin is yours, and you will be the one to blame, and if you insist on fighting, the common people will be guiltless.[217] Cleanse yourself then of the wealth of others! I hereby place my wealth before you. Take of it whatever you want, until such time as God delivers his verdict.[218] Farewell.

When the letter reached the Successor and he had apprised himself of its contents, he tore it up and sent no answer. His evil deeds grew in number and those who complained about him multiplied. The sultan therefore sent the *malik* of the northern region, who was known in the army as the Tikináwi, against him. The Tikináwi went after him and caught up with him at a place called Bawwā. When the Successor saw the army had come, he drew up his ranks and stood his ground till it reached him. Then the two hosts joined battle. The Successor's army had been cowed by the battle of Tāldawā and was on the verge of defeat, but the Successor steadied them and waded into 2.3.11

فأراد الانهزام فثبّتهم الخليفة واقتحم الحرب بنفسه هو وجماعة من تِرْبِه فكان كلّما حلّ في جهة يفرّون منه حياء لا خوفاً حتّى دخل في القلب ووصل إلى التكنياوي فقال له يا عبد السوء ألست عبد أبي تغدر وتقاتلني وجرّد حسامه وضربه حتّى قتله وحين خرّ قتيلاً تشوّش صفّه وانهزم جنده وتبعهم عسكر الخليفة فأخذوهم قتلاً وأسراً ونهباً ولم ينج من الفَلّ إلّا القليل وغنم الخليفة خيلهم وسلاحهم وماكان معهم فانجبر خاطره وأمل النصرة على عمّه وتقوّى بما حصل له من الغنيمة

١٢،٣،٢ وبلغ ذلك السلطان عبد الرحمن فاغتاظ ثمّ أرسل أخاه ريفا مع جيش آخر فأدرك الخليفة في بوّا أيضاً وحين رآه الخليفة رتّب صفوفه وعبّأ عساكره وكان قد أعدّ كميناً في محلّ منخفض وقال لهم إنّي أتقهقر بالعساكر وهم يطمعون فيّ ويأتون خلفي فإذا رأيتموهم فعلوا ذلك فاصبروا حتّى تروهم أمامكم ثمّ كونوا[1] من خلفهم وانزلوا فيهم وأثخنوا فيهم ونحن نرجع عليهم فنكون أمامهم وأنتم خلفهم فلا يفلت منهم أحد وكان الأمر كذلك فحين التقى الجمعان تقهقر جماعة الخليفة فظنّ جماعة السلطان أنّه انهزم فأوغلوا فيهم حتّى صاروا أمام الكمين وهم لا يعلمون فخرج الكمين عليهم وأثخنوا فيهم بالقتل وكرّ الخليفة راجعاً فتضعضع جيش السلطان واختلّ أمرهم وتشوّش صفّهم وقُتِلَ باسي ريفا أخو السلطان وأمير[2] الجيش وقتل أكثر الجيش ولم ينج منهم إلّا القليل وحينئذ قويت شكيمة الخليفة وطمع في أن يرجع إلى السلطان ويقاتله وما علم أن الأمور بالخواتيم ولمّا سمع السلطان بموت أخيه ريفا اغتمّ غمّاً شديداً ولام نفسه على القعود عن الحرب وقال لو لم أسمع كلام الناس وتوجّهت بنفسي لم يحصل هذا الأمر ﴿وَكَانَ أَمْرُ اللهِ قَدَراً مَقْدُوراً﴾ ثمّ ارتحل من يومه وقصد جهة الخليفة بجيش يسدّ السهل والوعر وجاءت عيون الخليفة

١ الأصل: كنوا. ٢ الأصل: أمير.

the battle himself, along with the men his age, but whenever he appeared, the enemy would run away from him, out of embarrassment, not fear. In the end, he plunged into the middle of the army and reached the Tikináwi, to whom he said, "Evil slave! Didn't you belong to my father? Would you turn traitor and fight me?" And he drew his sword and struck him dead. When the Tikináwi fell, his battle formation was disrupted and his troops defeated. The Successor's soldiers pursued them, either killing them, taking them captive, or robbing them for plunder. Only a small number of the vanquished survived, and these the Successor despoiled of their horses, weapons, and everything they had with them. This consoled him and he looked forward to victory over his uncle, reinforcing himself with the spoils he'd taken.

News of this reached Sultan ʿAbd al-Raḥmān and he became furious. He 2.3.12 sent his brother Rīfā with another army. Rīfā caught up with the Successor at Bawwā again, and when the Successor saw him he drew up his ranks and put his army into a state of readiness, having previously prepared an ambush in a depression; he told them, "I shall withdraw with my soldiers and they, being eager to seize me, will come after me. When you see that they've done so, wait till they are in front of you. You'll be behind them and you can fall on them and harass them, and we shall wheel around and attack them. We shall be in front of them, and you behind, and no one will escape." And that is what happened. When the two hosts met, the Successor's men retreated, and the sultan's men, thinking them defeated, pressed on among them till they found themselves, all unawares, before the ambush. At this, the troops who were lying in wait emerged and put them to the slaughter. Wheeling around, the Successor returned to the charge, and the sultan's army was thrown off balance. It became disordered, and its ranks fell into disarray. Báási Rīfā, the sultan's brother, was killed, as were most of the army, leaving only a few survivors. At this, the Successor's energy was revived, and he became eager to go once more against the sultan and fight him, giving no thought to the fact that the affairs of men are decided by powers beyond their control. When the sultan heard of his brother's death, he grieved greatly and blamed himself for staying at home and not going to war. He said, "If I'd refused to listen and gone myself, this would not have happened—«and the command of God is a decree determined.»"[219] That same day he departed for the Successor's territory, with an army so immense it filled mountain and plain. When the Successor's spies came, they saw the sultan's

فرأوا جيش السلطان وما فيه من العساكر التي لا يقدر الواصف على وصفها والعادّ على حصرها وأسرعوا بالخبر إليه

فخاف على نفسه وجماعته فأصبح راحلاً قاصداً بلاد الزغاوة لأنّ ملكها خاله يريد أن ينزل عليه ليمدّه بجند من عنده فسار يقطع الأرض ليلاً ونهاراً والسلطان على أثره لأنّ الجواسيس أخبروه بقصده فخاف السلطان أنّه إذا وصل إلى زغاوة يمدّه خاله بجيش ويعسر أمره ويطول الحال بينهما فجدّ في طلبه حتّى أدركه بمحلّ يقال له جَرَكو وكان في طليعة جيش السلطان الأمين محمّد دُكّي بن الأمين عليّ ود جامع الذي سمّ نفسه في كردفال كما سبق فلمّا التقى الجمعان ظنّ الخليفة أنّ الجيش هذا فقط فكرّ راجعاً عليهم وناوشهم القتال وقاتل بنفسه ففرّت الناس أمامه حتّى وصل إلى الأمين محمّد دكّي فوقف أمامه وصار يضربه بالسيف ويقول له يا عبد يا خائن يا غدّار ألك عين ترفعها تخون نعمتي ونعمة أبي وتأتي لقتالي والأمين ساكت لا يتفوّه بحلوة ولا مرّة لكن كان لابساً درعين فلم يعمل سيف الخليفة فيه شيئاً فلمّا أعيا الخليفة أمره تركه وأراد أن يذهب فصبر عليه الأمين محمّد حتّى التفت وضربه على عاتقه الأيمن بالسيف وكان ذا قوّة فكسر عظم تَرْقُوَتِهِ وانكسر السيف من مقبضه وطار في المجال فخدرت يد الخليفة وأرخى ذراعه وعلم بذلك الأمين محمّد فطمع فيه وأراد أن يقبض عليه فأدركه جماعته فخلّصوه منه وانهزم حينئذ جيش الخليفة وتبعه الأمين محمّد بجيشه وأرسل السيف المكسور إلى السلطان عبد الرحمن يعلمه بما وقع فأرسل السلطان في الحال للأمين محمّد سيفين عظيمين مُحَلَّيَيْنِ وأمره بالمسير خلفه وأنّه على أثرهم ١٣،٣،٢

وكان حينئذ بالعسكر رجل من أبناء العرب يقال له زَبادي قيل إنه من فلّاحين مصر وكان يصطاد بالبندق ويصيب فتجاسر على السلطان وقال له يا مولاي إن ١٤،٣،٢

army and all the soldiers in it, who were too many for any describer to describe or counter to count, and they hurried to take him the news.

He then feared for his life and his men's lives, and he set off the next morning, striking camp and making for Zaghāwah territory: its overlord was his maternal uncle and he wanted to stay with him, hoping his uncle would provide him with some of his own troops. Through the land he rode, by day and by night, the sultan following in his tracks as his spies had told him of the Successor's intended destination. The sultan was afraid that, if he reached Zaghāwah, the Successor's uncle would indeed provide him with an army. Then he'd find himself in a difficult position, and the conflict between them would be prolonged. The sultan therefore pressed on, hard in his pursuit, and eventually caught up with him at a place called Jarkū. In the vanguard of the sultan's army was Counselor Muḥammad Dukkumī, son of Counselor ʿAlī wad Jāmiʿ who had poisoned himself in Kordofan, as mentioned earlier. When the two sides met, the Successor thought that was all there was to the army, so he wheeled round, attacked them, and skirmished with them, joining in the fighting himself. Everyone fled before him until he reached Counselor Muḥammad Dukkumī, where he halted and began striking at him with his sword, saying, "Slave! Betrayer! Traitor! Have you the gall to covet my wealth and that of my father?" But the counselor remained silent, uttering not a single word, bitter or sweet. He was, however, wearing two coats of mail so the Successor's sword had no effect on him. When the Successor got fed up with this, he decided to leave him be and was about to go. Counselor Muḥammad Dukkumī waited until he turned and then struck him on his right shoulder with his sword and broke his collarbone (he was a strong man), the sword breaking at the hilt and flying off into the field. The Successor's hand went numb and his arm went slack. Counselor Muḥammad noticed this and was eager to take him, but the Successor's men freed him just as the counselor was about to seize him. The Successor's army was now defeated, and Counselor Muḥammad sent his own after it, dispatching the broken sword to Sultan ʿAbd al-Raḥmān to inform him of what had happened. Immediately, the sultan sent to Counselor Muḥammad two mighty swords set with gems, ordered him to march after the Successor, and told him he was following their tracks. 2.3.13

There was at that time a man among the native Egyptian soldiery[220] called Zabādī who was said to be an Egyptian fellah. He hunted using a musket[221] and always hit his mark. He went boldly up to the sultan and said to him, "My Lord, 2.3.14

أرحتك من عدوّك في هذه الساعة فماذا يكون لي عليك قال السلطان عبد الرحمن له إذا أرحتني منه لك عليّ مائة رأس رقيق فقال أرسلني إلى الأمين لأكون في عسكره وترى ما يصير اليوم فأرسله في الحال إلى الأمين بكتاب من عند السلطان يقول فيه إنّ زبادي قد التزم براحتنا من عدوّنا والتزمنا له الجزاء في ذلك وطلب أن يكون في عساكرك فها هو واصل إليك فإن التمس منك شيئاً فساعده وأكرمه وإنّي على أثركم وركب زبادي على هجين ولحق بعسكر الأمين فأعطاه أمر السلطان فقرأه ورحّب به وسار في الجيش وبالأمر المقدر أنّ الخليفة آلمه ذراعه وأراد أن ينزل للراحة فمنعه أرباب دولته عن النزول فقال لهم ولِمَ تمنعوني فقالوا إن الأمين محمد قاف أثرنا بجيشه والقتال بيننا وبينه دائر فغضب وقال ألم يرجع عنّا فقالوا لا فكرّ راجعاً على عسكر الأمين فتعرّضوا له أيضاً فقال ولا بدّ

وبينما هو ينازعهم على الرجوع ويلاطفونه في الترك إذ جاء زبادي وتأمل الخليفة وعرفه وأخذ عليه النيشان وأطلق البندقيّة فأصابته قيل في صدره وقيل في رأسه فخرّ فأسندوه ومشى قليلاً وصار يجود بنفسه فحين رأى أرباب دولته أنّه يجود بنفسه نصبوا له سرادقاً وأدخلوه فيه ووقف الجيش يذبّ عنهم والقتال دائر بين فريقين حتّى وصل الأمين فرأى العسكر وقوفا ونار الحرب تستعر فسأل عن الخبر فقيل له إنّ الخليفة أصيب بالرصاص وهو يجود بنفسه وعجز عن الحركة فنصبوا له هذا السرادق ووقف جيشه يذبّ عنه فقال أمّا إذا كان الأمر كذلك فاتركوا القتال وأحيطوا بهم حتّى ننظر ما يكون وأرسل إلى السلطان يعلمه أن الخليفة أصيب برصاصة من زبادي وهو يجود بنفسه فإن كان يمكن مولانا أن يحضره قبل إزهاق روحه فليفعل وبعد ذهاب الرسول إلى السلطان بقليل قضي على الخليفة وأعلن بالبكاء ونزل الجيش الذي كان يقاتل من ظهور الخيل وكذا نزل جيش الأمين مفرد [بسيط] ١٥،٣،٢

if I rid you of your enemy right now, what will you give me?" The sultan answered, "If you rid me of him, I'll give you a hundred slaves." "Send me to the counselor's army," said the man, "so that I can be among his soldiers, and you shall see what will happen this day." The sultan sent him right away to the counselor with a letter in which he stated, "Zabādī has undertaken to rid us of our enemy, and we have undertaken to reward him for doing so. He asked to be with your soldiers, and now has reached you. If he requests anything of you, help him, and treat him well. I am coming along behind you." So Zabādī mounted a swift camel and caught up with the counselor's army and gave him the sultan's order. The counselor read it and welcomed him, and he joined his forces. Now, the Divine Will had ordained that the Successor's arm should hurt him, making him want to dismount and take a rest, but the high officers of the state forbade him to do so. "Why do you prevent me?" he asked them. "Counselor Muḥammad is pursuing us with his army," they replied, "and the fighting between us continues." The Successor grew angry and said, "He still has not turned back and left us alone?" They said, "No." So he wheeled around to attack the counselor's soldiers. His high officials opposed him in this too, but he said, "It must be so."

While he was arguing with them that they should turn back, and they were trying to persuade him with gentle words to abandon the idea, Zabādī arrived, recognized and picked out the Successor, took aim, fired, and hit the target, some say in the chest, others in the head.[222] The Successor fell, but they propped him up. He walked a little way and started to expire. When the officials saw he was dying, they set up a large tent for him and set him down in it. The army halted and warded off their attackers, but the fighting between the two sides went on. Eventually the counselor arrived and saw that the soldiery had halted and that the battle was ongoing. He asked what was happening and was told that the Successor had been hit by a bullet, was expiring, and was unable to move. That was why they'd erected this tent for him and the army had halted to defend him. "Stop fighting, then," he said, "and encircle them and let us wait and see what happens," and he sent word to the sultan that the Successor had been injured by a bullet fired by Zabādī and was dying and that "if it is possible for our lord to go to him before he gives up the ghost, he should do so." Shortly after the messenger was sent to the sultan, the Successor died, loud weeping was heard, and the soldiers who had been fighting dismounted from their horses, as did the counselor's soldiers. As the poet says: 2.3.15

لا يَأْمَنِ ٱلدَّهْرَ ذو بَغْيٍ وَلَوْ مَلِكًا   جُنُودُهُ ضَاقَ مِنْهَا ٱلسَّهْلُ وَٱلْجَبَلُ

مفرد لكاتبه [الشطر الأول من الكامل والشطر الثاني من الطويل]

لا يَمْنَعُ ٱلْجَيْشُ ٱلْكَثِيفُ مِنَ ٱلرَّدَى   وَلا يَمْنَعُ ٱلْمَقْدُورَ بُرْجٌ مُشَيَّدُ

١٦،٣،٢ وبعدها بقليل حضر السلطان وجيشه فاخترق الصفوف وحين رآه جيش الخليفة أعطوه الطاعة فدخل السرادق هو والأمين محمّد وجماعة من أرباب الدولة وكشف الغطاء عن وجه الخليفة وبكى بكاءً شديداً وقال يا ولدي أنت فعلت هذا بنفسك ونصحناك فلم تقبل ﴿وَكَانَ أَمْرُ اللهِ قَدَراً مَقْدُوراً﴾ ثمّ التفت إلى أرباب دولة الخليفة وقال لهم لقد زيّنتم القتال لولدي حتّى قتلتموه أما فيكم ذو عقل يكفّه وينصحه فحلفوا كلّهم أنّهم برآء ممّا كان فيه وأنّهم نصحوه فلم يقبل وقالوا له يا سيّدنا نحن تقلّدنا نعمته وقاتلنا عنه حتّى قضى الله فيه وما خنّاه وإن أنت قبلتنا نقاتل عنك كذلك ولو خنّاه وخدمناك نخونك أيضاً فعرف صحّة قولهم وقال قد عفوت عنكم فمن أراد أن يكون معي منكم فهو على رتبته ومقامه ومن أبى يلقَ خيرًا ثمّ أمر بدفن الخليفة في ذاك المحلّ وأبى يدفنه في مقبرة الملوك وقال هذا عاقٌّ لا يُدْفَنُ في مقابرنا فدُفِنَ هناك

١٧،٣،٢ وأقام السلطان بقية نهاره وليلته وأصبح قافلاً إلى الفاشر محفوفاً بالنصر مستبشرًا بذهاب العسر[١] كأنّ أبا الطيب رآه على تلك الحال حين أنشد وقال [كامل]

سِرْ حَيْثُ شِئْتَ تَحُلُّهُ ٱلْأَنْوَارُ   وَأَرَادَ فِيكَ مُرَادَكَ[٢] ٱلْأَقْدَارُ
وَإِذَا ٱرْتَحَلْتَ فَرَافَقَتْكَ سَلامَةٌ   حَيْثُ ٱتَّجَهْتَ وَدِيمَةٌ مِدْرَارُ

١ الأصل: عسر. ٢ الأصل: مراده.

No evildoer escapes Fate, though he be a king
whose troops fill plain and mountain!

And the writer of these words has said:

No army, though mighty, can fend off destruction
nor well-built tower Fate!

Soon after, the sultan and his army arrived and broke through the opposing ranks: when the Successor's army saw him, they surrendered. With Counselor Muḥammad and a group of high officers of the state, the sultan entered the tent, lifted the covering from the face of the Successor, and wept bitterly, saying, "My son, you did this to yourself. We gave you advice but you refused it, «and the command of God is a decree determined.»"[223] Then he turned to the high officers of the Successor's court and told them, "You made fighting seem so attractive to my son that you killed him. Wasn't there even one among you with the good sense to deter him and advise him more wisely?" They all swore that they were innocent of what he'd done and that they'd advised him against it, but that he'd refused to accept their advice. They told him, "Our Lord, we accepted his favor and we fought for him until God brought about his death, and we did not betray him. If you accept us, we will fight for you in the same way. If we'd betrayed him and then entered your service, we would have ended up betraying you too." The sultan saw the truth of their words and said, "I pardon you. Any of you who wants to be with me retains his rank and standing and any who does not, let him meet with nothing but good." Then he ordered that the Successor be buried in that same place and refused to let him be buried in the tombs of the kings, saying, "He was a rebel, and is not to be buried in our tombs."[224] So he was buried there. 2.3.16

The sultan stayed there the rest of the day and the following night, and in the morning set off to return to his seat, trailing clouds of victory, happy that the time of hardship was over—as though it were he whom Abū l-Ṭayyib al-Mutanabbī had in mind when he said:[225] 2.3.17

Go where you will—there shall light alight
and the fates ensure your hopes come true,
And when you depart, may safety be your companion
where'er you go, and a steady, quiet rain that never flags.

وَصَدَرْتَ أَغْنَمَ صَادِرٍ مِنْ مَوْرِدٍ   مَرْفُوعَةٌ لِقُدُومِكَ ٱلْأَبْصَارُ
أَنْتَ ٱلَّذِي لَهِجَ ٱلزَّمَانُ بِذِكْرِهِ   وَتَزَيَّنَتْ بِحَدِيثِهِ ٱلْأَسْمَارُ
وَإِذَا تَنَكَّرَ فَٱلْفَنَاءُ عِقَابُهُ   وَإِذَا عَفَا فَعَطَاؤُهُ ٱلْأَعْمَارُ
وَلَهُ وَإِنْ وَهَبَ ٱلْمُلُوكُ مَوَاهِبٌ   دَرُّ ٱلْمُلُوكِ لِدَرِّهَا أَغْبَارُ
لِلَّهِ قَلْبُكَ لَا يَخَافُ مِنَ ٱلرَّدَى   وَيَخَافُ أَنْ يَدْنُو إِلَيْكَ ٱلْعَارُ
وَتَحِيدُ عَنْ طَبْعِ ٱلْخَلِيقَةِ كُلِّهِ   وَيَحِيدُ عَنْكَ ٱلْجَحْفَلُ ٱلْجَرَّارُ
يَا مَنْ يَعِزُّ عَلَى ٱلْأَعِزَّةِ جَارُهُ   وَيَذِلُّ فِي سَطَوَاتِهِ ٱلْجَبَّارُ
كُنْ حَيْثُ شِئْتَ فَمَا تَحُولُ تَنُوفَةٌ   دُونَ ٱللِّقَاءِ وَلَا يَشِطُّ مَزَارُ

١٨،٣،٢ وكان الفاشر إذ ذاك بالمحلّ المسمّى قِرْلي وكان فاشر السلطان تيراب بالرِيل وفاشر الخليفة بجديد راس الفيل ثمّ انتقل بعد ذلك وجعل الفاشر بالمحلّ المسمّى تندلتي وهو فاشر ابنه الآن ولم يعهد للفور إقامة في فاشر كإقامتهم في فاشرهم هذا المسمّى تندلتي

١٩،٣،٢ ولمّا أراح قلبه من قتال الخليفة وسكن جأشه نظر في أمر الرعيّة فأبطل المكوس ورفع المظالم وولّى المناصب وانتبه لعمار البلاد ورفاهيّة الحال وقطع الإعلان بشرب الخمر والزنا وأمن الطرق وكانت مخوّفة فبعد ذلك صارت أمنًا حتّى أنّ المرأة كانت تسافر من أقصى البلاد إلى أدناها محمّلة من الحلي والمتاع لا تخشى إلّا الله وكثرت التجارات وتتابع الخصب وأظهر العدل التامّ فكان لا يكرم ظالمًا ولا يعينه ولو كان من ذوي قرابته

٢٠،٣،٢ ولقد أخبرني الثقة أنّ أعرابيّين تعرّضا له يوم وكان قادما من الصيد فقال له أحدهما أنا مظلوم يا رشيد الله يخلّيك يا رشيد أنا مظلوم ومن عادتهم أن المظلوم

From any source you plunder you will emerge the richest,
all eyes raised to watch your coming.
You are he with talk of whom time is besotted,
with talk of whom men's evenings are adorned.
Should you remove your favor, death's the penalty you mete out,
should you be forgiving, longevity's your gift—
And kings may give gifts, but to the favored you give gifts
beside which the best of what kings may give is dust.
God save your heart! It fears not ruin,
only that shame come near you.
You have turned aside from all that marks man's mortal nature,
while before you mighty armies with all their panoply swerve aside.
O you, whose protégé lords it o'er the powerful
while the tyrant before his assaults is brought low,
Where'er you be, no desert shall come between us,
and our meeting, and the place where we shall visit you, are not far off.

At the time, the sultan's seat was at a place called Qirlī, while Sultan Tayrāb's seat had been at Rīl,[226] and that of the Successor at Jadīd Rās al-Fīl. Later, Sultan ʿAbd al-Raḥmān moved and made his seat at a place called Tandaltī, which is now the seat of his son. It was never before the custom of the Fur to remain in one capital as they have in the place called Tandaltī.[227] 2.3.18

After the sultan had rested and recovered from fighting the Successor, and his agitation had abated, he turned his attention to the condition of his subjects. He abolished local tolls, removed illegal imposts, filled offices, and attended to the country's prosperity and affluence. He prohibited the consumption of alcohol[228] in public, and fornication, and reestablished security on the highways, which had been terrifying places but which now became so safe a woman could walk from one end of the country to the other loaded with jewelry and carrying goods and fear none but God. Trading activities increased, the land produced crops without interruption, and the sultan displayed perfect justice, neither honoring nor aiding oppressors, even when they were his relatives. 2.3.19

A trusted source told me that one day two Bedouin crossed the sultan's path, as he was returning from the hunt. One of them told him, "I have suffered an injustice, Rashīd! God keep you, Rashīd, I have suffered an injustice!" 2.3.20

إذا جاء أمام السلطان يضع إصبعَيْ يده اليمنى أي السَبّابة والإبهام على شدقَيْه ويردّدهما مع إخراج صوت عال فيه كاف واحدة وراءات كثيرة مضمومة فيخرج من فيه صوت يقال له الكُرُوراك وهذا الصوت لا يصوّت[1] به أحد إلّا إذا كان أصيب بمصيبة فكان الأعرابيّ يصوّت كذلك ويقول بعد كلّ صوت الله يخلّيك يا رشيد أنا مظلوم وشغل عنه السلطان إما لأمر قام به أو لأنّه لا يسمعه لكثرة الطبول والغناء وأصوات الجند فكرورك الأعرابيّ مراراً فلمّا لم يجبه السلطان قال له صاحبه خلّه عنك رشيد لنفسه لا لك فسمعه السلطان فوقف وسأل الأعرابيّ عمّا قال فقال إنّ أخي هذا كورك مراراً واشتكى لك وهو ينادي يا رشيد أنا مظلوم فلمّا لم تجبه قلت له خلّه فإنّه رشيد لنفسه غير رشيد لك فضحك السلطان وقال بل أنا رشيد لك أيضاً قل لي من ظلمك قال ظلمني باسي خبير وكان باسي خبير من أقاربه فقال وما أخذ منك قال أخذ منّي خمس نياق فوقف مكانه ودعا باسي خبير وسأله فاعترف فأمر أن يدفع له عشر[2] نياق خمسا حقّه وخمسا تأديبا له فدفعها وذهب الأعرابيّان وهما في غاية الغبطة والسرور

٢١،٣،٢ وفي أيّامه تلك نصب محمّد كرّا في منصب الأب الشيخ وهو أجلّ المناصب هناك صاحبه مطلوق السيف له دولة كدولة السلطان وشارات كشاراته ومن عادة هذا المنصب أنه[3] لا يتولّاه إلا خصيّ لأنّه يخشى من غير الخصيّ إذا تولّاه وقويت شكيمته أن يصادر السلطان ويطلب الملك لنفسه وبعد تولية الأب الشيخ محمّد كرّا وجّهه إلى البلاد فنزل في أبي الجدول وسلك طريق العدل في العالم وضبط الأمور حتّى أنّه قتل أناساً كثيرين لما وقع منهم من الظلم

٢٢،٣،٢ ولمّا ظهر عدل السلطان وحبّه للعلماء وأهل الفضل والأشراف وفد عليه الأشراف والعلماء من جهات عديدة فكان أوّل وافد عليه والدي عليه سحائب الرحمة

[1] الأصل: يصوته. [2] الأصل: عشرة. [3] أضيف للسياق: أنه.

It is their custom, if one of them finds himself in the presence of the sultan, to place two fingers of his right hand, namely, the index finger and the thumb, against the corners of his mouth and to flick them, producing a loud sound that contains a *k* and lots of *r*s followed by *u*.[229] This sound that emerges from the mouth they call *karawrāk*, and it is made only by one who has been afflicted by some disaster. The Bedouin made this sound and every time he did so he would say, "God keep you, Rashīd! I have suffered an injustice!" The sultan, however, paid him no attention, either because he was busy or because he couldn't hear him above all the drumming and singing and the clamor of the troops. The Bedouin performed the *karawrāk* several times, and when the sultan did not respond, his friend said to him, "Leave him be. He's 'rightly guided' when it comes to his own interests, not yours."[230] The sultan heard him, halted, and asked the other Bedouin why he'd said that. "My brother here," replied the man, "has performed the *karawrāk* several times and complained to you, crying out, 'Rashīd, I have suffered an injustice.' When you failed to respond to him, I told him, 'Leave him be: he's "rightly guided" when it comes to his own interests, not when it comes to yours.'" The sultan laughed and said, "Not at all. I'm rightly guided when it comes to yours too. Tell me who has done you this injustice." "Báási Khabīr has done me an injustice," said the man (Báási Khabīr was a relative of the sultan's). "What did he take from you?" he asked. "He took five she-camels from me," the man said. The sultan stayed where he was, summoned Báási Khabīr, and questioned him. He confessed, and the sultan ordered him to pay ten she-camels, five as the man's right and five as a punishment. He paid, and the Bedouin left in transports of joy.

It was now that he appointed Muḥammad Kurra to the office of shaykh-father, the highest office in Darfur. Its occupant exercises rights over life and death, has a government apparatus like that of the sultan, and insignia like those of the sultan. It is customary for this office to be occupied by a eunuch and only a eunuch, since it's feared that if any other occupies it and his sense of his own importance grows, he may set himself up against the sultan and seek to take the realm for himself.[231] Once Shaykh-Father Muḥammad Kurrā had been appointed, the sultan sent him out into the country,[232] and he stopped at Abū l-Judūl, where he established justice among the people and set things to rights, to the extent of having many men executed for injustices they'd committed. 2.3.21

When the sultan's justice became plain for all to see, and scholars, the learned, and the sharifs all began to love him, sharifs and scholars came from 2.3.22

والرضوان وكان حين قدومه إلى دارفور نزل بكوبيه على الفقيه حسن ود عَوُوضة وبلغ أهل كوبيه أنّه جاءهم رجل عالم من تونس فاجتمع عليه أكابرهم كالفقيه محمّد كُرَيْتِيم والشريف سرور بن أبي الجود وعبد الكريم بن الفقيه حسن ود عووضة وأضرابهم وطلبوا منه قراءة مختصر الشيخ خليل فقرأ لهم منه ربع العبادات ووصل خبره إلى الفقيه مالك الفوتاويّ فأعلم به السلطان فأرسل إليه فذهب له فأكرمه وأعطاه عدّة جواري وأمره أن يكون عند الفقيه نور الأنصاريّ زوج ابنته الميرم حوّاء وكان رجلا من سلالة الأنصار محبّا لأهل العلم وفيه فقه فقرأ على والدي نبذة من صحيح البخاريّ

٢٣،٣،٢ وأعلم السلطان بعلميّته وأنّه ماهر في العلوم العقليّة والنقليّة فأحضره لديه وقرأ عليه في شهر رمضان جزءًا من الحديث وتعلّقت به آمال الفقيه مالك فأمر أولاده أن يحضروا عليه فحضر عليه من إخوانه الفقيه إبراهيم والفقيه مدنيّ والفقيه يعقوب ومن أولاده الزاكي والسنوسيّ ومحمّد جلال الدين وابن أخيه الفقيه محمّد البَرَكاويّ وحضر عليه الفقيه حسين ود تُورِس وأمره السلطان أن يكتب على الخصائص التي ألّف متنها مُغُلْطايْ التركيّ فكتب عليها شرحاً عظيماً نحو ستّة عشر كرّاساً سمّاه الدرّة الوفيّة على الخصائص المحمديّة وسأله في شرح على مختصر الشيخ خليل المالكيّ في الفقه فكتب عليه شرحاً في مجلّدين سمّاه الدرّ الأوفاق على متن العلّامة خليل بن إسحاق وكتب على الآجرّوميّة شرحاً كبيراً أدخل فيه نحو مائتي بيت من ألفيّة ابن مالك فأتى مجلّداً ضخماً ثمّ اختصره في كراريس وكتب على السُلّم المُرَوْنَق شرحاً لطيفاً في كراريس وألّف رسالة في علم الكفّ[1]

٢٤،٣،٢ ووفد على السلطان عبد الرحمن الفقيه الزاهد الناسك الشيخ تَمُرّو[2] الفُلّانيّ ووفد عليه الفقيه النبيه الشيخ حسين عماريّ الأزهريّ ووفد عليه من أشراف مكّة

---

١ الأصل: الكتف. ٢ الأصل: التمُرّو.

many parts of the country to pay him their respects. The first to go was my father, may clouds of mercy and acceptance hover over him. When he first arrived in Darfur, my father stayed at Kūbayh with Faqīh Ḥasan wad ʿAwūḍah, who informed the people of the town that a man of learning from Tunis had arrived.[233] Their great men, such as Faqīh Muḥammad Kuraytīm, Sharif Surūr ibn Abī l-Jūd, ʿAbd al-Karīm (Faqīh Ḥasan wad ʿAwūḍah's son), and their like, came to see him and asked him to give lessons in Shaykh Khalīl's *Epitome,* so he took them through the section on acts of worship. Word of my father reached Faqīh Mālik al-Fūtāwī, who told the sultan about him, and the latter summoned my father. My father went to him and the sultan did him honor, gave him several female slaves, and ordered him to stay with Faqīh Nūr al-Anṣārī, the husband of his daughter, Mééram Ḥawwāʾ. He was descended from the Anṣār—a lover of the learned and a knowledgeable man. He studied under my father a portion of al-Bukhārī's collection of hadiths of the Prophet titled *The Reliable Compendium.*

The holy man told the sultan of my father's qualifications as a scholar and that he was skilled in both the rational and the transmitted sciences.[234] 2.3.23 So he had him brought before him and, during the month of Ramadan, studied under him some of the hadiths of the Prophet. Faqīh Mālik pinned his hopes on him and ordered his sons to attend his classes. Of Faqīh Mālik's brothers, Faqīh Ibrāhīm, Faqīh Madanī, and Faqīh Yaʿqūb attended his classes, and of his sons, al-Zākī, al-Sanūsī, and Muḥammad Jalāl al-Dīn, as well as his nephew Faqīh Muḥammad al-Barkāwī. Faqīh Ḥusayn wad Tūris also attended. In addition, the sultan ordered him to write a commentary on Mughulṭāy al-Turkī's *Qualities,* so he wrote an enormous commentary on it in some sixteen fascicules that he called *The Perfect Pearl Regarding the Qualities of Muḥammad.* He also asked him for a commentary on the *Epitome* of Shaykh Khalīl al-Mālikī concerning jurisprudence, so he wrote a two-volume commentary on it that he entitled *The Perfectly Matched Pearls on the Text of the Erudite Khalīl ibn Isḥāq.* He also wrote a large commentary on *Ibn Ājurrūm's Text* within which he included about two hundred lines from *The One-Thousand-Line Poem* of Ibn Mālik, which made up a huge volume that he subsequently abridged in several fascicules. And he wrote a graceful commentary on *The Glittering Ladder,* in fascicules, and he authored an epistle on palmistry.[235]

Sultan ʿAbd al-Raḥmān was also visited by that ascetic and reclusive man 2.3.24 of religion Shaykh Tamurrū al-Fullānī, and likewise by the distinguished man

الشريف مساعد يقال إنّه من أولاد الشريف سرور وكان قاضيه الفقيه النزيه الشيخ عزّ الدين الجامعيّ وهو قاضي القضاة بدارفور وأعمالها وكان السلطان عبد الرحمن جوادًا كريمًا عادلًا عفيف النفس وكان وسط القامة شديد السواد قد وَخَطَه الشيب أبحّ الصوت شديد الغضب سريع الرضا ذا تدبير حسن فمن حسن تدبيره أنّه لمّا دخلت الفرانساويّة مصر وهرب الغُزّ عنها توجّه إلى دارفور منهم كاشف يسمّى زَوانه كاشف قيل إنّه من مماليك مراد بيك أو هو أحد كشّاف الألفيّ ومعه أكثر من عشرة مماليك ومعه أمتعة زائدة وجمال وخدم وطبّاخ وفرّاش وسيّاس وأخذ معه مدفعًا وهاون بُنّ فحين حلّ بدارفور أكرمه السلطان عبد الرحمن وأحسن ملقاه وأنزله نُزُلًا حسنًا وأجرى عليه من الأرزاق شيئًا كثيرًا حتّى صار لا يعرف رقيقه كثرته ثمّ طلب من السلطان أن يبني بيتًا كبيوت مصر فأذن له في ذلك فضرب الآجر واستخدم العبيد في قطع الأحجار وصنع بيتًا جميلًا وسوّره بسور وجعل السور عريضًا وجعل فيه مزغلتين مقابلتين لبيت السلطان يضع في إحداهما المدفع وفي الأخرى هاون البنّ

٢،٣،٢٥ وكان محلّ هذا البيت أعلى من محلّ بيت السلطان بحيث كان يرى السلطان حين يدخل وحين يخرج فسوّلت له نفسه أن يقتل السلطان ويملك البلد بأن يرصده[١] وهو داخل أو خارج ويطلق عليه مدفعًا يهلكه به لكن خاف إن قتل السلطان لا يطيعوه[٢] أهل المملكة وأرباب الدولة فاحتال أن اجتمع بالفقيه الطيّب ود مصطفى وكان هذا الفقيه وزير السلطان تيراب وصهره أعني أنّ السلطان تيراب كان متزوّجًا بأخته وأتت منه بولد فلمّا اجتمع عليه زوانه كاشف فشى سرّه له بعد أن عاهده على الكتمان وقال له إنّه قد بلغني أنّ ابن أختك ابن السلطان وأريد أن تجعل يدك معي فنقتل هذا ونولّي ابن أختك وتصير المملكة بيننا فرضي الفقيه الطيّب بذلك ثمّ قالوا إنّ هذا الأمر لا يتمّ لنا إلّا بإدخال بعض الناس الذين تكون لهم

١ الأصل: يرصد. ٢ الأصل: يطعوه.

of religion Shaykh Ḥusayn ʿAmmārī al-Azharī. Another who came to pay his respects was the Meccan sharif Musāʿid, who I was told was a son of Sharif Surūr.[236] Sultan ʿAbd al-Raḥmān's judge was that irreproachable man of religion Shaykh ʿIzz al-Dīn al-Jāmiʿī, who is currently chief judge of Darfur and its territories.[237] Sultan ʿAbd al-Raḥmān was generous, noble, just, and unassuming. He was of medium height, extremely black, with gray hair; he was fierce in his anger, quick to be reconciled, a good manager of affairs. One example of that last trait is that when the French entered Egypt and the Turkish soldiery fled, a certain *kāshif* named Zawānah Kāshif,[238] who was said to be one of Murād Bayk's Mamluks or one of al-Alfī's *kāshif*s, came to Darfur, bringing with him more than ten Mamluks and a large quantity of baggage, as well as camels, servants, a cook, a housekeeper, and grooms. He also brought a cannon and a mortar. When he stopped in Darfur, Sultan ʿAbd al-Raḥmān treated him as an honored guest and gave him a warm welcome, putting him up in a good hostelry and providing for him so well that the man ended up with so many slaves he couldn't tell one from the other. Then he asked the sultan if he might build a house like those in Egypt, and the sultan gave him permission to do so. He cast bricks, used the slaves to cut stones, and made a beautiful house, which he surrounded with a wall, which he made thick, with two loopholes in it, opposite the sultan's house. In one of these loopholes he placed the cannon and in the other the mortar.

This house was on higher ground than the sultan's, allowing him to observe 2.3.25
the sultan's comings and goings. He then let himself be seduced by the idea that he could kill the sultan and rule the country by watching him as he went in and out, firing the cannon at him, and killing him. At the same time, he was afraid that if he killed the sultan, the people and the high officers of the realm would refuse to obey him, so he arranged to meet privately with Faqīh al-Ṭayyib wad Muṣṭafā, who had been a vizier of Sultan Tayrāb's and was his in-law, by which I mean that Sultan Tayrāb was married to his sister, who had borne him children. When Zawānah Kāshif met with him, he confessed his secret, after making him promise to tell no one, and said, "I'm told your sister's son is a son of the sultan. I want you to join forces with me in killing the latter so your nephew can assume power and the realm can be ours." Faqīh al-Ṭayyib agreed to this. Then they said, "This will not work unless we involve people who have soldiers." "That's up to you to arrange," said Zawānah, "for you know the people better." So Faqīh al-Ṭayyib set about cozening people and bringing

عساكر فقال زوانه ذاك إليك وأنت أعرف الناس به فصار الفقيه الطيّب يخادع الناس ويأتي بهم إلى الكاشف والكاشف يعطيهم الأموال ويحلّفهم أن يكونوا معه حتّى أدخلوا في أمرهم عدّة رجال

٢،٣،٢٦ واتّفق أنّ رجلاً من الأمراء خادعه الفقيه الطيّب وجاء به إلى الكاشف فأعطاه عطيّة سنيّة وأطلعه على الأمر وحلّفه على الكتمان فحلف وأخذ العطاء وتوجّه به إلى السلطان وأطلعه على جليّة الأمر وحقيقته فقال له السلطان خذ عطاءك واذهب وكن معهم على ما أنت عليه وإيّاك أن تخبر أحداً أنّك أتيتني ولمّا كان من الغد جاء زوانه الكاشف إلى بيت السلطان فأكرمه أكثر ممّا كان يكرمه وأعطاه في ذلك الوقت مائة عبد ومائة جارية ومائة ناقة ومائة جرّة سمناً ومثلها عسلاً ومائة حمل دخناً وكساه كشميرًا أحمر وجوخة حمراء وقلّده سيفاً وأعطاه جواداً سرجه من ذهب وتوجّه الكاشف إلى منزله مغتبطاً بما حصل له من السلطان وقال هذه أموال ساقها الله إليّ أستعين بها على هذه المصلحة ولمّا أمسى المساء وكان بعد العشاء أمر السلطان بإحضار ملك من الملوك بعسكره وأمره أن يقف حتّى يرى الكاشف داخل دار السلطان فيعقبه[1] ويضبط جميع ما في بيت الكاشف من الأموال وحذره من[2] أن يفلت منه شيء ثمّ أرسل للكاشف غلاماً يقول له إن سيّدي جلس للسمر وقد أراد أن تحضر مجلسه الآن ورتّب عبيداً للقبض عليه عند أمر السلطان به

٢،٣،٢٧ فذهب الغلام وأخبره بمقال السلطان فحضر معه ولمّا دخل على السلطان أكرمه وكان معه بعض من الخدم دخلوا معه بابين ومُنعوا أن يدخلوا من الثالث وقيل لهم اصبروا هنا حتّى يأتي سيّدكم فكدّسوا مكانهم[3] وجلس السلطان يتحدّث مع الكاشف حتّى فاتت من الليل حصّة فقال السلطان إنّي جائع والتمس ما يؤكل فأتي بلحم نصيص أي حنيذ غير مقطّع فالتمسوا سكّيناً فلم يجدوا فأخرج الكاشف سكّيناً

١ الأصل: يعقبه. ٢ الأصل: عن. ٣ الأصل: بايين ومنع أن يدخل من الثالث وقيل له اصبر هنا حتى يأتي سيدك فكدس مكانه.

them to the Kāshif, and the Kāshif would award them goods and make them swear to be with him. Eventually, they involved a number of men in the matter.

Now, it happened that Faqīh al-Ṭayyib cozened one of the army commanders and brought him to the Kāshif, who gave him a handsome gift, let him in on what was planned, and swore him to secrecy. The man swore, took the gift, and took it to the sultan, and revealed the full extent and truth of the matter. The sultan told him, "Take your gift, go, and be with them just as you are now, and be sure not to tell anyone that you came to see me." The following morning, Zawānah Kāshif came to the sultan's house and the latter did him even more honor than before, giving him, on this occasion, one hundred male slaves and one hundred female, one hundred she-camels, one hundred jars of clarified butter, one hundred of molasses, and one hundred loads of millet, and he clothed him in a red cashmere shawl and a coat of red broadcloth and presented him with a sword and gave him a fine steed with a saddle of gold. The Kāshif left for his house overjoyed at what the sultan had given him, saying, "These are assets God has put in my way to use for this business." That evening, after the prayer, the sultan ordered that one of the petty kings, along with his soldiery, be brought to stand and wait until he saw the Kāshif entering the sultan's house, and then, while he was away, go in and seize everything of value that was in the Kāshif's house, warning him to let nothing escape him. After that, he sent a boy to the Kāshif to tell him, "My master has taken his seat for his evening gathering with his friends and has expressed the desire that you attend his assembly, now." And the sultan placed slaves in position to arrest him whenever he should give the order. 2.3.26

The boy went and told the Kāshif what the sultan had said, and the man went back with him. When he entered the sultan's presence, the latter treated him with honor. With him were some servants, who passed through two doors with him but were prevented from going through the third.[239] They were told, "Wait here till your master comes back," so they huddled there together. The sultan sat conversing with the Kāshif until a part of the night had passed, and then the sultan said, "I'm hungry," and requested something to eat, so some roast meat of the sort called *naṣīs*, meaning the kind that's roasted on hot stones, was brought, uncut. They called for a knife but no one could find one, so the Kāshif pulled out a knife he had on him and was about to cut up the meat when one of those present swore that he mustn't do so and that he'd see to it, and he took the knife from him and started cutting up the meat. Then the 2.3.27

كان معه وأراد أن يقطع اللحم فحلف عليه بعض الحاضرين ألّا يفعل وأنّه هو الذي يقطع فأخذ منه السكّين وصار يقطع بها فأخذ الكاشف الخنجر فأخذه آخر وحينئذ أمر السلطان بالقبض عليه فلمّا قبض عليه قال له السلطان أيّ ذنب جرى لك منّي حتّى أنّك تريد قتلي وتغوي عساكري وتخادعهم فقال أقلني فقال لا أقالني الله إن أقلتك وأمر بذبحه في الحال فذبح كالشاة وفي الحال جيء بأمواله وما كان عنده من رقيقه وغيره حتّى لم يبق في البيت شيء وأمر السلطان بهدم بيته فهدم ومحيت رسومه وكأنّه لم يكن وقبض على أتباعه في تلك الليلة وباتوا محبوسين ولمّا أصبح الصباح دعا بهم السلطان فحضروا فعفا عنهم وأطلقهم وأمر عليهم خازندار الكاشف وكان يسمّى يوسف[1] ثمّ تتبّع جميع من تعاهد مع الكاشف وقبض عليهم واحداً بعد واحد حتّى لم يبق منهم أحد وكان آخرهم الفقيه الطيّب فإنه قبض عليه وقتله أشرّ قتلة وسجن ابن أخته سجن الدوام إلى أن يموت

٢٨،٣،٢ وكيفيّة القبض على الفقيه المذكور أنه أرخى له العنان وبذل له الأموال وأظهر له الودّ التامّ بحيث أنّ الفقيه الطيّب لم يخطر بباله أنّ السلطان معه علم بأنّه كان مع زوانه كاشف ومضت على ذلك مدّة حتّى كان في بعض الأيّام حضر الفقيه الطيّب دار السلطان وكان السلطان جالساً في ديوانه وحضرت له إبل موقورة عسلاً فأعطاها للفقيه الطيّب وأمر له بكسوة فأحضر له كشمير أحمر وكسوة جليلة فلبسها ودعا للسلطان بدوام العزّ وجلس ومن عادة ملوك الفور إذا كسوا إنساناً كسوة حمراء فإنّهم في غضب عليه ولا بدّ ما يقتلونه وتذكّر السلطان ما كان منه ونفاقه مع الكاشف في آخر المجلس فالتفت إلى الحاضرين وقال لهم أشهدكم بالله هل هذا الفقيه في أيّام أخي أرفه حالاً وأكثر مالاً أم هذا الوقت فقالوا كلّهم لا والله بل في هذا الوقت أرفه وأغنى وأنفذ كلمة فقال السلطان سلوه حينئذ لم خانني وتواطأ مع الكاشف على قتلي وخراب داري فسألوه فأقسم على السلطان بالله العظيم

١ الأصل: يوسفا وثم.

Kāshif took out his dagger and another took that from him and at that point the sultan gave the order to arrest him. Once he'd been seized, the sultan asked him, "What wrong did I do you that you should want to kill me and mislead and cozen my soldiers?" "Pardon me!" said the man. "May God not pardon me if I pardon you!" said the sultan, and he ordered that he be slaughtered on the spot, and he was, like a sheep. Right away, his possessions were brought too, along with his slaves and other things he possessed, so that in the end there was nothing left in the house. The sultan ordered that the house be torn down, so it was torn down and all vestige of it erased, as though it had never been, and his followers were seized the same evening and spent the night as prisoners. Next morning, the sultan summoned them, and when they were before him, pardoned them and released them, placing the Kāshif's treasurer, whose name was Yūsuf, in command of them. Then he pursued all those who had made a pact with the Kāshif and seized them one by one till none were left. The last to be arrested was Faqīh al-Ṭayyib. He arrested him and made him suffer the worst of deaths, and he imprisoned the man's nephew for life, till he should die.

The arrest of the aforementioned Faqīh took place in the following manner. **2.3.28**
The sultan gave him complete freedom to do what he wanted, bestowing wealth on him and showing him the utmost affection, so that it never occurred to Faqīh al-Ṭayyib that the sultan had any awareness that he'd been involved with Zawānah Kāshif. Things went on like this till a day came when Faqīh al-Ṭayyib was present in the sultan's house. The sultan was seated in his court and some camels loaded down with honey were brought him, so he gave them to Faqīh al-Ṭayyib and ordered that he be given a set of clothes, and they brought him a fine set of clothes and a red cashmere shawl. He put these on and called down blessings on the sultan, calling for the preservation of his rule, and then sat; it is a custom of the petty kings of the Fur that if one of them dresses someone in red clothes, it means he's angry with him and has decided to kill him. At the end of the gathering, the sultan recalled what the Faqīh had done and his duplicitous behavior with the Kāshif and he turned to those present and said, "I ask you, in God's name, to bear witness: was this Faqīh more comfortably off or wealthier in the days of my brother than he is now?" They all responded, "No, by God. He's more comfortably off, wealthier, and more influential now!" "Ask him, then," said the sultan, "why he betrayed me and plotted with the Kāshif to kill me and bring ruin to my house." They asked him, and the man adjured the sultan by Mighty God to kill him rather than force him to answer

أن يقتله ولا يكلّفه جواب هذا السؤال لأنّ الموت عنده أهون من ذلك فأبرّ السلطان قسمه حينئذ وأمر فذُبح كالشاة وأخذ جميع ما عنده من الأموال والضياع ولم يفلت منه شيء وقد سمعت أنّه أرسل العساكر لأخذ ماله من ضياعه قبل ذلك بمدّة وعيّن لهم أن يكبسوها في ذلك اليوم بعينه خوفاً أن يطيش الخبر ويفلت منها شيء وذلك كلّه من سعادته ومن سعادته أيضاً أن جميع من رامه بسوء يخذل ويمكّنه الله منه

٢،٣،٢٩ ومن ذلك ما حصل من إياكري كِنانة أم حبيب المتقدّم ذكرها وذلك أنّ السلطان تغافل عنها ولم يف بما وعدها به إمّا لأمر قام به أو خوفاً على نفسه منها أو من ولدها فلمّا رأت تغافله لها وكانت في دار السلطان وابنها حبيب متأهّل في دار له عقدت له بالمكاتبة مع بعض الملوك عقداً واتّفقت معه أن يساعد حبيباً ليتولّى سلطاناً خصوصاً وقد[1] انقطع أملها حين رأت أن السلطان ولد له فخافت على ولدها لكنّ السلطان وإن كان تغافل عنها إلّا أنّه كان مبقيها في منصبها آمرة ناهية مقاليد أمور الدار كلّها بيدها

٢،٣،٣٠ فلمّا نوت الغدر بالسلطان استأذنته في أنّ حبيباً[2] يريد أن يصنع وليمة وأريد أن أمدّه بطعام من هنا فأذن لها السلطان في ذلك فصنعت الطعام وصارت تأتي بالجفنات وتضع الدروع في الجفنة ثمّ تجعل الطعام فوقها بحيث أنّ من يرى الجفنة لا يظنّ أنّ فيها غير الطعام وكانت تضع في واحدة دروعاً وفي أخرى سيوفاً فأخرجت ما يزيد عن مائة جفنة بهذه الصورة ثمّ مكثت مدّة أيّام واستأذنت له في وليمة أخرى فأذن لها ولم يخطر بباله شيء ممّا في نفسها لأنّه كان سليم الصدر غير ظنّان بالسوء ففعلت كما فعلت بالمرّة الأولى وبعد أيّام أيضاً استأذنته كذلك وقبل إبراز الوليمة الثالثة كانت عندها بنت من بنات الأكابر جميلة الصورة تربّيها فرآها السلطان على حين

[1] الأصل: قد. [2] الأصل: حبيب.

that question, since to die, he thought, would be easier. The sultan honored his wish and gave the order, and he was slaughtered like a sheep. The sultan took all his property and estates; nothing escaped him. I heard that he'd dispatched the soldiers to take his property from his estates some time previously and gave the order to seize them on that precise day, for he was afraid that otherwise word would get out and something escape him. This was an example of the good fortune that accompanied him always. Another example of this good fortune was that everyone who sought to do him ill failed and God delivered them into his hands.

Another example of that same good fortune was the incident with Iyā Kurī Kinānah, mother of Ḥabīb, who was mentioned earlier.[240] What happened was that the sultan ignored her and failed to fulfill his promise to her, either because he was too busy or because he was afraid that either she or her son would try to kill him. When she saw how he ignored her (she was living at that time in the sultan's house while her son Ḥabīb had been provided with his own), she made a contract with some of the members of the royal family that they would support her son and agree to let them help Ḥabīb rule when he was sultan—her hopes had been dashed on her discovery that the sultan had had more sons, making her fear for her own. The sultan, though he ignored her, had left her in office—she had power to command and forbid, and the reins of household affairs were still entirely in her hands. 2.3.29

When she made up her mind to betray the sultan, she asked his permission to allow her son Ḥabīb to fulfil his wish to hold a banquet, saying, "I'd like to provide him with food from here." The sultan agreed, so she started to bring in huge bowls, placing chain mail coats in them and putting food on top in such a way that anyone who looked at a bowl would think that there was nothing in it but food;[241] in one she would put coats of chain mail, in the next swords. She was able to send out more than a hundred bowls in this way. She waited and, after a few days, asked his permission for another banquet, which he gave without giving the matter a second thought, for he was openhearted and harbored no suspicions of evil. And she did as she had the first time. A few days later she asked for permission again, but before the third banquet was announced it happened that the sultan unexpectedly set eyes on a daughter of one of the notables, a pretty girl she was raising, and he fell in love with her and made up his mind to speak to the Iyā Kūrī about her and become engaged to her. Umm Ḥabīb[242] must have sensed this in the sultan 2.3.30

غفلة فأحبّها ونوى في نفسه أن يخاطب إيا كري في شأنها ويعقد عليها وكأنّ أمّ حبيب فهمت من السلطان ذلك فصارت تؤذيها لأنها أعدّتها لولدها حبيب فلم تطق البنت الأذيّة خصوصاً وقد انكشفت على غدرها بالسلطان وما تريد أن تصنعه معه فاختلست نفسها وقابلت السلطان على خلاء وأخبرته أنّ أمّ حبيب أخربت خزينة السلاح والأمتعة وأنّ الولائم كلّها مملوءة بالدروع والسيوف وأنّها تعاقدت مع الملك فلان وفلان بأنّهم يساعدوها على قتلك وتولية حبيب الملك وإن كنت في شكّ ممّا أقوله اقلب جَفْنة من الجِفان التي تخرج في الوليمة في غد فإنّك تعلم صحّة قولي فقال لها السلطان ارجعي إلى مقرّك وإيّاك أن تقولي إنك أعلمتيني بشيء فرجعت وضاق صدر السلطان لذلك وأخبر بعض الخدمة أن أخبرني في غد قبل خروج الوليمة إلى حبيب واستكتمه فكتم

٢،٣،٣١ وبقي الحال كذلك حتّى أصبح الصباح وصنعت الوليمة ونادت العبيد والجواري يرفعن الجفنات فأخبره الخادم بأنّ الوليمة قد تجهّزت فدخل فرأى أمّ حبيب ترتّبها للحمل فقال على رِسلكم ثمّ قال ارفعوا الأغطية وأروني وليمة ولدي حبيب فرفعوا الأغطية فرأى طعاماً حسناً فجاء إلى جفنة فيها طعام يحبّه وقال اتركوا هذه لي واجعلوا ما فيها في أوانٍ صغار لآكل منها أنا وبعض أضياف لي فقالوا سمعاً وطاعة وجاءت أمّ حبيب حين بلغها ذلك وقالت فداك أبي وأمّي عندنا من نوع هذا الطعام كثير فليترك مولاي الجفنة ونحن نأتيه بكثير منه فقال قد علمت وإنّما نفسي طلبت من هذه ولعلّ ما تأتون به وإن كان من هذا بعينه لا تتوق إليه نفسي فحينئذ لم تجد بدّاً من طاعته وقالت دع الخدم يرفعن هذه الجفنات واحبس أنت هذه فقال لا بل حتّى تفرغ هذه الجفنة وتملأ كما كانت ويحمل كلّه مرّة واحدة

٢،٣،٣٢ ولمّا جيء بالأواني واغترف من الجفنة ظهر الدروع من تحت الطعام فنادى يا أمّ حبيب ما هذا فخجلت ولم تُحِرِ جواباً فعند ذلك أمر بالقبض عليها وقلب جميع

and she started mistreating the girl whom she'd been grooming to marry her son Ḥabīb. The girl couldn't stand the mistreatment, especially since she'd discovered the Iyā Kūrī's betrayal of the sultan and what she wanted to do to him. She therefore slipped away, met with the sultan in private, and told him that Umm Ḥabīb had broken into the weapons and supplies storehouses, that the vessels for the banquet had all been filled with chain mail and swords, and that she'd engaged with Malik So-and-so and Malik So-and-so "to help her kill you and make Ḥabīb sovereign, and if you doubt what I say, overturn any of the bowls that are sent out for the banquet tomorrow and you'll see my words are true." "Go back to your place," said the sultan, "and be careful not to let anyone know that you've told me anything." She went back, and the sultan, angry at what he had heard, said to one of his servants, "Inform me tomorrow before the food for the banquet is sent over to Ḥabīb's," telling him to keep it to himself, which he did.

This was how things stood when morning came, when the banquet was laid out and Umm Ḥabīb summoned the men and women slaves to carry the bowls. The servant told the Sultan then that the banquet was ready, so he went in and saw her organizing the food for delivery. "Not so fast!" said the sultan, and then, "Lift the covers and show me my son Ḥabīb's banquet." They lifted the covers and he saw fine food. Going over to a bowl that contained a kind of food that he liked, he said, "Set this aside for me and put the contents into small dishes so that I and some of my guests may partake of it." "We hear and obey!" they replied. When word of this reached Umm Ḥabīb, she came and said, "I swear on my father and mother, we have lots of that dish! May my lord leave that bowl, and we'll bring him a great quantity of it." "No doubt," he replied, "but I've taken a fancy to this: perhaps what you send me may not be as good, and, even if it's the very same dish, may not appeal to me." At this, she could think of no alternative but to do as he asked, and said, "Allow the servants to remove these other bowls while you keep this one aside." "No," said he. "This bowl must be emptied and filled just as it was and then all the food loaded up at one time." 2.3.31

When the small dishes were brought and the food was being ladled out of the bowl, the chain mail came into view from beneath the food, and he called out, "Umm Ḥabīb, what is this?" Abashed, she said nothing. He ordered, therefore, that she be seized and all the bowls turned upside down, and discovered all the chain mail coats, swords, French dollars, and so on. "What wrong did I do you 2.3.32

الجفنات فوجد فيها كلّها دروعا وسيوفاً وريالات فرانسا ونحو ذلك فقال لها أيّ ذنب وقع منّي حتّى دبّرتي على هلاكي فلم تردّ جواباً فأمر بقتلها في تلك الساعة فقتلت وفي الحال أرسل ملكاً من ملوكه إلى بيت حبيب بعد أن دعا حبيباً إليه فحضر على حالة الطمأنينة فلمّا مثل بين يدي السلطان أمر بالقبض عليه فوُضِعَ في المحبس ثمّ أرسله تحت جنح الليل إلى جبل مرّة واستصفى ما عنده من المال ورد الدروع والسلاح إلى مقرّها ثمّ قبض على جميع من تواطأ مع حبيب ولم يبق منهم أحداً

٢،٣،٣٣ وتمهّدت أموره واستوزر الفقيه مالك الفوتاويّ لظنّ علميّته وصلاحه وكان يدّعي أنّه يعرف سرّ الحرف وعلم الأوفاق مع أنّه كانت فيه عاميّة وكثيراً ما كان يظهر الورع والصلاح ويُبطن ضدّه وكنت أظنّ ذلك منه حتّى حقّق الله ظنّي فيه في مجلس واحد وذلك أنّه لمّا ترقّى الوزارة أدخل جميع قبيلة الفُلّان التي بدارفور تحت أمره وصار يذبّ عنهم عند السلطان كلّما وقع منهم أمر مع أعدائهم من القبائل الأخر وحرّرهم عند الدولة حتّى صار لا يُجبى منهم مال وكلّ ما[1] نهبوه من غيرهم من القبائل برد لهم حتّى صاروا من أقوى القبائل وأغناها

٢،٣،٣٤ فاتّفق أنّ قبيلة الفلّان أغاروا على قبيلة المساليط وقتلوا منهم خلقاً كثيراً ونهبوا منهم أموالاً جمّة من بقر وخيل ورقيق وجاء رئيسهم وكان يسمّى بجِدّ العيّال وأتى بخيل وبقر ورقيق من المنهوب هديّة إلى الفقيه مالك ليذبّ عن القبيلة وكان في شهر رمضان وكان وقت العصر والفقيه مالك إذ ذاك يقرأ في تذكرة القرطبيّ في صفة أهل النار فأتى على قوله ولا زالت النار تقول يا ربّ زدني حتّى يضع الرحمن فيها رِجلَهُ والرِجل هي الجماعة من الناس وعليه قول الشاعر [طويل]

فَمَرَّ بِنَا رِجْلٌ مِنَ ٱلْحَيِّ وَٱنْزَوَى

[1] الأصل: وكلما.

that you should plot my destruction?" he asked her. She didn't answer, so he ordered her to be killed there and then, and she was. Then he immediately sent one of his chiefs to Ḥabīb's house, having first invited Ḥabīb to come to him. Ḥabīb came, thinking nothing was amiss. When he appeared before him, the sultan ordered that he be seized, and he was placed in the lock-up. Then he sent him under cover of night to Jabal Marrah,[243] stripped him of all his wealth, and had the chain mail and weapons returned to their place. Subsequently, he seized all those who had conspired with Ḥabīb and left not a single one alive.

Now that order was restored, Sultan ʿAbd al-Raḥmān appointed Faqīh Mālik al-Fūtāwī as vizier, because he believed him to be a scholar and a righteous man; al-Fūtāwī also claimed to know the "secret of the letter" and the science of talismans,[244] even though he was in fact a man of mediocre literary culture and would often make a show of being God-fearing and righteous while concealing the opposite in his heart. This was something I suspected of him, and then God proved the truth of my suspicions at a single gathering. The way this came about was that when he was promoted to the viziership, the entire Fullān tribe in Darfur fell under his command, and he started taking their side with the sultan whenever there was some incident between them and their enemies among the other tribes. He also released them from their obligations to the state to the point that no taxes were collected from them and everything they took as plunder from other tribes stuck with them. As a result, they became one of the most powerful and richest tribes. 2.3.33

Now it happened that the Fullān raided the Masālīṭ, killing many of them and taking a large portion of their wealth in the form of cattle, horses, and slaves. The head of the Fullān, whose name was Jidd al-ʿAyyāl,[245] came, bringing as a gift for Faqīh Mālik some of the horses, cattle, and slaves that had been plundered, so that he would defend the tribe's interests. It was the month of Ramadan and late afternoon, and at that moment Faqīh Mālik was reading from al-Qurṭubī's *Memorandum*, where it describes the people of hellfire. He came to the place where the author says, "And the fire keeps saying, 'O Lord, add to me,' until the Merciful puts His *rijl* in it, a *rijl* being a company of people, as evidenced by the verse: 2.3.34

> And a company of the clan passed by us (*fa-marra binā rijlun*) and
> retired."[246]

فقال ولا زالت النار تقول يا ربّ زدني وكان من عادته أن يقول بعد كلّ كلمة أو كلمتين أي نعم قال الكتّاب فقال ولا زالت النار تقول يا ربّ زدني أي نعم قال الكتّاب ولا زالت النار تقول يا ربّ زدني أي نعم قال الكتّاب حتّى يضع الرحمن فيها رِجْله أي نعم قال الكتّاب والرِجْل هي الجماعة من الناس أي نعم قال الكتّاب وعليه قول الشاعر أي نعم قال الكتّاب فِرّ[1] بنا رِجَل أي نعم قال الكتّاب وكرّرها مراراً فقال له السنوسيّ ولده يا أَبّو فِرْ! بنا رَجُلٌ! فقال أي نعم فِرْ بنا رَجُلٌ وكرّرها مراراً وكنت جالساً ولم يسعني السكوت فأخذت نسخة من رجل بجانبي فرأيت فيها فَمرّ بنا رِجْلٌ من الحي البيت فقلت يا أبو فَمَرَّ بنا رِجْلٌ فقال لي اسكت أنت الآن صغير عن هذا وأمثاله مع أنّ هذا هو الذي يصلح لأن يكون شاهداً فسكتّ

ومن عاميّته ما حكى لي والدي عليه سحائب الرحمة والرضوان أنّ السلطان التمس من الفقيه المذكور أن يخطب يوم العيد فقصد والدي أن يؤلّف له خطبة فألّفها وكتب في آخرها تمّت على يد مؤلّفها الفقير إلى المنّان عمر التونسيّ[2] ابن سليمان في يوم وسنة كذا وأعطاها إيّاه فلمّا كان يوم العيد صلّى بالسلطان ثمّ رقي المنبر فخطب وبعد الخطبة قال تمّت إلى آخر ما كتب ولم يتفطّن أنّ هذه الكلمات خارجة عن الخطبة وكان من أغنى أرباب الدولة وكان له من الأقطاع ما ينوف عن خمسمائة بلد وذلك غير أقطاع إخوانه ٢،٣،٣٥

ثمّ السلطان أجلّ مقام الأب الشيخ محمّد كرّا وأعلى كلمته حتّى صار لا تعلى[3] على كلمته كلمة وبلغه أنّ هاشم المسبّعاويّ ملك كردفال رجع إليها وأخذها من يد عامل السلطان فجهّز جيشاً كثيفاً لنظر الأب الشيخ محمّد كرّا فتوجّه إلى كردفال وأغنى غناء حسناً وأخذ كردفال من يد السلطان هاشم وقتل عساكره وشرّده في القفار واستوطن كردفال مدّة سبع سنين وفيها أرسل للسلطان أموالاً جمّة من رقيق ٢،٣،٣٦

١ الأصل: فَرَّ. ٢ الأصل: التنسي. ٣ الأصل: تعلّى.

The Faqīh read out "And the fire keeps saying, 'O Lord, add to me'" and—it being his habit to repeat after every word or two "Yes, indeed! Thus sayeth the book!"—he said, "And the fire keeps saying, 'O Lord, add to me.' (Yes, indeed! Thus sayeth the book!) And the fire keeps saying, 'O Lord, add to me.' (Yes, indeed! Thus sayeth the book!) until the Merciful puts his *rijl* in it (Yes, indeed! Thus sayeth the book!), a *rijl* being a company of people (Yes, indeed! Thus sayeth the book!) as in the verse (Yes, indeed! Thus sayeth the book!), 'And a man ran off with us' (*farra binā rajulun*) (Yes, indeed! Thus sayeth the book!)." He repeated this numerous times until his son, al-Sanūsī, said to him, "*Abbo! Fir! Binā rajulun!* ('Sir! Flee! There's a man upon us!')" and the Faqīh repeated "Yes, indeed!—*Fir! Binā rajulun*" and said it several times. I was sitting there and couldn't keep silent, so I took a copy from a man who was next to me and saw written, "*fa-marra binā rijlun min al-ḥayy*," etc., so I said, "*Abbo*, it's *fa-marra binā rijlun*," but he said to me, "Shut up. You're still too young to understand these things; plus, he's the one who has the qualification to be a witness." So I shut up.[247]

Another example of the mediocrity of his literary culture is contained in the story told to me by my father, may clouds of mercy and acceptance hover above him, to the effect that the sultan asked the same Faqīh to preach on the day of the Feast, so he went to my father and asked him to write him a sermon. This my father did, putting at the end, "Composed by the one in need of his Bountiful Lord, ʿUmar al-Tūnisī ibn Sulaymān, on such and such a day and year," and gave it to him. On the day of the Feast, the Faqīh prayed with the sultan, then mounted the pulpit and gave the sermon, saying at the end, "Composed by . . . ," etc., without realizing that these words weren't part of the sermon. He was one of the richest high officers of state and held about five hundred villages as fiefs, not counting those held by his brothers. 2.3.35

The sultan granted Shaykh-Father Muḥammad Kurrā exalted status, giving his word authority greater than any other's. He received news that Hāshim al-Musabbaʿāwī, King of Kordofan, had returned and taken it back from the sultan's governor. He therefore equipped a massive army under the command of Shaykh-Father Muḥammad Kurrā, and the latter went to Kordofan, where he scored a great success, wresting it from Sultan Hāshim's control, killing his soldiers, and chasing him into the desert. Shaykh-Father Muḥammad Kurrā made Kordofan his home for seven years,[248] during which time he sent the sultan vast wealth in the form of slaves, gold, and other things. Some of his enemies told tales 2.3.36

وذهب وغيره وسعى به بعض من أعدائه إلى السلطان فأرسل السلطان الأمين محمّد ابن الأمين عليّ ود جامع بجيشه إليه وأرسل معه قيداً وقال له خذ هذا القيد وقيّده به وأرسله مع جيشه وكان ذلك امتحاناً من السلطان فلمّا وصل الأمين محمّد إلى كردفال ظنّ في نفسه أنّ الأب الشيخ محمّد يعارضه أو ينازعه فلم يفعل شيئاً من ذلك بل حين وصل إليه قال له بماذا أمرك السلطان قال بتقييدك[1] وإرسالك إليه فقال سمعاً وطاعة هات القيد فأعطاه إيّاه فأخذه وقيّد نفسه بيده ودعا الحدّاد وأمره أن يسمّره ويبرّد عليه امتثالاً لأمر السلطان ففعل وأصبح مسافراً والقيد في رجليه حتّى وصل إلى دارفور وحين أخبر السلطان بقدومه أرسل له من ينزع القيد من رجليه وقال أمّا قلت لكم إنّ محمّد كرّا لا يعصا فيّ ثمّ أمره أن يأتي إلى الفاشر في موكبه فأتى على أحسن حالة وخرج إليه السلطان وأحسن ملقاه وسوّره بسوار من ذهب أمام الوزراء والحاضرين وبالغ في إكرامه وردّه إلى منزلته بل صار أعظم ممّا كان وكان هذا الفعل من السلطان هو عين البخت التامّ لابنه محمّد فضل فإنّه لمّا توفّي السلطان قام بأمره الأب الشيخ محمّد كرّا ولولاه لما نظر إليه أحد ولا عُنِيَ به

٣٧،٣،٢ وكيفيّة ذلك أنّ السلطان لمّا ثقل به مرضه دخل عليه الفقيه مالك الفوتاويّ فوجد الأب الشيخ محمّد كرّا عنده فقال له الفقيه مالك يا سيّدي إنّ الوصيّة فيها خير عظيم وإنّك فعلت مع الناس من المعروف ما لا يوصف وكلّ وزرائك وأهل مملكتك راضون عنك فإن وصّيت بشيء أظنّه بل أتحقّقه أنّه يُنفذ ولا بدّ فأوص لعلّ ولدك ينتفع بوصيّتك فقال ومن يتوكّل على الله فهو حسبه فأعاد عليه الفقيه مالك هذا القول ثانياً فقال هو ذلك أيضاً فأعاد عليه ثالثاً فقال ذلك أيضاً فتركه بعد الثالثة ثمّ قضى نحبه عليه سحائب الرحمة فحين توفّي بكى عليه الأب الشيخ والفقيه مالك وبعد البكاء قال الفقيه مالك للأب الشيخ ماذا أنت صانع الآن قال

[1] الأصل: بتقيدك.

against him to the sultan,[249] so the sultan dispatched Counselor Muḥammad,[250] the son of Counselor ʿAlī wad Jāmiʿ, and his army against him. He gave him a pair of shackles and told him, "Take these shackles and put them on him." Then he sent him off with his army. This was a test on the part of the sultan. When Counselor Muḥammad reached Kordofan, he expected Shaykh-Father Muḥammad would oppose or resist him, but he did nothing of the sort. On the contrary, when the counselor reached him, he said, "What did the sultan order you to do?" "To shackle you," he said, "and send you to him." "I hear and obey," he responded. "Give me the shackles." Counselor Muḥammad gave them to him and the shaykh-father took them and put them on with own hands and then summoned the blacksmith and ordered him to close them with a pin and file it down, in compliance with the sultan's order. The man did so, and the next day Shaykh-Father Muḥammad left on his journey, wearing the shackles on his feet all the way to Darfur. When the sultan was informed of his coming, he sent him someone to strike the shackles from his feet and said, "Didn't I say Muḥammad Kurrā would never disobey me?" Then he ordered him to come, with his entourage, to where the sultan was holding court. He arrived in great state, and the sultan went out to meet him and made much of him, in front of the viziers and those present, giving him gold bracelets to wear, going to the greatest lengths to honor him, and restoring him to his previous status; indeed, he now became greater than ever before. This act of the sultan's was the luckiest thing that could have happened to his son Muḥammad Faḍl, because when the sultan died, Shaykh-Father Muḥammad Kurrā took up his cause. If he had not, no one would have spared him a glance or cared about him one way or the other.[251]

This came about as follows. When the sultan's last illness grew serious, Faqīh Mālik al-Fūtāwī went in to see him and found Shaykh-Father Muḥammad Kurrā with him. He told the sultan, "My master, there is much to be gained by stating one's last wishes. Your kindnesses to the people are beyond description and all your viziers and all the inhabitants of your realm think well of you. If, therefore, you express a wish, I believe—in fact, I am certain—that it will be put into effect without demur. So tell us your wishes; your children may well benefit from your doing so." The sultan replied, saying, "And who would want to play the role of God? He alone is equal to it." Faqīh Mālik repeated what he had said, and the sultan responded as before. Then he said it a third time, and the sultan responded as before. After the third time, Faqīh Mālik left him. Then the sultan, may clouds of mercy hover above him, died. When he died, 2.3.37

الأب الشيخ سأريك ما أصنع فقام من وقته ودخل الدار ودعا محمّد فضل وكان أكبر ولديه لأنّه لم يترك من الذكور إلّا محمّد فضل وبخاريّ ومن الإناث حوّى وست النساء وأمّ سلمى فأقعد محمّد فضل ولبّسه الخاتم وعمّمه وقلّده السيف وأجلسه على كرسيّ السلطنة وأدخله في حجرة وأرخى عليه سترًا وأرسل في الحال إلى جماعته فحضروا متقلّدين سيوفهم شاكّين السلاح فأوقفهم على الأبواب ورتّب منهم جماعة يحرسونه ونفعه في ذلك باب سرّ كان بين بيته وبيت السلطان بحيث أنّ العساكر دخلت منه ولم يشعر بها أحد

٣٨،٣،٢ ثمّ أرسل إلى أكثر الوزراء جماعة وأقواهم شوكة الملك إبراهيم ود رَماد إنسانًا يقول له إنّ السلطان يأمرك بالذهاب إليه فجاء فلمّا دخل الباب وجد العساكر وقوفًا فراعه أمرهم ولم يجد بدًّا من الدخول ولمّا وصل إلى محلّ السلطان وجد الأب الشيخ محمّد كرّا والفقيه مالك جالسين والسلطان بينهما مسجّى فلمّا رآه كذلك بكى ثمّ بعد استرجاعه قال له الأب الشيخ إنّ السلطان قد توفّي فماذا ترى فقال لا أرى سوى[1] رأيك فقال له الأب الشيخ اتعاهدني على ذلك قال نعم فحلّفه وأخذ مواثيقه أنّه لا يتعدّى رأيه ثمّ رفع الستر وقال هذا السلطان يعني محمّد فضل فقال الملك إبراهيم وهو كذلك فقال قم فبايعه فبايعه حينئذ وجلس ثمّ أرسل إلى الوزراء والملوك واحدًا بعد واحد وكلّما جاءه أحد فعل معه كما فعل بالملك إبراهيم حتّى استوثق من أكابر الدولة كلّهم ولم يترك منهم إلّا من لا قوّة له

٣٩،٣،٢ ثمّ أعلن بموت السلطان وضربت طبول الحزن وسمعها أولاد السلاطين فركبوا وجاءوا شاكّين السلاح هاجمين على دار السلطان فرأوا الأمر مهولًا والجند محيطًا بها حارسًا لها منهم ومن غيرهم فلمّا لم يجدوا إلى الدخول سبيلًا ضربوا في البلاد

[1] الأصل: سوء.

the shaykh-father and Faqīh Mālik wept. When they had done, Faqīh Mālik said to the shaykh-father, "What are you going to do now?" and the shaykh-father said, "I will show you what I shall do," and that second he entered the sultan's house and called for Muḥammad Faḍl, who was the elder of the dead sultan's two sons, for the sultan had left behind him only two male offspring (Muḥammad Faḍl and Bukhārī[252]) and three female (Ḥawwā, Sitt al-Nisāʾ, and Umm Salmā). He sat Muḥammad Faḍl[253] down, placed the seal ring on his finger and the turban on his head, girded him with the sword, and made him sit on the sultan's throne. Then he took Muḥammad Faḍl into a chamber, covered the doorway with a curtain, and immediately sent for his men. These came, wearing their swords, bristling with weapons, and he stood them at the doors,[254] detailing a group to act as his personal guard. He was helped in this by a secret door between his house and that of the sultan by which the soldiers entered undetected.

Then he sent someone to Malik Ibrāhīm wad Ramād, the most powerful of the viziers in terms of the number of men he commanded and the one with the fiercest fighting spirit, and said, "The sultan commands your presence." So Malik Ibrāhīm went, and when he passed through the door, he found the soldiers standing there. Their presence took him by surprise, so he could see no alternative but to go on in. When he reached where the sultan was, he found Shaykh-Father Muḥammad Kurrā and Faqīh Mālik sitting, the dead sultan wrapped in a shroud between them. Seeing him thus, he wept. When he'd recovered, the shaykh-father said to him, "The sultan is dead. What do you think we should do?" "I think we should do whatever you think."[255] "Will you give me your word on that?" asked the shaykh-father. "Yes," he said. So he made him swear and accepted his assurances that he wouldn't oppose his opinion, and then raised the curtain and said, "This is the sultan," meaning Muḥammad Faḍl. "So be it," said Malik Ibrāhīm. Then the shaykh-father said, "Arise and give him your oath of allegiance," so he gave him his oath of allegiance then and there and sat down again.[256] Then the shaykh-father sent for the viziers and petty kings, one after another, and did with each as he had done with Malik Ibrāhīm until all the great men of the state had given their assurances, and the only ones left were those who had no power. 2.3.38

He now announced the death of the sultan, and the mourning drums were beaten. On hearing these, the sons of the sultans[257] mounted and rode, bristling with weapons, to launch an attack on the sultan's house. They found 2.3.39

وصاروا ينهبون أموال الناس وتجمع عليهم الغوغاء حتّى صاروا في جند كثيف وثقلت وطأتهم وعظم شرّهم فجهّز لهم الأب الشيخ جيشاً لنظر الملك دَلدَن الذي أسلفنا ذكره وهو ابن عمّة السلطان محمّد فضل فخرج إليهم وأوقع بهم وانهزمت الغوغاء الملتفّة عليهم وقتل منهم كثير وظفر بأولاد السلاطين وجيء بهم إلى الأب الشيخ مصفّدين فأرسلهم الأب الشيخ إلى السجن في جبل مرّة وسكنت الفتنة وتمهّدت الأمور ثمّ أمر السلطان بالقراءة وطلب العلم لصغر سنّه وعدم خبرته بالأمور فثقل ذلك عليه ولم يجد بدّاً من الامتثال فكابد مشقّة التعليم نحو سنتين وقتل الأب الشيخ محمّد كرّا في تلك المدّة بعض الملوك لفتنة وقعت منهم ورمى بعضهم في السجون وكلهم من أسرة السلطان وعصابته وولّى مناصبهم لجماعته فثقل ذلك على أرباب الدولة وخافوا شرّه فأغروا السلطان على قتله أو سجنه فوقع بينهما الحرب وقتل كما قدّمنا ذلك كلّه والله أعلم

things in a state that caused them dread, with troops surrounding it and guarding it, against them and any others besides. When they couldn't find a way to get in, they attacked the town and started looting property, and the mob rallied to them, turning them into a massive army—terrible was the damage they did, and great the harm. The shaykh-father equipped an army against them under the command of Malik Daldan, whom we have mentioned above,[258] the son of Sultan Muḥammad Faḍl's aunt, and he went out against them and attacked them, and the mob that had gathered around them was defeated. Many were killed, and the sons of the sultans were overwhelmed and brought to the shaykh-father in irons. The shaykh-father sent them to prison in Jabal Marrah,[259] the uprising died down, and order was restored. Then the shaykh-father ordered the sultan, in view of his youth and lack of experience, to devote himself to study and the pursuit of learning. The boy found this tedious but had no choice but to obey, and he put up with the drudgery of education for about two years. During this period, Shaykh-Father Muḥammad Kurrā killed some maliks who staged an uprising, threw others into prison—all of them of the sultan's family and lineage—and appointed his own men to their positions. The high officers of state found this intolerable and feared what he might do to them, so they urged the sultan to kill or imprison him. Eventually, war broke out between them and he was killed, all of which we have already described,[260] though God knows best the truth of the matter.

Notes

1 Q Quraysh 106:2; the reference is to the two yearly trading caravans that set off from Mecca in the days before Islam, one in the winter, to Yemen; the other in the summer, which went first to Tābūk, then bifurcated, part going to Buṣrā (then a Ghassanid capital of Provincia Arabia, today a provincial center in southern Syria) and part to Gaza. The reference—like the others in this preamble—serves to introduce the theme of "journeying," signaling that the author viewed this as the work's dominant motif.

2 The Prophet Muḥammad is said to have traveled with trading caravans to Buṣrā as a youth, first with his uncle Abū Ṭālib, later on behalf of his first wife, Khadījah.

3 Q An'ām 6:11.

4 A *sayyid* is a "descendant of the Prophet Muḥammad." The placement of al-Tūnisī ("of Tunis") in the middle rather than at the end of the name allows the author to rhyme *al-mannān* ("most gracious") with *Sulaymān*.

5 The author begins his life story in the middle: the period to which he refers was that between his return to Tunis in 1813 after his sojourn in Darfur and Wadai and his subsequent move to Egypt and entry (probably in or shortly after 1823) into the service of its ruler, Muḥammad ʿAlī (r. 1805–48; d. 1849). His account of his birth and early years is to be found in the Prolegomenon, Chapter 1 below.

6 Literally "the banner is knotted for . . . ," an idiom meaning that the subject is offered a position of leadership, or promoted.

7 Attributed to Imam Muḥammad ibn Idrīs al-Shāfiʿī (150–204/767–820).

8 A proverb: "appearances may be deceptive" (see al-Maydānī, *Majmaʿ al-amthāl*, 2:156).

9 Attributed to Imam Muḥammad ibn Idrīs al-Shāfiʿī.

10 Meaning, presumably, getting flogged.

11 I.e., Muḥammad ʿAlī, viceroy of Egypt. The verses are presumably the author's.

12 As a vassal of the Ottoman sultan, Muḥammad ʿAlī sent troops to the Hejaz in a campaign lasting from 1811 to 1818 and recovered Mecca and Medina from the forces of the first Saudi state.

13 Muḥammad ʿAlī's eldest son, Ibrāhīm Pasha, took Syria and Lebanon from the Ottomans and occupied them from 1831 to 1840.

14 Egyptian intervention in the Morea, intended to suppress Greek resistance to Ottoman rule, began in 1823 and ended in 1828.

15 Egypt's first modern medical school opened at Abū Zaʿbal, northeast of Cairo, in 1827 (Heyworth-Dunne, *History of Education*, 125).

16 On Nicolas Perron and his role in the creation of this text, see Introduction, pp. xxvi–xxvii.

17 A pedagogical poem by Muḥammad ibn al-Ḥasan ibn Durayd (222–312/838–933).

18 Earlier editors have identified the final chapter of the lithographic edition with this conclusion (al-Tūnisī, *Tashḥīdh*, 1965, 303, n. 1). However, that chapter does not bear this title and the abruptness with which the text ends may indicate that the author never in fact wrote a conclusion. In this edition, the final chapter is treated as such (as the Book Proper, chapter 4: see volume two).

19 The line is from a longer poem by Abū l-Ṭayyib al-Mutanabbī (see *al-ʿArf al-ṭayyib fī sharḥ dīwān Abī l-Ṭayyib*, 96).

20 I.e., Muḥammad III ibn ʿAbd Allāh (r. 1171–1204/1757–90), of the Alawite dynasty.

21 Pilgrims often took, and still take, the opportunity to engage in trade offered by the presence of large numbers of people from all over the Islamic world.

22 Meaning the clamor of voices exclaiming, "We have obeyed your call, O God, we have obeyed your call" and the sacrifice of sheep, both activities to which pilgrims are bidden.

23 I.e., *hādhī* ("this") preceding *al-Kuthub* is a variant of *hādhihi*.

24 The Beloved is the Prophet Muḥammad; his two companions are the caliphs Abū Bakr al-Ṣiddīq (r. 11–13/632–34) and ʿUmar ibn al-Khaṭṭāb (r. 13–23/634–44), who are buried next to him.

25 Attributed, with variants, to Imam Muḥammad ibn Idrīs al-Shāfiʿī.

26 Attributed, with variants, to Imam Muḥammad ibn Idrīs al-Shāfiʿī.

27 Q Baqarah 2:261.

28 The verses are from al-Ḥarīrī's *Maqāmah on a Gold Piece* (*al-Maqāmah al-dīnāriyyah*), the third of his fifty *maqāmah*s (see al-Ḥarīrī, *Maqāmāt al-Ḥarīrī*, 19–25).

29 Al-Ḥarīrī puns on the similarity between the words *badr* (literally "full moon")—a conventional term for a beautiful girl or boy—and *badrah* ("a purse," i.e., ten thousand dirhams).

30 By other accounts, Ḥusayn Pasha was ʿAlī's uncle (al-Sharīf al-Hādī, *Tārīkh Tūnis*, 84).

31 ʿAlī invaded Tunis in 1735; according to other accounts, however, Ḥusayn was not killed in 1735, but fled to Qayrawān in central Tunisia and was finally defeated and decapitated in 1740 (al-Sharīf al-Hādī, *Tārīkh Tūnis*, 84).

32 The *qawwāṣ* (more correctly spelled *qawwās* and meaning "archer") was an armed escort who provided protection to and cleared the way on the street for important persons and Europeans, and was known to the latter as a "kavass."

33 I.e., Muḥammad ʿAlī; in fact, it was Khusraw Pasha, viceroy from 1802 to 1803, who failed to pay the Albanian irregular forces in Egypt their wages, thus triggering the series of events that led in 1805 to the assumption of power by their commander, Muḥammad ʿAlī. Khūrshīd Pasha (1804–5) was the viceroy who replaced Khusraw and stepped down in Muḥammad ʿAlī's favor.

34 Unidentified; according to Umar ("Travels," 54, n. 4), the title al-Amīr al-Kabīr ("the Great Prince") indicates that this person was the head of the syndicate of descendants of the Prophet. By "our shaykh of shaykhs" the author probably means "the greatest teacher of our day."

35 "regency": Arabic *al-ʿamal*, which, in grammatical parlance, means the "regency" exercised by one word over the form of another (as when a preposition requires that the noun it governs be in the genitive case), but in nontechnical terms means "employment, work," with here the connotation of "work as a *ʿāmil*," i.e., a political agent. In contrast, the negative particle *mā* does not change the form of the word that follows it.

36 An error for Maḥmūd (ibn Bakkār) al-Jallūlī (Ibn Abī l-Ḍiyāf, *Itḥāf ahl al-zamān bi-akhbār mulūk Tūnis wa-ʿahd al-amān*, 3:23); al-Jallūlī's son Muḥammad features below.

37 This incident took place on Jumada al-Thani 16, 1206/February 10, 1792 (Ibn Abī l-Ḍiyāf, *Itḥāf*, 3:20).

38 On this idiom, see n. 6.

39 I.e., he became the cynosure of all eyes.

40 The battle took place on July 13, 1807 (see Ibn Abī l-Ḍiyāf, *Itḥāf*, 3:47, where the name of the site of the battle is given as Salāṭah).

41 The author confuses al-Ḥājj Abī l-Ḍiyāf (d. 1838), chief secretary to Yūsuf the Seal Bearer and the person intended here, with his son Aḥmad ibn Abī l-Ḍiyāf (1217/1802–3 to 1291/1874), who wrote a history of the Tunisian state entitled *Itḥāf ahl al-zamān bi-akhbār mulūk Tūnis wa-ʿahd al-amān* (*A Presentation of the History of the Kings of Tunis and the Covenant of Security to the People of the Age*); see Ibn Abī l-Ḍiyāf, *Itḥāf*, 3:96.

42 According to Ibn Abī l-Ḍiyāf, that year was not the date of the death of Ḥammūdah's father, ʿAlī Pasha II, but the one in which he designated his son as his heir (*Itḥāf*, 3:11). Ḥammūdah's actual rule began with his father's death in 1196/1782.

43 Following an invasion by the forces of the Ottoman provincial authorities of Algiers in 1756, Tunis had become a vassal of the latter. In 1807, Ḥammūdah Pasha rebuilt the walls of the citadel of al-Kāf (Le Kef), just east of the border with Algeria, which had been destroyed by the Algerians, and reestablished the independence of Ḥusaynid Tunis (see al-Sharīf, *Tārīkh Tūnis*, 86, 90).

44 The mosque—Masjid Ṣāḥib al-Ṭābiʿ—was built between 1808 and 1814 and survives.

45 Chronograms are poems in which certain words may be read both as words and as dates, using the system known as *ḥisāb al-jummal* (see n. 47); they are a common feature of congratulatory poetry from the ninth/fifteenth century onward.

46 "Yūsuf, counselor of Him Who Is Most Content with God's Favors" (*Yūsufu khōjatu l-raḍiy*): a play on the seal bearer's name plus the title *Khōjah*, a Turkish-Persian loanword, meaning, in origin, "teacher," afforded persons of substance of foreign origin and used of Yūsuf below (§2.1.25); *al-raḍī* refers to Ḥammūdah Pasha, as does *al-bahī* in the following hemistich.

47 Under a system known as *ḥisāb al-jummal* (see *EI2*, art. "Ḥisāb al-d̲j̲ummal"), letters of the alphabet are assigned numerical values and the letters grouped for mnemonic purposes into clusters forming pseudo-words. In the western (i.e., Maghrebi) system, these mnemonics are *ayqash-bakar-jalas-damat-hanath-waṣakh-za'adh-ḥafaḍ-ṭaghaẓ*, where ا = 1, ي = 10, ق = 100, ش = 1,000 (for remaining *ayqash* values, see al-Tūnisī, *Tashḥīdh*, 1965, 26, n. 1). Here, بشربه ("on drinking of it") provides the following numerical values: ب = 2 + ش = 1,000 + ر = 200 + ب = 2 + ه = 5, i.e., 1209 (= AD 1794–95).

48 Both the structure and the building remain unidentified; the area in which the fountain was located was cleared in a series of demolitions that started in the 1920s and continued until the 1950s, creating the present-day square in front of the shrine.

49 Or, punningly, "His way is inclined to good works, [that] Maḥmūd."

50 This and the following chronograms use, in contrast to the preceding, the eastern version of *ḥisāb al-jummal* (see n. 47), whose mnemonics are *abjad-hawwaz-ḥuṭṭī-kalaman-sa'faṣ-qarshat-thakhadh-ḍaẓagh*, where the first ten letters in the sequence equal one through ten, the next nine indicate the decades, the next nine the hundreds, and *gh* equals one thousand.

51 I.e., from Ibrāhīm (Abraham), who is described in the Qur'an as the friend (*khalīl*) of God (see, e.g., Q Nisā' 4:125). Ibrāhīm is represented in the sanctuary surrounding the Kaaba ("the Sacred House" and "the House of God") by a small open-sided building (*maqām*) in which is kept a stone on which the patriarch is said to have stood while he supervised its construction, along with his son Ismā'īl (Ishmael) (Q Baqarah 2:127).

52 Presumably, this stood next to the tomb of Shaykh al-'Afīfī, which survives, close to the later mausoleums of the khedivial royal family in the area of the tomb of Qāyitbāy in Cairo's Lesser Cemetery.

53 Al-Suhā (Alcor, or Ursa Major 80), from a root denoting "inattention, failure to notice" is a dim star that forms a pair with a brighter star called al-Mi'zar (the Waist Wrapper). The ability to distinguish al-Suhā from al-Mi'zar was considered proof of excellent eyesight. Thus, the author means that al-Maḥrūqī's glory was so bright that it was visible even at a vast distance.

54 Yūsuf died on Safar 12, 1230/January 23, 1815 (Ibn Abī l-Ḍiyāf, *Itḥāf*, 3:110).

55 Meaning "he after whom none more noble will come" and a punning allusion to his office of seal bearer.

56 *Bandar* is a Persian loanword that the author feels the need to explain (possibly to Perron, the copyist, rather than to his potential Egyptian readers, since the word is used in Egypt).

57 Sinnār is referred to as an island because it was embraced by the Blue and White Niles, in the cotton-producing region of modern Sudan still known as al-Jazīrah ("the Island").

58 Al-Quṣayr is on the coast of the Red Sea. Travelers would have taken a boat up the Nile to Qūṣ or Qinā in Upper Egypt and from there crossed the Eastern Desert to the port. It would have been while crossing the former that the author's father and grandfather crossed paths, as described below.

59 Attributed to the panegyricist Abū l-Fatḥ Maḥmūd ibn al-Ḥusayn al-Ramlī (ca. 360/970–71), of Mosul and then Aleppo, known as Kushājim.

60 Browne mentions that "I have observed that the people of our caravan, in such places as afforded stones for the purpose, used to collect four or five large ones, thus raising small heaps at proper distances from each other. This affords them some satisfaction at their return; but in many places, where the sand is loose and deep, it becomes impracticable . . . . Three times, in the course of our journey, the caravan was quite at a loss for the road, though some of the members of it had made ten or twelve journies to and from Dar-Fûr" (*Travels in Africa*, 248).

61 North Africans were famed for their curative talismans.

62 The Islamic day starts at sunset of the day before (according to Western reckoning) and is divided into two twelve-hour periods. "The third hour" of a Friday therefore refers to either the third hour after the sunset on the preceding Thursday, or to the third hour, i.e., sometime in the morning, of the Friday itself, which is probably what is meant here, as the author does not specify otherwise. The Friday closest to the fifteenth day of Dhū l-Qaʿdah (the eleventh month of the Islamic year) fell on the seventeenth of that month and was equivalent to July 30, 1790.

63 See n. 34.

64 Students resident at al-Azhar lived in halls or hostels (*riwāq*, pl. *arwiqah*) organized on sectarian and/or regional lines. There was no hall exclusively for Maghrebi *sayyid*s, so the author may not be using the term literally here.

65 The third surah of the Qur'an.

66 I.e., al-Ṭāhir was passing through Cairo on his way from Tunis to the Hejaz.

67 In 1212 H, the pilgrimage month (Dhū l-Hijjah, the last of the Islamic year) started on May 17, 1798.

68 France's three-year occupation of Egypt, led by Napoleon Bonaparte, began in July 1798.

69 A combined Ottoman-British force retook Egypt from the French in 1216/1801 and Ottoman rule through viceroys sent from Istanbul was restored. Egyptians frequently referred to the viceroy as "the vizier" or minister, since many viceroys held that rank in the Ottoman hierarchy.

70 I.e., to Paradise.

71 The first and third lines of a poem by Kamāl al-Dīn Abū l-Ḥasan ʿAlī ibn Muḥammad ibn Nabīh (560/1164–65 to 619/1222–23).

72 Abū Tammām Ḥabīb ibn Aws al-Ṭāʾī (ca. 189–232/805–45) (cf. al-Ṣūlī, *The Life and Times of Abū Tammām*, 306/7).

73 The caravanserai was located in the Ṣanādīqiyyah quarter in the heart of Cairo and served as the main distribution point for all goods from Sudan (Walz, "Wakalat al-Gallaba: The Market for African Goods in Cairo" 263–86; Abū l-ʿAmāyim, *Āthār al-Qāhirah al-islāmiyyah fī l-ʿaṣr al-ʿUthmānī*, 3/2:237).

74 Al-Fusṭāṭ, the first capital of Islamic Egypt, close to today's Miṣr al-ʿAtīqah (Old Cairo), was the location of the customs office and all boats coming from the south had to stop there to be assessed and taxed, while all travelers for Upper Egypt embarked there.

75 I.e., our ship.

76 Q Hūd 11:40. The reference is to Noah's ark.

77 I.e., the antagonism between the black races (the "sons of Ḥām (Ham)") and the Semites (the "sons of Sām (Shem)").

78 See n. 2.

79 These verses appear, with differences, in the collected works of Muḥammad ibn Idrīs al-Shāfiʿī, where they are described as being of dubious attribution (al-Shāfiʿī, *Shiʿr*, 265).

80 These lines and those immediately following are from al-Ṭughrāʾī's *The Non-Arabs' Poem in Lām* (*Lāmiyyat al-ʿAjam*) (lines 33, 34, and (for the following) 3), written in conscious imitation of al-Shanfarā's celebrated *The Arabs' Poem in Lām* (*Lāmiyyat al-ʿArab*) and famous for its arcane vocabulary.

81 I.e., if the nobility bestowed by place were sufficient to ensure the satisfaction of aspirations, the sun would never leave the domain of Aries—the ram, a noble creature—said domain being the first month after the vernal equinox (March 21–April 20).

82 The words echo the well-known saying "I have no she-camel in the affair and no he-camel," i.e., "I have no stake in the matter."

83 The verses occur with many variants and are attributed to Imam Muḥammad ibn Idrīs al-Shāfiʿī.

84 Perhaps the "Azharī shaikh" and "Shaikh Muṣṭafā" mentioned by Heyworth-Dunne as being attached to the veterinary school at Abū Zaʿbal (Heyworth-Dunne, *History of Education*, 133–34).

85 The poem contains a series of clues to words meaning "ship." In all cases, in this and the poems that follow, it is the consonantal skeleton of the word that matters; the unwritten short vowels between the consonants are not counted and may be changed to fit the author's needs.

86 The literal meaning of *kassāb* is "acquirer," allowing the author to pun on Muṣṭafā Kassāb's name.

87 The author means *fulk* ("ship"); however, the same consonants, revoweled as *falik*, yield "one with large buttocks," while *falaka thadyuhā* means "her beasts rounded out," which explains the references to the heart being tormented. There is an additional clue in the fact that *qalb* ("heart") also means "inversion (of the order of the root consonants of a word)," while *k-l-f*, root consonants of *kalifa* ("is enamored"), if read backward, yield *f-l-k*, root consonants of *fulk* ("ship").

88 *Fulk* occurs twenty-five times in the Qur'an, the first occurrence being Q Baqarah 2:164. It is this that those such as the addressee "constantly recite," etc.

89 I.e., *jāriyah*, which means both "ship" and "girl" (or "slave girl").

90 The radicals are *j-r-y*, from which *jārin*, meaning "runner," may be derived; *muhadhdhib* is the active participle of *hadhdhaba* meaning "(of a man and other things) to move fast (*asraʿa*)" (al-Fīrūzābādī, *Qāmūs*, s.v. *h-dh-b*).

91 I.e., *markib*, which, when spelt without short vowels, appears identical to *murakkab*, the last word in the line, thus forming a visual pun.

92 I.e., is one meaning represented by several different words.

93 I.e., this poem, or the letter that contained it.

94 The characteristics that follow may be applied to either a ship or a girl (see n. 89).

95 I.e., the girl, in her clothes, struts, etc., while the ship, when it raises its sails, moves fast.

96 I.e., the ship, when its sails are lowered, does not move, while the girl, when stripped of her clothes, is paralyzed by embarrassment.

97 I.e., the ship carries large, heavy goods that no human could lift, while, when the girl becomes pregnant, she bears something no man can: the wonder of a fetus.

98 I.e., the ship moves forward on its hull while the girl, in her efforts to make her way in this world (*fī saʿyihā*), progresses by lying on her back.

99 In terms of the ship, the reference may be to the oars of a galleon being arranged so as to allow them to wallop the water; in terms of a girl, the meaning may be that she opens her legs wide (on either side of her body) to allow herself to be "walloped."

100 In the first hemistich, which refers to the ship, *hawā* does duty for *hawā'* ("wind"), while in the second, which refers to the girl, it is to be taken in the sense of "love."

101 Cf. Q Hūd 11:37–38.

102 Cf. Q Hūd 11:41.

103 If the consonants of *baḥr* are reversed, the resulting word may be realized as either *ruḥb* or *raḥab*, both meaning "an open-armed welcome."

104 Again, *baḥr* ("sea"), spelled backward, can yield *raḥuba* "to be spacious or roomy."

105 I.e., if you remove the first letter of بحر (*baḥr*, meaning "sea") you are left with حر (*ḥarr*, meaning "heat").

106 I.e., if its letters are read out of order, the words *ḥabr*, meaning "an eminent scholar," *ḥibr*, meaning "ink," and *ḥarb*, meaning "war," may be formed.

107 I.e., بحر (*baḥr*) becomes بر (*barr*), meaning "dry land."

108 I.e., its wick.

109 The first two letters of *miṣbāḥ*, namely, *m* and *ṣ*, may be read on their own as *maṣṣ*, meaning "sucking," associated in Arabic poetry with saliva.

110 The remaining letters are *bāḥ*, which may be read as *bāḥa*, meaning "to divulge a secret."

111 If you remove the first consonant of *miṣbāḥ*, the remaining letters read *ṣabāḥ*, meaning "morning."

112 Q Nūr 24:35 *Allāhu nūru l-samāwāti wa-l-arḍi mathalu nūrihi ka-mishkātin fīhā miṣbāhun al-miṣbāhu fī zujājatin* . . . («God is the light of the heavens and the earth; the likeness of His Light is as a niche wherein is a lamp (the lamp in a glass . . .)» (Arberry, *The Koran Interpreted*, 356–57).

113 I.e., stars.

114 E.g., Q Baqarah 2:19 and frequently elsewhere.

115 If the first and last letters of *mudām* are dropped, one is left with *dā*, equal for these purposes to *dā'*, meaning "disease."

116 If the last letter of *mudām* is dropped, one is left with *mudā*, which is the plural of *mudyah*, meaning "knife."

117 Or, punningly, and referring to *mudām* rather than *mudyah*: "It entails the *ḥadd* penalty [meaning that the drinking of wine is an offence the penalty for which is specified in the Qur'an]—such is [the] incisiveness of the law."

118 If the first letter of *mudām* is dropped, one is left with *dām(a)*, meaning "to last."

119 Meaning that these members of the former Mamluk military elite had turned into defectors and freebooters taking advantage of the chaos that reigned in Egypt, and especially Upper Egypt, between the departure of the French in 1801 and the seizure of power by Muḥammad ʿAlī in 1805.

120 Manfalūṭ was safer than al-Minyā, not being controlled by rebellious Mamluks.

121 The author's memory apparently betrayed him: Abīrīs (today called Bārīs) is farther from al-Khārijah than Būlāq.

122 Browne writes, "This is a wretchedly poor place, the houses being only small square pieces of ground inclosed with a wall of clay, or unburned bricks, and generally without a roof. It furnishes good water, and the people live by the sale of their dates" (Browne, *Travels in Africa*, 186).

123 According to ancient Arabian legend, Luqmān the Long-lived, a pre-Islamic figure to whom wise sayings are attributed, was granted as a reward for his piety a life as long as that of seven named vultures (the vulture being a popular symbol of longevity among the Arabs). The last vulture was named Lubad; when Lubad died, so did Luqmān.

124 *Shabb* means "alum"; the French translation glosses the name as ʿAyn al-Shabb, or "the Alum Spring" (El-Tounsy, *Voyage au Darfour*, 30, n. 1).

125 Browne reports further of Salīmah that "the jelabs [traders] related many fables concerning it; as that it had of old been inhabited by a princess who, like the Amazons, drew the bow, and wielded the battle-axe, with her own hand; that she was attended by a large number of followers, who spread terror all over Nubia, &c.; and that her name was Selimé" (*Travels in Africa*, 187).

126 According to Browne, the natron mined in the vicinity was exported to Egypt, where it was mostly used in the manufacture of snuff and fetched a high price (*Travels in Africa*, 186–87).

127 On this seal, see O'Fahey and Abu Salim, *Land in Darfur*, 28–29.

128 "loved scholarship and . . . hated ignorance": i.e., promoted Islam and combated paganism.

129 See Prolegomenon, Chapter 3.

130 Bīr al-Zaghāwī . . . Bīr al-Malḥah: al-Zaghāwī's Well . . . Salt Flat Well.

131 Most of the remaining fifty-six would have been loaded with trade goods.

132 Horses from Dongola, on the Nile in Nubia, were prized because of their large size compared to the native Darfurian breed; armored, they were used there as heavy cavalry (see O'Fahey, *Darfur Sultanate*, 196–98).

133 "Sweini is the general resort of the merchants trading to Egypt, both in going and returning, and thence derives its chief importance" (Browne, *Travels in Africa*, 237).

134 The delay may have been due to the fact that, at al-Suwaynah, "all strangers, as well as merchants of the country, coming with the caravan, are obliged to wait, till the pleasure of the monarch in disposing of them be known" (Browne, *Travels in Africa*, 189).

135 Jadīd al-Sayl (literally "the new place by the seasonal watercourse"): the term *jadīd* ("new (place)"), as here and in Jadīd Karyū, occurs frequently in western Sudan, reflecting the impermanence of human settlement.

136 Aḥmad Zarrūq was probably the son of the author's grandfather Sulaymān by the Ethiopian woman whom he married in Sinnār.

137 I.e., the Prophet Muḥammad, ʿAdnān being his ancestor in the twentieth degree.

138 Slaves were measured in handspans from their heels to their earlobes (see §3.3.44); a *sudāsī* ("sixer") measured six spans. A slave taller than seven spans was considered to be an adult and fetched a lower price (El-Tounsy, *Voyage au Darfour*, 39, n. 1). Thus the slaves mentioned here would have been young boys, as confirmed by Browne, who speaks of "a male slave, *sedasé*, about twelve to fourteen years of age" (*Travels in Africa*, 308).

139 Cf. Q Naml 27:17 «And there were gathered unto Solomon his armies of the jinn and humankind, and of the birds, and they were set in battle order.»

140 "Nature's tongue" (*lisān al-ḥāl*) is the faculty by which nonhuman and even inanimate actors are supposed to express themselves. Sulaymān (Solomon) is supposed to have been able to understand the speech of animals.

141 Meaning his "honorary uncle," his father's friend Sayyid Aḥmad Badawī.

142 Q Ḥujurāt 49:6.

143 Meaning here Darfurian Arabic.

144 Browne describes Kabkābiyyah as "the key to the Western roads [i.e., the western trade routes], as Sweini [al-Suwaynah] of the Northern" (*Travels in Africa*, 238).

145 Cf. §3.1.10 and following sections.

146 "the Sultanic Portals" (*al-aʿtāb al-sulṭāniyyah*): the name, while appropriate enough to a palace whose doorways had ceremonial importance (see §3.1.77), also evokes "the Sublime Porte" (*al-Bāb al-ʿĀlī*), as the palace of the Ottoman sultan in Istanbul was commonly known. Another Ottoman honorific appropriated by the sultans of Darfur was "Khāqān" (see §3.1.17).

147 Thus the author first met Shaykh-Father Muḥammad Kurrā in 1803, i.e., during the period between 1800 and 1804 when, as regent of Sultan Muḥammad Faḍl (whom he had been instrumental in installing), he was at the height of his powers and exercised nearly complete ascendancy over the sultanate. During this time, according to Nachtigal, he was honored as though he were the sultan and "the people fell back at a distance from his path, and squatted on one side, brushing the ground with the palms of their hands" (*Sahara and Sudan*, 299; see also O'Fahey, *Darfur Sultanate*, 61).

148 On this person, a close associate of Sultan ʿAbd al-Raḥmān, who raised him to high status and gave him great wealth, and on the prominent family of holy men, the Awlād ʿAlī, to which he belonged, see O'Fahey, *Darfur Sultanate*, 63 and, especially, O'Fahey, "The Awlad ʿAli."

149 Though the author describes Mālik al-Fūtāwī as his father's agent, from the latter's perspective he would have been his father's sponsor at court.

150 It may seem strange that the author identifies Mālik al-Fūtāwī as being of Arab descent almost in the same breath with which he states that he belonged to the Fullān (Fallātā), who are largely non-Arabic-speaking tribes originating in the western Sahel; however, the Fullān do indeed claim descent from ʿUqbah ibn Nāfiʿ (d. 63/683), conqueror of North Africa and a member of the Prophet's tribe of Quraysh.

151 Various sources attribute various origins to Muḥammad Kurrā (see O'Fahey, *Darfur Sultanate*, 66, n. 7).

152 See §§2.2.48–64 and §§2.3.1–39.

153 According to O'Fahey, the word is of uncertain origin and applied originally to the area in front of the sultan's compound where he gave audience (*Darfur Sultanate*, 308). O'Fahey describes the *fāshir* as "an enormous complex of buildings and courtyards housing the sultan, his family and *harim*, stores of food, weapons and trade goods and a host of palace officials and their retinues; at a reasonable guess its personnel cannot have numbered much under three to four thousand" ("Slavery and the Slave Trade in Dar Fur," 88).

154 Nachtigal describes the cashmere shawl as "the principal ornament of the inhabitants of Darfur" (*Sahara and Sudan*, 248).

155 I.e., descendant of the Prophet Muḥammad; see n. 137.

156 I.e., descendants of the Prophet Muḥammad.

157 Perron spells the name "Homaydah" (El-Tounsy, *Voyage au Darfour*, 48), though Ḥumaydah is usually a male name, Ḥamīdah a female name.

158 The not very learned Faqīh Mālik presumably was mixing up the Qur'anic verse that refers to *kawāʿiba atrābā* (Q Naba' 78:33), or "young maidens of equal age," with that which refers to *yatīman dhā matrabah* (Q Balad 90:16), or "a needy person in distress." Thus what he meant to convey was that he had given the author a pretty young girl (*kawāʿib* may also be translated as "buxom maidens") of the sort mentioned in the Qur'an. Ironically, the author himself makes a mistake when he states that the singular of *kawāʿib* is *kāʿibah*—the correct form is *kāʿib*—and is wrong again when he says that *matrabah* occurs, like *kawāʿib*, in the Qur'an's descriptions of houris—the verse cited here is its sole occurrence. However, *atrāb* ("of equal age"), from the same root, does occur in the Qur'an in this context, at Q Ṣād 38:52 and Q Wāqiʿah 56:37, in addition to the verses cited above. For another example of Faqīh Mālik's flawed literary Arabic, see §2.3.34.

159 I.e., an assignment of land (*iqṭāʿ*) granted by the sultan to a favored person in return for political loyalty and a specified portion of the revenue. "Grants of land or privilege were used to accommodate newcomers, pre-eminently the *fuqara* and merchants" (O'Fahey, *Darfur Sultanate*, 137), to both of which categories the author's father belonged.

160 The inhabitants of Qirlī, close to Jabal Marrah, probably spoke Fur.

161 I.e., a little over 40 liters; thus, his father would harvest some 560 liters of cotton a day in this season.

162 Many such land grants are translated and reviewed in O'Fahey and Abu Salim, *Land in Darfur*.

163 Malik Khamīs 'Armān: the name is given as Malik Khamīs 'Irfān in Perron's Arabic text (al-Tūnisī, *Tashḥīdh*, 1850, 65) but appears in his French translation as "Armân" (El-Tounsy, *Voyage au Darfour*, 51) and again as 'Armān at §4.48. O'Fahey has described how a fief from the sultan was assigned and demarcated by court officials such as, presumably, the person mentioned here (see "Awlad 'Ali," 158–59).

164 "staple grains" (*'aysh*): in Darfur, the term *'aysh* covers any grains used to make bread (mostly sorghum, millet, and maize) (cf. Qāsim, *Qāmūs*).

165 Thus Muḥammad may have spent no more than a scant two months with the father he had traveled so far to see, as indicated by the facts that, three days after he had been reunited with him at Ḥillat Jūltū (§2.2.28), he was dispatched by his father to Tandaltī on Sha'ban 1, 1218 to present himself to the authorities there (§2.2.30); father and son then spent the following month of Ramadan together, after which his father first traveled himself to Tandaltī (§2.2.33), then "in the shortest possible time" (§2.2.34) left for Tunis.

166 If this is true, Muḥammad Kurrā would have been proposing, as O'Fahey points out, "a dynastic change for the first and only time in the sultanate's history" (*Darfur Sultanate*, 61). With respect to affording Muḥammad Kurrā's brother the exclusively royal title "Báási," either the author is mistaken or its use by Muḥammad Kurrā was an indication of his aspirations for just such dynastic change.

167 According to O'Fahey, matters came to a head when Muḥammad Kurrā, presumptuously and no doubt provocatively, invited the sultan to eat with him, in violation of the taboo against the sultan's eating in public (*Darfur Sultanate*, 61).

168 In Sudanese Arabic, *rahad* means a depression that fills with water during the rainy season.

169 For a different account of this battle and of Muḥammad Kurrā's relations with Sultan Muḥammad Faḍl in general, see Nachtigal, *Sahara and Sudan*, 298–301.

170 Eunuchs of high rank, such as Muḥammad Kurrā, sometimes married, in order to appear to conform to social norms. The epithet Shīlfūt means in Arabic "take-and-go" and was a tribute to his boldness (El-Tounsy, *Voyage au Darfour*, 55 [54, n. 1]).

171 'Umar, known as 'Umar Lēl (or Lēle) ('Umar the Donkey, because of his stubbornness), was Aḥmad Bukur's grandson rather than his son, and succeeded his father, Muḥammad Dawrā (r. ca. 1720–30), whom the author does not mention. 'Umar Lēl was succeeded by his uncle (rather than, as given here, his brother) Abū l-Qāsim (r. ca. 1739–52), and

Abū l-Qāsim was succeeded by Muḥammad Tayrāb (r. ca. 1752–53 to 1785–86) (for a genealogical table of the Keira dynasty, see O'Fahey, *Darfur Sultanate*, 40). Aḥmad Bukur is said, in fact, to have had over a hundred sons, of whom those named here were only, presumably, the most prominent; other sultans had even more (O'Fahey, *Darfur Sultanate*, 90). O'Fahey states that this great mass of "sons of the sultans" formed a distinct group within the state and as such "were provided with estates and revenues, as were their sisters, but rarely with commands or administrative responsibilities" (O'Fahey, *Darfur Sultanate*, 9).

172 In the French translation, "sultan Mohammed-Djaoudeh" (El-Tounsy, *Voyage au Darfour*, 56).

173 The equation of Dār Barqū with Dār Wāddāy is problematic: Nachtigal indicates that Borku, as he spells it, was in present-day northern Chad and not part of Wadai, being in the territory of the Ennedi, to the north. Volume II of his *Sahara and Sudan* is subtitled "Kawar, Bornu, Kanem, Borku and Ennedi."

174 According to Browne, whose sources seem to have been less sympathetic than the author's to the dominant narrative concerning Darfur's rulers, Sultan Tayrāb acquired his name because of his "habit of rolling in the dust when a child" (*Travels in Africa*, 277).

175 I.e., "seed grain."

176 I.e., Sultan Muḥammad Tayrāb.

177 I.e., before the amulet that had been tied in her hair as a child had been removed, which happens at puberty. The amulet would consist of a piece of paper bearing names of God or Qur'anic verses and be concealed in a small leather pouch.

178 I.e., a boy of the best of the line of Hāshim ibn ʿAbd Manāf, eponym of the clan of the tribe of Quraysh to which the Prophet Muḥammad belonged.

179 I.e., the Prophet Muḥammad, who is buried in Medina.

180 The anecdote is anachronistic: Abū Bakr al-Ṣiddīq died in 13/634, while Muḥammad ibn al-Qāsim was born *ca.* 72/695.

181 The sense of the maxim seems to be that women are dangerous, whether a man falls in love with one of them or she sets her sights on him.

182 The passage is not entirely clear; the words "as they would say" have been added in the translation and the likely sense of *durā l-ʿiyāl* is "children of the place," meaning here "children of the palace." The *soom*, located within the *fāshir*'s public area, was, according to Nachtigal, "the assembly place where the people come together for conversation or for a common meal" (*Sahara and Sudan*, 335); according to O'Fahey, it also functioned as a school where the palace pages or cadets were taught (*Darfur Sultanate*, 310).

183 On the office of counselor (*amīn*), see §3.1.56.

184 According to Nachtigal, the departure of the Fur tribe known as the Musabbaʿāt ("the Massabat") from their ancestral home in Jabal Marrah was the result of a succession struggle (*Sahara and Sudan*, 355); O'Fahey describes them as "in origin Keira adventurers who had been cast out or fled the sultanate" (*Darfur Sultanate*, 53). Eventually, the Musabbaʿāt became "a tribal designation for a group of communities stretching from Darfur to Kassala in the eastern Sudan" (*Darfur Sultanate*, 53–54).

185 According to Perron, the Shāyijiyyah lived "between Darfur and Kordofan but closer to the former" (El-Tounsy, *Voyage au Darfour*, 67, n. 1), but the name is not found in other sources. It seems likely that Perron misconstrued the name "al-Shāyiqiyyah," with *q*, which the author no doubt pronounced in the Sudanese fashion as *g*, and interpreted the latter as the letter *jīm*, pronounced as *g* in Egypt (where Perron lived). This is especially likely given that the progression in this list from Dongola to the Rizayqāt Arabs is otherwise from east to west. The Shāyiqiyyah are a tribe who live on the Nile in northern Sudan.

186 "Hashim . . . attempted . . . to create a state in central and eastern Kordofan that would rival or possibly supplant Darfur and Sinnar" (O'Fahey, *Darfur Sultanate*, 54).

187 See §2.2.38.

188 See §2.2.40.

189 I.e., all the sons of Sultan Aḥmad Bukur who were still in line of succession and their offspring.

190 Following Muḥammad Tayrāb's successful invasion of Kordofan in 1785, Darfurian rule continued there until 1821, when it fell to Egyptian forces.

191 On Sultan Muḥammad Tayrāb's strategy of strengthening the ties between his eldest son and the children of his viziers, presumably in the hope of forming a loyal, cohesive elite around his designated successor, see §2.2.40.

192 This is the penultimate line of the "suspended ode" (*muʿallaqah*) of Zuhayr ibn Abī Salmā (d. AD 609).

193 Al-Mutanabbī, *al-ʿArf al-ṭayyib*, 522.

194 According to Perron, who presumably had it from the author, the reference is to a well-known fable: a sheep was waiting to be slaughtered but the knife had been lost in the sand; the would-be butcher had abandoned the idea of killing the sheep when the latter, pawing at the sand, uncovered the knife; it was then slaughtered.

195 Abū l-Fatḥ al-Bastī (ca. 400/1010); the second hemistich of the Arabic forms a visual pun: *arā qadamī arāqa damī*.

196 See n. 137.

197 According to O'Fahey, the title means "powerful mother" (*Darfur Sultanate*, 116) and the holder was responsible for the production of food for the royal household (personal communication).

198 Muḥammad Kurrā's patron (see §2.2.44).

199 Umar ("Travels," 145, n. 1) identifies this person with Nachtigal's "Hasseb el-Agaran," the son of the sultan's uncle, Sultan Hārūt/Khārūt of the Zaghāwah of Kobe (*Sahara and Sudan*, 287). O'Fahey refers to him as "a military leader" (*Darfur Sultanate*, 56–57).

200 Perron renders this name "Djoutâ," i.e., Jūtā.

201 For the author to refer to Muḥammad Dukkumī, son of ʿAlī wad Jāmiʿ, at this point as a counselor is anachronistic, though he was eventually to become one (see §2.3.6 below).

202 I.e., to the grandsons of Sultan Aḥmad Bukur, all of whose fathers were referred to as "sultans," even though they might never have ruled as such.

203 O'Fahey outlines the dynamic underlying the conflicts among the "sons of the sultans," which lasted for approximately the first sixty years of the eighteenth century, by describing how "an old order of powerful Fur chiefs, strongly based on local loyalties, serving a sultan who was but *primus inter pares*, gave way to new institutions, a supratribal bureaucracy, maintained by grants of land and tax-rights, slave troops and increasing Islamisation, all centred on the sultan" (*Darfur Sultanate*, 45). In O'Fahey's analysis, ʿAbd al-Raḥmān (the Orphan), who "was poor, lived in obscurity, and had no children," appealed to the elite since "he would be in a weaker position to establish new lineages to compete with the old" (*Darfur Sultanate*, 56). O'Fahey also points out that "the civil war that followed was in effect between two generations, that of Ahmad Bukr and that of Tayrab" (*Darfur Sultanate*, 58).

204 See §2.2.38 and n. 171.

205 A less flattering portrait of Sultan ʿAbd al-Raḥmān is painted by Browne, who may have been influenced by his generally dyspeptic attitude to Darfur, just as the author may have been influenced by his situation as a client of ʿAbd al-Raḥmān's son and successor. Browne, who calls the sultan "the Usurper," writes that "after the victory [by which he gained the throne] . . . judging it right to maintain for a time the shew of moderation and self-denial, he employed that dissimulation for which his countrymen are famous, in persuading them that his affections were fixed on the blessings of futurity, and that he was indifferent to the splendor of empire. . . . At length, finding his claim unquestioned, and his authority firmly established, the veil of sanctity, now no longer necessary, was thrown aside, and ambition and avarice appeared without disguise" (Browne, *Travels in Africa*, 279). Nachtigal's judgment is more balanced than either the author's or Browne's. He writes: "He had indeed his faults, and if his principles were just, he was also resentful and vindictive; he never forgave acts of hostility, and repaid them in his own time

(*Sahara and Sudan*, 293) . . . [He] died after a prosperous reign of fourteen years . . . one of the best of Darfur's rulers, who had combined prudence and good sense with energy" (*Sahara and Sudan*, 296).

206 Perron spells the name "Djiddau" (El-Tounsy, *Voyage au Darfour*, 87).

207 The onlookers presumably meant that the moon was the last of the month (cf. "Orphan Friday," the last Friday of Ramadan).

208 On the importance of having a good excuse for not eating food offered by the sultan, see §3.1.43.

209 O'Fahey gives the name as "Umm Buza" (Darfur Sultanate, 51, 119).

210 Q Shuʿarāʾ 26:227.

211 I.e., carry out no orders but his.

212 According to Nachtigal, the name of this person was Ḥājj Mufliḥ (*Sahara and Sudan*, 290).

213 The war between ʿAbd al-Raḥmān and Isḥāq over the succession was to last for three years.

214 A set phrase that also occurs in the Qurʾan (Q Āl ʿImrān 3:155, 166); other occurrences have been left unnoted.

215 "God is greater" (*Allāhu akbar*): i.e., God is greater than all else.

216 The master of the tax collectors (*malik al-jabbāyīn*) was responsible for "the collection and storage of the revenues . . . throughout the state. . . . He was one of the greatest of the state officials and controlled an extensive hierarchy of subordinates" (O'Fahey, *Darfur Sultanate*, 203). Nachtigal states that "The taxes which these people had to pay consisted chiefly of tribute in the form of corn and cattle, property tax customs dues and the so-called *diwan*," the latter being a levy imposed every four years "according to the occupations of the tribes and the yield of the regions" (*Sahara and Sudan*, 358–59). For a comprehensive review of the tax system in Darfur, see O'Fahey, *Darfur Sultanate*, 202–12.

217 I.e., they will be guiltless if they rise up against you.

218 "until such time as God delivers his verdict": meaning, with perhaps deliberate ambiguity, either "until God decides between us in battle" or "until the Day of Judgment."

219 Q Aḥzāb 33:37.

220 The Arabic term *abnāʾ al-ʿArab* (literally "Sons of the Arabs") was commonly used in Egypt at the time (e.g., in the 1848 census) to distinguish Arabic-speaking from Turkish-speaking Egyptians.

221 A "trickle" of guns was imported to Darfur each year, but these appear to have been used, as is implied here, mainly for hunting (O'Fahey, *Darfur Sultanate*, 200, n. 22).

222 In an appendix to his French translation of this work, Nicholas Perron mentions, as an extreme illustration of the absolute inviolability of the person of the sultan and all his family, that Zabādī, after receiving the reward he had been promised, was executed (El-Tounsy, *Voyage au Darfour*, 376–77).

223 Q Aḥzāb 33:38.

224 The ancestral tombs of the Keira sultans were located at Ṭurrah in Jabal Marrah, where on important occasions sacrifices were made and prayers offered for their souls.

225 See, e.g., al-Mutanabbī, *al-ʿArf al-ṭayyib*, 308–9, with differences. The fourth (or, in some editions, the third) line of the poem is missing. It runs: *wa-arāka d-dahru mā tuḥāwilu fī l-ʿidā / ḥattā ka'anna l-ṣurūfa anṣārū* ("And Fate will show you what you seek in your enemies / as though even its twists were allies").

226 "Rīl is the key of the South and East roads" (Browne, *Travels in Africa*, 239).

227 According to O'Fahey, the establishment of the sultan's seat at Tandaltī, which lies east of Jabal Marrah, consolidated the reorientation of the sultanate to the east and to Nilotic Sudan. Tandaltī was strategically placed, close to the main west-east route through Jabal Marrah and provided with water by the *rahad*, or seasonal lake. It was also only a day's journey to the southeast from the trade entrepôt of Kubayh and close enough to the rain-fed area of the mountains to be supplied with agricultural products (*Darfur Sultanate*, 64–65).

228 Browne makes it clear that the alcohol in question was millet beer (*marīsah*) (*Travels in Africa*, 224–25)—which al-Tūnisī gives the more literary name of *mizr*—and dates the edict to March 1795 (*Travels in Africa*, 291). Millet beer is a lightly fermented beverage widely drunk in sub-Saharan Africa and regarded by some as an important component of the diet in protein-poor environments.

229 One supposes that the sound must be something like *krrrrruuuu*.

230 Here and in the rest of the passage, the Bedouin plays on the literal meaning of Sultan ʿAbd al-Raḥmān's epithet, al-Rashīd. The epithet was not merely a sign of his subjects' adulation but a title awarded the sultan by his Ottoman counterpart in thanks for a gift of ivory and ostrich feathers (O'Fahey, *Darfur Sultanate*, 69). Browne claims that, before receipt of the gifts, the Ottoman sultan had been unaware of Darfur's existence (Browne, *Travels in Africa*, 215).

231 I.e., he may start to think of establishing a dynasty of his own.

232 On becoming shaykh-father, Muḥammad Kurrā would have automatically taken charge of the territories pertaining to that office, i.e., Dār Dālī, the lands to the east of Jabal Marrah.

233 The point of the following passage may be to demonstrate ʿUmar al-Tūnisī's right to be numbered among the scholars who paid allegiance to the sultan and who were supported by him.

234 The rational sciences include mathematics, astronomy, logic, philosophy, and medicine. The transmitted sciences are those concerned with matters of faith, in particular, the Qur'an, the Hadith, and law.

235 ʿUmar al-Tūnisī's works have not survived.

236 Umar believes that Musāʿid, a son of Sharif Surūr, head of the Dhawī Zayd dynasty that then ruled Mecca, had probably fled to Darfur to escape family conflicts ("Travels," 182, n. 4).

237 The administration of justice lay largely in the hands of the sultan and the local authorities, in concert with the *fuqarā'*, who together ruled in most cases according to Fur customary law, though the influence of Islamic law increased with time. This system "was only partly modified by the appointment of some of the latter [i.e., the *fuqarā'*] as *qāḍī*s [judges]" (*Darfur Sultanate*, 217), most of whom were attached to the entourages of the same authorities. A few judges, such as ʿIzz al-Dīn al-Jāmiʿ (here called al-Jāmiʿī), did, however, hold fairly independent positions (same reference).

238 O'Fahey identifies this person with Aḥmad Aghā, an associate of Murād Bayk (the Mamluk leader who in collusion with the British tried to return Egypt to Mamluk rule following Napoleon's departure), sent by the latter to spy on Darfur ("The Affair of Ahmad Agha," 202–3).

239 I.e., the servants were prevented from entering the courtyard that contained the sultan's living quarters; see the Plan of the Sultan's Seat (§3.1.91).

240 See §2.2.57.

241 The kind of bowl referred to, the *jafnah*, is defined as holding enough to satisfy ten men (see Lane, *Lexicon*, s.v. *j-f-n*).

242 Literally the Mother of Ḥabīb, the term that would have been used habitually to refer to her.

243 No doubt to the caves there where princes were imprisoned; see §3.1.16, §3.1.24.

244 The "secret of the letter" (*sirr al-ḥarf*), also called "the science of letters" (*ʿilm al-ḥurūf*), deals, in its cosmological aspect, with the relationship between divine speech and the manifest world, and, as an occult practice, with the making of talismans such as "magic squares" formed of letters (*awfāq*, sg. *wafq*).

245 The name is written so in the lithograph, but should perhaps be Jidd al-ʿIyāl ("the Grandfather of the Little Children").

246 The quotation is a paraphrase of one in the *Memorandum on the Conditions of the Dead and Matters Pertaining to the Hereafter* (*al-Tadhkirah fī aḥwāl al-mawtā wa-umūr al-ākhirah*) of Muḥammad ibn Aḥmad ibn Abī Bakr ibn Farḥ al-Anṣārī al-Qurṭubī (d. 671/1273), a leading Andalusian Mālikī scholar (*al-Tadhkirah*, 513–14). In this passage, al-Qurṭubī reports a hadith, on the authority of Muslim on the authority of Anas, that runs, in one version, "Hell will continue to have people thrown into it and will say, 'Are there more?' until the Lord of Might puts his *qadam* [in other versions, *rijl*] into it, when it will draw back upon itself and say, 'Enough! Enough!'" Since both *qadam* and *rijl* might be understood in their common sense of "foot," al-Qurṭubī points out that both also have the sense given here and must be so understood, since God does not possess limbs (same reference, 513).

247 The story demonstrates the Faqīh's stupidity because, when al-Sanūsī addresses him (in mixed Darfurian and literary Arabic, as signaled in the Arabic text by the voweling *Fir* rather than the correct form *Firra*), he takes his son's words *Fir! Binā rajulun* to be a rereading of the phrase *fa-marra binā rijlun* and accepts it as correct, whereas the son is in fact trying to draw his attention to the arrival of Jidd al-ʿAyyāl, whose appearance at the head of a host of men and animals must have scared the youth. Al-Sanūsī must have been at least eighteen years of age, the age of majority, and hence of validity as a witness, according to the Mālikī rite. Perron understands the anecdote, which he relegates to an appendix (see El-Tounsy, *Darfour*, 119 and 425), slightly differently.

248 This second invasion of Kordofan took place in about 1206/1791–92 (O'Fahey, *Darfur Sultanate*, 66). The appointment of Muḥammad Kurrā as governor of Kordofan would have followed naturally from his position as governor of eastern Darfur.

249 Nachtigal says that Muḥammad Kurrā "made himself and the extreme east of the country more independent than Abd er-Rahman could allow . . . the *abu shaykh* undertook military expeditions in all directions on his own initiative . . . while he restricted himself to sending tribute to Abd er-Rahman, but no longer obeyed his orders" (*Sahara and Sudan*, 294–95).

250 On the enmity between Counselor Muḥammad (Dukkumī) and Muḥammad Kurrā, see §2.2.62.

251 O'Fahey comments that "There was no precise or automatic rule of succession" (*Darfur Sultanate*, 59). Sultan ʿAbd al-Raḥmān is said to have had four sons. One of these, Muḥammad Abū l-Madyan (of whose existence al-Tūnisī may have been unaware), eventually escaped from Darfur only to return in 1843 as an Egyptian-backed pretender; his campaign to unseat Muḥammad Faḍl failed (Nachtigal, *Sahara and Sudan*, 303, n. 1).

252 Perron gives the latter's name as Muḥammad Bukhārī.

253 Nachtigal estimates that Muḥammad Faḍl was eleven or twelve at the time (*Sahara and Sudan*, 298).

254 I.e., at the doors to the sultan's house.

255 According to Nachtigal, Muḥammad Kurrā had previously approached each of the royal princes in secret and "and promised the government to each of the most eligible, persuading the others to agree to whatever he, Kurra, would propose. Accordingly, to the question which he put to them publicly, they were unanimous in answering, 'We are all content, *abu shaykh*, with whatever you will do'" (*Sahara and Sudan*, 298–99).

256 Against this account, Nachtigal states that Malik Ibrāhīm was the only one of those summoned to oppose the shaykh-father's selection, telling him that "he saw blood in the features of the royal boy . . . and of blood Darfur had . . . had enough" (*Sahara and Sudan*, 299). Malik Ibrāhīm also warned that the shaykh-father that he "should take heed of what he was doing, for at some time he would himself be the man who had most to fear from the young prince" (same reference).

257 I.e., Muḥammad Faḍl's cousins, sons of the other sons of Sultan Aḥmad Bukur.

258 See §2.2.36.

259 See §3.1.16, §3.1.24.

260 See §2.2.37.

Glossary

Names of persons are alphabetized by the first element of the name. Names are given in the form in which they appear in the text, which generally reflect al-Tūnisī's spelling. Other spellings found in the literature (especially O'Fahey, Nachtigal, and Browne) are given in parentheses, e.g., "Fartīt (elsewhere Fertit)." The ascription "Fur" in parentheses after an item indicates that the word is used in the Fur language, but not necessarily that it is ultimately of Fur origin (many terms used in Fur are also used by other ethnic groups). The names of beads, other accessories, and perfumes are ever changing. Items (such as certain plants and diseases) that it has proven impossible to identify satisfactorily are omitted here and dealt with in the notes.

Ab Sanūn a people, also called Kodoi, related to the royal family of Wadai.

ába dima'ng (Fur) see Dār Ába Dima'ng.

ába poor-ii (Fur) according to the author, a title of the kaamíne.

ába umá (elsewhere abbo uumo*; Fur)* commander of the rearguard of the army and hereditary ruler of Dār Umá (Dar Uumo), one of the four primary provinces of Darfur, southeast of Jabal Marrah.

abbo (Fur) a title of respect.

'Abd al-Raḥmān al-Rashīd sultan of Darfur (r. 1202/1787 to 1218/1803–4).

Abīrīs (= Bārīs) an outlying oasis west of the al-Khārijah group, fifty-four miles from the town of al-Khārijah.

abū abāṭ Indian corn, maize (*Zea mays*).

Abū 'Abd Allāh Muḥammad al-Wirghī (d. 1190/1776) Tunisian chancellery secretary and poet.

Abū l-Judūl an estate or group of villages near Tandaltī (El-Fasher) granted to the author's father as a fief and where the author lived during his stay in Darfur.

Abū Muḥammad Ḥammūdah Pasha Ḥammūdah Pasha ibn 'Alī II (r. 1196–1229/1782–1814), ruler of Tunis.

Abū l-Qāsim sixth historical sultan of the Keira dynasty (r. ca. 1739–52); preceded by ʿUmar Lēl and succeeded by Muḥammad Tayrāb.

Abū l-Ṭayyib al-Mutanabbī see al-Mutanabbī.

abū ṣaffayr (so voweled in the original) jaundice.

abū l-ṣufūf pleurisy.

Abū Zaʿbal a locality north of Cairo, where the first modern Egyptian medical school was opened on February 28, 1827, attached to a military hospital; the school was transferred to Qaṣr al-ʿAynī in Cairo in 1837.

Ādam Adam, father of humankind; also a male given name.

Adiqiz (Agadez) formerly a city-state, now a region of central Niger.

ʿAdnān putative ancestor of the Northern Arabs, i.e., those who speak Arabic as it is commonly known, versus the Southern Arabs, who speak the now largely extinct South Arabian languages.

ʿAfnū Hausaland.

Aḥmad Bukur (or Bukr) (r. ca. 1700–20) third of the historical Keira sultans, associated with the second phase of Islamization of the Darfur state.

Aḥmad ibn Sulaymān a teacher in Tunis and the maternal uncle of the author's father.

Aḥmad Zarrūq an uncle of the author's; presumably a son, born in Sennar, of his grandfather Sulaymān.

al-Alfī Muḥammad Bayk al-Alfī (d. 1226/1811), a Mamluk army commander who, shortly before the events described by the author, had played a role in the failed attempt to restore Mamluk control over Egypt; his sobriquet, from *alf* ("one thousand"), means "purchased for a thousand dinars."

ʿAlī, Imam ʿAlī ibn Abī Ṭālib, cousin and son-in-law of the Prophet Muḥammad and fourth caliph (r. 35–40/656–61), famed for his wise sayings.

ʿAlī al-Darwīsh ʿAlī ibn Ḥasan ibn Ibrāhīm al-Ankūrī al-Miṣrī (1211–70/1797–1853), Egyptian poet, laureate to the viceroy ʿAbbās I.

ʿAlī al-Ghurāb ʿAlī ibn al-Ghurāb al-Ṣafaqisī (d. 1183/1769), poet from Sfax, known for eulogies of the rulers of Tunis and bawdy verse.

ʿAlī Pasha I ʿAlī I ibn Muḥammad (r. 1148–70/1735–56), second Ḥusaynid ruler of Tunis.

ʿAlī wad Jāmiʿ a grandee at the court of Sultan ʿAbd al-Raḥmān and patron of Shaykh-Father Muḥammad Kurrā.

Anbūsah (elsewhere *Umm Būsa*) a slave woman belonging to Sultan ʿAbd al-Raḥmān and mother of his successor, Sultan Muḥammad Faḍl.

ʿandurāb a tree: either *Cordia monoica*, "snot-berry tree," or *Cordia sinensis*, "gray-leaved cordia."

ʿanqallū green fruit of the Jericho balm tree (*hijlīj*).

the Anṣār literally "the helpers"; i.e., the men (of the peoples of Aws and Khazraj) of Medina who supported the Prophet Muḥammad, as distinguished from the Muhājirūn or "emigrants," i.e., his Meccan followers who moved with him to Medina.

ʿaqīq round agate beads.

ʿArafah al-Dusūqī al-Mālikī Muḥammad ibn Aḥmad ibn ʿArafah al-Dusūqī (d. 1230/1815), a prominent Mālikī jurisprudent and scholar of his day.

al-Azhar the premier mosque and teaching institution of premodern Cairo, built 361/972.

báási (Fur; approx. "royal") a title originally given the brother of the sultan and later extended to apply to all his male relatives.

Bāb al-Muʿallā Mecca's most ancient cemetery.

Banī ʿAdī a town in Upper Egypt near the west bank of the Nile in the governorate of Banī Suwayf and the terminus of the so-called Forty Days Road (*Darb al-Arbiʿīn*) between Egypt and Darfur.

the Banū Ḥalbah cattle-herding nomads living south of Jabal Marrah.

the Banū Jarrār cattle-herding nomads belonging to the Fazārah group.

the Banū ʿUmrān cattle-herding nomads belonging to the Fazārah group.

al-Bāqirmah (Bagirmi) formerly, a state southeast of Lake Chad in what is now Chad.

Baradiyyah in the Wadai sultanate, a goblet drum.

the Barajūb probably, the swamps of Baḥr al-Ghazāl and Baḥr al-Jabal, south of Darfur.

the Barqū a people, originally from Wadai, with many communities in Darfur (cf. Dār Barqū, a name for Wadai).

the Bartī (Berti) a people living in eastern Darfur, formerly speakers of a now-extinct Nubian language.

al-Basūs, War of a pre-Islamic intertribal conflict fought toward the end of the fifth century AD that lasted forty years and was blamed on an old woman called al-Basūs whose camel had been killed by a member of a rival tribe.

baṭṭūm a tree: probably terebinth (*Pistacia terebinthus*).

Bawwā a wadi in northern Darfur, perhaps the same as the "Wadi Howa" on modern maps.

the Bidāyāt a non-Arabic-speaking people found in northwestern Darfur.

bindilah a kind of dance.

Bingah a Fartīt people living on the southern fringes of the sultanate.

the Bīqū (Beigo) a Dājū-speaking people of originally servile status living in southern Darfur.

Bīr al-Malḥah ("Salt Flat Well") alternative name of Bīr al-Zaghāwī.

Bīr al-Zaghāwī ("al-Zaghāwī's Well") a well on the road from Asyut to Darfur south of Laqiyyah, also called Bīr al-Malḥah.

the Birqid a people living east of Jabal Marrah and south of Tandaltī (El-Fasher) who spoke a Nubian language.

Bornu (Barnaw) from 1380 to 1893, an empire that at its height incorporated parts of what are now Nigeria, Chad, Cameroon, and Niger; in the author's day, the state immediately west of Wāddāy (Wadai).

al-Bukhārī, Muḥammad ibn Ismāʿīl (194–256/810–70) author of an authoritative collection of some eight thousand sound prophetic hadiths.

Būlāq (1) the name of two localities in Cairo, one (Būlāq Abū l-ʿIlā) being the city's port, on the east bank of the Nile; the other (Būlāq al-Dakrūr) a settlement on its west bank, in Giza; (2) a village on the caravan route from Asyut to Darfur, seventeen miles west of al-Khārijah.

al-burjuk scarlet fever.

būzah in Egypt, barley beer; elsewhere usually spelled *būẓah.*

the Caravanserai of the Jallābah (Wikālat al-Jallābah) a *wikālah* was a combined warehouse and hostel for merchants; the *jallābah* were traveling merchants drawn largely from Upper Egypt and northern Nilotic Sudan who traded between the Sudanic countries and Egypt. The greater part of their trade from Darfur was in slaves, but ivory, ostrich feathers, wild-animal parts, camels, and other merchandise were also taken to Egypt, while beads, tin, cloth, swords, coffee, paper, and more were taken from Egypt to Darfur.

counselor (Arabic: amīn, pl. umanāʾ) a confidential advisor to the sultan of Darfur.

the Dājū a people living in southern Darfur whose ancestors are said to have ruled the first Darfurian state and who were superseded in the sixteenth century by the Tunjūr.

al-Dalīl, Judge chief judge of Wadai, who passed through Cairo in October 1841 on his way to Mecca and there met with both the author and Nicolas Perron.

dallūkah set of three goblet drums.

dam-l-raʿāf (= *dam al-ruʿāf*, literally "nosebleed blood") a kind of coral bead.

damsuga (Fur) personal spirit guardian purchased from the jinn.

Dār literally "house" and, when followed by the name of a group or individual, "land of, territory of"; hence Dār Fartīt ("the Land of the Fartīt"), Dār Bagirmi ("the Land of the Bagirmi"), Dār Wāddāy ("Wadai"), Dār al-Tikináwi (Darfur's northern province, governed by the Tikináwi).

Dār Ába Dima'ng (Dar Aba Dima; Fur) literally "The Land of the Lord of Dima'ng"; an autonomous area southwest of Jabal Marrah ruled by a line of hereditary chiefs.

Dār Bandalah a Fartīt people, non-Muslims living on the southern fringes of the sultanate.

Dār Mallā (Mali) formerly (tenth to fifteenth centuries AD), a western Sudanic empire between the Upper Senegal and Upper Niger rivers.

Dār Qimir (Dar Qimr) a sultanate subject to Darfur, north of Dār Masālīṭ and south of Dār Zaghāwah, ruled by a dynasty allegedly originating from the Jaʿaliyyīn ethnic group in the Nilotic Sudan.

Dār al-Rīḥ literally the Land of the Wind; an alternative name for Dār al-Tikináwi, the sultanate's northern province.

Dār Rūngā the territory of a Fartīt (non-Muslim) people living on the southwestern fringes of the sultanate.

Dār Silā (Dar Sula) a Dājū-speaking kingdom lying between Darfur and Wadai and paying tribute to both.

Dār Ṣulayḥ (also Dār Ṣaliḥ) an alternative name for (Dār al-) Wāddāy (Wadai), either because its inhabitants claimed descent from one Ṣāliḥ (of which Ṣulayḥ is the diminutive) ibn ʿAbd Allāh ibn ʿAbbas, or because its second founder, Sultan Jawdah (r. ca. 1747–75), bore the epithet al-Ṣāliḥ, meaning "the Righteous."

Dār Tāmā, Dār Tāmah an area between Darfur and Wadai in the west, never comfortably part of Darfur or of Wadai; it takes its name from the Tāmā (Tāmah) people of Jabal Tāmā.

Dār Tunbuktū (Timbuktu) a state on the Niger River, today in Niger.

darat a period of extreme heat lasting about forty days from the end of the rainy season (see *kharīf*), during which the sorghum ripens.

Darfur a formerly independent sultanate located between al-Wādday (Wadai, now eastern Chad) on the west and Kordofan on the east; since 1916, part of Sudan. The name is a contraction of Dār al-Fūr, the Land of the Fur.

darmūdī member of an outcast group of hunters and smiths.

dawdarī kind of *waykah* (q.v.) made from bonemeal.

dééng saaya (Fur) a slightly fermented drink of rice, sugar, and water (= Arabic *sūbiyā*).

dhikr Sufi ceremony that, through rhythmic movement and sound, allows the participant to achieve mystical unity with God; the specifically Fur form of the *dhikr* described by the author differs, however, from this norm.

difrah a grain; probably sawa millet.

dimlij (pl. damālij) literally "bracelet"; subchief under the authority of a *shartāy*.

dinbī "dimbi," a cultivar of pearl (bulrush) millet.

dinjāyah a mud-brick storehouse within the *fāshir* (q.v.) of the sultan of Darfur.

dinqār a large wooden drum of state.

Dongola a town on the Nile in Sudanese Nubia.

dullong (Fur) a kind of small clay pot.

al-duqrī osteomyelitis.

durdur a circular wall of mud forming the foundation of the walls of the houses of members of the elite.

durrāʿah a length of cloth wound around the upper half of a woman's body.

durzūyah a wooden pillar used to support the roof of a *tukultī* (q.v.).

emir army commander.

The Epitome (al-Mukhtaṣar) an authoritative handbook of Islamic law according to the Mālikī school of jurisprudence by Khalīl ibn Isḥāq al-Jundī (d. 776/1374).

Fallātā, Fallātah (from Kanuri, "people"; Fellata) name of a nomadic people found from Mauritania to eastern Sudan, who call themselves Fulbe (sg. Pullo); also called here Fullān (sg. Fullānī), from the Hausa.

the Fanqarū (Fongoro) a people living in southern Dār Ába Dima'ng.

faqīh (1) (used of non-Darfurians; plural *fuqahā'*) a man trained in Islamic legal science, a jurisprudent (2) (used of Darfurians; plural, anomalously, *fuqarā'*) a holy man, i.e., a man, not necessarily learned, from a family, usually of non-Darfurian origin, credited with religious charisma (*barakah*) and supernatural powers who often acted as a village schoolmaster.

the Farāwujayh (Feroge) a Fartīt (non-Muslim) people living south of Baḥr al-ʿArab.

fardah apron-like garment worn by women.

Fartīt non-Muslim peoples living on the southern margins of Darfur; they were regarded as enslaveable by the raiders from the north; despite this, it was recognized that in some way the Fartīt were related to the Fur.

fāshir the compound forming the seat of the sultan's government, in former times itinerant but from 1791 located permanently at Tandaltī (now known as El-Fasher, capital of the federal state of North Darfur); the term, which is used from Lake Chad to the Nile, is of unknown origin and seems to have referred in the first instance to the open space before the encampment of a king or chief.

the Fazārah a generic term for the cattle-owning, Arabic-speaking nomads of southern Darfur.

feathers (Arabic: rīsh) (1) "the feathers": the sultan's ceremonial fan; (2) a kind of bead.

Fezzan Libya's southwestern province.

Fullān (Fulan, Fulani, Fulbe) an alternative name for the Fallātā (q.v.).

fuqarā' see *faqīh*.

Fur the largest ethnic group in Darfur, forming about one third of the population and speaking a Nilo-Saharan language. Sultans from the Fur ruled Darfur from the mid-seventeenth century until 1916.

al-Fusṭāṭ site of the first capital of Egypt under Muslim rule, just south of Cairo.

The Glittering Ladder *The Glittering Ladder on Logic* (*al-Sullam al-murawnaq fī l-manṭiq*) by ʿAbd al-Raḥmān ibn Muḥammad al-Akhḍarī (918–83/1512–75), a well-known didactic poem on logic.

the Ḥabbāniyyah (Habbania) an Arab-speaking, cattle-herding, semi-nomadic people of southern Darfur.

al-habūb wind trapped in the lower belly.

Hadith the corpus of reports (hadiths) of the words or actions of the Prophet Muḥammad.

the Hafsids the dynasty that ruled Tunisia and eastern Algeria from 627/1229 to 982/1574.

al-Ḥājj title of Muslims who have made the pilgrimage to Mecca.

al-Ḥajjāj al-Ḥajjāj ibn Yūsuf (ca. 41/661 to 95/714), governor of Iraq, who brutally crushed several revolts against Umayyad rule.

Ḥalfāwīn a historic district of Tunis (Halfaouine).

Ḥalq al-Wād the fortified port of Tunis (La Goulette).

Ḥammūdah Pasha see Abū Muḥammad Ḥammūdah Pasha.

ḥarāz a tree: apple-ring acacia (*Faidherbia* (or *Acacia*) *albida*).

al-Ḥarīrī al-Qāsim ibn ʿAlī al-Ḥarīrī (446–516/1054–1122), Iraqi prose writer, poet, and civil servant, author of fifty immensely popular *maqāmāt* (compositions in a highly polished style), which he arranged in a work of the same name.

ḥarish a kind of bead worn by poor women and used in certain localities as currency.

Ḥasan wad ʿAwūḍah chief imam of Kūbayh under Sultan ʿAbd al-Raḥmān.

al-ḥaṣar leukorrhea.

ḥashāb a tree: gum acacia (*Senegalia* (or *Acacia*) *senegal*); elsewhere spelled *hashāb*.

ḥashshāshah a kind of iron hoe.

al-hayḍah cholera.

Ḥawwāʾ the first woman, the Qurʾanic equivalent of Eve; also a given name.

the High Plain (al-Ṣaʿīd) the name given in Darfur to the area from Rīl south to the farthest limits of the country.

hijlīj a tree: Jericho balm (*Balanites aegyptiaca*).

Ḥillat Jūltū village in the district of Abū l-Judūl.

ḥummayḍ a tree: marula (*Sclerocarya birrea*).

al-Ḥusayn, Shrine of mosque in Cairo containing a tomb said to hold the head of al-Ḥusayn, grandson of the Prophet Muḥammad.

Ḥusayn ʿAmmārī al-Azharī Bedouin shaykh from Kordofan, known as the introducer of tobacco to Darfur.

Ḥusayn Pasha al-Ḥusayn I ibn ʿAlī al-Turkī (r. 1117–48/1705–35), founder of Tunis's Ḥusaynid dynasty.

Ibn Ājurrūm's Text (al-Ājurrūmiyyah) widely used brief compendium of Arabic grammar, formally entitled *al-Muqadimmah al-Ājurrūmiyyah*, by Abū ʿAbd Allāh Muḥammad ibn Dāʾūd al-Sanhājī (672–723/1273–1323), known as Ibn Ājurrūm.

Ibn Ḥajar Aḥmad ibn Muḥammad ibn ʿAlī ibn Hajar al-Haythamī al-Makkī al-Ansārī (909/1503–4 to 973/1565–66), an influential Shāfiʿī jurist.

Ibrāhīm the builder of the Kaaba, identified with biblical Abraham; also a male given name.

Ibrāhīm al-Riyāḥī Ibrāhīm ibn ʿAbd al-Qādir ibn Aḥmad al-Riyāḥī al-Tūnisī (1180–1266/1766–1850), Mālikī jurist, chief mufti of Tunis, and poet.

Ibrāhīm wad Ramād powerful Fur clan chief and Master of the Drums during the reign of Sultan ʿAbd al-Raḥmān; his name, "son of Ashes," alluded to his illegitimacy.

the Illumined City Medina.

Imruʾ al-Qays (sixth century AD) celebrated pre-Islamic Arabian poet.

the ʿIrayqāt (Ireigat) an Arabic-speaking, camel-herding people forming part of the Northern Ruzayqāt.

irdabb a dry measure equal to 198 liters.

iyā kurī (Fur: "mother" + "power") title of the sultan's premier wife.

ʿIzz al-Dīn al-Jāmiʿī (elsewhere, al-Jāmiʿ) a judge during the reign of Sultan ʿAbd al-Raḥmān and later chief judge of Darfur and its territories; member of the Jamāwiʿah family of holy men whose ancestor came from the east and was invited to settle in Darfur by Sultan Sulaymān Solóng.

Jabal Marrah mountain range in western Darfur; homeland of the Fur and cradle of the Keira dynasty of Darfur sultans (see O'Fahey, *Darfur Sultanate*, 3, 33–36). The author refers to a specific peak within the range as "the true Marrah" and on his map of Darfur draws a Little Jabal Marrah (presumably the same) about halfway between the north and south ends of the range but slightly to the west. It has not proven possible to identify this peak.

Jabal Tāmah see Dār Tāmah.

(Jadīd) Karyū a village south of Tandaltī, on the estate of Faqīh Mālik al-Fūtāwī.

(Jadīd) Rās al-Fīl a village in southeast Darfur, northeast of Rīl; formerly a *fāshir* (q.v.).

Jadīd al-Sayl a village near Tandaltī (El-Fasher).

jallābah (sg. jallāb) traveling merchants trading between Egypt and Sudan.

Jarkū perhaps modern Jarkul, near Mellit.

jêl (Fur) kind of dance.

al-jiqqayl a sexually-transmitted disease; probably syphilis or gonorrhea.

jūghān or jūkhān a tree: jackalberry (*Diospyros mespiliformis*).

kaamíne (kamni, kamene; Fur) the "shadow sultan," an ancient ritual title of enormous prestige but little power.

ka'b al-ṭīb literally "the best of perfumes": a perfume made from a certain root.

the Kabābīsh an Arabic-speaking group of camel nomads living between Kordofan and Sennar.

kabartū in the Wadai sultanate, officers of the law, executioners, and musicians of a low caste.

Kabkābiyyah (Fur; literally "they threw down their shields") a town ninety-two miles west of Tandaltī (El-Fasher), named in reference to the defeat of invading Wadaian forces by those of Darfur under Sultan Aḥmad Bukur.

al-Kāf a city in northwest Tunisia (Le Kef).

Kalīlah and Dimnah (Kalīlah wa-Dimnah) a book of animal fables translated by 'Abd Allāh ibn al-Muqaffa' (second/eighth century) from the Persian and ultimately of Indian origin.

kalkaf a fine cotton cloth.

kamkūlak in the Wadai sultanate, a counselor attending the sultan at audience; or one of four with this title, one of whom was in charge of the administration of the sultan's palace while the other three assisted with the administration of the sultan's estates; said to mean "sweeper of the sultan's house" (same reference).

kanfūs (pl. kanāfīs) women's breechclouts.

Karakriit one of the three great sections of the Fur; the Karakriit live in and to the east of Jabal Marrah.

karbābah reed hut.

karnū a variety of jujube.

kāshif literally "uncoverer, inspector"; in contemporary Egypt, governor of a minor province, as a rule drawn from the Turkish-speaking military elite.

the Kashmirah a people living in Wadai.

Katakū (Kotoko) formerly a kingdom covering parts of modern Cameroon, Nigeria, and southwest Chad.

katkāt a kind of heavy *tukkiyyah* (q.v.) of a compact weave.

kawal either of two bushes (*Cassia absus* and *Cassia tora*) and the condiment made from their fermented leaves and stalks.

kenykenya (Fur) a kind of candy made from dried jujube seeds.

Khabīr literally "expert"; title of the leader of a desert caravan; also a given name.

khaddūr kind of bead worn by poor women and used as currency for small purchases; Nachtigal describes the beads as large and made of clay.

Khalīl [ibn Isḥāq al-Jundī] (Khalīl al-Mālikī) (d. ca. 1365), author of *The Epitome* (q.v.).

kharīf the rainy season in Darfur, which starts between September and October and ends between November and December depending on latitude.

Khāqān a title of the sultans of Darfur, as also of the Ottoman sultan.

al-Khārijah (Kharjah) a group of oases in Egypt west of Asyut.

khayriyyah an Egyptian gold coin of the value of nine piasters (see Lane, *Manners*, 573).

Khūrshīd Pasha Aḥmad Khūrshīd Pasha, Ottoman governor of Egypt from 1804 until ousted by Muḥammad ʿAlī in 1805.

kilí a tree (unidentified) producing a drink used to determine the innocence or guilt of accused persons.

kīm horn bracelets worn by women.

Kīrī a village; according to informants it is close to Qirlī at the foot of Jabal Marrah.

kitir a tree: blackthorn (*Senegalia mellifera*).

kóór kwa (Fur) literally "spearmen"; slaves with spears who stood behind the sultan as part of his bodyguard when he held audience and surrounded him when he rode out; among them were young boys who sang and made music with whistles and maracas. They were also used as messengers and for other services.

Kordofan the region from Darfur's eastern border almost to the Nile; unlike Darfur, and Sennar to its east, Kordofan never underwent a process of state formation. Today, as part of Sudan, the area is divided into the federal states of North and South Kordofan.

Kūbayh (Kobbei, Kobbé) a town, now abandoned, thirty-five miles northwest of Tandaltī (El-Fasher). Kūbayh formed the southern terminus of the trade route between Asyut in Egypt and Darfur (the "Forty Days Road"), was inhabited almost exclusively by traders, and constituted the commercial capital of Darfur; in its heyday in the eighteenth and first half of the nineteenth centuries, it may have been the largest town in the sultanate, with six to eight thousand inhabitants.

the Kūkah a people of southwestern Wadai.

kumbā (or kanbū: both occur in the text; from Fur kômbo*)* as defined by the author, a liquid extracted from the ash of the *hijlīj* tree (Jericho balm, *Balanites aegyptiaca*) and used as a salt substitute.

Kunjáara (Kunjaara, Kunyjaara) one of the three great sections of the Fur people and that to which the Keira dynasty belonged; the Kunjáara live in and to the east of Jabal Marrah.

kūrāyāt literally "grooms"; four high officials in charge of the sultan's horses and servants. The word, though presumably Fur, was not recognized by informants.

kūrayb either of two grasses that are used for fodder and as famine foods: Egyptian crowfoot grass (*Dactyloctenium aegyptium*) and dropseed grass (*Sporobolus festivus*).

kurnug a kind of house resembling a *tukultī* but whose roof is raised on four rather than two wooden pillars (see §3.1.86, images).

Kusā a region of central Darfur.

laddāy a woman's headpiece of silver wire and beads.

lanngi (Fur) a dance.

Laqiyyah (Leghea, Laguyeh, Lagia) an uninhabited oasis on the route from Asyut to Darfur, south of Salīmah and close to the northern marches of Dār Zaghāwah.

lawī a variety of the cotton known as "Indian."

liqdābah (apparently from Fur libdenga*)* a roofed, open-sided structure within the sultan's compound used as an audience hall, mess, etc.

Little Jabal Marrah (Jubayl Marrah) the author's name for the peak, probably that usually referred to on modern maps as the Deriba Caldera, that lends its name to the entire Jabal Marrah mountain range and plateau.

Lubad According to ancient Arabian legend, Luqmān the Long-lived, a pre-Islamic figure to whom wise sayings are attributed, was granted, as a reward for his piety, a life as long as that of seven named vultures (the vulture being a popular symbol of longevity among the Arabs). The last vulture was named Lubad; when Lubad died, so did Luqmān.

madīdah a broth made from pounded desiccated watermelon.

madraʿah a bead bracelet worn by women.

Magian literally "Zoroastrian"; applied in Darfur to the pagan peoples on its southern borders.

the Maḥāmīd cattle-herding nomads of the Fazārah group.

the Majānīn Arabic-speaking camel-herding nomads living in eastern Darfur and western Kordofan.

Makk a title, equivalent to "king," used by rulers in the Nile Valley, such as the Makk of Sennar; also used by the chief of the Birgid of Darfur.

the Malanqā (also Mananqah) a subgroup of the Ab Sanūn (q.v.).

malik a title used of (1) a king; (2) a tribal chief or person related to the royal family to whom some of the accoutrements of Sudanic royalty (such as the possession of copper war drums) pertained; (3) an official in charge of a significant place or specialized group. See further Volume One, Note on the Text, pp. xliii–xliv.

Mālik al-Fūtāwī Mālik ibn ʿAlī ibn Yūsuf al-Fūtāwī (d. ca. 1820), a prominent member of the Awlād ʿAlī family of holy men and an influential vizier at the court of Sultan ʿAbd al-Raḥmān; sponsor of the author's father.

Mālikī follower of the school of jurisprudence established by Mālik ibn Anas (179/795); most African Muslims, apart from those of Egypt, are *Mālikī*s and the designation often appears in names, e.g., Shaykh ʿArafah al-Dusūqī al-Mālikī.

the Mananqah see Malanqā.

Mandarah a kingdom (ca. 1500–1893) and people in what is today northwest Cameroon.

Manfalūṭ a city in Upper Egypt on the west bank of the Nile north of Asyut.

manjūr a bead worn by women of the middle class.

manṣūṣ (literally "squashed") round, flattened amber beads.

maqāmah a short independent narration written in ornamental rhymed prose with verse insertions, a common plot-scheme, and two constant protagonists: the narrator and the hero.

al-Maqs (Macs, Maghs, Mughess) the southernmost oasis of the Khārijah complex, uninhabited in the author's day.

al-Marbūṭah a village on the banks of Wādī l-Kūʿ not far from Tandaltī (El-Fasher).

marhabayb a species of thin cane (*Cymbopogon nervatus* and/or *proximus*) with which houses are roofed; elsewhere sometimes spelled *marḥabayb*.

mārīq a generic name for sorghum.

Marrah see Jabal Marrah, Little Jabal Marrah.

the Masālīṭ (Maṣālīṭ, Mesalit) a large people with its own language living to the west of Jabal Marrah.

al-Mazrūb a well marking the northern entry into Darfur for those coming from Asyut in Egypt.

mééram (Fur) a title given to the daughter of the sultan of Darfur or to younger marriageable women of the royal family in general, as opposed to the *habbūbāt*, and to the representative of the bride and her friends at a wedding.

The Memorandum (al-Tadhkirah) see al-Qurṭubī.

the Mīdawb (Meidob) a people living on Jabal Mīdawb in far northeastern Darfur who speak a language of the Nubian group.

mīdawbī a kind of naturally occurring salt.

the Mīmah a people centered on the town of Wadaʿah east of Wādī Kuʿ in eastern Darfur.

al-Minyah a city in Upper Egypt on the west bank of the Nile.

mishāhrah a bead worn by women.

the Misīriyyah (Misiriyah, Messiria) the Brown Misīriyyah (al-Misīriyyah al-Ḥumr) are camel nomads living in northern Kordofan, the Black Misīriyyah (al-Misīriyyah al-Zurq) are cattle nomads living in southern Kordofan; both peoples have offshoots in Darfur.

mooge (singular and plural; Fur—pronounced as two syllables) jester cum eulogist cum crier who shouted the praises of his master (for example, the sultan) on public occasions, was licensed to speak audaciously, and sometimes acted as public executioner.

the Mother of the Book the Qurʾan.

mudd measure of volume used for grain; Perron states, on the author's authority, that the Sudanese *mudd* was equal to the Egyptian *malwah*, i.e., 4.125 liters.

Mughulṭāy al-Turkī Mughulṭāy ibn Qalīj ʿAbdullāhi al-Bakjarī al-Miṣrī (689–762/1290–1361), Egyptian historian and Hadith scholar of Turkic origin, also known for his book on martyrs for love, *al-Wāḍiḥ al-mubīn fīman ustushhida min al-muḥibbīn* (*The Clear Exposition Concerning Those Who Gave Their Lives for Love*).

mughrah a stone from which a red pigment is obtained.

al-Muhallabī, the vizier al-Ḥasan ibn Muḥammad al-Muhallabī (291–352/903–63), administrator and general for the Buyid princes of Baghdad, and a litterateur.

Muḥammad ʿAlī (r. 1805–48) ruler of Egypt under the nominal suzerainty of the Ottoman state.

Muḥammad Daldan (Fur: Daldang) wad Binayyah (d. 1804?) Keira warlord and slave trader, styled "King" because he was a grandson of Sultan Muḥammad Tayrāb.

Muḥammad Faḍl (elsewhere usually al-Faḍl) ninth sultan of Darfur of the Keira dynasty (r. ca. 1730–39), preceded by his father, ʿAbd al-Raḥmān, and succeeded by his son, Muḥammad al-Ḥusayn.

Muḥammad al-Ḥasanī Muḥammad III ibn ʿAbd Allāh (r. 1171–1204/1757–90), ʿAlawid ruler of Morocco.

Muḥammad ibn al-Qāsim ʿImād al-Dīn Muḥammad ibn al-Qāsim al-Thaqafī (ca. 695–715), a Muslim general best known for the conquest, at an extremely young age, of Sindh and Multan.

Muḥammad al-Jallūlī Ḥusaynid governor of Sfax in Tunisia in the late eighteenth or early nineteenth century.

Muḥammad Kurrā (d. 1804) in Fur "Muḥammad the Tall"; a palace servant in the days of Sultan Muḥammad Tayrāb who rose to become, despite temporary setbacks, shaykh-father under sultans ʿAbd al-Raḥmān and Muḥammad Faḍl and, for a time, master of Kordofan. His rivalry with Muḥammad Faḍl led to his death. The author was a protégé of Muḥammad Kurrā's associate Mālik al-Fūtāwī and met Muḥammad Kurrā shortly before the shaykh-father's death.

Muḥammad al-Maḥrūqī likely the leading merchant of that name (d. 1232/1816–17) appointed by Muḥammad ʿAlī to advise his son Ṭūsūn when the latter was given responsibility for the campaign (1811–16) against the Āl Saʿūd rulers of the Hejaz.

Muḥammad al-Muknī nineteenth-century governor of Fezzan (southern Libya).

Muḥammad Órré Dungo a eunuch belonging to Sultan Muḥammad Tayrāb and a shaykh-father.

Muḥammad Shihāb al-Dīn al-Miṣrī Muḥammad ibn Ismāʿīl ibn ʿUmar (1210–74/1795–1857), known as Shihāb al-Dīn al-Miṣrī, a scholar and poet who became coeditor of the official *Egyptian Gazette* (*al-Waqāʾiʿ al-Miṣriyyah*), was associated with the royal family, and wrote much occasional verse.

Muḥammad Tayrāb (r. ca. 1752–53 to 1785) third son of Aḥmad Bukur to become sultan of Darfur; invaded Kordofan toward the end of his reign and incorporated it into the sultanate, thus creating the largest premodern state within what is now the Sudan.

mukhkhayṭ a tree: *Boscia senegalensis.*

Murād Bayk Murād Bayk al-Qazdaghlī, a Mamluk who ruled Egypt in partnership with Ibrāhīm Bayk from 1784 until the French invasion in 1798.

muʿrāqī literally "rooter"; one skilled in the gathering and use of medicinal plants.

al-Musabbaʿ brother of Sultan Sulaymān Solóng (q.v.); left Darfur for western Kordofan, parts of which his descendants thereafter ruled.

al-Musabbaʿāwī, Hāshim (fl. 1770–1800) a descendant of al-Musabbaʿ who, during the reign in Darfur of Sultan Muḥammad Tayrāb, attempted to create from his base in Kordofan a state that would rival or supplant that of Darfur.

Musāʿid (ibn Surūr) a member of the family of the Dhawū Zayd dynasty of rulers of Mecca resident in Darfur during the author's time there.

al-Mutanabbī Aḥmad ibn al-Ḥusayn Abū l-Ṭayyib al-Mutanabbī (ca. 303–54/915–65), a renowned poet of the Abbasid era.

nārah a love potion.

Nufah (Nupe) a state, founded in the mid-fifteenth century, in what is now north-central Nigeria.

Numlayh a village in Jabal Marrah, in the area inhabited by the Karakriit, a clan of the Fur (not to be confused with Nimule, a town in South Sudan).

Nūr al-Anṣārī a holy man living in Kubayh and married to the daughter of Sultan ʿAbd al-Raḥmān.

nyúlmá (Fur) sesame lees.

The One-Thousand-Line Poem (al-Alfiyyah) a popular textbook of grammar in the form of a poem of some thousand lines, by Muḥammad ibn Mālik (ca. 600–72/1203–74).

ŏrnang (Fur) the representative of the men at a wedding and organizer of hunting parties for the young men of a village; the ŏrnang may be evidence of a residual age-grade system, comparable to that of the Maasai or the Zulu, in which he acted as a war leader.

orondolong (Fur) literally "the door posts"; the highest officer of state, also known as "the sultan's face" (or "the sultan's head"). In peace, he acted as majordomo of the sultan's compound and the main intermediary between sultan and subjects; in war, he marched at the head of the sultan's army. He also governed four tribal territories.

órré bayyâ (Fur) literally "the narrow door," but generally referred to as "the women's door": the southern entrance to the sultan's compound or *fāshir*; also, in the author's usage, the superintendent of the *warrābāyah*, who supervised the eunuchs of the harem and acted as jailer and executioner.

órré dee (Fur) "the men's door": the northern entrance to the sultan's compound or *fāshir*.

órré'ng ába (Fur) a title listed by the author as that of a member of the state hierarchy who governed two tribal territories, without further explanation of the title's meaning or its holder's role.

păw (Fur) artificial coral.

Perron, Nicolas (1798–1876) the translator from Arabic into French of *The Land of the Blacks* (*Voyage au Darfour*) and other works. See Volume One, Introduction.

The Poem on Words Ending in -ā and ā' (al-Maqṣūrah) a pedagogical poem by Mūhammad ibn al-Ḥasan ibn Durayd (223–321/838–933).

pôlgo (Fur) kind of manufactured salt, sold in finger-shaped pieces.

poora'ng ába (Forrang Aba; Fur) literally "Father of the Fur"; the guardian of Fur law and custom, a ritual title dating from the Fur state's remote past.

Preserved Tablet the urtext of the Qur'an, preserved in Heaven.

the Protected City an epithet of Cairo.

qafal a tree: perhaps in this context frankincense (*Boswellia papyrifera*) or African myrrh (*Commiphora africana*); identification is tentative as the word was applied to a number of trees used in perfumes, medicines, and incense.

qanā savannah bamboo (*Oxytenanthera abyssinica*).

qaraẓ the pods of the sant acacia (*Acacia nilotica*), used for fodder.

Qimir see Dar Qimir.

Qirlī (Gurly, Gerli, Gerle) a settlement, now disappeared, that the author places between the northern end of Jabal Marrah and Kabkābiyyah on the west, site of a *fāshir* of Sultan Muḥammad Tayrāb.

The Qualities *The Prophetic Qualities* (*al-Khaṣā'iṣ al-nabawiyyah*), a work on the qualities of the Prophet Muḥammad by Egyptian historian and Hadith scholar Mughulṭāy al-Turkī.

qudānī an indigo-dyed cloth.

quffah in Egypt, a large basket.

qūqū the practice of carrying a baby by tying it to its mother's back.

al-Qurṭubī Muḥammad ibn Aḥmad ibn Abī Bakr al-Anṣārī al-Qurṭubī (d. 671/1273), author of a renowned commentary on the Qur'an and other works, including his *Memorandum on the Conditions of the Dead and Matters of the Hereafter* (*al-Tadhkirah fī Aḥwāl al-Mawtā wa-Umūr al-Ākhirah*); originally from Cordoba, Spain, he relocated to Egypt.

al-Quṣayr a port on Egypt's Red Sea coast, the point of embarkation for pilgrims going to the Hejaz.

Quss Quss ibn Sā'idah (sixth century AD), a pre-Islamic Arabian Christian renowned for the eloquence of his preaching.

rabdā' (of an ostrich) having four small, pure-white plumes.

Rajab seventh month of the Islamic calendar; it has the epithet "the Separate" because, under the pre-Islamic system according to which no fighting was allowed during certain months, it was the only such month that was neither preceded nor followed by another sacred month.

Rās al-Fīl see Jadīd Rās al-Fīl.

al-Raṭlī Pond one of thirteen ponds or lakes that existed in Cairo until the nineteenth century.

réëka (Fur) a kind of large basket.

The Reliable Compendium (*al-Jāmi' al-ṣaḥīḥ*; *al-Ṣaḥīḥ*), a collection of some eight thousand sound hadiths, by Muḥammad ibn Ismā'īl al-Bukhārī (194–256/810–70).

Rīfā a son of Sultan Aḥmad Bukur who was passed over for the succession in favor of 'Abd al-Raḥmān.

Rīl town in southeast Darfur (Dār Birqid); formerly a *fāshir*.

Rīz a son of Sultan Aḥmad Bukur who was passed over for the succession in favor of 'Abd al-Raḥmān.

Rizayqāt (Rizayqat, Rizeigat) a group of nomadic Arabic-speaking peoples with northern (camel-herding) and southern (cattle-herding) sections, the former living in the north and west, the latter in the south and southeast of Darfur.

rub' a measure of volume used for grain, equivalent to 8.25 liters.

Rūngā a town in Dār Rungā (q.v.).

ruqād al-fāqah (literally "restful sleep") a kind of large bead worn by the women of the rich.

Ṣābūn, Muḥammad sultan of Wadai (r. ca. 1805–16).

the Sacred House the Kaaba at Mecca.

al-Ṣaftī probably Aḥmad al-Sāʾīm al-Saftī, shaykh (rector) of the mosque-university of al-Azhar in Cairo from 1838 to 1847.

Salīmah (Selima) an uninhabited oasis on the route from Asyut to Darfur, between al-Shabb and Laqiyyah.

sangadiri (Fur) a dance.

ṣanṭ sant acacia (*Vachellia* (or *Acacia*) *nilotica*).

Sarf al-Dajāj town northwest of Jabal Marrah and west of Kabkābiyyah; according to Perron, *sarf* (Fur) means "brook"; thus the name means "Chickens' Brook."

ṣarīf internal fence within a homestead acting as a dust-break for the huts.

sayāl umbrella thorn tree (*Vachellia/Acacia tortilis*).

sayyid male claiming descent from the Prophet Muḥammad; also the title of such a man, used interchangeably in this work with "Sharif."

sequin gold coin minted in Venice.

al-Shabb (Sheb) literally "alum"; a small oasis north of Salīmah on the road from Asyut to Darfur.

al-Shāfiʿī, Muḥammad ibn Idrīs (150–204/767–820) a leading jurist from whose teachings emerged one of the four canonical schools of legal interpretation, and a much-quoted poet.

al-Shaʿīriyyah a village near Tandaltī (today's El-Fasher).

Shālā a Fartīt people living on the southern fringes of the sultanate.

shallāngīn (Arabization of Fur *sagala kin*) traditional eye doctors specializing in the removal of cataracts.

shaʿlūb a vine (*Leptodenia arborea*).

sharāmīṭ literally "shreds": jerked meat.

sharif a male claiming descent from the Prophet Muḥammad; also, the title of such a man, used interchangeably in this work with "Sayyid."

shartāy (pl. sharātī) head of a *shartāyah*, one of the districts into which the provinces of the sultanate of Darfur were divided. The *shartāy* was the representative of the ruler and his village was the center for the collection of taxes, the administration of justice, and the levying of troops.

shāshiyyah in Tunisia, a rigid red felt cap similar to that called a tarboosh in Egypt.

shāw a tree: arak (*Salvadora persica*).

shawtar (pl. shawātir) a kind of camlet (a fine woolen fabric, originally of camel hair), sometimes dyed blue, and used in some areas as currency.

shaykh-father (Arabic: al-ab al-shaykh; Fur: abbo shaykh (daali)) chief eunuch and traditionally governor of the eastern region (Dār Dālī); the holder, though not necessarily himself a slave, was head of the slave hierarchy. Arabic *ab* "father" assimilates Fur *abbo*, a title of respect.

shīkah a kind of raw calico (*tukkiyyah*) of light, loose weave.

Shīth Seth, third son of Ādam and Ḥawwā' (Adam and Eve) and one of the first prophets.

shūsh small red seeds used to make amulets and as hair decorations for women.

shuwūr a bead bracelet worn by women (synonym of *madraʿah*).

Silā see Dār Silā.

Sinnār (Sennar) a town in the area between the Blue and White Niles now known as al-Jazīrah; home of the Funj sultanate, which lasted from 1504 until its conquest by Egyptian forces under Muḥammad ʿAli's son Ibrāhīm in 1821.

Ṣirāṭ a promontory on the coast of Tunisia between Sejnane and Tabarka (Cap Serrat).

Sodom apple a tree (*Calotropis procera*; Arabic: *ʿushar*).

soom'íng dogólá (Fur) the pages' house (literally "the children's house"). The author describes these pages or cadets as agents who oversaw the sultan's business. The *soom*, located within the *fāshir*'s public area, was also the assembly place where the people came together for conversation or for a common meal; it also functioned as a school where the palace pages or cadets were taught.

soomiit (Fur) a kind of bead.

sūbiyā in Egypt, a cold, thick nonalcoholic drink of slightly fermented rice, sugar, and water.

sudāsī (fem., sudāsiyyah) literally a "sixer": a slave measuring six handspans from heel to earlobe.

suktāyah a kind of house (see §3.1.86, images).

Sulaymān al-Azharī father of the author's teacher Aḥmad ibn Sulaymān, and the maternal grandfather of the author's father.

Sulaymān ibn ʿAbd al-Malik ibn Marwān sixth caliph of the Umayyad dynasty (r. 96–99/715–17).

Sulaymān Solóng (r. ca. 1660–80) founding father of the Keira dynasty in its historical manifestation. This sultan, generally known as Sulaymān Solongdungo (meaning "the Arab" and/or "of reddish complexion"), who ruled from ca. 1660 to 1680, though regarded as the first historically documented sultan of the Keira dynasty, is said, in Fur tradition, to have been preceded by at least three earlier sultans. With his two immediate successors, Mūsā and Aḥmad Bukur, he was responsible for the transformation of their Fur tribal kingdom into a multiethnic empire and played a major role in the Islamization of the Darfurian state.

Sulaymān al-Tūnisī the author's paternal grandfather

suspended ode (muʿallaqah) one of the seven renowned poems by seven renowned poets that (according to legend) hung in the Kaaba in the days before Islam.

al-sūtiyyah inflammation of the knee joint.

al-Suwaynah (Sweini) the first village in Darfur reached by caravans coming from Asyut.

al-Suyūṭī, Jalāl al-Dīn a prolific Egyptian polymath (d. 911/1505).

tābā tobacco.

ṭabābī a practitioner of the science of magic (*ṭibb*).

tabaldī a tree: the baobab (*Adansonia digitate*).

Tabaldiyyah a place northeast of Nyala where Sultan ʿAbd al-Raḥmān inflicted a defeat on his rival Isḥāq.

Ṭāhir a son of Sultan Aḥmad Bukur to whom Muḥammad Kurrā allegedly pledged allegiance when the latter revolted against Sultan Muḥammad Faḍl.

al-Ṭā'if a city in the Hejaz ninety miles northeast of Mecca.

takākī see *tukkiyyah*.

al-Takrūr a name used in northern Africa to designate West Africans in general; now pronounced Dakrūr.

Tāldawā a hill northeast of Nyala.

ṭalḥ a tree: red acacia (*Vachellia* (or *Acacia*) *seyal*).

Tāmā, Tāmah see Dār Tāmā, Dār Tāmah.

Tamurrū al-Fullānī a holy man known for his skill as a magician.

Tandaltī a town east of Jabal Marrah where Sultan ʿAbd al-Raḥmān established his *fāshir*, or royal compound, in 1206/1791–92. Subsequent sultans maintained the tradition; El-Fasher is now the name of the capital of North Darfur State.

Tărne (Tarni; Fur) a village southwest of Tandaltī (today's El-Fasher).

tărne (Fur) a ring of tin used as currency.

tawse (Fur) a dance, performed by slaves.

Ṭaybah a name for Medina, site of the tomb of the Prophet Muḥammad.

thawb a large wrap worn by women.

ṭibb magic.

*tikináwi (*takanawi*; in the author's spelling* takaniyāwī*; Fur)* title of the hereditary governor of Dār Zaghāwah in the sultanate's northern region (also known as Dār al-Tikináwi); the tikináwi had a position of command in the army and was known as "the Sultan's Left Arm."

tindinga (Fur) a dance.

togjêl (Fur) a kind of goblet drum.

Tomorókkóngá (Tamuurkwa; Fur) one of the three great sections of the Fur people; the Tomorókkóngá live to the west of Jabal Marrah.

the Tubū (Toubou, Tebou) an ethnic group speaking a Nilo-Saharan language that inhabits parts of today's Chad (where they are concentrated in the Tebesti region), Libya, Niger, and Nigeria.

al-Ṭughrā'ī Mu'ayyid al-Dīn Abū Isma'īl al-Ḥusayn ibn 'Alī al-Ṭughrā'ī (453/1061 to 514/1120–21), Arab poet and administrator under the Saljuq sultans of Mosul and Baghdad.

al-Tuhāmī Abū l-Hasan 'Alī al-Tuhāmī (d. 416/1025); poet and scholar of Yemeni origin.

tukkiyyah (pl. takākī) raw or unbleached calico; bolts of the latter ten cubits in length and one in breadth were used by poor women to make their robes and also, especially in the area around the sultan's capital, as currency.

tukultī a kind of house with a roof raised on two wooden pillars (see §3.1.86, images).

al-Tūnisī, 'Umar ibn Sulaymān see 'Umar ibn Sulaymān al-Tūnisī.

al-Tūnisī, Sulaymān see Sulaymān al-Tūnisī.

Tunjūr a people living in central Darfur who in the sixteenth century superseded the Dājū as its rulers and as rulers in Wadai; in the mid-seventeenth century, they were themselves succeeded in Darfur by Fur sultans of the Keira dynasty.

Turqunak in the Wadai sultanate, one of sixteen freeborn men, four of whom acted as overseers of persons of the royal blood and four as captains of the sultan's bodyguard, while eight assisted the *kamkūlak*s (q.v.) in the provinces.

Turūj a generic and pejorative term applied by Darfurians to enslaveable tribes living south of Kordofan.

al-Ṭuwayshah a town close to Umm Kidādah on Darfur's border, and its surrounding district.

'Umar ibn Sulaymān al-Tūnisī the author's father.

'Umar Lēl (or Lēle) (r. ca. 1730–39), fifth historical sultan of the Keira dynasty, preceded by his father Muḥammad Dawra and succeeded by his uncle Abū l-Qāsim.

umm bulbul literally "Mother Nightingale"; a kind of barley wine.

the Victorious (al-Manṣūrah) smallest and most sacred of the royal kettledrums of the Darfur sultans.

vizier a general title (rather than an office) of high officials in the courts of Tunis, Darfur, and elsewhere.

al-Wāddāy (Waddāy, Wadadāy) Wadai, formerly a sultanate immediately to the west of Darfur, also called Dār Ṣulayḥ or Dār Ṣalīḥ; today part of Chad.

Wādī l-Kūʿ a seasonal watercourse running south from Jabal Sī (north of Jabal Marrah), on whose banks at Tandaltī Sultan 'Abd al-Raḥmān built his *fāshir*.

Wārah the capital of the sultanate of Wadai.

warrāniyyah a meal eaten in addition to regular meals.

waykah a dish made from rehydrated ingredients, most commonly okra.

Yājūj and Mājūj monstrous peoples who, according to the Qur'an and the Torah (where they are called Gog and Magog), will invade the world on the last days before the Day of Judgment; they are said by some to number 400,000, by others to be nine times as numerous as humans

Yūsuf Pasha Yūsuf Pasha al-Karamanlī (1795–1832), hereditary governor of Libyan Tripoli.

Yūsuf the Seal Bearer (Muhurdār) Yūsuf Ṣāḥib al-Ṭābiʿ (ca. 1765–1815); a slave, possibly Moldovan, bought at around age thirteen in Istanbul by Bakkār al-Jallūlī, an army commander and rich merchant of Sfax. Yūsuf was raised in the Jallūlī household and presented to Ḥammūdah Pasha, ruler of Tunis, when he was eighteen; he rose to be the latter's principal minister and the country's most powerful figure, with control over much of the economy. He was assassinated not long after his sponsor, Ḥammūdah Pasha, died.

al-Zaghāwah peoples speaking a language of the Nilo-Saharan family and living on the northern marches of Darfur and in Wadai.

al-Zaghāwī (or, Bīr al-Zaghāwī) a well on the road from Asyut to Darfur south of Laqiyyah, also called Bīr al-Malḥah.

zaghāwī a kind of naturally occurring salt.

zakat a property tax disbursed by the state in the form of alms for specified categories of persons.

ẓalīm (of an ostrich) having four large and four small pure-white plumes.

zarībah a fence of thorny branches surrounding a homestead.

al-Zarqā' a spring in Medina.

the Zayādiyyah Arabic-speaking camel-herding nomads of the Fazārah group living in the northeast of Darfur.

ẓufr literally "fingernail"; *Unguis odoratus*: fragments of the operculum, or plug, of certain kinds of mollusks, which when broken up resembles blackish fingernails and which is used in perfumes.

Index

Mu'ayyid al-Dīn Abū Isma'īl al-Ḥusayn ibn 'Alī al-Ṭughrā'ī. *See* al-Ṭughrā'ī
Muftāḥ (general of 'Abd al-Raḥmān al-Rashīd), §2.3.8, 202n212
Mughulṭāy al-Turkī, §2.3.23
al-Muhallabī (vizier), §2.1.7
Muḥammad (the Prophet), §1.1, §2.1.7, §2.1.33, §2.2.2, §2.2.23, §2.2.41, §2.3.5, §2.3.22, 187n2, 187n4, 188n24, 189n34, 196n137, 197n150, 197n155, 197n156, 199n178, 199n179
Muḥammad (older paternal uncle of the author), §§2.1.26–27, §2.1.32, §2.2.33
Muḥammad (cousin of the author), §2.1.33
Muḥammad III ibn 'Abd Allāh. *See* Muḥammad al-Ḥasanī
Muḥammad Abū l-Madyan, xxiii, 205n251
Muḥammad 'Alī Pasha, xvi, xxii–xxiii, xxvi, §1.5, 187n5, 187n11, 187n12, 187n13, 189n33, 195n119
Muḥammad al-Amīr al-Kabīr, §2.1.32, 189n34, verses by §2.1.13
Muḥammad al-Barkāwī, §2.3.23
Muḥammad Daldan [wad Binayyah], §2.2.36, §2.2.39
Muḥammad Dardūk, §2.3.2
Muḥammad Dawrā, xii, 199n171
Muḥammad Dukkumī, §2.2.62, §2.3.6, §§2.3.13–16, §2.3.36, 201n201, 205n250
Muḥammad (al-)Faḍl (sultan of Darfur), xvi–xvii, xviii, xxiii, §2.2.15, §2.2.29, §§2.2.35–38, §2.3.4, §§2.3.36–39, 196n147, 198n167, 198n169, 205n251, 205n253, 206n257
Muḥammad al-Ḥasanī (sultan of Morroco), §2.1.1, 188n20
Muḥammad al-Ḥusayn, xiii, xvii
Muḥammad ibn Aḥmad al-Qurṭubī. *See* al-Qurṭubī
Muḥammad ibn al-Ḥasan ibn Durayd, *See* Ibn Durayd
Muḥammad ibn Idrīs al-Shāfi'ī. *See* al-Shāfi'ī
Muḥammad ibn Ismā'īl al-Bukhārī. *See* al-Bukhārī
Muḥammad ibn Ismā'īl ibn 'Umar. *See* Shihāb al-Dīn al-Miṣrī
Muḥammad ibn al-Qāsim, §2.2.41, 199n180
Muḥammad ibn 'Umar al-Tūnisī. *See* Muḥammad al-Tūnisī
Muḥammad Jalāl al-Dīn, §2.3.23
Muḥammad [Maḥmud] al-Jallūlī, §2.1.14, §§2.1.16–18, 189n36
Muḥammad Kuraytīm, §2.3.22
Muḥammad Kurrā (shaykh-father), xvi, §§2.2.29–38, §§2.2.43–47, §§2.2.57–62, §2.3.21, §§2.3.36–39, 196n147, 197n151, 198n166, 198n167, 198n169, 198n170, 201n198, 203n231, 204n232, 205n248, 205n249, 205n250, 205n255, 206n256
Muḥammad al-Maḥrūqī, §2.1.24
Muḥammad al-Muknī, §2.1.9
Muḥammad Sanjaq, xliii, §2.2.19
Muḥammad Shihāb al-Dīn al-Miṣrī. *See* Shihāb al-Dīn al-Miṣrī
Muḥammad Shīlfūt, §2.2.37, 198n169
Muḥammad Ṭahir (al-Ṭahir) (younger paternal uncle of the author), §§2.1.26, §§2.1.32–34, §2.2.33, 191n66
Muḥammad Tayrāb (sultan of Darfur), xii–xiii, §2.2.29, §§2.2.38–40, §§2.2.43–44, §2.2.47, §§2.2.48–60, §§2.2.62–64, §§2.3.4–6, §2.3.18, 199n171, 199n174, 200n190, 200n191, 201n203

About the NYU Abu Dhabi Institute

The Library of Arabic Literature is supported by a grant from the NYU Abu Dhabi Institute, a major hub of intellectual and creative activity and advanced research. The Institute hosts academic conferences, workshops, lectures, film series, performances, and other public programs directed both to audiences within the UAE and to the worldwide academic and research community. It is a center of the scholarly community for Abu Dhabi, bringing together faculty and researchers from institutions of higher learning throughout the region.

NYU Abu Dhabi, through the NYU Abu Dhabi Institute, is a world-class center of cutting-edge research, scholarship, and cultural activity. The Institute creates singular opportunities for leading researchers from across the arts, humanities, social sciences, sciences, engineering, and the professions to carry out creative scholarship and conduct research on issues of major disciplinary, multidisciplinary, and global significance.

About the Typefaces

The Arabic body text is set in DecoType Naskh, designed by Thomas Milo and Mirjam Somers, based on an analysis of five centuries of Ottoman manuscript practice. The exceptionally legible result is the first and only typeface in a style that fully implements the principles of script grammar (*qawāʿid al-khaṭṭ*).

The Arabic footnote text is set in DecoType Emiri, drawn by Mirjam Somers, based on the metal typeface in the naskh style that was cut for the 1924 Cairo edition of the Qur'an.

Both Arabic typefaces in this series are controlled by a dedicated font layout engine. ACE, the Arabic Calligraphic Engine, invented by Peter Somers, Thomas Milo, and Mirjam Somers of DecoType, first operational in 1985, pioneered the principle followed by later smart font layout technologies such as OpenType, which is used for all other typefaces in this series.

The Arabic text was set with WinSoft Tasmeem, a sophisticated user interface for DecoType ACE inside Adobe InDesign. Tasmeem was conceived and created by Thomas Milo (DecoType) and Pascal Rubini (WinSoft) in 2005.

The English text is set in Adobe Text, a new and versatile text typeface family designed by Robert Slimbach for Western (Latin, Greek, Cyrillic) typesetting. Its workhorse qualities make it perfect for a wide variety of applications, especially for longer passages of text where legibility and economy are important. Adobe Text bridges the gap between calligraphic Renaissance types of the 15th and 16th centuries and high-contrast Modern styles of the 18th century, taking many of its design cues from early post-Renaissance Baroque transitional types cut by designers such as Christoffel van Dijck, Nicolaus Kis, and William Caslon. While grounded in classical form, Adobe Text is also a statement of contemporary utilitarian design, well suited to a wide variety of print and on-screen applications.

Titles Published by the Library of Arabic Literature

For more details on individual titles, visit www.libraryofarabicliterature.org

Classical Arabic Literature: A Library of Arabic Literature Anthology
Selected and translated by Geert Jan van Gelder (2012)

A Treasury of Virtues: Sayings, Sermons, and Teachings of ʿAlī, by al-Qāḍī al-Quḍāʿī, with the **One Hundred Proverbs** attributed to al-Jāḥiẓ
Edited and translated by Tahera Qutbuddin (2013)

The Epistle on Legal Theory, by al-Shāfiʿī
Edited and translated by Joseph E. Lowry (2013)

Leg over Leg, by Aḥmad Fāris al-Shidyāq
Edited and translated by Humphrey Davies (4 volumes; 2013–14)

Virtues of the Imām Aḥmad ibn Ḥanbal, by Ibn al-Jawzī
Edited and translated by Michael Cooperson (2 volumes; 2013–15)

The Epistle of Forgiveness, by Abū l-ʿAlāʾ al-Maʿarrī
Edited and translated by Geert Jan van Gelder and Gregor Schoeler (2 volumes; 2013–14)

The Principles of Sufism, by ʿĀʾishah al-Bāʿūniyyah
Edited and translated by Th. Emil Homerin (2014)

The Expeditions: An Early Biography of Muḥammad, by Maʿmar ibn Rāshid
Edited and translated by Sean W. Anthony (2014)

Two Arabic Travel Books
Accounts of China and India, by Abū Zayd al-Sīrāfī
Edited and translated by Tim Mackintosh-Smith (2014)
Mission to the Volga, by Aḥmad ibn Faḍlān
Edited and translated by James Montgomery (2014)

Disagreements of the Jurists: A Manual of Islamic Legal Theory, by al-Qāḍī al-Nuʿmān
Edited and translated by Devin J. Stewart (2015)

Consorts of the Caliphs: Women and the Court of Baghdad, by Ibn al-Sāʿī
Edited by Shawkat M. Toorawa and translated by the Editors of the Library of Arabic Literature (2015)

What ʿĪsā ibn Hishām Told Us, by Muḥammad al-Muwayliḥī
Edited and translated by Roger Allen (2 volumes; 2015)

The Life and Times of Abū Tammām, by Abū Bakr Muḥammad ibn Yaḥyā al-Ṣūlī
Edited and translated by Beatrice Gruendler (2015)

The Sword of Ambition: Bureaucratic Rivalry in Medieval Egypt, by ʿUthmān ibn Ibrāhīm al-Nābulusī
Edited and translated by Luke Yarbrough (2016)

Brains Confounded by the Ode of Abū Shādūf Expounded, by Yūsuf al-Shirbīnī
Edited and translated by Humphrey Davies (2 volumes; 2016)

Light in the Heavens: Sayings of the Prophet Muḥammad, by al-Qāḍī al-Quḍāʿī
Edited and translated by Tahera Qutbuddin (2016)

Risible Rhymes, by Muḥammad ibn Maḥfūẓ al-Sanhūrī
Edited and translated by Humphrey Davies (2016)

A Hundred and One Nights
Edited and translated by Bruce Fudge (2016)

The Excellence of the Arabs, by Ibn Qutaybah
Edited by James E. Montgomery and Peter Webb
Translated by Sarah Bowen Savant and Peter Webb (2017)

Scents and Flavors: A Syrian Cookbook
Edited and translated by Charles Perry (2017)

Arabian Satire: Poetry from 18th-Century Najd, by Ḥmēdān al-Shwēʿir
Edited and translated by Marcel Kurpershoek (2017)

In Darfur: An Account of the Sultanate and its People, by Muḥammad ibn ʿUmar al-Tūnisī
Edited and translated by Humphrey Davies (**2 volumes; 2018**)

English-only Paperbacks

Leg over Leg, by Aḥmad Fāris al-Shidyāq (**2 volumes; 2015**)
The Expeditions: An Early Biography of Muḥammad, by Maʿmar ibn Rāshid (2015)
The Epistle on Legal Theory: A Translation of al-Shāfiʿī's *Risālah*, by al-Shāfiʿī (2015)
The Epistle of Forgiveness, by Abū l-ʿAlāʾ al-Maʿarrī (2016)
The Principles of Sufism, by ʿĀʾishah al-Bāʿūniyyah (2016)
A Treasury of Virtues: Sayings, Sermons and Teachings of ʿAlī, by al-Qāḍī al-Quḍāʿī with the **One Hundred Proverbs**, attributed to al-Jāḥiẓ (2016)
The Life of Ibn Ḥanbal, by Ibn al-Jawzī (2016)
Mission to the Volga, by Ibn Faḍlān (2017)
Accounts of China and India, by Abū Zayd al-Sīrāfī (2017)
A Hundred and One Nights (2017)
Disagreements of the Jurists: A Manual of Islamic Legal Theory, by al-Qāḍī al-Nuʿmān (2017)
What ʿĪsā ibn Hishām Told Us, by Muḥammad al-Muwayliḥī (2018)

About the Editor–Translator

Humphrey Davies is an award-winning translator of some twenty works of modern Arabic literature, among them Alaa Al-Aswany's *The Yacoubian Building*, five novels by Elias Khoury, including *Gate of the Sun*, and Aḥmad Fāris al-Shidyāq's *Leg over Leg*. He has also made a critical edition, translation, and lexicon of the Ottoman-period *Hazz al-quḥūf bi-sharḥ qaṣīd Abī Shādūf* (*Brains Confounded by the Ode of Abū Shādūf Expounded*) by Yūsuf al-Shirbīnī and compiled with Madiha Doss an anthology entitled *Al-ʿāmmiyyah al-miṣriyyah al-maktūbah: mukhtārāt min 1400 ilā 2009* (*Egyptian Colloquial Writing: selections from 1400 to 2009*). He read Arabic at the University of Cambridge, received his Ph.D. from the University of California at Berkeley, and, previous to undertaking his first translation in 2003, worked for social development and research organizations in Egypt, Tunisia, Palestine, and Sudan. He is affiliated with the American University in Cairo.

CPSIA information can be obtained
at www.ICGtesting.com
Printed in the USA
LVHW051124090523
746502LV00013B/72/J

9 781479 876389